W9-BOO-807

WITHDRAWN

APR 2014

24.95

THE
COMPLETE
BEER COURSE

THE COMPLETE BEER COURSE

BOOT CAMP FOR BEER GEEKS:
FROM NOVICE TO EXPERT IN TWELVE TASTING CLASSES

JOSHUA M. BERNSTEIN

STERLING EPICURE
New York

HIGHLAND PARK PUBLIC LIBRARY
494 LAUREL AVE.
HIGHLAND PARK, IL 60035-2690
847-432-0216

641.23
B531

STERLING EPICURE
New York

An Imprint of Sterling Publishing
387 Park Avenue South
New York, NY 10016

STERLING EPICURE is a trademark of Sterling Publishing Co., Inc. The distinctive Sterling logo is a registered trademark of Sterling Publishing Co., Inc.

© 2013 by Joshua M. Bernstein

All rights reserved. No part of this publication may be reproduced, stored in a retrieval system, or transmitted in any form or by any means (including electronic, mechanical, photocopying, recording, or otherwise) without prior written permission from the publisher.

Some of the selections were previously published in different form as follows: Parts of "Bring It on Home" were published as "Where There's Beer, There's a Whey" in *Imbibe*. Sections of "Around the World in 80 Pints" were adapted from "As American as IPA" in *Imbibe* and "On Garde" in *Culture*. Parts of "Take It From the Bottom" were adapted from "In from the Cold" in *Imbibe*.

ISBN 978-1-4027-9767-5

Illustration by Christian Barr
Design and Layout by Rachel Maloney
A complete list of picture credits appears on pages 319–320.

Distributed in Canada by Sterling Publishing
c/o Canadian Manda Group, 165 Dufferin Street
Toronto, Ontario, Canada M6K 3H6
Distributed in the United Kingdom by GMC Distribution Services
Castle Place, 166 High Street, Lewes, East Sussex, England BN7 1XU
Distributed in Australia by Capricorn Link (Australia) Pty. Ltd.
P.O. Box 704, Windsor, NSW 2756, Australia

For information about custom editions, special sales, and premium and corporate purchases, please contact Sterling Special Sales at 800-805-5489 or specialsales@sterlingpublishing.com.

Manufactured in China

2 4 6 8 10 9 7 5 3

www.sterlingpublishing.com

*For all the drinkers demanding,
and brewers creating, better beer.*

CONTENTS

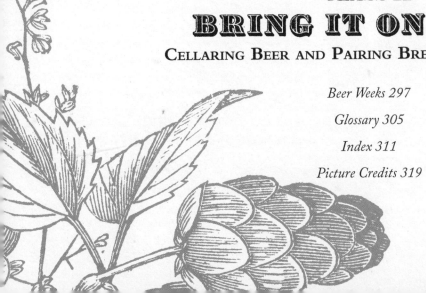

ACKNOWLEDGMENTS

MONTHS BEFORE MY FIRST BOOK, *Brewed Awakening*, hit stores, my publishers propositioned me: "Would you like to do a second book?" they asked. My eyes blazed like Times Square on New Year's Eve, and I soon affixed my John Hancock to the contract.

How simple the plan seemed. I'd promote the first book while spending my free time penning the follow-up! Then *Brewed Awakening* was released. Life became a beer-fueled Tilt-a-Whirl. I was soon crisscrossing the United States, visiting its finest beer bars and breweries, spending nights knocking down brews and chatting up the country's most passionate brewers and fans of carbonated culture. This seems like heaven. For writing, it was hell. Months disappeared as easily as a pint of IPA, and my sum total of words written was zero.

If anything helps a writer shrug off procrastination, it's an ironclad deadline. The terrific team at Sterling Publishing, in particular Carlo Devito and Diane Abrams, installed a finish line. Words flowed as fast as a mudslide, massaged into tip-top shape by my patient, tireless editor, Pam Hoenig. Brita Vallens proved to be a picture-perfect photo researcher, Scott Amerman pored over the layout to ensure proper punctuation, and Rachel Maloney tied the whole package together with another winning design. I owe all of you a beer.

I'll keep the tab running for all the brewers, bar owners, friends, homebrewers, fellow scribes, beer drinkers, photographers, and historians who have helped me on this hop-fueled literary ride. Your insights, talents, and time spent sharing just one more beer were crucial to creating this book.

And finally, thanks to my wife, Jenene, for her unshakable support and love, even as I spent multiple months unshaven, drinking beer at 2 p.m., and spouting unmentionables at my computer screen. You and Sammy make every day memorable.

TOP FIVE BEERS CONSUMED WHILE WRITING *THE COMPLETE BEER COURSE*

I largely penned this book during the hottest summer on record, in a century-old Brooklyn apartment without air-conditioning. These beers kept me cool and sane:

1. Victory Prima Pils: prickly pilsner perfection
2. Lagunitas Little Sumpin' Sumpin' Ale: smooth, hoppy wheat bomb
3. Tröegs Perpetual IPA: West Coast–style bitter beauty from Pennsylvania
4. Sierra Nevada Kellerweis: pure unfiltered hefeweizen refreshment
5. Allagash White: aromatic, thirst-quenching witbier

INTRODUCTION:
BEYOND THE LIGHT BEER

DURING MY WASTED YOUTH, I was the classic quantity-over-quality imbiber, pooling together my nickels, dimes, pennies, and quarters to purchase beers whose chief selling point was that they were cheap and cold. Or at least lukewarm. I was far from picky.

Come drinking time, an arbitrary hour that began at 1 p.m., 7 p.m., or even 11 a.m., I would crack endless cans of Busch Light, Natural Light, and Schlitz. I do not recall relishing drinking these low-cost lagers or the occasional 40-ouncer of malt liquor. To me, beer was beer. It was a flavor-deprived means to, more often than not, a hangover-filled end.

As college relented to reluctant adulthood, I gradually saw the light. More specifically, I saw that there was more to beer than Coors Light. Instead of buying 99-cent cans of fizzy, lightly boozy water, I forked over a few extra quarters and sampled inky stouts, bitter India pale ales, and barley wines as warming as an armchair next to a roaring fireplace in February. Each new beer was a revelation, leading to a realization: if the beer family resided in a sprawling mansion, I'd been confining myself to one cramped basement corner.

It was time to unlock those doors and start exploring beer's nooks and crannies. I grew obsessed, spending my eves bending elbows at better-beer saloons. My days were devoted to perusing bottle shops with the same fervor I once did record stores, as well as interviewing passionate brewers, forward-thinking bar owners, and restaurateurs who believe that great grub deserves equally great beers. Through my exhaustive hands-on—and stomach-first—investigations, I was consumed by one crucial question: What makes each beer delicious and different?

UNIQUELY FLAVORFUL

More than ever, that's a tough query to answer concisely. Over the last decade, American brewing has changed more drastically than at any time since Prohibition. In 1980, there were fewer than 50 breweries in the United States, with most making the same crisp everyman beer advertised during the Super Bowl. Today there are more than 2,500 American-based breweries, with hundreds, if not thousands, more in the pipeline. From locally rooted brewpubs to regional powerhouses such as Oregon's Ninkasi, Michigan's Bell's, and New Hampshire's

Smuttynose and new-breed national brands such as Rogue and Stone, American craft brewing is in full bloom.

With the chain of tradition severed by Prohibition, American brewers have free creative rein to reinvent the very notion of beer, and this has inspired a global brewing revolution bubbling up on almost every continent. (Antarctica *still* does not have a brewpub.) Across the world, the bitter India pale ale has birthed red, white, and black varieties and the potent, superaromatic double IPA. Alcohol percentages have climbed above 10 percent—on a par with wine—and those strong brews are now as welcome as Rieslings and Cabernet Sauvignons at the dinner table. Low-alcohol beers now have big flavor. Wild yeasts and bacteria are used to create rustic beers as sour as lemonade (that's a good thing). And brewmasters have begun aging their creations in wooden casks that once contained bourbon, brandy, Chardonnay, or rum.

CHOICES, CHOICES, CHOICES

It's the best time in history to be a beer drinker. It's also the most confusing time. Stroll into any craft-beer bar or beer distributor and you're forced to sift through a dizzying array of dozens, if not hundreds, of singular brews. A marketplace of overwhelming choice can lead to paralysis and settling for the same old, same old. Repetition can be comforting; that is why I always purchase the same pair of jeans at the department store.

Do not make the same mistake with craft beer, where curiosity rewards the intrepid imbiber. In *The Complete Beer Course*, I demystify the beverage, elementally breaking down the grains, yeast, hops, and techniques that cause beer's flavor to spin into thousands of distinctively delicious directions. After outfitting you with the tools to taste, smell, and evaluate brews, the book will lead you on a flavorful trek through the most critical styles of beer. Structured around a series of easy-to-follow classes, you'll hop from lagers and pilsners to hazy wheat beers, aromatic pale ales and bitter IPAs, Belgian-style abbey and Trappist ales, roasty stouts, barrel-aged brews, belly-warming barley wines, and mouth-puckering sour ales. Through a sequence of suggested targeted tastings, you'll learn which flavors are appropriate and which ones signify that you should dump those beers down a drain.

Not every beer is worthy of residing in your stomach. Years of experience and sampling have given me the confidence to pass on certain beers and seek out others as rabidly as my dog does a chicken bone. The key is being armed with the necessary knowledge. That means learning the ropes, loosening your lips, and trying one beer after another, and another. Something tells me you'll like taking *The Complete Beer Course*, where earning extra credit has never been so much fun.

Until next beer.

SUPPORT
THE SESSION BEER PROJECT

nks,

GOLDEN ROAD
BREWING

GYO ✓ GYO ✓ GYO ✓ GYO ✓ G

CHATOE
ROGUE
GROW THE REVOLUTION

First Growth
Roguenbier Rye A

Dream Rye, Independent Hops, Dare & Risk

POINT I
POINT THE WAY │││ INDIA PALE ALE │││ BREWED A

AT GOLDEN ROAD BREWING, WE LOVE THE HOPPY GOODNESS O
THAT CAPTURED THOSE FLAVORS WITH A 5.2% ALCOHOL CONT

16 FL. OZ   ONE PINT   5.2% ALC./ OL

THE BEER ESSENTIALS

UNDERSTANDING AND APPRECIATING THE WORLD'S GREATEST BEVERAGE

 I CLEARLY RECALL THE DAY WHEN a know-it-all friend revealed the secret inside the energy drink Red Bull, ruining it for me forever.

"It's an organic acid called taurine, which was discovered in bull bile," my friend said, pointing at the cylindrical can as if it were weeks-old trash. "That's why they call it Red *Bull*."

"How do they get the bile?" I wondered. I envisioned a farm filled with angry bulls prodded with sharp sticks by brave, if underpaid, men.

"Taurine is synthetically manufactured," he explained, sending my flight of fancy crashing back to earth.

Our conversation ended, as did my late-night dance with Red Bull and other 7-Eleven beverages concocted in a science lab, which, very fortunately for me, do not include beer.

You don't need a master's degree to understand beer's four essential ingredients: hops, grain, yeast, and water, with occasional aid from supporting adjuncts. In the hands and brains of brewers, those raw materials are transformed into endless flavor profiles. Sour, bitter, sweet, chocolaty, coffee, salty—dream it, brew it, drink it. For brewers, choosing the right blend of aromatic hops, grains, and yeast strain is an art, a series of carefully deliberated selections that ideally, when put through a process that's remained largely unchanged for centuries, results in a perfectly unique potable. But why do these ingredients cause beers to taste and smell so different? Follow me along brewing's flavorful path to find out how brewers get from grain to glass.

GOING WITH THE GRAIN

One of the foundation stones of beer is barley, which is transformed into brew-ready malt by taking a bath in hot water. This causes the grain to create the enzymes that transform proteins and starches into fermentable sugars, which yeast will later feast on to create alcohol.

With brewing, top billing on the grain bill usually is reserved for barley malts. This is due to an evolutionary advantage: barley contains husks, which keep the *mash* (the grains steeped in boiling water) loose and permit drainage of the *wort*—the broth that becomes beer. For flavor, brewers often blend the lead grain barley with a host of supporting fermentable grains (such as rye and wheat).

BARLEY

There's no global system for classifying the hundreds of varieties of barley, but they can be condensed into several broad categories.

BASE MALTS: These compose the bulk of the grain bill. Typically lighter-colored, these workhorse malts provide the majority of the proteins, fermentable sugars, and minerals required to create beer.

SPECIALTY MALTS: These auxiliary grains are great for increasing body, improving head retention, and adding color, aroma, and flavor, such as coffee, chocolate, biscuit, and caramel. Specialty grains are blended to achieve unique flavor profiles and characteristics. Popular varieties include the following:

- *Crystal (or caramel) malts*, specially stewed to create crystalline sugar structures within the grain's hull. They add sweetness to beer.

- *Roasted malts*, kilned or roasted at high temperatures to impart certain flavor characteristics. Coffee beans undergo a similar transformation.

- *Dark malts*, highly roasted to achieve the robust flavors associated with stouts, schwarzbiers, bocks, and black IPAs.

UNMALTED BARLEY: This imparts a rich, grainy character to beer, a key characteristic of styles such as dry stout. Unmalted barley helps head retention, but it will make a beer hazier than Los Angeles smog.

OTHER COMMONLY USED BREWING GRAINS

CORN: When used in beer, corn provides a smooth, somewhat neutral sweetness. It is utilized to lighten a beer's body, decrease haziness, and stabilize flavor.

OATS: Used in conjunction with barley, oats create a creamy, full-bodied brew that's as smooth as satin. Stouts are a natural fit.

RICE: As a beer ingredient, rice imparts little or no discernible taste. Instead, the grain helps create snappy flavors and a dry profile as well as lighten a beer's body.

RYE: Working in conjunction with barley, rye can sharpen flavors and add complexity, crispness, and subtle spiciness as well as dry out a beer. The grain also can be kilned to create a chocolate or caramel flavor. Its shortcoming: since rye is hull-less, using large percentages of the grain during brewing can cause it to clump up and turn to concrete.

WHEAT: Packed with proteins, this grain helps create a fuller body and mouthfeel and a foamy head as thick and lasting as Cool Whip. A large proportion of wheat can result in a smooth, hazy brew such as a hefeweizen or a witbier. Wheat can impart a slight tartness.

SORGHUM: Sorghum (which is actually a grass indigenous to Africa, not a grain) is a gluten-free alternative to barley and other grains. It's used to

WASTE NOT

The brewing process creates vast amounts of spent grain. Instead of sending it to a landfill, breweries have begun exploring alternative uses for excess grain. Many breweries give it to farmers for animal feed, and bakers are occasionally recipients of the used grain: it can make great bread or pizza dough as well as waffles and even dog biscuits (pictured).

create gluten-free beer, sometimes adding a sour edge. Most breweries use prepared sorghum syrup, which is highly concentrated wort.

NO GRAIN, NO PROBLEM: GLUTEN-FREE BEERS

It almost seems like an existential question: If a beer does not contain barley, is it still beer? More important, will it taste any good?

Increasingly across America, the answer to both questions is yes. That's great news for the estimated 3 million people with celiac disease, an autoimmune disorder that leaves them unable to digest gluten easily. Ingesting a food or a beverage that contains gluten, one of several different proteins found in cereal grains such as rye, wheat, spelt, and barley, can wreak havoc on digestive systems and cause paralyzing stomach pain. This nixes pizza. Fresh-baked bread. A bowl of spaghetti. And beer. Sipping a single pint could leave a person with celiac disease sicker than someone who drank the better part of a bottle of bourbon.

Ten years ago, the term *tasty gluten-free beer* was mainly an oxymoron. As was the case with large-scale lagers such as Budweiser and Miller Lite, breweries that concocted barley-free beer aimed for the middle ground to reach the widest swath of consumers. That meant drinkable if middle-of-the-road products such as Anheuser-Busch InBev's sorghum-based Redbridge. Sure, it approximates beer, but for drinkers accustomed to vibrant craft beer, merely having a serviceable alternative is not enough.

As celiac disease becomes more visible, and as health-conscious consumers restrict gluten from their diets, brewers are rising to meet the demand for gluten-free brews as flavorful and inventive as anything found in the craft-beer aisle. Accomplishing that is not as effortless as omitting barley or wheat from a brew kettle, which would be like building a table without legs. The grains supply the sugars yeasts require to kick-start fermentation.

As an acceptable alternative, brewers lean on gluten-free alternatives such as millet, buckwheat, rice, flax, and, most commonly, sorghum grass, which has a high sugar content. Processed sorghum extracts such as Briess Malt & Ingredients Co.'s white sorghum syrup, are essentially brew-ready wort. Sorghum syrup mimics standard malt extracts, though its drawbacks include creating hazy beer and imparting a sour note.

Instead of fighting sorghum's natural flavor, some brewers use it to their advantage. In its Celia Saison, Vermont's The Alchemist utilizes sorghum in conjunction with orange peel, Celia hops, and a Belgian yeast strain to create

The Alchemist's John Kimmich started brewing gluten-free beers after his wife, Jennifer, was diagnosed with celiac disease. Though Hurricane Irene wiped out the couple's brewpub in Waterbury, Vermont, in 2011, their production brewery escaped unscathed. The Alchemist is now home to Prohibition Pig, a restaurant with world-class beer.

a spicy, somewhat tart gluten-free beer with a farmhouse feel. Colorado's New Planet Beer does a nice job with its fruity 3R Raspberry Ale and decently hopped Off Grid Pale Ale, and England's Green's Gluten-Free Beers manufactures an assortment of Belgian-style ales. Instead of sorghum, Utah's Epic Brewing turns to brown rice, millet, molasses, sweet potatoes, and heaps of hops to make Glutenator. (Since Widmer Brothers makes Omission Lager and Omission Pale Ale with barley that has had its gluten removed, the government does not allow that brewery to label its beer as gluten-free.)

Probably the surest sign of gluten-free beer's ascension is Harvester Brewing in Portland, Oregon. All its beers are celiac-friendly, relying on gluten-free oats, pure cane sugar, sorghum, Pacific Northwest hops, and locally sourced roasted chestnuts to supply color and flavor to its Pale, Red, and Dark ales as well as its rotating experimental series. Going without gluten no longer means going without good beer.

FLOWER POWER: HOPS

Hops are the female flowers—aka *cones*—of *Humulus lupulus*, a creeping bine. (Instead of using tendrils or suckers, a bine climbs by wrapping itself around a support.) Hops are a brewer's Swiss Army knife: they flavor beers, provide bitterness, and enhance a beer's head retention, and their preservative powers keep unwanted bacteria at bay. Hop resins possess two primary acids, alpha and beta. Beta acids contribute to a beer's bouquet. Alpha acids serve as a preservative and contribute bitterness early in the boil, flavor later in the boil, and aroma in the last minutes of a boil.

During hop harvest season in late August and early September, the moist and sticky flowers typically travel straight from field to kiln, where they're dried to prevent spoilage. That's done because hops are like cut grass. Initially, the smell is superb, but the flowers rapidly go rotten.

HOP-GROWING REGIONS

By weight, the top hop-producing country is Germany. In America, California, Oregon, Washington, and Idaho have a lockdown on hop production. It took root in the Pacific Northwest in the 1850s, and within 50 years the region was leading the nation in producing beer's crucial bittering agent. The farms survived Prohibition by primarily exporting hops overseas, and when that national scourge was eradicated

BEER TERROIR-IST

The term *terroir* describes the unique characteristics that soil and climate give agricultural products. The phrase has been used traditionally in reference to coffee, tea, and especially wine. But brewers have begun laying claim to the term, using locally sourced barley, inoculating beers with native yeasts, flavoring beers with locally harvested fruits and vegetables, and using hops that were grown specifically for or by a brewery.

Some breweries, such as California's Sierra Nevada and Oregon's Rogue Ales, run their own farming operations. However, this is the exception to the rule. Most often, terroir in beer expresses itself in brewers incorporating ingredients that speak of the region. In the Northeast you'll see beers made with maple syrup. Spruce tips are popular in Alaskan ales. Sweet potatoes, satsumas, and peaches often appear in Southern craft beers. In southeastern Ohio, many brewers add pawpaw, America's largest tree fruit. For a taste of terroir, try Sierra Nevada Estate Homegrown Ale, a selection from San Francisco's rigorously local, farm-to-bottle Almanac Beer, or Rogue's GYO—grow your own—range of Chatoe Rogue beers.

WEEDING OUT THE TRUTH

When it comes to beer, my wife's taste buds verge toward the illicit. "I like beers that smell like marijuana," she explains, thumbing her nose at pilsners and stouts. Instead of seeking out beers made with cannabis, she turns to dank, pungent IPAs and double IPAs. That's because, genetically speaking, hops and cannabis are both members of the Cannabaceae family. Just don't go sparking a hop spliff: hops contain zero mood-altering THC.

The first documented case of hop cultivation was in 736, in the Hallertau region of what is now known as Germany.

The French WORD FOR HOP IS *houblon.*

in 1933, hop acreage quickly expanded. Today, Washington's Yakima Valley accounts for about 75 percent of domestic hop production. (During the late nineteenth century, New York State was America's hoppy epicenter, growing up to 90 percent of the nation's supply. However, diseases such as powdery and downy mildew, followed by industrialization and Prohibition, effectively killed that part of the agricultural industry. Slowly and steadily, farmers are attempting to revitalize hop growing in New York.)

Internationally, other crucial hop-growing countries include New Zealand, where a lack of natural pests and no known hop diseases means Kiwi hops are largely pesticide-free, and the United Kingdom, which is recognized for its fruity, earthy hops. The Czech Republic and Germany are famed for their noble hops, delicate European varieties that offer intense aromas paired with dialed-back bitterness. The four classic varieties, Hallertau, Tettnanger, Spalt, and Saaz, are named after the German and Czech regions or cities where they originally were grown.

SPECIAL LITTLE FLOWERS

Each hop variety is unique, with its own distinctive gifts to bestow upon beer. Some are better suited to providing astringent bitterness; others are utilized for their aromas of citrus, tropical fruit, or perhaps pine. There are two main categories of hops:

AROMA: These hops add bouquet and flavor, not bitterness. They are higher in beta acids. To prevent their delicate, fragrant essential oils from evaporating, they're added on the back end of the boil.

BITTERING: These hops add bitterness, not aroma. They are higher in alpha acids. To maximize the bitterness, they're added earlier in the boil, which causes the hops' delicate essential oils to evaporate.

Like a switch-hitter in baseball, some do-it-all hops provide flavor, aroma, and bitterness. These are known as *dual-purpose hops.*

KNOW YOUR HOPS

HERE ARE SOME OF THE MOST POPULAR HOP VARIETIES POPULATING BEER, THEIR FLAVOR CHARACTERISTICS, AND THEIR PRIMARY USES IN THE BREWING PROCESS.

AHTANUM
This variety is fairly grapefruity and floral, alongside notes of pine and earth. Its bitterness is relatively low.
USE: *aroma and flavor*

AMARILLO
Amarillo is semisweet and supercitrusy, verging on oranges. Consider it Cascade (see right) on steroids.
USE: *flavor and aroma*

APOLLO
This potent variety contributes notes of resin, spice, and citrus—mainly orange.
USE: *bittering*

BRAVO
Bravo presents an earthy and herbal, lightly spicy aroma suited to brash IPAs.
USE: *bittering*

BREWER'S GOLD
This is a complex, pungent variety with a spicy aroma and flavor as well as a fruity current of black currant.
USE: *bittering*

CALYPSO
This new variety's fruity aroma recalls pears and apples.
USE: *aroma, bittering*

CASCADE
Popular in American pale ales and IPAs, this floral hop smells strongly of citrus, sometimes grapefruit.
USE: *flavor, aroma, bittering*

CENTENNIAL
This variety offers over-the-top citrus flavor and aroma with a relatively restrained floral nose.
USE: *flavor, aroma, bittering*

CHALLENGER
The robust aroma offers a polished, spicy profile that can verge on fruity; the bitterness is clean and present.
USE: *flavor, aroma, bittering*

CHINOOK
Chinook provides an herbal, earthy, smoky, piney character with some citrus thrown in for fun.
USE: *aroma, bittering*

CITRA
This variety provides a heavy tropical aroma of lychee, mango, papaya, and pineapple. A full-on fruit attack.
USE: *aroma*

CLUSTER
A pure, gently floral bitterness makes it suited to a wide variety of beer styles.
USE: *aroma, bittering*

COLUMBUS (ALSO KNOWN BY THE TRADE NAME TOMAHAWK)
This variety is earthy and mildly spicy with subtle flavors of citrus; very similar to Zeus hops.
USE: *aroma, bittering*

CRYSTAL
This one is floral and spicy, somewhat reminiscent of cinnamon and black pepper.
USE: *flavor, aroma*

DELTA
The bouquet is a blend of fruit, earth, and grass—flavor-wise, subdued citrus with an herbal edge.
USE: *flavor, aroma*

EL DORADO

Released in fall 2010, this new variety presents a perfume of pears, watermelon candy, and tropical fruit.

USE: *flavor, aroma, bittering*

FALCONER'S FLIGHT

This floral proprietary blend provides plenty of grapefruit, lemon, citrus, and tropical fruit; perfect for IPAs.

USE: *aroma, bittering*

FUGGLES

Traditionally used in English-style ales, this hop is earthy, fruity, and vegetal.

USE: *flavor, aroma, bittering*

GALAXY

This new Australian cultivar stands apart with its profile of citrus crossed with passion fruit.

USE: *flavor, aroma*

GALENA

This hop provides clean, pungent bitterness that plays well with other hop varieties. There is also a Super Galena variant.

USE: *bittering*

GLACIER

Glacier is a mellow hop with an agreeable fragrance that flits between gentle citrus and earth.

USE: *aroma*

GOLDINGS

The traditional English hop, its flavor is smooth and somewhat sweet; it's called East Kent if grown in that region.

USE: *flavor, aroma, bittering*

HALLERTAUER

Hallertauer presents a mild, agreeable perfume that's floral and earthy with a spicy, fruity component. One of Germany's famed noble hops. Hallertauer encompasses several varieties; the term *Hallertau* often signifies hops grown in America.

USE: *flavor, aroma*

HERSBRUCKER

Its pleasant, refreshing scent offers hints of grass and hay. A noble hop.

USE: *aroma*

HORIZON

This hop offers a tidy, uncluttered profile that's equal parts citric and floral; its bitterness is smooth, not abrasive.

USE: *flavor, bittering*

LIBERTY

Liberty presents a mild, dignified aroma of herbs and earth.

USE: *flavor, aroma*

MAGNUM

The acutely spicy aroma recalls black pepper and perhaps nutmeg; there's a touch of citrus too.

USE: *bittering*

MOSAIC

Released in 2012, this new American hop has a spicy, tropical scent with an earthy edge and a hint of citrus as well.

USE: *aroma*

MOTUEKA

This lively, Saaz-like New Zealand variety is loaded with lemon, lime, and tropical fruit.

USE: *aroma, bittering*

MT. HOOD

Earthy and fresh, this hop offers a restrained spicy nose that evokes noble hops.

USE: *aroma*

MT. RAINIER

This hop's nose pulls a neat trick: black licorice cut with a kiss of citrus.

USE: *aroma, bittering*

NELSON SAUVIN

Partly named after the Sauvignon Blanc grape, New Zealand's Nelson is bright, juicy, and packed with the flavor of passion fruit.

USE: *flavor, bittering, aroma*

NORTHERN BREWER

This multipurpose hop's fragrant aroma leans toward earthy, woody, and rustic. Maybe some mint too.

USE: *aroma, bittering*

NUGGET
This way-bitter hop has a heavy herbal bouquet.
USE: *bittering*

PACIFIC GEM
This is a woody hop that provides a brisk, clean bitterness and subtle notes of blackberry.
USE: *bittering*

PALISADE
Expect a lovely grassy, floral scent with a hint of apricot.
USE: *aroma*

PERLE
This all-purpose variety has a clean, green bitterness verging on mint; it's somewhat spicy and floral as well.
USE: *flavor, aroma, bittering*

PRIDE OF RINGWOOD
Used in many Australian beers, it presents a forthright earthy, herbal, woody scent.
USE: *bittering*

RIWAKA
This New Zealand gem smells strongly of grapefruit.
USE: *aroma*

SAAZ
This noble hop has a distinctly clean, cinnamon-spicy bouquet and typically is used in pilsners.
USE: *flavor, aroma*

SANTIAM
Its herbal, floral perfume is reminiscent of a noble hop.
USE: *aroma*

SIMCOE
Pine, wood, and citrus drive this bittering hop's profile.
USE: *aroma, bittering*

SORACHI ACE
This Japan-bred hop has a strong lemony aroma; it can also taste buttery.
USE: *aroma*

SPALT
A spicy and delicate scent defines this German noble hop.
USE: *aroma*

STERLING
An alternative to European hops, it has a spicy, sophisticated scent and assertive flavor.
USE: *aroma, bittering*

STYRIAN GOLDINGS
This Slovenian Fuggles variant has a sweet, resinous, pleasingly spicy aroma with a little floral edge.
USE: *flavor, aroma, bittering*

SUMMIT
Summit presents an up-front perfume of orange and tangerine.
USE: *bittering*

TARGET
This hop has an intense grassy, herbal, mineral-like character and a floral scent more indebted to Britain than to the West Coast.
USE: *bittering*

TEAMAKER
Originally developed for its antimicrobial properties, this hop variety provides green tea–like aromas and no bitterness.
USE: *aroma*

TETTNANGER
This noble hop has a full, rich flavor mixed with a spicy, flowery nose that verges on herbal.
USE: *flavor, aroma*

TOPAZ
Topaz contributes an earthy character and a fruitiness that recalls lychee.
USE: *aroma, bittering*

WARRIOR
This hop offers a clean, smooth bitterness that works in hop-forward ales.
USE: *aroma, bittering*

WILLAMETTE
The aroma is decidedly herbal, earthy, and woody, with a little floral fruitiness to boot.
USE: *flavor, aroma*

THE BREWING PROCESS

 MILLING: The barley malt is run through a mill, which converts it into crushed grain known as *grist*.

 MASHING: In a vat called a *mash tun*, the grist is steeped in hot water to convert its starches into fermentable sugars.

 LAUTERING: In a *lauter tun* (a vessel that allows liquids to flow through the slotted bottom), the solid grains are separated from the sugary broth, which is called *wort*. Next, hot water is trickled through the grain to extract the remaining sugars, a process called *sparging*.

 BOILING: The wort is transferred to a boil kettle, where it's boiled and hops are added at different stages to impart both bitterness and aroma.

 WHIRLPOOL: During this phase, the hopped wort is spun in a whirlpool. This removes spent hops and coagulated proteins.

 WORT COOLING: Before the yeast can be added, the wort must be chilled to the appropriate fermentation temperature. To accomplish that, the wort is run through a heat exchanger.

FERMENTING: The wort is transferred to fermentation tanks, and then yeast is added. The sugary liquid begins its transformation into beer.

 CONDITIONING: After the yeast has ceased gorging on sugar, fermentation slows down and the yeasts start descending to the bottom of the fermentation tank. To encourage this settling, the beer is cooled to near freezing and then transferred to a conditioning, or bright, tank for flavor maturation, continued clarification, and/or carbonation. (Some breweries only chill beers in the conditioning tank.)

 FILTERING AND PACKAGING: For a final polish, some beers are filtered for optimum clarity. Others are sent directly to cans, bottles, and kegs, ready for your consumption.

WITHOUT YEAST, YOU'RE NOTHING

In 1949 in New York City, a strike shuttered breweries for 81 days. One of the many casualties was the yeast strain of Brooklyn's popular Trommer's Evergreen Brewery. When production restarted, the brewers were forced to introduce a new strain. The beer tasted drastically different, its popularity plummeted, and by 1951 the brewery had been sold.

Researchers at the University of Florence discovered that during the winter, Saccharomyces cerevisiae has a safe, warm refuge in the guts of wasps.

YEAST OF EDEN

A beer's flavor, aroma, mouthfeel, and finish are the result of a complex stew of hops, grains, yeast, and even the water used—its properties and mineral content play a significant role in brewing. Of those four ingredients, yeast steers the oxcart of aroma and flavor. Yeast is a beer's beating heart. It's why a hefeweizen recalls cloves or bananas and why some sour beers' flavors are more in line with stinky cheese.

There are two families of yeast. *Ale yeasts* favor warmer temperatures, reclining at the top of a fermentation tank and creating flavors and aromas that are slightly estery—that is, fruity. Ales encompass a colossal range of styles, ranging from golden IPAs to dark-as-night stouts, and are often sweeter and fuller-bodied than the second main family, lagers. Like polar bears, bottom-fermenting *lager yeasts* prefer cooler temperatures. Lagers are typically crisp, delicate, and as refreshing as swimming in a pool on a hot summer day.

Yeast is introduced to the wort after it has been cooled to the appropriate temperature; each yeast grows best in a different temperature range. Wort that is too hot can kill or stress yeast, resulting in unwanted flavors. Wort that is too cold can make yeast sluggish, increasing the fermentation time and potentially allowing unwelcome bacteria to infiltrate the liquid. (For centuries, Belgium's Senne region has specialized in spontaneously fermented brews known as *lambics*. After the wort has cooled, the brewery allows wild yeasts to settle naturally in the beer. See page 229 for more on lambics.)

After fermentation is complete, many breweries harvest a beer's yeast, store it, and repitch it in a new batch of beer. According to the yeast supplier Wyeast Laboratories, breweries can reuse the same batch of yeast safely 7 to 10 times before it must be discarded. (Over time, the yeast can mutate or become contaminated.)

Finally, although lagers are synonymous with Germany and the Czech Republic, researchers recently discovered that the yeast strain actually hails from Patagonia in South America. The yeast probably hitched a ride on an oceangoing vessel, over time finding its way to Bavaria. There it fused with the top-fermenting *Saccharomyces cerevisiae* yeast strain, creating the *S. uvarum* strain and clearing the path for the rise of lager in the fifteenth century.

FERMENTATION

Fermentation is the primary reason people wear lampshades on their heads and grope for aspirin in the morning.

Scientifically speaking, fermentation is the process in which yeasts convert sugars into carbon dioxide and alcohol. Historically, alcohol has played a crucial role in ensuring that Western civilization did not drop dead of cholera, dysentery, and other devastating waterborne diseases. These days in America, we can turn on a tap and reasonably expect that the gushing water will not contain killer microbes. Until recent times, however, water often was contaminated or dangerous to drink. Not so beer. During its production water is boiled, assassinating many lurking microbes. Then alcohol performs its antiseptic duties, keeping wicked pathogens from setting up camp in beer and making it safe to drink—in moderation, mind you.

How long does yeast take to turn wort into bottle-ready beer? That answer can be broken down by families of beer. Ales can be ready to consume in as little as two or three weeks, whereas lagers take up to six weeks or longer, hence their name: *lagern* means "to rest" in German. (Before the advent of refrigeration, lagers were fermented underground in caves or stone cellars.) Spontaneously fermented beers do not follow such rigid timelines. Naturally infected with wild yeast and bacteria, these sour, funky beers sometimes take years to fully develop the desired flavors.

ALCOHOL

A beer's degree of booziness is measured by its percentage of ABV, or alcohol by volume, which signifies the proportion of the total volume of liquid that is alcohol.

Calculating ABV requires a hydrometer. By using flotation, it measures the difference in gravity—that is, density—between unadulterated water and water containing dissolved sugar. At 60°F, the hydrometer is calibrated to measure 1.000 in pure water; a denser liquid results in a higher reading. After boiling the grains and creating wort, brewers cool the sugar-filled broth and take an initial measurement of what's known as *original gravity*. Next, the yeasts are unleashed in the beer and attack the sugary buffet as ravenously as a pack of starving high schoolers, creating CO_2 and blessed alcohol.

When fermentation is finished, the now-boozy beer is measured with a hydrometer again. The *final gravity*, as the number is known, is subtracted from the original gravity and multiplied by 131. The result is ABV. Though ABV is the customary craft-brewing standard measurement, some brewers still use alcohol by weight (ABW). Don't let this flummox you. Here's a quick way to convert ABW to ABV: multiply by 1.25. Alcohol is about 80 percent the weight of water, making a 6 percent ABV beer about 4.8 percent ABW.

NO BREWERY, NO PROBLEM

Mystic Brewery in Boston is a curious brewery operation. The married owners, Bryan and Emily Greenhagen, do not brew. Instead, the MIT grads and scientists (he worked in commercial yeast strain development, and she spends her days turning agricultural waste into ethanol) use local fruit to isolate, cultivate, and propagate their own yeast strains to make Mystic beer. Oh, and they don't have a brewery on site: they get their wort from elsewhere and focus on the fermentation. Their saisons and abbey ales are worth seeking out on your next trip to the Northeast.

Attenuation *measures the percentage of the wort's sugars that the yeast consumes, usually 65 to 85 percent. A lower percentage results in a maltier, fuller-bodied brew, whereas a higher percentage creates a drier beer with dialed-down sweetness.*

THIRST FOR EDUCATION

In San Diego, yeast supplier White Labs runs a tasting room designed to demonstrate how yeast strains and fermentation techniques affect beer, brewing multiple versions of the same beer and dosing them with different yeasts. It's part classroom, part pub, and all fun (*whitelabs.com*).

Chris White is the cofounder of White Labs.

ABV AND FLAVOR

Generally, a higher ABV signifies a sweeter and more full-bodied taste because it is malt that drives the boozemobile. The more malts that are used, the more sugars are available for yeast to eat, leading to more alcohol. To balance out the sweet surplus, brewers turn to bitter hops.

That doesn't mean that low-strength beers lack flavor. Instead of overdosing on malt, brewers use yeast strains, hops, and specialty grains to concoct flavorful beers in the shallow end of the alcohol pool. They're called session beers, since you can have several of them in a drinking session without sliding off your stool. As Chris Lohring, the founder of Massachusetts's session-focused Notch Brewing, says: "Craft beer enhances our time together; session beer extends it. Who doesn't want to extend the good times?"

In the United Kingdom, session beers typically tip the scales at less than 4 percent ABV, accounting for most of that country's milds and bitters. (Low alcohol is a by-product of convivial pub culture and tariffs, in which beers are taxed according to alcohol level.) In the United States, the Brewers Association guidelines state that a session beer must range between 4 and 5.1 percent ABV. That's a tad high for my taste. Instead, I prefer the philosophy preached by the Philadelphia-based beer writer Lew Bryson, whose online Session Beer Project (*sessionbeerproject.blogspot.com*) touts the charms of beers that are "low alcohol but not low taste." According to Bryson, session beers should be "4.5 percent alcohol by volume or less, flavorful enough to be interesting, balanced enough for multiple pints, conducive to conversation, and reasonably priced." *Session* is a catchall phrase applied to styles ranging from dry Irish stouts to hoppy pale ales and everything in between. Bryson would be the first to admit that the ABV may be arbitrary, but a line had to be drawn, and I'll proudly join him in waving the 4.5 percent flag.

AN EXTREME COMPETITION

For yeasts, alcohol can be too much of a good thing. Each strain has a certain alcohol tolerance: a point at which the microorganisms refuse to create more booze no matter how much wort you feed them. (Carbonation is also curtailed or even eliminated in the presence of ramped-up alcohol.) This places a natural limit on a beer's strength. Of course, for modern breweries, a barrier is merely an excuse to seek a taller ladder.

To create the rich, roasty World Wide Stout (its ABV ranges from 15 to

WE SUPPORT THE SESSION BEER PROJE

Thanks, I'll Have Another

sessionbeerproject.blogspot.com

SERVED HERE

20 percent), Dogfish Head uses six different yeast strains over seven months of fermentation. Sam Adams enlisted an ale yeast and a special strain reserved for Champagne to make the 2012 version of its blended, barrel-aged Utopias, which measured 29 percent ABV—that is, stronger than port. (Utopias is released biannually.) That's the current record holder for naturally fermented beer. Freeze-distilled beers make those numbers seem downright quaint. Here are some of the strongest beers ever brewed. Note: Most of these beers were made once and then retired.)

29%: Dave, **HAIR OF THE DOG BREWING COMPANY**
This English-style barley wine was frozen three times, resulting in the concentrated nectar. It debuted in 1994, but owner Alan Sprints occasionally releases limited quantities of Dave.

39%: Black Damnation VI–Messy, **DE STRUISE BROUWERS**
For this one-off, the Belgian brewers sent an imperial stout through a double-eisbock process, miraculously retaining the carbonation.

40%: Schorschbock 40%, **SCHORSCHBRÄU**
Known for its strong beers, this German brewer entered an alcohol arms race with . . .

41%: Sink the Bismarck!, **BREWDOG**
. . . this cheeky Scottish brewery, which has made its name with marketing gimmicks.

43%: Schorschbock 43%, **SCHORSCHBRÄU**
Not to be outdone, the Germans' syrupy release wrested away the world's strongest beer title from BrewDog—temporarily.

55%: The End of History, **BREWDOG**
Stuffed inside a dozen taxidermied stoats and squirrels, the beer was both monstrous and monstrously strong.

57.5%: Finis Coronat Opus, **SCHORSCHBRÄU**
This beer's name translates to "the end crowns the work." The battle was won . . .

60%: Start the Future, **'T KOELSCHIP**
. . . until the Dutch brewery one-upped them. Still, victory soon turned to defeat…

65%: Armageddon, **BREWMEISTER**
…at the hands of *another* ABV-crazed Scottish brewery. The title is safe. For now.

TYPICAL ALCOHOL RANGES OF SELECTED BEERS

LAGERS AND PILSNERS
4% to 5.5%

HEFEWEIZEN
4% to 6%

WITBIERS
4% to 6%

PALE ALES
4% to 6%

PORTERS AND STOUTS
4% to 7%

AMERICAN INDIA PALE ALES
5.5% to 7.5%

DOUBLE/IMPERIAL PALE ALES
7.5% to 12%

IMPERIAL STOUTS
8% to 12%

BARLEY WINES
8% to 15%

In 1612, Hans Christensen
and Adrian Bloch opened
the first brewery in British
North America in New
Amsterdam—the future
home of New York City. By
the 1620s, Dutch settlers
had started planting hops
in Manhattan. That's right:
America's beating heart
of commerce was once an
agrarian paradise.

CARBONATION

Effervescence is a critical component of every beer. Bubbles affect mouthfeel and the perception of bitterness as well as the formation of the beer's foamy head. Although some beer drinkers consider the head wasted space, a foamy cap—caused by CO_2 rising to the surface—captures many of a beer's volatile compounds, offering a more appealing aroma.

There are two main techniques to fizz brew. The first is *forced carbonation*. Beer is pasteurized and filtered to remove yeasts, resulting in a clearer, more consistent, shelf-stable product that will not evolve; it's effectively dead. Because the technique nixes carbonation, the beer is chilled to serving temperature and introduced to compressed CO_2, which is absorbed into the beer via osmosis. *Et voilà!* Bubbles. (Most draft beer is force-carbonated.)

Second, there is *bottle conditioning*, which keeps yeast in beer. The liquid is sealed in a bottle alongside an addition of sugar or wort and perhaps extra yeast. (Brewers sometimes filter beer for clarity and then add a new yeast dose.) The microorganisms munch the sugar, creating natural carbonation as a by-product; the

ABV is not radically altered. It can take several weeks for beer to reach optimal effervescence, and so this is not an option for brewers rushing to meet a production schedule. You can identify a bottle-conditioned beer by the layer of sediment at the bottom of the bottle. That's perfectly acceptable and will not slay your insides. If you're curious, swirl your beer to incorporate the yeast and then take a sip.

Alternatively, if you pour an unpasteurized and unfiltered beer into a *firkin*—a wood, plastic, or, more often, metal keg that holds 10.8 gallons, also called a *cask*—the live yeasts develop a gentle natural carbonation, creating what is known as cask ale. Because firkins aren't pressurized, hand-pumped "beer engines" or gravity dispenses the nectar. Cask ale is best savored at 55 degrees, a moderate temperature that accentuates the nuanced flavors, softer mouthfeel, and fragrant aromas. The beer is alive, developing and changing flavor every day, even after it has been tapped. Long a tradition in Britain, cask ale is becoming a mainstay at better American alehouses.

Guinness, too, is a bar stalwart. Its staying power is due largely to its luscious, creamy head and mouthfeel. This is achieved via nitrogenation, in which the beer is carbonated with a 70/30 or 75/25 mixture of nitrogen and carbon dioxide. When it's dispensed on draft, a similar blend of "beer gas" is used to push the beer from the keg and through a special tap outfitted with a small disc called a restrictor plate. This slows the flow of beer, channeling it through small holes and a narrow nozzle. The dissolved nitrogen cascades down the side of the glass and then bubbles up through the center. Nitrogen has smaller bubbles than carbon dioxide, resulting in the trademark pillowy foam. Besides stouts, bars are serving nitrogenated IPAs and cream ales, bringing the tiny bubbles to a bigger audience.

PACK IT UP, PACK IT IN

Beer packaging used to be so simple: cheap lagers were sold in aluminum cans, and craft brews and imports were put in 12-ounce glass bottles. No longer. Today's beers are sold in an impressive array of glass and aluminum packages, each with its own distinct merits.

ALUMINUM CANS: These easily crushable containers have long been derided for the tinny taste they impart. That's been eliminated by a water-based polymer lining that prevents beer from coming into contact with the aluminum. In addition, cans are easily recyclable, are able to travel where bottles can't tread (backpacking, the lake, the beach, stadiums), and keep light from striking beer, ensuring a fresher and more flavorful product. Craft brewers have even started using 16-ounce cans, putting a pint in your palm. Yes, there are trace amounts of bisphenol A (BPA) in a can's epoxy-resin lining, but you'd need to drink more than 450 cans of beer to exceed the daily recommended dose, according to the U.S. Environmental Protection Agency (EPA).

BOTTLES: When the craft-beer movement kicked off, brewers turned to brown bottles, in part to distinguish their products from green-bottled foreign imports (Heineken, Grolsch) and mass-market macrobrews. However, the classic, elegant craft-beer packaging is not without its drawbacks. The breakage-prone bottles' caps are not always sealed properly, letting carbonation and beer leak out. Plus, whether the glass is brown, green, or clear, every bottle lets in ultraviolet (UV) light, which can cause beer to smell skunky. That's a result of the presence of hops, which, when boiled, release isohumulones. When light strikes these chemicals, they create chemical compounds that are also found in skunks' spray.

Golden Road Brewing is one of the bright lights of Los Angeles's beer scene. Their beers are primarily released on draft and in 16-ounce cans, including Point the Way IPA, which smells of peaches and passion fruit, and refreshing, lightly tart Golden Road Hefeweizen.

Beer bottles are most definitely not "one size fits all."

- *12-ounce bottle (355 ml):* The standard bottle size in the United States and what's commonly found in a six-pack. Also called a longneck because of the bottle's elongated neck. In Europe, the standard bottle is 11.2 ounces, or 330 ml. Many beers also are sold in 500-ml, or 16.9-ounce, bottles.

- *22-ounce bottle (650 ml):* Also called bombers, these large-format bottles often contain higher-alcohol beers that are best shared with a friend or two.

- *750-ml bottle (25.4 ounces):* Presenting a dinner table–worthy appearance, these wine-size bottles typically are sealed with a Champagne cork and a wire cage. The format often is used for stronger or more effervescent brews, such as sour ales or Belgian-style beers.

GROWLERS: Used to be, if you wanted a pint of fresh draft beer, you had to sidle up to a bar. Now beer shops, breweries, restaurants, and bars are selling draft beer by the growler. It's a reusable 64-ounce (1.9-liter) glass jug—often decorated with the logo of a brewery, brewpub, or beer shop—that can retain the crispness of keg-fresh brew for around a week (after opening, about 36 hours). Containing four pints, the glass jug is the perfect size for sharing with fellow beer lovers. When your growler is empty, do not let it marinate with the dregs of the beer. As soon as possible, rinse out the jug with hot water and turn it upside down to dry. A moldy growler is a major no-no. If that happens, just add a few drops of bleach, fill the jug with warm water, and give it a serious swirl. Then rinse, rinse, rinse.

The standard measurement for brewery production is the barrel. A barrel is equal to 31 gallons (117 liters) of beer. The standard keg (you know, the kind seen at college parties across the country) is a half barrel, holding 15.5 gallons (58.5 liters) of beer.

RECOMMENDED SERVING TEMPERATURES

Though taking beer's temperature would be a wildly funny visual, I don't expect you to insert a thermometer into your brew. However, not every beer should be served ice-cold. In fact, some beers do not reveal their true personality and character fully until they've warmed up—kind of like people.

Light beers, advertisements tout, are crisp, easy drinking, and best served at temperatures penguins can appreciate. Here's why: frosty temps mute a beer's aroma

RECOMMENDED SERVING TEMPERATURES

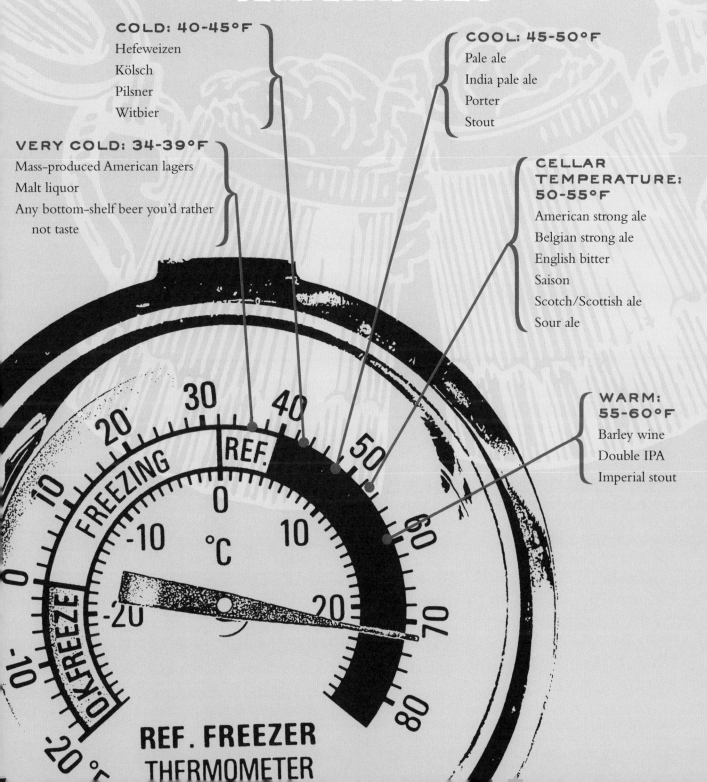

COLD: 40-45°F

Hefeweizen

Kölsch

Pilsner

Witbier

COOL: 45-50°F

Pale ale

India pale ale

Porter

Stout

VERY COLD: 34-39°F

Mass-produced American lagers

Malt liquor

Any bottom-shelf beer you'd rather
not taste

CELLAR TEMPERATURE: 50-55°F

American strong ale

Belgian strong ale

English bitter

Saison

Scotch/Scottish ale

Sour ale

WARM: 55-60°F

Barley wine

Double IPA

Imperial stout

FREEZING

REF.

O.K.FREEZE

°C

REF. FREEZER
THERMOMETER

AN IMPORTANT DATE

To ensure freshness, opt for beers that are stored in coolers and check the can or bottle for the packaging date. More delicate, aromatic styles such as lagers, pilsners, pale ales, and IPAs should be consumed as close to the bottling date as possible.

How clean are your beer glasses? To test them, rinse out a glass and sprinkle it with salt; wherever the seasoning does not stick is dirty. Sometimes oils or soap remains behind, affecting head formation.

* * *

There's no need to blow your bank account on glassware. The Core Four are a pilsner, weizen, pint (either shaker or nonic), and a goblet or chalice.

and flavor while amplifying carbonation's trademark tingle. But as a beer warms, it loses carbonation and aromas become more apparent. That's why Bud, Miller, and Coors suggest that you sip their beer ice-cold. (Most bars serve draft beer at 38°F.) Without that tingle, you're left with a warm, flavor-deprived beer.

Behold, a basic primer for serving temperatures, with an important caveat: do not worry about matching the temps to the degree. An easy rule of thumb is that stronger beers can and should be served a touch warmer, and freezing temperatures are not your friend.

AT YOUR SERVICE

From coast to coast, there's one commonality in American bars: the pint glass. The sturdy, conical cylinder from which you sip beer originally was designed to mix drinks with a larger metal cup and thus was dubbed the *shaker pint*. American bartenders loved the vessels' stackability and started using them to serve beer—about 16 ounces, though thick-bottomed glasses that hold 14 ounces or less are increasingly common. Across the Atlantic, the British imperial pint is a government-regulated 19.2 ounces (568 ml). Barkeeps use authorized glasses etched with the word *pint* and European Union's official "CE" mark.

Although the utilitarian pint glasses are omnipresent, they're not always the best vessel for savoring beer. Certain glasses have been designed to capture and concentrate a beer's aroma, help retain a fluffy head, or simply showcase the breakneck bubbles and color. Though I'm not so snobby as to snub a beer straight from a can or bottle, I believe brews are best guzzled in glassware. Partly this is for visual pageantry.

A beer is designed to engage your senses of smell, taste, sight, and touch. By keeping beer confined to a light-blocking brown bottle, you lose the visual component, the ability to observe clarity or the lack thereof. Furthermore, a little head is a good thing, allowing you to get a solid snoutful of aromatic yeast by-products such as fruity esters and alcohol, hop oils, and/or spices. A final point to remember: do not freeze your glasses before pouring beer into them. Frozen glasses can create ice crystals in beer, which affect foaming, and frost can absorb flavors from your freezer.

GLASSWARE

FLUTE: *Although closely associated with Champagne, the flute lends itself well to lively beers such as Belgian lambics, American sour and wild ales, and fruit-driven beers. The glass's long, slender shape enhances and displays carbonation as well as concentrating the aroma.*

GOBLET AND CHALICE: *Looking a bit like peg-legged soup bowls, goblets and chalices are engineered to help beers retain their head. Linguistically speaking, goblets are the thinner and more delicate of the two. However, the glassware is basically interchangeable. They're ideal for burly Belgian ales.*

NONIC PINT: *The handsome, all-purpose glass's bulge serves both to improve grip and to prevent glasses from clinging together when stacked and chipping, hence, "no nick"—the origin of the name. This glass is aces for a session beer.*

PILSNER: *Tall, narrow, and tapered, this runway model serves to highlight a pilsner's seltzer-like effervescence and golden hue as well as maintain a pillowy head.*

SHAKER PINT: *The general beer glass. Though durable and workaday, the shaker's shape does not enhance a beer's aromas or flavors.*

SNIFTER: *Classically used for cognac and brandy, the balloon-shaped snifter is ably suited for strong ales such as imperial stouts, double IPAs, and barley wines. The snifter's tapered shape ensnares the volatiles, and it's suited for swirling—and not spilling on yourself, might I add.*

STANGE: *This narrow cylindrical glass traditionally is used to serve Germany's delicate, summer-friendly kölsch beer, highlighting its subtle nuances. Fun, if unsurprising, fact: stange means "stick."*

STEIN: *I like to think of the handled mug as a good-time friend. It's sturdy enough to withstand a long afternoon of clinking lagers, and the wide mouth means that more beer will slide into your stomach.*

TULIP: *Named after the flower, the stemmed tulip's body helps captures aromas, and the flared lip helps maintain a thick head. The tulip is tops for potent, malty beers such as double IPAs, Scotch ales, and strong Belgian ales.*

WEIZEN GLASS: *This tall, curvaceous glass is great for serving a cloudy, refreshing hefeweizen. The large size (usually a half liter) allows people to anoint the handsome wheat beer with a kingly crown of foam.*

*Throughout the book,
I include personal
impressions of some of my
favorite examples of each
beer style. Consider them
broad impressions, not the
gospel. Trust your own nose
and tongue. In the long run,
they're far more important
than mine.*

ON TASTING BEER

No matter where I travel, I'm always asked the same two questions: Why are you not fat? and How can I get your job?

The answer to the first query is genetics and a healthy dose of bicycling. As for the second, I imbibed tons of beer and actually woke up the next morning to write about my experiences. (Hey, being witty with a brain-melting hangover takes, uh, talent.)

To this day, I've yet to turn my back on drinking a beer. However, I've met plenty of beers that I don't want to drink twice or that I've dumped down a drain. And that's okay. There are thousands of beers brewed around the world, with hundreds more released every month. Some are bound to be duds, and others simply will not tickle your particular taste buds. The key to increasing your carbonated knowledge is to sample as many different beers as you can stomach. It's tough work, I know, but I believe you're up to the task.

Tasting beer can be broken down into three steps: appearance, swirl and smell, and taste. Crack open a bottle and follow along.

APPEARANCE

Sometimes at bars, I have a staring problem. When a beauty interests me, I'll train my gaze on her form, letting my eyeballs wander from top to bottom and back again. Only when I've examined every inch of the stunner do I make my bold move. I part my lips, reach out, and grab the . . . glass.

When it comes to beer, looks are important. Its color, clarity, and head speak volumes about the awaiting taste. Begin by pouring enough beer for several sizable mouthfuls into the proper glassware (see page 33), making sure to generate a sizable head. You don't want a glass full of foam, but a creamy cap is crucial to an assessment.

Before pouring beer, I tilt the glass to a 45-degree angle and slowly dispense till the glass is halfway filled. Then I bring the glass upright and pour the remainder of the beer straight down, creating foam. (Some highly carbonated beer styles, such as hefeweizens, produce great poofs of foam and may not require you to tilt the glass upright.)

Now, take a good look at your glass:

1. First, evaluate the beer's tint. Hold it up to a light and observe the hue. Red often signifies rich caramel flavor, whereas black usually denotes coffee or chocolate. But don't let the tint color your perception. Sometimes the darkest beers will drink dainty and light and pale-gold brews will sit on your tongue like a sack of bricks.

2. Next, note the clarity of the beer. Many brews are filtered, which removes yeast and lets their natural colors shine—it's a bit like polishing jewelry. Because bottle-conditioned beer and cask ale keep their yeast, they can have a cloudy appearance. Remember that certain beer styles, such as German hefeweizens and Belgian witbiers, are hazy by design.

3. Finally, examine the head of foam. Its color can range from bone-white to tan, with a creamy texture like meringue pie or perhaps thin bubbles like dish soap. Note whether the head lasts a long time or disappears in a flash. Does the foam lace a glass when it vanishes? What do I mean by that? When foam dissipates, it often clings to the glass in a pattern that resembles lace as frilly as a lady's finest undergarment. Regard lacing as a mark of quality. Foam is a key signifier of the quality of beer.

SWIRL AND SMELL

After you've gotten an eyeful of your beer, put your snout to work. Gently swirl the glass, which helps oxygen mix with the beer. This agitates its volatile compounds, releasing a more pronounced aroma. Now take a series of short and long sniffs, sending beer molecules traveling to the northernmost reaches of your nasal cavity. That rarefied area is where olfactory receptors reside, rendering molecules' raw chemical data into digestible electrical signals that are transmitted to the brain.

Do not worry if the terms required to describe a beer escape you. Tying smells to words is tough, and I'm often left marble-mouthed. Start by trying to ID the beer style, then work your way into descriptors that the brew exhibits—or is lacking. There are two key terms to remember: *bouquet* refers to the aromatics that the hops contribute, and *aroma* signifies the overall smell of the beer, encompassing the grains, yeast, *and* hops.

Smelling beer is a crucial step in the tasting process and one that people often rush through to get that luscious nectar between their lips. Your nose is a marvel, able to perceive several thousand unique scents—aroma is estimated to make up 80 percent of flavor. I like to smell a beer at least two or three times. This may seem like overkill, but consider that a beer's aroma changes as it warms and the volatile aromas dissipate. New scents appear, and old ones disappear. For the second tasting, try holding the glass in your hand to warm the beer slightly. Cover the glass and swirl again, capturing the volatile aromas beneath your palm. When you're ready, release your hand and inhale deeply. Understanding a beer's aroma will help you identify flaws or defects.

Scientists from The Johns Hopkins University School of Medicine recently discovered the brain's "nose plug," a mental switch that allows people to stop smelling the same odor even if it is, well, right beneath our nose. This response short-circuits sensory overload, desensitizing us to subtle variations. To avoid that, sniff something totally different, like a pen, in between whiffs of your beer.

* * *

Recent studies have shown that when judging beer, women may have a more acute sense of smell and taste than men. Underscoring that, every year SABMiller runs an international competition among its 2,000 beer tasters to uncover the company's best taste buds. In 2009 and 2010, the winner was Poland's Joanna Wasilewska; the Canary Islands' Carmen Herrera Benitez took the title in 2011.

One important note: don't worry if you are unable to smell what someone else does in a beer. Olfactory receptors differ from person to person and can be affected by sickness, exposure to irritants or allergens, and even spicy food.

TASTE

Now comes the moment that every beer drinker awaits: the taste. Sip a solid mouthful—no more than an ounce, my thirsty friend—and let the liquid slide over your lips and entire tongue, slowly allowing it to waterfall down your throat and into your stomach. Wine drinkers spit, but beer drinkers happily swallow. Doing so provides a full snapshot, from the first bubbles to the last lingering blast of bitterness. Besides, why waste delightfully drinkable beer?

After the first taste, pause to reflect, then repeat. For me, three is the magic number of sips for acclimating my palate. What's foreign becomes familiar, and only then do I understand a beer's nuances, pleasures, and shortcomings. Your tongue can identify five basic tastes: salty, sweet, sour, bitter, and umami (translated from the Japanese as "savory," it's found in soy sauce, shiitake mushrooms, and miso). Make the most of them. And forget everything you were taught in your school textbooks.

For decades, health and science books have drilled into students' brains that tastes can be experienced only on certain parts of the tongue. The front was for sweetness, and bitterness backed up the rear. This is all wrong, so very wrong. Science has debunked the tongue map, discovering that we experience taste equally across the tongue's landscape. The front half of the tongue registers all tastes evenly, the sides better perceive sourness, and the back is more sensitive to bitterness.

During moments of extreme thirst or after a hard day's work, I've been known to gulp beer as greedily as a desert traveler discovering water in an oasis. However, I make this my exception, not the rule. Appraising a beer's taste requires thought and deliberation, not just a mainline hit to the pleasure receptors. Furthermore, when sipping a beer, it's important to understand your personal thresholds and prejudices. For example, extreme bitterness may rub you the wrong way, but it's the right flavor for a double IPA. Bypass first-sip conclusions and instead carefully consider these common taste components:

ACIDITY: Although acidity in the average beer will indicate a tragic infection or disaster, sourness is accepted in Belgium's gueuzes, lambics, krieks, and Flemish sour ales as well as Germany's gose and Berliner weisse and American sour ales.

AFTERTASTE: These are the flavors that linger in your mouth long after the last sip. Is it pleasant and balanced? Or is it harsh and lacking? An aftertaste is what compels you to take one sip after another, a reminder of the awaiting pleasure—or it's a sign that perhaps the beer should be sentenced to the sink's drain. Also known as *finish*.

BITTERNESS: Bitterness is marked by a dry, harsh taste. It's lauded in IPAs and barley wines but can overwhelm lighter styles. Roasted malt can supply appropriate bitterness to porters and stouts.

MOUTHFEEL: The sum perception of the beer's body, carbonation, and afterfeel (the latter ranges from to oily to sticky to astringent). This will be felt across your tongue and palate. A beer's body can range from wan and watery to as viscous as used motor oil. The standard terms are *light*, *medium*, and *full*, and fuller-bodied beers will be sweeter.

SWEETNESS: Malts supply sweetness, and stronger, barley-heavy beers sometimes sock you with residual sugars. Do they overwhelm, or are they balanced by bitterness?

TERMS TO KNOW: NEGATIVE QUALITIES

Here's the language you need to describe why your beer is lousy.

ACETALDEHYDE: This by-product of fermentation creates aromas and flavors of green apples. Though it is great for keeping doctors away, you do not want green apple in your beer.

ACETIC: The flavors and aromas recall vinegar; it's the result of aerobic bacteria producing acetic acid.

ASTRINGENT: A harsh, puckering, drying sensation that verges on tannic, it's caused by brewers mishandling grain. Imagine gnawing on grape skins.

CLOYING: Overly sweet; the beer equivalent of watching Saturday morning cartoons while eating Lucky Charms.

DIACETYL: An aroma or flavor of butterscotch or buttered popcorn. It's acceptable in certain beer styles, but it's a defect in others. Personally, I despise diacetyl.

DIMETHYL SULFIDE (DMS): Think cooked sweet corn; DMS is a sulfur compound caused by a bacterial infection or problems while boiling the grain.

A SIP OF **WATER** *or an* **UNSALTED CRACKER** WILL SERVE TO **clear** your **palate**.

Go to the nearest mirror and take a close look at your tongue. The raised bumps you see are not taste buds but rather papillae, which contain 50 to 150 taste buds apiece. The average person comes equipped with around 10,000 taste buds.

ESTERY: Fruity aromas that arise from ale fermentation; the scent recalls strawberries, pears, peaches, apples, bananas, or papayas. It's common in British and Belgian-style beers but a defect when present in other styles.

FUSEL: You'll know it by the solvent-like scent; a fusel-y beer is like a hot plate for your palate. It can be caused by too-warm fermentation temperatures or excessive yeast.

GRAINY: Astringent flavor of raw grains caused by grain husks or toasted malt; often used negatively.

GRASSY: Flavors that recall fresh-cut grass or chlorophyll; poorly stored grains and hops are the culprit. When used in abundance, certain American and British hops varieties produce grassy notes that are appropriate.

METALLIC: Flavor of copper, coins, or—eww—blood. Only vampires willingly drink blood. The off flavors can be caused by improperly stored grains, high iron content in water, brewing equipment, and even bottle caps.

OXIDIZED: Exposing beer to oxygen creates a musty, papery flavor reminiscent of wet cardboard or perhaps sherry; can be found in past-their-prime beers.

PHENOLIC: The smell of Band-Aids, plastic, or medicine. Beer should be medicine, not taste like it.

SKUNKY: When a beer is exposed to ultraviolet light, it creates a chemical compound found in skunks' spray. Clear- and green-bottle beers such as Corona and Heineken are susceptible to this defect.

SOUR: Acidity is pungent, and notes of vinegar signify acetic acid; sourness can also be lactic, like yogurt. It occurs when beers are infected with unwanted—or desired—bacteria and yeast.

SULFUR: Think matches, rotten eggs, Old Faithful.

VEGETAL: Recalls cooked vegetables such as celery, onions, and cabbage; appetizing, eh?

YEASTY: Like drinking liquefied bread dough. It can be caused by unhealthy yeast or beer that has been in contact with dead yeast for too long; the yeast devours itself in a process called autolysis, creating harsh, sulfury flavors.

Try this fun trick: take turns closing a nostril with an index finger and smelling your beer. Detect anything different? Each nostril can discern different scents.

TERMS TO KNOW: POSITIVE QUALITIES

BANANAS AND CLOVES: A classic profile of a hefeweizen; the aroma comes courtesy of a yeast strain.

BARNYARD: Sour ales and lambics that have been spiked with *Brettanomyces* yeast often have aromas that recall a frolic through an animal-filled farm—in a good way!

BISCUITY: A lightly toasted malt creates flavors of fresh-baked biscuits or Saltine crackers.

CLEAN: Free of unpleasant aromas and flavors.

CREAMY: A pleasingly soft, smooth mouthfeel and appealing texture.

CRISP: Bone-dry and effervescent, with very little sugar. I liken it to drinking seltzer with a boozy edge.

DRY: A sharp finish lacking sweetness.

EARTHY: Aromas and flavor reminiscent of a stroll through a forest.

FLORAL: Used to describe hop flavor and aroma.

HERBACEOUS: Used to describe hop flavor and aroma.

NUTTY: Aromas and flavors that call to mind nuts; comes from grains.

PINEY: Used to describe hop bitterness, flavor, aroma.

PUNGENT: Used to describe hop bitterness, flavor, aroma.

RESINOUS: Used to describe hop bitterness, flavor, aroma.

SHERRY-LIKE: Hold on: oxidization isn't totally terrible. The aromas and flavors of dry sherry are welcome in strong old ales and barley wines.

SILKY: A slick and smooth mouthfeel, often courtesy of oatmeal.

SPICY: Used to describe hop bitterness, flavor, aroma.

TANGY: A pleasingly sharp flavor that's not as intense as tart (see below).

TART: A strongly acidic sensation; often found in sour beers.

TOAST: A malt trait typically associated with darker beers.

VINOUS: Aromas and flavors reminiscent of wine.

FEST IS BEST

Throughout the book, you will notice that I often make a special mention of whether a beer won a medal at the Great American Beer Festival (GABF). Here's why that's such a big deal: since brewing guru Charlie Papazian founded the GABF in Colorado in 1982, the annual event has grown into the country's most prestigious beer festival. Each fall, around 50,000 microbrew enthusiasts descend on Denver's Colorado Convention Center for a three-day extravaganza featuring more than 2,700 different beers poured by nearly 600 breweries spanning the country. But what sets the GABF apart is the Olympics-worthy judged competition in which breweries vie for gold, silver, and bronze medals in 84 categories. Winning a medal can change a brewery's fortunes in an instant. You have to be quick on the draw to grab a ticket. In 2012, the festival sold out in 45 minutes.

SAVOR

After you've sampled your fill of beer, allow yourself to kick back and savor the flavor. Now's the time to ponder what you imbibed, trying to answer the all-important question: Would I buy this beer or one similar to it ever again? Let these questions whittle your impressions into a sharp point:

- What did you enjoy most about the beer? Chocolaty malts? Floral bouquet? Grapefruit bitterness? A brisk finish?

- Was the beer light-, medium-, or full-bodied?

- What kind of food would you enjoy with the beer?

- If anything, what rubbed your taste buds the wrong way?

- For the style, was the beer well balanced?

- For your taste buds and wallet, was this worth the bucks spent?

- Lastly, would you serve this beer to your friends or family? Or is it something you'd serve your archnemesis?

HOW DO YOU KNOW IF A BEER IS ANY GOOD?

Do you want another? Then that's a good beer. Taste is subjective, and one drinker's bliss is another's dirty dishwater. When I lead tastings and talk to fellow imbibers, I never bad-mouth a beer even if it's a shotgunned can of Bud Light. Each beer, even godforsaken malt liquor, possesses merits that appeal to someone.

NOTES ON THROWING A TERRIFIC TASTING PARTY

My favorite type of dinner party is the potluck. If you've never attended one, here's a rule refresher: every invitee brings a different dish, usually oriented to a theme. Maybe it's Mexican for Cinco de Mayo, rib-clinging southern grub, or a soup party, which is an annual tradition in the Bernstein household. Bite after bite, slurp after slurp, diners are able to sample a broad array of food. It's dinner by a thousand nibbles.

A beer-tasting party is no different. With an endless army of unique brews being released every day, there's no conceivable way you could sample them all in your lifetime—and trust me, I'm trying. Although quantity is an issue, a bigger concern is many beers' head-crushing quality. The marketplace is crammed with beers sold in 22-ounce bottles that boast ABVs above 10 percent. That's not a beer

In 2012, Merriam-Webster added "craft beer" to the dictionary. The definition: "a specialty beer produced in limited quantities."

I want to drink by myself. But share with a friend? That's the point of a tasting party, a low-key sharing of information, opinions, and beer.

At its simplest, a tasting party can be a free-flowing bottle share in which guests break out special beers, perhaps ones hunkering in a fridge or a looker that caught their eye at a beer shop. (Every beer lover I know saves bottles for a special celebration; make this tasting event the celebration.) For a slightly more structured event, orient the evening to a theme, perhaps regional or stylistic. Ask guests to bring a beer from, say, Belgium or the West Coast. Or work your way up the alcoholic ladder from pale ales to IPAs and double IPAs. Remember to keep the pours to a couple of ounces per brew, and so using tumblers, goblets, or chalices is perfectly fine. Instead of absentmindedly glugging, the goal is to sample and discuss, keeping conversation and the beers flowing in equal measure as the evening dissolves into night.

HOW TO USE *THE COMPLETE BEER COURSE*

To get the most from this book, I'm ordering you to drink. A lot. As you read *The Complete Beer Course*, you'll notice the sections marked "Two to Taste" that accompany the beer categories. These are the beers I feel best highlight and embody each selected style's flavor, aroma, and mouthfeel. While reading or shortly afterward, you should try at least one of these suggested beers, if not two—twist your arm, right? (I've also listed beers within the text as well as backup beers in case my selections are not available in your city.) Reading these words is just the first step to broadening your beer knowledge. Sampling, savoring, and evaluating these brews will give you a deeper understanding of each style's variations and nuances. The perfect beer is a matter of taste, and training your taste buds matters most.

AN IMPORTANT NOTE ON STYLE

In the beer world, there's been much hullabaloo about the utility of style. Why do beers have to fit within neatly defined parameters? Short answer: they don't. To me, styles prove their worth as a general framework, a reference point for discussion, and a launch pad for future innovation. Consider style to be like an elastic waistband, stretching to accommodate a range of beers.

TAKE IT FROM THE BOTTOM

LAGERS, PILSNERS, AND MORE PLEASURES OF COLD FERMENTATION

HERE'S NO DENYING THE UBIQUITY and dominance of lagers. Belly up to any bar anywhere in the world, from Iceland to India to China, and you'll probably be offered the local low-strength lager, be it Viking, Taj Mahal, or Tsingtao. Their appeal is understandable. Done properly, a crisp, nuanced lager is an easy-drinking thing of beauty. It's not tough to love a lager.

The lager was probably the first beer you drank. I remember mine: Busch Light, bought by the 30-pack and guzzled from a beer bong built from a funnel and plastic tubing. A lager was merely a cold, clear highway to intoxication, a belief underscored by the puny price tag and endless advertising campaigns. It can be tough to love a lager.

Lagers, especially the dominant American lagers, have been dulled down to appeal to the widest range of people, with continent-spanning breweries focusing less on flavor development than on swaying drinkers with the latest flashy commercial. The end result is that the lager has been reduced to the lowest common denominator. In the brew kettles of beer behemoths the lager lost its way, and *lager* became synonymous with *lowbrow*. It's time to reboot that opinion and remind you that more than 150 years ago, lagers and their offspring, the pilsner, revolutionized global beer drinking.

Lagers are born from cold fermentation. The brewing process was perfected in Germany centuries ago and spread across Europe and America, branching out and supplying drinkers with lagers of wildly varying strengths, colors, and flavors suited for every season and drinking occasion. In this chapter I'll introduce you to the surprising world of lagers: strong bocks, dark Munich dunkels, coal-black schwarzbiers that drink unexpectedly light, Oktoberfest-friendly märzens, and the Czech pilsner, all of which set the template for the crisp, clear lager. I'll also be talking about other cold-fermented delights, including altbier, kölsch, and cream ale, a uniquely American construct that does not contain a dollop of dairy. Come on, bud. It's time to shine a light on lagers.

BRING ON THE DARKNESS

Do not let a lager's tint color your taste assumptions. Not every darker-shaded lager is a rich indulgence, ready to overwhelm you with intensely roasty flavors. Make sure your mind is as open as your mouth.

MUNICH DUNKEL

For millennia, German beer was synonymous with dark-hued brews. However, roasting malt over a blazing fire was a difficult thing to accomplish properly. Fermentation was tricky too. Beer could easily and often did go sour. Whatever the reason, brewers often needed to mask off flavors in their beer and did so by adding a proprietary mixture of herbs and spices called *gruit*— or worse. Soot, chalk, chicken blood, poisonous mushrooms, and ox bile were common additives.

That all ended in 1516 when William IV, Duke of Bavaria, introduced

the Reinheitsgebot. The Purity Law's mission was threefold. First, it mandated fixed prices for beer during the wintertime and summertime. Second, it forbade brewers from using wheat or rye to prevent price competition with bakers so that bread remained affordable. Third, it ruled that beer could be prepared only from hops, water, and barley. (The law predated scientific understanding of yeast, which has since been added to the list. Brewers of yore created a new brew by using, unbeknownst to them, the yeast-packed sediment from a previous batch of beer.)

Without recourse to blood, rye, and bile, what were brewers to do? Improve the quality of their beer. During this era, brewers already had begun lagering beer,

partly out of necessity and geography. What is now the state of Bavaria (whose capital is Munich) is in southeastern Germany and encompasses the Bavarian Alps. Winters are glacial. Summers are sweltering. To insulate beers from infection and scorching temperatures, brewers stored it in the cool local caverns. That did the trick, with added benefits. The brewers discovered that long cold storage worked wonders for the beer's maturation, allowing the yeast to sink out of suspension and improve the beer's stability. Inadvertently, the code for bottom-fermented brews was cracked.

Over the centuries, Munich's brewing reputation became tied to this dark lager known as the Munich dunkel (which means "dark" in German). Today,

To put on your bucket list: attending Oktoberfest in Munich.

Nearly five centuries later, some Germans are still not placing a premium on pure ingredients. In 1985, Dr. Helmut Kieninger, a professor who was known as Bavaria's "Beer Pope," was arrested for recommending the use of illegal—and toxic—chemicals that could extend a beer's shelf life and keep it from going bad. While in a Munich jail, he committed suicide.

the smooth beer is known for its lovely bready nose; rich and multifaceted flavors of caramel, coffee, or nuts; gently roasty finish; and a lightness and low ABV that belie the dark-brown, ruby-tinted hue. Dunkel's flavor profile is largely the result of a nineteenth-century invention known as the indirect-heat malt kiln. This coffee roaster–like device gave the barley maltsters greater control over the roasting process, allowing them to pinpoint the malt's flavors and tint. This led to the creation of the sweet and complex Munich malt, the soul of the Munich dunkel. The popularity of the refined style continued through the nineteenth century, when dark lagers relented to light and the brewing world was tossed deliciously topsy-turvy.

BOCK

Lagers get a bad rap for being light, watery, and as boring as C-SPAN. A pointed rebuttal is the bock, a malty and robust lager closely aligned with a head-butting goat. The origin: in the fourteenth century, brewers in the handsome medieval city of Einbeck in what is now the state of Lower Saxony in Germany began brewing an ale unlike any other (remember, this was long before the Reinheitsgebot was enacted). During that era, dark and murky beers that often tasted sweet or tart were the norm. By contrast, Einbeck's liquid wares were made with somewhat lighter malts and about one-third wheat (it added an appealing softness). Contemporary European brewers flavored beers with

TWO TO TASTE: MUNICH DUNKEL

SPATEN MUNCHEN DUNKEL
Spaten-Franziskaner-Bräu
ABV: 5.2%

The pride of Munich presents itself with the color of root beer, topped by a dense and short head that'll disappear faster than my friends when we're settling a bar tab. The scent is baked bread cut with herbal hops and caramel candy, flavors that you'll find as you take each slick, well-carbonated sip.

DARK
Harpoon Brewery
ABV: 5.5%

Boston's first commercial brewery knocks it out of Fenway Park with the medium-bodied Dark, a rich dunkel that delights with its earthy, chocolaty flavors mixed with a splash of coffee. Instead of following a strict Munich script, the lager deviates with a refreshing bit of bitterness.

BACKUP BEERS: *Mother Earth Brewing Dark Cloud, Pennsylvania Brewing Company Penn Dark, Port Brewing Hot Rocks Lager, Saranac Brewery Lake Effect Lager, Staatliches Hofbräuhaus Hofbräu Dunkel, Warsteiner Premium Dunkel*

THE PURITY STING

Before the unification of Germany in 1871, Bavaria insisted that every independent state agree to follow the Reinheitsgebot. This was not to ensure that breweries used first-rate ingredients; instead, Bavaria wanted to curtail competition from beers brewed elsewhere with a wider palette of ingredients. Brewers outside Bavaria were up in arms. Agreeing to the Reinheitsgebot, which was extended to cover all of Germany by 1906, spelled the end of interesting regional styles such as the cherry-flavored Kirschenbier and Braunschweiger Mumme, a thick, sweet, boozy, and bitter ale favored on seafaring treks to the tropics. Germany's ale tradition was slowly extinguished, with the gose, Berliner weisse (see pages 94 – 98), kölsch, and altbier some of the only surviving remnants (more on them on pages 79 and 81). In 1993, the Reinheitsgebot was replaced by the *Vorläufiges Deutsches Biergesetz*, or Provisional German Beer Law, which allows brewers to use yeast (imagine that!), different grains, and, for top-fermenting beers, additional sugars.

A sunny afternoon. An excellent mustache. A full stein of beer. How could life be any better for a German man of a certain age?

gruit, but Einbeck brewers favored hops, which grew well in the region. The flowers' preservative powers prevented spoilage, a critical trait for what came next.

At the time, brewing was mainly a local business, with beers rarely venturing beyond the borders of the towns in which they were made or even beyond people's homes. But Einbeck beers' extended shelf life allowed them to be shipped far and wide. As a member of the Hanseatic League, an economic alliance of cities that dominated the trade of northern Europe from the Baltic to the North Sea (the league's heyday was from the thirteenth century to the seventeenth century), Einbeck sent its strong beer far afield to England, Russia, and Scandinavia. The Einbeck brews became some of the league's most lusted-after exports, winning over drinkers and bestowing the town with the pleasing nickname "city of beer."

Imbibers in southern Bavaria also enjoyed the brawny brew from

It's a little-know fact that when Greece became a monarchy in 1832, the first king was Otto, a prince imported from Bavaria. Otto enforced the Reinheits-gebot, which governed Greece's beer production for more than a century until 1987.

the city they pronounced Ein-*bock*, eventually shortening the beer's name to *bock*—that is, a billy goat. Einbeck's reign did not endure. The Hanseatic League crumbled, and Bavaria tired of importing Einbeck beer at the expense of its local brewing industry. Instead, in the early seventeenth century, Duke Maximilian I of Munich launched a search for Germany's best brewer. Expert Einbeck brewmaster Elias Pichler was lured to Munich, where he was appointed brewmaster at the Hofbräuhaus, the royal brewery founded in 1589 by Wilhelm V, Duke of Bavaria. During Pichler's tour of duty, he re-created his city's famous beer, which in time evolved into a new beer style: the lager. Today's cold-fermented bocks are stronger than the standard-issue lager, navigating the color range from chestnut red to pumpernickel brown. Rich malt is the star of the flavorful show, and bitterness appears only in a supporting role.

> *The German monk and theology professor Martin Luther, who started the Protestant Reformation, once proclaimed: "The best drink known to man is called Einbecker beer."*

TWO TO TASTE: BOCK

EINBECKER UR-BOCK DUNKEL
EINBECKER BRAUHAUS
ABV: 6.5%

The birthplace of bock does not disappoint with the self-named "original" offering, a garnet looker topped by a tight, creamy head. The sweet and toasty aroma skips from caramel to brown sugar, leading to a full body and somewhat sticky flavors of molasses, bready malt, and raisins. You'll dig the dry and spicy finish.

PANDORA'S BOCK
BRECKENRIDGE BREWERY
ABV: 7.5%

To survive a snow-swept Colorado winter (or just an afternoon on the slopes), may I suggest Colorado-based Breckenridge's Pandora's Bock? The mahogany lager's flavor is caramel to the core, presenting a perfume like a holiday snack bowl: toasted pecans and walnuts and dark fruit. Consider the alcohol a concealed weapon.

BACKUP BEERS: *Anchor Brewing Bock Beer, Mahr's Bräu Christmas Bock, Millstream Brewing Company Schokolade Bock, Spoetzl Brewery Shiner Bock, Sprecher Brewing Company Winter Brew, Yuengling Bock*

TWO TO TASTE: DOPPELBOCK

AYINGER CELEBRATOR
BRAUEREI AYING
ABV: 6.7%

In my book, the ne plus ultra of doppelbocks is Ayinger Celebrator. This striking mocha-brown brew delivers a nose of Christmas fruitcake and cocoa. Celebrator drinks nice and silky, with lip-licking flavors of chocolate, coffee, and all the dark fruits you could ever desire. P.S. Each bottle comes with a collectible goat trinket. My wife has several.

DOUBLE BOCK
SAMUEL ADAMS
ABV: 9.5%

This doppelbock is a love letter to malt, with around half a pound of barley required for each 12-ounce bottle of the crimson-brown beer. As a result of the gargantuan grain bill, there's plenty of rich and chewy candy-shop sweetness to be savored. Caramelized sugars and molasses are underscored by a subtle balancing bitterness. Double Bock will warm you like a wool sweater.

BACKUP BEERS: *Atwater Brewery Voodoo Vator Dopplebock, Brauerei Tucher Brau Bajuvator Doppelbock, Paulaner Brauerei Salvator, Smuttynose Brewing Company S'muttonator, Thomas Hooker Liberator Doppelbock, Tröegs Brewing Company Troegenator Double Bock*

DOPPELBOCK

If the bock is a beefed-up lager, the massively rich and malty doppelbock ("double bock") would be a world-class weight lifter. The style tips the scales at anywhere from 7 percent to 10 percent ABV, a strength that underscores its original purpose: to keep monks alive during Lent's 46 days of fasting—Sundays are excluded—leading up to Easter.

Beer, as countless rotund bellies can attest, is chock-full of calories. The more potent the beer is, the more calories are contained therein. Thus, a lager of sizable potency could theoretically sustain food-shunning holy men. In the seventeenth century, the brothers of Munich's St. Francis of Paula (aka the Paulaner monks) were granted a papal dispensation to brew a strong beer suited for consumption during Lent. The beer was known as Sankt Vaterbier, or Holy Father Beer, until the name was corrupted into Salvatorbiere— that is, Salvator, or "savior."

At some point, the brothers began

For more than a century, the Spoetzl Brewery in Shiner, Texas, has been brewing won- derful German beers such as Shiner Hefeweizen, Oktoberfest, and the iconic Bock, which is so ubiquitous in Texas, it might as well be the official state beer.

selling their beer outside the brewery, a no-no because they did not possess the proper permits. In 1780, they finally received an official permit to sell and distribute their doppelbock. The citizens of Munich clamored for this seasonal treat until Napoleon rolled around and banned churches from owning property, levying taxes, or earning a few bucks from a side business—like brewing beer. In 1799, the monastery and brewery were shut down, becoming the property of the Bavarian state.

In 1806, the brewery was rented to the secular brewer Franz-Xaver Zacherl, who licensed the rights to produce the doppelbock. (He bought the brewery in 1813.) Salvator was sold around Easter, and competing breweries soon cottoned to the name. It nearly became as generic as Band-Aid or aspirin, but Zacherl's successors, the Brothers Schmederer, trademarked Salvator in 1896. Their competitors' response was to attach the -*ator* suffix to their doppelbocks,

In 2011, Iowa newspaper editor J. Wilson spent the 46 days of Lent subsisting on a homebrewed doppelbock. Check out an account of his tale, Diary of a Part-Time Monk *(diaryofaparttimemonk .wordpress.com).*

SANTA'S BEER

Though it's often described as a doppelbock, Samichlaus Bier resists neat categorization. Each year on December 6, Austria's Brauerei Schloss Eggenberg brews Samichlaus (Santa Claus in Swiss-German, which is spoken in Austria), a knockout lager with a 14 percent ABV. The beer ages for 10 months before it's bottled, creating a robust, warming elixir that's suitable for savoring now or saving for Christmases to come. Consider Samichlaus the gift that keeps giving.

a tradition that continues for both American and German brewers today.

Befitting a beer that's supposed to nourish fasting monks, the hefty doppelbock has a darker tint than the standard bock; a rich gold to a deep, ruby-hinting brown are standard hues. As for the flavors and aromas, malt sweetness stars, with caramel, dark fruits, and chocolate tagging along and hop bitterness lagging far, far behind.

Still, I'm sure drinking a doppelbock will make you believe in a higher power.

MÄRZEN

Before the modern invention of artificial refrigeration during the nineteenth century, Bavarian lager brewers faced a conundrum. If they brewed during the spring and summer, bacteria and wild yeasts would infiltrate their beers and wreak havoc. Warm temperatures rolled out a welcome mat for infection.

Eventually, as you learned earlier in this chapter, Bavarian brewers discovered that if they cooked their lagers during the late winter or early spring and sent them to slumber in cool caves or cellars until the fall, the beers that emerged were crisp, flavorful, and superfresh. This runaround laid the framework for the creation of fall's signature lager, the full-bodied, malt-forward, and lightly sweet märzen—that's German for March, the month in which many märzens traditionally were brewed.

The märzen is an ideal transitional

The opening parade for Munich's Oktoberfest features decorated beer wagons drawn by a team of Clydesdale horses (left). Around 1.5 million people live in Munich (above), which was founded in 1158 by a Benedictine order of monks and, as its coat of arms, features a monk dressed in black and holding a red book. The city's name is derived from the ancient German word **Munichen,** *which is loosely translated to "monks' place."*

beer, matching summer's favored crispness with the hearty richness required for the cooling nights of autumn. In time, the beer style became closely aligned with another beer-centric rite of the season, Oktoberfest (which traditionally occurs in September, mind you). Munich's weeks-long celebration of sausage, beer, and Bavarian culture was born in 1810 to commemorate the epic wedding of Crown Prince Ludwig I of Bavaria and Princess Therese of Saxe-Hildburghausen.

The first beers served at the festival were märzens, which in time came to be identified under the Oktoberfest

OKTOBERFEST'S
MASSIVE ONE-LITER
BEER STEIN
is known as a Mass.

Munich's Oktoberfest kicks off every year with a 12-gun salute, followed by the city's mayor tapping the first keg of Oktoberfest beer and proclaiming, "O'zapft ist!"—"It is tapped!" The first beer is served to Bavaria's minister-president, and then the revelry begins. The celebration normally welcomes more than 7 million visitors annually.

TWO TO TASTE: MÄRZEN

ORIGINAL OKTOBERFEST
HACKER-PSCHORR BRÄU
MÜNCHEN
ABV: 5.8%

This Bavarian brewery offers a textbook example of the classic Oktoberfest lager. The tawny märzen makes itself known with a clean, toasty-sweet scent tempered by a touch of spicy hops. The taste is what you should expect but rarely receive: smooth and pleasantly sweet (honey, nuts) with a dry close. Savor it alongside a bratwurst.

OKTOBERFEST
BROOKLYN BREWERY
ABV: 5.5%

Brooklyn Brewery does a splendid job with traditional German lagers, including a Vienna-style beauty, a snappy pilsner, and the Oktoberfest, which was first introduced in 2000. Brewmaster Garrett Oliver relies on Bavarian heirloom Munich and pilsner malts and German noble hops to create this full-bodied lager with bready notes and a scintilla of bitterness.

BACKUP BEERS: *Ayinger Oktober Fest-Märzen, Great Divide Brewing Co. Hoss, Left Hand Brewing Company Oktoberfest, Spaten Oktoberfest Ur-Märzen, Summit Brewing Company Oktoberfest Märzen Style*

mantle. And herein begins a bit of tricky business. In 1841, the legendary Austrian brewer Anton Dreher unveiled the lightly sweet, gently hopped, amber-tinted Vienna lagers, which rose to fame in the mid-1800s and later flourished in Texas and Mexico (see page 54). In 1872, the Munich brewer Josef Sedlmayr (he worked for Franziskaner, which is today part of Spaten) released a German spin on the Vienna style, a lager he called *Ur-Märzen*—original märzen. It quickly became the festival's gold standard and continues to set the Oktoberfest template today.

Though the märzens no longer are brewed in March (few breweries can afford to let lagers hibernate in precious fermentation tanks for six months), they remain a delicious reminder of spring to keep you company during the fall—ideally, with a sausage at your local Oktoberfest celebration.

Austrian brewer Anton Dreher was the father of the Vienna lager, which led to the creation of the traditional Oktoberfest lager known as the märzen.

Boston's Harpoon Brewery makes a heck of an Octoberfest lager and during the last weekend of September hosts the rollicking Harpoon Octoberfest, an annual tradition since 1990. Expect oompah bands, chicken dancing, keg bowling, and plenty of beer.

VIENNA LAGER

The grand brewing archives are stuffed to the gills with the exploits and inventiveness of brewers from Germany, England, and Belgium. Austria rarely gets mentioned, an oversight I aim to rectify right now.

One of the brightest minds of European brewing in the nineteenth century was the Austrian brewer Anton Dreher, who owned Schwechat Brewery, near Vienna, which was the headquarters of his family's sprawling brewing enterprise that stretched across the Austro-Hungarian Empire. One of Dreher's close friends was Gabriel Sedlmayr, a fellow brewer based in Munich, Germany. (Yes, that was his son Josef who developed the modern template for märzen.) Both colleagues were eager to improve the quality of the lager, with Gabriel pioneering production techniques at his brewery, Spaten, where he was instrumental in advancing the dark, cold–fermented beer that came to be known as the Munich dunkel (see page 44).

In contrast, Dreher decided to use paler malts, the sort that were popular in English ales. He cooked up the

The original allure of Oktoberfest was not beer but horse racing, which has since been eliminated.

TWO TO TASTE: VIENNA LAGER

NEGRA MODELO
GRUPO MODELO S.A. DE C.V.
ABV: 5.4%

Mexican cuisine is brimming with inventive flavors. Mexican beer? Not so much. When I'm craving an accompaniment to my carne enchilada tacos, I skip Corona and Pacifico, instead selecting the best of the bunch, the burnt sienna Negra Modelo. Equipped with toasty malt sweetness and a slight, nine-volt shock of bitterness, this simple beer is the personification of smooth drinkability.

TOASTED LAGER
BLUE POINT BREWING COMPANY
ABV: 5.5%

Named after an acclaimed oyster breed, Blue Point has been one of Long Island's leading breweries since Mark Burford and Peter Cotter took over an old ice factory, bought secondhand equipment, and in 1998 started brewing. The flagship is Toasted Lager, which is made on Blue Point's signature direct-fire brick brew kettle. White-hot flames impart a toasted quality to the beer, which pairs well with a profile of toast, caramel, and a lick of grassy bitterness.

BACKUP BEERS: *August Schell Brewing Co. FireBrick, Brooklyn Brewery Brooklyn Lager, Karl Strauss Brewing Company Amber Lager, Snake River Brewing Snake River Lager, Thornbridge Brewery Kill Your Darlings, Trader Joe's Vienna Style Lager*

HOLD THE LIME

Mexican beer has not always been so boring. During the nineteenth century, the nation was sprinkled with dozens of breweries that, just as in the United States, made full-flavored beer. But just as in the States, consolidation winnowed the marketplace, leading to two conglomerates—Cuauhtémoc Moctezuma and Grupo Modelo—ruling the country's brewing roost. Their power is amplified by the fact that they own most of Mexico's alcohol licenses, which the corporations dole out only if a bar agrees to sell certain brands; this is why Tecate, Corona, and Sol are ubiquitous. Though the odds are stacked against them, Mexican craft breweries such as Cerveza Cucapá, which makes Chupacabras American Pale Ale and a rare tequila barrel–aged barley wine, and Cervecería Minerva (the brewery's products include a kölsch and an Irish-style stout) are ever so slowly changing the perception of Mexican beer. Still, it's too early to discard the lime wedges and start to celebrate: according to the Mexican microbrewers association, for every 100,000 beers consumed in Mexico, only 8 are considered craft beers.

Schwechater Lagerbier, a copper-red lager with a soft, graceful malty character and a firm but restrained bitterness for balance. The landmark beer, which came to be known as Vienna lager, enjoyed widespread popularity across Europe in the second half of the nineteenth century. But as the Austro-Hungarian Empire disintegrated and even paler styles such as the pilsner, Munich helles, and Dortmunder Export rose to prominence, the Vienna lager lost its luster. The style waned, though it did not disappear.

In Mexico, of all places, a brewer by the name of Santiago Graf kept the Vienna lager's flame burning. In the late 1800s, he imported high-quality hops and rich, aromatic, and lightly toasty Vienna malt from Europe and even purchased refrigeration equipment to produce lagers properly in a less-than-chilly climate. (During that era, immigrant brewers from Austria also relocated to Mexico.) The Vienna lager

During Munich's Oktoberfest, only beer brewed within the city limits can be served. The six permitted breweries are Staatliches Hofbräu-München, Augustiner-Bräu, Spatenbräu, Hacker-Pschorr-Bräu, Paulaner-Bräu, and Löwenbräu.

took off in Mexico and parts of Texas, largely as a result of Graf's exacting standards.

Though American Prohibition and Mexican political strife eroded Vienna lager's toehold in the Americas, echoes of Mexico's infatuation with the Austrian style can be found in Negra Modelo and Dos Equis Amber, though they're a bit sweeter than the historical standard. In America, the Vienna lager also has found its footing in the modern craft-beer landscape, where brewers interpret the style as crisp and full-bodied, with less sweetness, a nice hop zap, and a dry finish. In Texas, Live Oak plays the style closer to tradition with its smooth Big Bark Amber Lager, and Ohio's Great Lakes turns up the alcohol and hops a notch in its Eliot Ness. Most surprisingly, that all-American example of American beer, Samuel Adams Boston Lager, is in fact a Vienna-style lager.

Somewhere, I'm sure Anton Dreher is smiling.

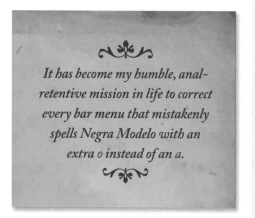

It has become my humble, anal-retentive mission in life to correct every bar menu that mistakenly spells Negra Modelo with an extra o instead of an a.

A DARK ALTERNATIVE

Breweries in eastern Germany used to make the hybrid alt-schwarzbier, which was brewed with special ale yeast (like the altbier; see page 81). The last brewery specializing in these beers closed several decades ago, but Louisiana's Bayou Teche Brewing has revived the style with its LA-31 Bière Noire, a dark, beguiling brew that calls to mind a cup of strong coffee.

Bayou Teche focuses on beers that complement Cajun cuisine.

TWO TO TASTE: SCHWARZBIER

KÖSTRITZER SCHWARZBIER

KÖSTRITZER
SCHWARZBIERBRAUEREI
GMBH & Co.

ABV: 4.8%

Founded in 1543, this German brewery is one of the nation's most august schwarzbier producers. Naturally, the flagship is nothing short of perfection. The nearly black beauty drinks dry, light, and smoother than a sailboat on a lake. The roasty notes of coffee and dark chocolate are buffed down with a mild rounded sweetness.

SESSION BLACK

FULL SAIL BREWERY

ABV: 5.4%

Black's perfume is an intoxicating muddle of roasted malts and Cocoa Puffs, childhood pleasures in an adult package. As for the taste, please strap in your taste buds: the crisp tongue tingler rides a flavor roller coaster across caramel and chocolate, with tangy floral hops hiding in the rumble seat. The throwback stubby bottles are also a nice touch. Grandpa would approve.

BACKUP BEERS: *Cervejaria Sul Brasileira Xingu Black Beer, Kulmbacher Brauerei AG Mönchshof Schwarzbier, The Duck-Rabbit Craft Brewery Duck-Rabbit Schwarzbier, Moonlight Brewing Company Death & Taxes Black Beer, Spoetzl Brewery Shiner Bohemian Black Lager*

SCHWARZBIER

In 1935, archaeologists unearthed a fascinating find. During a dig in northern Bavaria, near the city of Kulmbach, the explorers discovered a Celtic tomb that dated to around the eighth century BC. The grave contained an amphora, a vase-shaped container with handles and a narrow neck. A peek inside revealed charred, blackened crumbs of partially baked bread, one of the earliest known brewing ingredients. The bread was crumbled into water, whereupon passing yeasts hunkered down and fermented the mixture into something faintly—very faintly—resembling beer.

The possible remains of this ancient brew may be the forebearer of Germany's inkiest, most delicious beer style, the schwarzbier (pronounced "shvarts-beer"; *schwarz* is German for "black"). Over the ensuing centuries, the schwarzbier evolved into a coalition of dark and light: a crisp-drinking lager with roasty notes but little of the harsh, astringent bitterness that accompanies stouts and porters.

Brewers can achieve this by driving down one of two avenues. First, they can use dehusked malt, which dials down the burnt, roasty character. (This is accomplished by means of a process similar to rice polishing.) Alternatively, brewers can borrow a trick from cold-brewed coffee. The dark-roasted malts are submerged in nonboiling water, drawing out the roasty flavors—and none of the unwanted acidity or bitterness. Whatever the path, the journey ends with a Darth Vader–colored brew that packs a bit of hop bitterness and appealing flavors of cocoa and coffee that don't sit on your tongue like an elephant herd.

Today the black lager remains popular in Germany, and it's increasingly become a fool-the-taste-buds favorite of craft brewers in the United States. The light-drinking dark brews are cropping up from coast to coast, with Magic Hat Howl, Uinta Brewing's organic Baba Black Lager, and Sprecher Brewing Black Bavarian all worthy of calling your stomach home. Once you go black, you may never go back.

RAUCHBIER

In more than a decade of professional beer writing and drinking, I've found few styles as divisive as the rauchbier, a smoke-drenched German kind of beer that's a bit like drinking Texas BBQ run through a blender.

For centuries, most beers were smoky by default. That was the case because the sprouted barley (called green malt) was dried over a roaring fire, imbuing the grains with a pronounced smokiness. The process started falling out of favor in the eighteenth and nineteenth centuries, when the advent of industrialization led to kiln drying germinated barley over indirect heat, pushing smoke away from the grains and curtailing the smoky character.

MEAT YOUR MATCH

"There's one camp that loves rauchbiers and thinks they're fantastic, while the other camp sees no utility in that style," says Rick Allen, the founder and brewmaster of McMinnville, Oregon's Heater/Allen Brewing, which makes Smoky Bob rauchbier. Allen suggests that, instead of drinking these beers by themselves, you make the smoke-drenched brew a mealtime mate. "If you drink it with smoky food, the smoke flavor in the beer disappears and you get the true beer flavor," he enthuses. Try a rauchbier or two during your next BBQ.

THE GREAT WHITE SMOKE

Since 1988, Alaskan Brewing has released its medal-winning Smoked Porter, a beer born of resourcefulness. Russian settlers as well as the Czech and German brewmasters who made their way to Alaska during the Gold Rush dried and roasted their malts over fire. To honor that tradition, Alaskan Brewing enlists a local smokehouse to smoke its grain over alder wood, then brews the porter with glacier water. Over the last 25 years, the trailblazing Smoked Porter has helped spark interest in smoked beers in the United States.

TWO TO TASTE: RAUCHBIER

AECHT SCHLENKERLA RAUCHBIER MÄRZEN
Brauerei Heller-Trum
ABV: 5.4%

Vegetarians may have a tough time wrapping their tongues around Schlenkerla's pungent märzen, which is made with beech wood–smoked malts. The aroma recalls bacon roasted over a bonfire, a hammy flavor that's highlighted by hints of dark fruit and even chocolate. It's intense yet surprisingly refreshing; however, it's best enjoyed with a meal.

Z SMOKED AMBER LAGER
Fort Collins Brewing
ABV: 5.4%

This Colorado brewery's lager pours out a clear copper, displaying a dapper off-white head with some nice staying power. Instead of incinerating your taste buds in a campfire's smoldering ashes, Z mutes the mesquite, cranks up the caramel, and closes clean and crisp. You need no BBQ to enjoy this beer.

BACKUP BEERS: *Bierbrouwerij Grand-Café Emelisse Rauchbier, Brauerei Spezial Rauchbier Lager, Jack's Abby Brewing Smoke & Dagger Black Lager, Les Trois Mousquetaires Série Signature Rauchbier*

Instead of kowtowing to modern times, the German city of Bamberg, in the Franconia region, proudly stuck to its smoky guns. Since the early 1500s, Bamberg breweries have been lauded for their smoldering brews, known as rauchbiers (*rauch* is German for "smoke"). The malts are dried over beech wood–stoked flames, imparting robust flavors and aromas to the beer that call to mind smoked meat or bacon.

Though any style can be classified as a rauchbier, it's most frequently a moderately strong, dark lager such as the märzen (see page 51). However, Bamberg's Schlenkerla also makes a lightly smoky Munich helles lager (see page 68) as well as a wheat beer. In the States, American craft breweries are coming back to the fire, using smoked malts in Caldera Brewing Company Rauch Ür Bock, Samuel Adams's

Germany's tiny Franconia region has around 300 different breweries, making it one of the most concentrated brewing centers in the world. In McKinney, Texas, about 30 miles from Dallas, Dennis Wehrmann pays homage to the area with his line of Franconia Brewing Company lagers and Bavarian wheat beers.

Bonfire Rauchbier, and Ballast Point Brewing's Abandon Ship Smoked Lager.

This certainly is one smoking habit I encourage everyone to pick up.

LET THERE BE LIGHT

Thanks to revolutionary malt-kilning techniques, the lager shed its dark skin in the nineteenth century and molted into these bright, light, easy-drinking delights. Summer-afternoon imbibing would never again be the same.

CZECH PILSNER

A beer must be royally mucked up before I'll dump it down the drain. An infection turned the flavors as funky as a postworkout armpit, or perhaps sunlight skunked the beer far worse than Pepé Le Pew ever could. In short, something has to be rotten in Denmark, just as it once was in Bohemia.

In 1838, the good people of Plzeň, Bohemia (now the Czech Republic), gathered in the town square and watched as 36 barrels of perfectly terrible beer were dumped out—a sharp indictment of the poor, declining quality of the local product. Though Bohemians had been brewing since the eleventh century, hundreds of years of practice could not prevent contamination and spoilage. A radical readjustment was required. A collective of independent Plzeň brewers gathered and decided on a drastic course

HEY, BUD, WHAT'S YOUR NAME?

The names of several prominent American lagers have their roots in the Czech Republic. Michelob stems from the town Michelovice, and Budweiser is derived from the town Ceske Budejovice, which is known as Budweis in German. There's still a pilsner produced in Southern Bohemia sold under the name Budweiser Budvar, though it's called Czechvar in the United States. In my opinion, it's leagues better than the Budweiser that was born in America.

TWO TO TASTE: CZECH PILSNER

PILSNER URQUELL
PILSNER URQUELL BREWERY
ABV: 4.4%

The classic Czech beer has been in production since 1842, back when the country was called Bohemia. Although the recipe has shifted over the ensuing 170 years, Urquell remains rock-solid. The snappy, golden pilsner—backed by a hint of grapes—is as fizzy and quenching as New York City seltzer. In 2012, the brewery started cold shipping the beer from the Czech Republic, ensuring a fresher product.

LAGUNITAS PILS CZECH STYLE PILSNER
LAGUNITAS BREWING COMPANY
ABV: 6.2%

"It's a beer built for someone who's not a hophead." That's how Lagunitas touts its glowing golden Pils with a bright and spicy bouquet—those are the Saaz hops talking. Though the ABV is a touch higher than I'd like, Pils wears its strength well and slakes thirst with its tingly carbonation and pure flavors of biscuits and a lemony snap.

BACKUP BEERS: *Budweiser Czechvar Original, Bull Jagger Brewing Company Big Claw Pilsner, Hopworks Urban Brewery Organic HUB Lager, Live Oak Brewing Company Pilz, Oskar Blues Mama's Little Yella Pils, Southern Tier Brewing Company Eurotrash Pilz*

of action: build a new brewery designed to produce a new class of lager.

For years, fermentation had been a fuzzy science. Brewers knew that yeast was crucial to beer's creation, but how it worked was a mystery. The German physiologist Theodor Schwann had an inkling. Though other scientists posited that fermentation was the result of yeast cells dying, Schwann's experiments proved that fermentation was a living process, with yeast cells growing and reproducing.

That crucial discovery helped the Bohemian brewers understand how yeast affected different styles of beer, and in 1840 the brewing collective bought a lusted-after strain of bottom-fermenting lager yeast from Bavaria. Two years later, the brewers were ready for production. A facility was built abutting the Radbuza River, close to a well and perched above a sandstone foundation carved into caverns suited for cold storage. A young Bavarian lager brewer named Josef Groll was imported and put in charge of the venture, finding a perfect storm of ingredients at his disposal.

He had soft well water, aromatic Saaz hops, that workhorse lager strain, and plenty of pale malts, the result of new kilning techniques. Those four ingredients worked in concert to create a thrilling new beer with a sparkling clarity, a color reminiscent of spun gold, an aromatic bouquet, and an incomparably light body. For European drinkers accustomed to dark, hazy brews, it was as if a ring of torches had been lit, heralding the arrival of Plzeň's singular new beer: Pilsner Urquell (*Urquell* is German for "original source").

The pale pilsner (now called a Czech or Bohemian pilsner) became the belle of European bars and soon the world. By 1859, the phrase *pilsner bier* was trademarked, and 1871 marked the beginning of exports to the United States. Brewing had entered its golden age. Soon competitors and imitators would follow.

GERMAN PILSNER

Brewing is a copycat profession. No sooner does a brewer make waves—and moolah—with a newfangled style than imitators follow the leader. This is not to slag brewers. The industry is built on innovation, then improvement, like the German chemical firm BASF and its catchphrase: "We don't make a lot of the products you buy. We make a lot of the products you buy better."

Speaking of Germans, that nation's brewers were knocked for a loop by the Bohemian pilsner. The gorgeous golden brew's popularity was widespread, particularly in the Saxony region abutting Bohemia. Buoyed by the success of pilsner, a gang of brewers from Radeberg, a suburb of Dresden, partnered to launch the Aktienbrauerei Zum Bergkeller brewery in 1872, later renamed the Radeberger Exportbier-

THAT'S SO RAD

One of my favorite lager-based drinks is the radler (German for "bicyclist"). It's a blend of brisk lager and tart lemonade that slakes thirst and, for lagging riders, provides a carb-packed energy boost. Britain offers the similar summer-friendly shandy, which is classically a 50–50 mixture of beer (often a light lager) and lemonade, citrus-flavored soda, or perhaps ginger ale.

TWO TO TASTE: GERMAN PILSNER

PRIMA PILS
VICTORY BREWING COMPANY
ABV: 5.3%

When I travel or just bend elbows at a bar, one of the most commonly asked questions is, "What's your favorite beer?" Though answering the question opens up a can of worms, I always reply that I prefer Prima Pils. This bracingly effervescent pilsner is overloaded with whole-flower European hops, resulting in a snappy, spicy beer with serious bite. The gently sweet aftertaste keeps me coming back for more.

RADEBERGER PILSNER
RADEBERGER EXPORTBIERBRAUEREI
ABV: 4.8%

Radeberger was Germany's first brewery to specialize in pilsners, finding a fan in King Friedrich August of Saxony. Radeberger remains a royal pleasure, as the golden brew possesses a complex herbal aroma—by turns spicy and sweet—with a bright, zesty flavor profile and just a touch of mild bitterness. Radeberger may not rock your world, but it's a dependable option at the bar.

BACKUP BEERS: *Jever Pilsner, Kulmbacher Brauerei AG EKU Pils, Mahr's Bräu Pilsner, Sly Fox Brewing Company Pikeland Pils, Trumer Pils, Utah Brewers Cooperative Squatter's Provo Girl Pilsner*

brauerei. Its trademark product became a slow-building success, a triumph that endures today: the gently grassy, decidedly golden, delicately bittered Radeberger Pils—a German pilsner.

To even the trained drinker, the German pilsner will not present a night-and-day distinction from its Czech sibling. The pale lagers share the same basic crisp and malty characteristics, though the German version's body and hue can skew somewhat lighter. The variances are due to the reliance on regional grains, yeast strains, and, most important, hops. Czech pilsners rely on the native Saaz hops, which impart a clean, cinnamon-spicy profile. By comparison, German pilsners make do with noble hops such as the floral and earthy Hallertauer, the spicy and delicate Spalt, and the green and floral Perle.

Don't worry if you can't tell the Czech from the German pilsner. After all, they share one central trait: both styles taste superb.

VICTORY BREWING COMPANY

DOWNINGTOWN, PENNSYLVANIA

Victory Brewing founders Ran Barchet (left) and Bill Covaleski met in grade school.

You do not arrive in Downingtown, Pennsylvania, by accident. The town of nearly 8,000 residents sits around 35 miles from Lancaster, Reading, and Philadelphia, far from the Pennsylvania Turnpike turnoff. After folks clock out at the Pepperidge Farm bakery or commute back from Philly, there's not much nightlife. But that lack of clubs and cocktail bars can be a blessing.

"We jokingly say, 'If you come to Downingtown, you have to make your own fun,'" says Bill Covaleski, the cofounder of Victory Brewing Company. Over the last 15 years, Covaleski and cofounder Ron Barchet have brewed up boatloads of fun, turning an old Pepperidge Farm factory into one of the country's most respected manufacturers of faultless German lagers and inspired ales.

Among my favorites, you'll find Lager, a bright, lean, and low-alcohol take on the Munich helles. Prima Pils has set the snappy, prickly template for the craft pilsner. St. Victorious Doppelbock is a warming winter tradition, and Festbier is a smooth amber companion to Oktoberfest. On the ale side, try the aromatic Hop Wallop double IPA, the fruity Belgian-style Golden Monkey, or the intense imperial-strength Storm King Stout.

Victory has a knack for producing winning beer.

GET ON THE BUS

Victory's roots stretch to 1973, when two fifth-graders by the names of Barchet and Covaleski boarded the same school bus. Their bond quickly cemented into a lifelong friendship. Not long after graduating from college in 1985, the friends began homebrewing, an after-work hobby for Covaleski, an advertising art director, and Barchet, a financial analyst. Corporate life soon was consumed by beer. Barchet quit his job and began apprenticing at Baltimore Brewing Company before leaving to study at the Technical University of Munich at Weihenstephan. Covaleski filled his open position, gravitating toward German-inspired beers.

"We fell in love with German imports in the early 1980s, when that was the only interesting thing going on in beer," explains Covaleski, who further polished his skills at Munich's famed Doemens Institute. After Barchet tended the kettles at Virginia's Old Dominion Brewing Company, helping increase production tenfold, the friends decided they were ready to combine their talents. Victory awaited.

But how best to spread the word? "When it came to my money, I was focused on the shortcoming of conventional advertising," Covaleski says. "I thought, What if we rolled up our sleeves and sold ourselves directly to the people coming in to visit us? They'd be introduced to Victory and, better still, leave money behind." When Victory's doors opened on February 15, 1996, customers could either dine in the restaurant or belly up to the handsome bar and sample the inaugural brews: HopDevil IPA, Brandywine Valley Lager (now retired), and Festbier. They were time-honored styles with a modern American twist.

"There are wonderful beer styles propagated by European breweries, but when they're shipped to America, they lose some of that vibrancy," Covaleski says. "Victory seized the opportunity to take the promise of European beer styles and deliver fresher beer to the American audience."

Crucial to Victory's formula were premium ingredients such as whole-flower hops, which the brewers believe lend a finer aroma and flavor. One taste of the brisk and biting Prima Pils and you'll probably agree. Additionally, the brewery relies on premium German malts and maintains a lab stocked with the more than 40 different unique strains of yeast employed in the brewery's ever-growing constellation of beers. "We invested our time and money in critical differences in brewing to make our beers more flavorful," Covaleski says. "We're committed to a high-quality product."

TASTY IN NUMBERS

Victory built its name on European-influenced lagers and ales, but the brewery does not pledge allegiance to a single style. Donnybrook Stout is a silky, compulsively drinkable dry Irish stout, and V-12 is a heady, intense Belgian-style ale that clocks in with a 12 percent ABV. Helios Ale is a spicy, refreshing saison, and Headwaters Pale Ale relies on tropical American-born Citra hops.

Many of these beers debut at Victory's brewpub, which doubles as a proving ground. "The brewpub is not only a focus group," Covaleski says, "it's a focus group where people are being honest"—a few pints make most people spill unvarnished opinions. "There's always someone telling you something that's very valuable."

Consumer input has caused Victory to change course on several of its beers. The dark and hoppy Yakima Glory black IPA was supposed to be a draft-only one-off, but the bitter, inky beer was so

well received that the brewery turned it into an annual winter seasonal. And the light, refreshingly aromatic Summer Love Ale has become an unexpected summertime hit.

Refusing to rest on its laurels makes smart business sense for Victory. Today, it's less common to rely on one or two beers to drive sales, and brand fatigue is not a question of if but when. "I can never imagine the day when we're draping the HopDevil in black and shoveling him in dirt, but you're fooling yourself as a business owner if you don't believe that brands have a shelf life," Covaleski says.

That's why the brewery keeps customers excited with draft-only releases such as the aroma-focused Ranch Double IPA series (Victory is working with small family-owned ranches and farms to source its hops) and the rotating Braumeister Pils, which highlights different European hops. Demand for Victory beers has been so intense that the brewery reached capacity in 2012, and a second production facility was opened nearby in 2013. "By no means are Ron and I reckless, but we're restless when we see opportunity. We want to drive the marketplace and offer the marketplace more widely distributed beer," Covaleski says. "I sometimes joke that if I were born ten years earlier, I'd be a drug dealer."

DORTMUNDER GOLD
GREAT LAKES BREWING COMPANY
ABV: 5.8%

In a beer world loaded with wallop-your-palate flavors, Gold shines because of its circus-worthy balancing act between sweetly honeyed malt and grassy aromatic hops; it's as brisk and gulpable as it is complex. The fat, creamy head will give you a beer mustache that will linger long after the dry, bitter conclusion. Sometimes you just want a beer you can knock back by the pint without blowing out your palate.

DOG DAYS DORTMUNDER STYLE LAGER
TWO BROTHERS BREWING COMPANY
ABV: 5.1%

To remedy the last endlessly oppressive stretch of summer, I must prescribe this lager with the color of Fort Knox's finest treasure. In Dog Days, the sibling-run Illinois brewery has devised a blend of caramel malts and German noble hops that drinks mellow and moderately bitter, presenting an appealingly earthy and mildly sweet grain profile. It's kind of like liquid bread.

BACKUP BEERS: *Appalachian Brewing Company Mountain Lager, Baltika Breweries No. 7 Export, Ayinger Jahrhundert-Bier, Dortmunder Actien-Brauerei DAB Original, Old Dominion Brewing Company Old Dominion Lager, Thirsty Dog Brewing Company Labrador Lager*

DORTMUNDER EXPORT

Though the German pilsner remains vital, another instrumental example of the late-nineteenth-century shift to paler-hued beers has seen its salad days come and go. Once upon a time, Dortmunder Export Lager was the pride of Dortmund, an industrial city known for its coal mines, steel mills, and breweries. Responding to the rise of golden pilsner, in 1873 the Dortmunder Union produced its own pale lager, Export.

Though slightly stronger and less dry than the Czech pilsner, Export largely played by the same rules: golden, crisp, and lightly bitter, though the local water's high concentration of calcium carbonate added sharpness and a slightly sulfuric character. The city's industrial laborers favored their indigenous lager, and the style reportedly became Germany's most popular.

Before making pale lagers, Dortmund breweries were known for producing Adambier. It was a strong, highly hopped ale that underwent a lengthy aging process, acquiring a sour tang. Hair of the Dog Brewing Company makes a modern version called Adam (see page 203).

However, the second half of the twentieth century brought the closure of the region's mills and mines, and Export, too, fell on hard times. The German pilsner ascended to the throne, and Export was left to limp along. Though it's still being produced, the style has fallen out of favor in Germany. Picking up the torch, a handful of American brewers are keeping Dortmunder's name alive, though the U.S. versions tend to be bolder than their German counterparts.

MUNICH HELLES

Back in the late 1800s, crisp, golden Bohemian pilsners bubbled across Europe, attracting drinkers en masse. To compete with the sparkling pilsner, brewers began cranking out pale lagers—but not in Munich. These Bavarian brewers were known for their amber and brown bocks, doppelbocks, and dunkel lagers. Breaking from tradition was verboten, which would explain why it took the city's brewers more than 50 years to muster a retort to pilsner. In 1894, Munich-based Spaten Brauerei tweaked its brown lager recipe, creating a brighter, lighter beer that shared pilsners' spicy hop characteristics but retained a balanced malty sweetness. When the first batches of the blonde brew were rolled out, the response was explosive.

On the one hand, drinkers loved the look and flavor of the light lager. On the other hand, Bavarian brewers were

UNFILTERED ACCESS

Fermentation tanks are equipped with a beer-sampling valve called the *zwickel*, which lends its name to the little-seen lager style zwickelbier. It's an unfiltered, unpasteurized, generally low-alcohol beer that rarely travels far from the brewery because of its short shelf life. A nearly identical style is the cloudy, similarly unfiltered kellerbier ("cellar beer"), which tends to be a touch stronger and have a more pronounced hop presence. Kellerbiers are uncommon, but if you spy a version at your local brewpub (or a bottle of Columbus Brewing Company Summer Teeth or a can of Surly Hell), give the unfiltered beer a go.

Each year, the Oregon Brewers Guild runs Zwickelmania, a tour of the state's breweries featuring tastes of beer straight from barrels or the zwickel (oregonbeer.org/zwickelmania). Here, Full Sail brewing supervisor Barney Brennan pours an Amber Ale off a zwickel.

TWO TO TASTE: MUNICH HELLES

GOLD LAGER

STOUDT'S BREWING COMPANY

ABV: 4.7%

One of the country's first—and finest—female brewmasters, Carol Stoudt, crafts a large lineup of German brews, including the Pils, Karnival Kölsch, Smooth Hoperator doppelbock, and this highly drinkable Munich helles. It's the color of summer sunshine with a light body, a morsel of sweet malt, and a swell hop snap. Naturally, Gold has won a number of medals.

ORIGINAL MÜNCHNER HELL

PAULANER BRAUEREI

ABV: 4.9%

First brewed in the late nineteenth century, the Original Münchner is now Germany's top-selling helles-style lager. Its popularity is understandable: The sparkling, good-looking blonde lager's got an enticingly bready fragrance with a trace of hay. A subtle jolt of lemon and hops provides tasty, unexpected nuance to the malty body.

BACKUP BEERS: *Augustiner-Bräu Wagner KG Lagerbier Hell, Cigar City Brewing Hotter Than Helles Lager, Staatliches Hofbräuhaus Hofbräu Original, Spaten-Franziskaner-Bräu Spaten Münchner Hell, Maui Brewing Co. Bikini Blonde Lager, Schlafly Helles-Style Summer Lager*

in a tizzy: some decreed that Spaten's creation was a pox upon tradition, but others understood that commerce and consumer demand should trump tradition. The bottom line prevailed, and soon Germany welcomed a new style, the Munich helles. (*Helles* is German for "light" or "bright.")

German drinkers flocked to the subtly flowery, sunshine-hued brew, which Bavarians preferred a touch maltier and less hop-focused than Bohemian pilsners. More than a century later, Munich helles remains a German favorite, with excellent renditions crafted by brewers such as Paulaner, Hofbräu, and Ayinger. In addition, growing ranks of American brewers have begun experimenting with Munich helles. In Texas, Rahr & Sons Brewing Company has the helles-style Blonde, and in Connecticut, Thomas Hooker turns out the fabulous floral-zinged Munich-Style Golden Lager.

It's one of the many good reasons why you should go to helles.

MAIBOCK

One of the least lauded pleasures of springtime drinking may be the maibock (*Mai* is German for "May"), an ideal encapsulation of the changing season. The gold- to amber-hued, nicely hopped maibock is nimble enough to savor while you're sitting in the sun, yet it remains potent enough to warm your cockles on a chilly evening.

The Hofbräuhaus of Munich claims to have released the first maibock in 1614, a beer so good that it helped keep the city from being razed during the Thirty Years' War. In 1632, history tells that the occupying Swedish army agreed not to pillage Munich in exchange for 1,000 pails of beer from the Hofbräuhaus, 361 of which were their maibock. This is a nice tale, but it doesn't explain how the maibock achieved its brighter hue. In the 1600s, beers were still pretty dark, and pale malts were not widespread until the middle to late nineteenth century. Most likely, the maibock was the offspring of the prevailing pale-lager trend.

Whatever the reason, maibock (also known as helles bock) is one of spring's delicious delights. I count down the days until I sip the year's first offering, a light yet strong lager laden with flavor and packing a deceptively strong alcohol load, calibrating malt sweetness with a bitter edge. It's sunshine wrapped in a warming coat. May you drink a good one.

AMERICAN LAGERS

If you drank beer in America at the turn of the twentieth century, the lager you would have enjoyed would have had little in common with today's watery mass-produced lagers. Pre-Prohibition lagers were flavorful and complex, crafted by European immigrants who arrived toting luggage packed with yeast cultures and brains stuffed with brewing expertise.

TWO TO TASTE: MAIBOCK

HOFBRAU MAIBOCK
STAATLICHES HOFBRÄUHAUS
ABV: 7.2%

During the last week in April, Munich's Hofbräuhaus taps the season's first barrel of maibock, a moment you might like to circle on your calendar. Hofbräu's clear copper maibock has a nose of honey, toffee, and toast as well as a sturdy malt backbone layered with caramel, brown sugar, and bitterness beneath the surface. The sweetness never gets cloying.

ANDYGATOR
ABITA BREWING COMPANY
ABV: 8%

I'm a lover of all things Louisiana, and that includes the brews of Abita, especially its hazy Satsuma Wit, bold Jockamo IPA, and toffee-touched Turbodog. Also winning is the Andygator, a golden, slightly bitter creature with a smidgen of citrus on its nose and a light body that tastes of pears and apples topped with a spoonful of sugar.

BACKUP BEERS: *August Schell Brewing Co. Maifest, Berkshire Brewing Company Maibock Lager, Capital Brewery Maibock, Einbecker Mai-Ur-Bock, Narragansett Bock, Rogue Dead Guy Ale, Victory Brewing Company St. Boisterous*

GET YOUR GOAT

On your marks, get set . . . goat! On the first Sunday of May, Phoenixville, Pennsylvania's Sly Fox Brewing Company hosts the Bock Fest & Goat Race. The rollicking daylong bash features brewmaster Brian O'Reilly's lineup of bocks, doppelbocks, eisbocks, and a maibock that's named after the race's hooved winner from the previous year.

On February 12, 1917, South Dakota governor Peter Norbeck signed the "bone dry" law that prohibited alcohol consumption—several years before the Eighteenth Amendment went into effect.

Soon after settling, those craftsmen began converting die-hard ale drinkers to lovers of lagers such as the strong, all-malt bock, a springtime favorite of New Yorkers that sometimes was marketed as a medicinal tonic. To sway fans of the once-dominant fruity ales, other lagers were spiced with orange peel and juniper berries. In the Midwest and on the East Coast, pale lager was the rage, largely as a result of the use of corn. Today, *corn* is a four-letter word and breweries that use it are derided for cutting corners. But this indigenous ingredient was vital for early lager brewers. They found American barley harsh, and European malt was cost-prohibitive to import. The runaround was blending American barley malt with corn, which added a calming sweetness that when combined with imported German hops created a robust lager that dominated the domestic market.

Lager's ascension was met by a swift downfall provoked by Prohibition (enacted by the Eighteenth Amendment,

The two oldest family-run breweries in the United States are Pennsylvania's D.G. Yuengling & Son and Minnesota's August Schell Brewing Co., which have, respectively, been in business since 1829 and 1860.

which went into effect on January 17, 1920, and was repealed on December 5, 1933) and aided by the Depression, as well as the Dust Bowl and World War II, both of which made beer ingredients scarce. Breweries closed or consolidated. Increasingly, lagers contained greater percentages of rice, mimicking the mild, less hoppy Western lagers that were popular on the West Coast, where rice was an indigenous ingredient. (Henry Weinhard's in Portland, Oregon, was a popular brewer and continues to produce lagers to this day, though the brand is now owned by MillerCoors.)

Rice helped create crisp, light, thirst-quenching lagers that appealed to a wide swath of consumers, paving the way to the rise of advertising-driven national brands such as Schlitz, Hamm's, Carling Black Label, and, of course, Budweiser. The die was cast for the clear, and clearly dominant, American lager.

CRAFT BREWING'S COLD SHOULDER

For much of the twentieth century, lagers defined American beer. If you were sipping a beer, you probably were drinking a lager. Thus, when the craft-brewing movement started percolating in the 1980s and 1990s, brewers did not mimic the mainstream. Back then, brewers were eager to return to the flavorful, fuller-bodied beers that the country had shunned. Sierra Nevada Pale Ale, Deschutes Black Butte Porter, and Stone IPA were drastic departures from

BOTTOMING OUT

When it comes to European lagers and ales, Will Kemper is a genius. At Bellingham, Washington's Chuckanut Brewery and Kitchen (which he owns with his wife, Mari), Will makes medal-winning, simply named standouts such as Vienna Lager, Dortmunder Lager, and Pilsner. If you're ever in Washington, seek out his European beers around the Puget Sound region. If you're on the East Coast, make note of Virginia's Devils Backbone Brewing Company. Brewer Jason Oliver also has a deft touch with bottom-fermented beers such as Gold Leaf Lager, Vienna Lager, and Old Virginia Dark lager.

During Prohibition, confiscated liquor and beer was often unceremoniously dumped out. Here, in 1924, barrels of beers are poured into Pennsylvania's Schuylkill River.

TWO TO TASTE: AMERICAN LAGER

SHIFT PALE LAGER
NEW BELGIUM BREWING
ABV: 5%

New Belgium may be known for its Belgian-style ales, but the brewery has a steady hand with bottom-fermented beers such as its Czech-style Blue Paddle Pilsener-Lager and this thirst-quenching pale lager. New Zealand's Nelson Sauvin hops give Shift a fruity, tropical profile, with notes of lychee and mango. The crisp drinker comes in cans, making it especially suited for sipping during sporting events.

1811 LAGER
FORT GEORGE BREWERY +
PUBLIC HOUSE
ABV: 5.1%

Brewed in honor of the bicentennial of Astoria, Oregon (Fort George's hometown), this lager sold in 16-ounce cans is crafted with a measure of corn—harkening back to early American brewing—and both Saaz and Centennial hops, resulting in a lively, zesty beer that'll knock any lingering lager prejudices for a loop. P.S. Fort George's Vortex IPA and Cavatica Stout are also sound selections.

BACKUP BEERS: *Bell's Brewery Lager Beer, Heater/Allen Coastal, Lightning Brewery Ionizer Lager, Pretty Things Beer & Ale Project American Darling, Shmaltz Brewing Albino Python (part of the Coney Island Craft Lager series)*

the status quo, demonstrating that beer and flavor were not mutually exclusive concepts.

This explains the rise and popularity of increasingly extreme, decidedly un-lager-like styles such as the double IPA, imperial stout, and barrel-aged sour and wild ales. How far could American brewers stretch the boundaries of beer? I don't believe we've reached the breaking point. However, I'm happy to report that American breweries are snapping back to the starting line, wholeheartedly embracing the maligned lager.

NOT YOUR FATHER'S LAGER
The revival is occurring on several fronts. First, breweries are traveling through time and reviving pre-Prohibition lagers. In addition to its series of Session lagers sold in stubby 11-ounce bottles, Oregon's Full Sail produces the LTD line of limited-edition lagers, and Nebraska's Lucky Bucket Brewing Co. boils up the floral, lightly malty Pre-Prohibition Lager. Craftsman Brewing Company in

One of New York City's most popular producers of lagers, including bocks, was Trommer's Brewery, which distinguished itself from other breweries by exclusively using malt.

Pasadena, California, makes 1903 Lager with a bit of corn, and the continued growth of Pennsylvania's 1829-born D.G. Yuengling & Son is due to demand for its flagship Yuengling Lager, which also contains corn.

Still, it would be folly to explain away the trend toward lagers as affection for the past. Craft brewers are applying the innovative thinking that once was reserved for ales to lagers, creating hoppy and unusual lagers that honor tradition yet leave it in the dust.

Chicago's Metropolitan Brewing focuses on German beers, both done according to style and with a twist, as evidenced by the brewery's limited-edition Urban Evolution experiments such as a Vienna lager spiced with chipotle and a dunkel-style dark lager spiked with rye. New Hampshire's Throwback Brewery "dry hops" its pilsner with roasted jalapeños to create the draft-only Spicy Bohemian. San Diego's Ballast Point produces a range of seven lagers throughout the year, including Abandon Ship Smoked Lager; brawny Navigator Doppelbock, which occasionally is aged in brandy barrels; and Fathom India Pale Lager.

There may be something brewing with India pale lager, which marries a fragrant IPA with a brisk lager. In Massachusetts, Jack's Abby Brewing makes the Hoponious Union, California's The Bruery crafts Humulus Lager, and Shmaltz Brewing uses eight different

Anchor Brewing's brew kettle sure is a beauty.

hops to hew its hoppy Sword Swallower lager (part of its Coney Island Craft Lager series). Flipping the formula, Stillwater Artisanal Ales uses the classic pre-Prohibition lager recipe of malt, corn, and rice and then ferments the beer with ale yeast and several strains of the wild yeast *Brettanomyces* to create Premium. It's the past reinvented for a delicious rule-breaking future.

CALIFORNIA COMMON

January 24, 1848, marked the beginning of a manic stretch of money madness in America. That day, a carpenter and sawmill operator by the name of James William Marshall, who was working at Coloma, California's Sutter's Mill, spotted gleaming flecks in the water. He collected the shiny, malleable rocks, and they were soon to put to the test. The results? Gold.

So commenced the California Gold Rush, a frenzied seven-year stretch that saw around 300,000 people pack their bags and head to the West Coast, hitching their wagons and boats to dreams of 24 karats. Counted among the California immigrants were brewers, who were seeking a gold rush of a different sort. The prospectors' long days and backbreaking labor certainly entitled them to a beer, or perhaps a half dozen. There was just one very glaring problem with the brewers' plans. They'd ferried lager yeast, which required cool

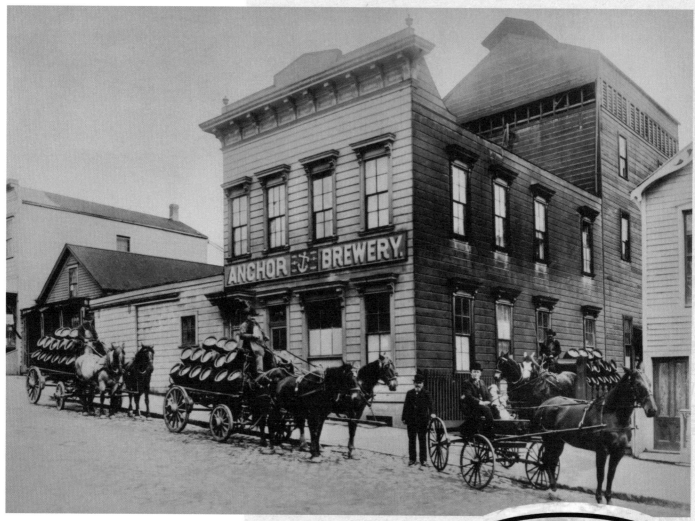

The original location of Anchor's brewery in San Francisco was formerly a beer-and-billiards saloon.

temperatures. The lack of cold caves, a steady supply of ice, and scientific means of mechanical refrigeration (still years away from being perfected) spelled doom for the bottom-fermenting yeast, which required cool temperatures for proper fermentation.

What followed was a merger of European brewing techniques and trademark American ingenuity and pluck. Forced to ad-lib and adapt to the

TWO TO TASTE: CALIFORNIA COMMON

STEAM ENGINE LAGER
STEAMWORKS BREWING COMPANY
ABV: 5.1%

At first, this Durango, Colorado, brewery called its California Common the Steam Engine Steam, a trademark-flaunting name that didn't tickle the fancy of Anchor's Fritz Maytag. Since rebranded, the balanced copper lager has become Steamworks' biggest seller owing to its robust caramel body, woody hops, and a sweetness-cutting finish that's pricklier than a pincushion.

ANCHOR STEAM BEER
ANCHOR BREWING COMPANY
ABV: 4.9%

The icon that kicked off the steam-beer revival remains as vital and vibrant as ever. The amber ale—er, lager—is topped by a creamy, lasting lid and has a sweetly inviting, cleanly hoppy scent. The taste smoothly carries you across biscuits, caramel, and citrus before closing good and dry. Though Anchor Steam seems simple by today's standards, it really was a revolutionary beer.

BACKUP BEERS: *Flat Earth Brewing Co. Element 115 Lager, Flying Dog Brewery Old Scratch Amber Lager, Furthermore Beer Oscura, Telegraph Brewing Company California Ale*

surroundings, brewers began experimenting with special lager yeast that thrived at a warmer temperature. One of their tricks for cooling the boiling wort (the sugar-rich soup that serves as a yeast feast) was to pump the scalding liquid to the rooftop, where big, shallow open bins awaited. Steady breezes from the Pacific Ocean dropped the temperature, creating an ideal, if originally unintended, environment for yeast. The end product of this compromise was a malty, liberally hopped amber beer with a refreshing effervescence. Miners appreciatively drank their share.

One of the drawbacks to this bubbly style was that when a keg was tapped, it had a propensity to spray like Champagne bottles after a World Series win. As a result of that or perhaps because of the steam rising off the rooftop-cooled wort (which also was fermented al fresco), the style came to be known as steam beer. (Additionally, this was the era of the steam engine, and *steam* was considered a cutting-edge adjective.) It was an affordable sop suited for workingmen, and steam beer did well by them until the twentieth century, when its fortunes slowly declined. Prohibition was a pain. Tastes changed.

The style was in danger of needing a tombstone when Fritz Maytag purchased San Francisco's struggling Anchor Brewery in 1965 and rejiggered the recipe for steam beer. First bottled in 1971, Anchor Steam singlehandedly performed CPR on the style. In time, other American brewers tried their hand at creating steam beer, though since Anchor Brewery trademarked the name, they were forced to market their offerings as California Common.

Today the California Common does not garner top billing at craft-beer bars. But look closely and you'll find examples worthy of slaking your thirst even if you didn't spend the day prospecting. Whatever you call it, the California-born beer is favored for its predictable fermentation time and smooth, easygoing flavor that's lightly malty and fruity with enough bitterness to keep you on your toes. Drinking one for the first time is not unlike striking gold.

IN FROM THE COLD

Lagers do not have a lockdown on a lengthy cold fermentation. The process also can be applied to ales, rounding

At a bar in Cologne, brusque waiters called Köbes, who wear blue shirts and long aprons, deliver beer drinkers their kölsch in circular trays. They'll keep bringing you kölsch until you slide a coaster over your glass.

In Cologne, there may not be a prettier sight in town than stanges—a narrow, cylindrical glass—filled with the city's snappy, refreshing kölsch. The 0.2-liter stanges (6.5 ounces) are delivered in a specially designed tray known as a kranz, which translates to "wreath."

TWO TO TASTE: KÖLSCH

GAFFEL KÖLSCH
Privatbrauerei Gaffel
Becker & Co.
ABV: 4.8%

Hailing from kölsch's birthplace of Cologne, this classic German quaff smells of honeysuckle, plum, and, ever so lightly, grapefruit. Gaffel's spunky carbonation leads to flavors of bready yeast and earthy hops, which slide into home with a twist of lemon. Gaffel is really great on draft.

SUMMERTIME
Goose Island Beer Co.
ABV: 4.7%

This Chicago-crafted kölsch is a sweet little session beer that's the color of Goldilocks's hair. Summertime's mellow scent of grass and lemon zest is partnered with an understated fruity flavor and downright gulpable drinkability. It'll go down your gullet as quickly as a little kid on a Slip 'n Slide.

BACKUP BEERS: *Coast Brewing Company 32°/50° Kölsch, Metropolitan Brewing Krankshaft Kölsch, Philadelphia Brewing Company Kenzinger, Reissdorf Kölsch, Saint Arnold Brewing Company Fancy Lawnmower, Samuel Adams East-West Kölsch*

down their fruity malts, aiding clarity, and imparting a snappy bite. These ales can't get enough of the cold.

KÖLSCH

For decades in the United States, summertime has meant a call to arms—and hands—for icy canned beers such as Bud Light and Coors Light. I love a frosty Silver Bullet tall boy as much as the next parched man sweating at the beach, but when it comes to that elusive balance of flavor and refreshment, I opt for one of Germany's lesser-known beer styles, kölsch.

Don't be frightened by the umlaut. Kölsch is as accessible as it is tricky to spell. Hailing from Cologne, Germany, this light, elegant beer is a study in equilibrium, restraint, and meticulous craftsmanship. Largely crisp lagers dominate in Germany. Rarer are ales, whose top-fermenting yeasts favor warmer temperatures, creating fruity flavors (a cloudy hefeweizen is an ale). Think of kölsch as an ale that has been adopted and reared by the cold-hearted lager clan.

To develop kölsch's gentle, lightly fruity profile, the subtly bittered ale is fermented at toastier temperatures. Afterward, a stint of chilly lagering smoothes out the sweet malts and adds a snappy character that is suited for summertime drinking. The pretty, pale result traditionally is served in a narrow, cylindrical glass called a stange.

Amid the tidal wave of burly

imperial stouts and dizzying double IPAs, the subtle pleasures of kölsch are often lost. But since this easy-sipping style is so summer-friendly, it's become an increasing favorite of American brewers searching for an offbeat hot-weather offering. But the new crop of kölsch beers often doesn't bear the umlaut-topped moniker. Instead, snag a stange and search for a beer named after summer, such as Harpoon Summer Beer and Alaskan Summer Ale. Accordingly, I recommend that you drink them cold.

CREAM ALE

I'll clear things up before you can ask the question: there's not a single drop of dairy in the confusingly named cream ale that, along with California Common, is one of the few indigenous styles in American brewing.

The refreshingly crisp and light cream ale is a beer born from competition. To better compete with American lager breweries in the Northeast and mid-Atlantic, ale brewers devised a hybrid style that wedded lager's crisp smoothness with the flavors of an ale. This was

Wisconsin-based New Glarus Brewing's smooth riff on the cream ale, Spotted Cow, is the state's best-selling craft beer on draft.

TWO TO TASTE: CREAM ALE

KIWANDA CREAM ALE
PELICAN PUB & BREWERY
ABV: 5.4%

I'll be mercilessly mocked for this pun, but Kiwanda is doubtlessly the cream of the crop. I fell under the sway of this cream ale at the Great American Beer Fest, where I returned to Pelican's booth time and again to guzzle the ale, which is as golden as an Olympic medal. Kiwanda's snippet of malt sweetness is complemented by a refreshing carbonation, delicately floral hops, and a honeyed finish. It's no wonder Pelican has crafted Kiwanda since 1996.

SUMMER SOLSTICE
ANDERSON VALLEY BREWING COMPANY
ABV: 5.6%

This California's brewery's Boonville home is a curious locale with its own lingo, Boontling. Therefore, I'll use the local dialect to describe the coppery ale with a creamy mouthfeel: "aplenty bahl steinber horn," which means "really great beer." On the palate, expect a medium body, lots of caramel malts, and a lick of citrus and sweetness that keeps Solstice compulsively sippable. You'll likely enjoy a heelch of 'em.

BACKUP BEERS: *Catawba Valley Brewing Company Farmer Ted's Farmhouse Cream Ale, Empire Brewing Company Cream Ale, Laughing Dog Brewing Cream Ale, New Glarus Brewing Company Spotted Cow, Sun King Brewery Sunlight Cream Ale, Terrapin Beer Co. Golden Ale*

FEELING FREE IN GERMANY

Sebastian Sauer and Peter Essel are on a mission to reverse the Reinheitsgebot. At Freigeist Bierkultur ("free spirit"), their revolutionary brewery in Cologne, Germany, the duo strive to revive and update forgotten and classic styles of German beer. Their releases include tart and smoky Abraxxxas, a take on an eastern German wheat beer once known as Lichtenhainer, and a traditional, unfiltered version of kölsch called Ottekolong, or "Eau de Cologne." This displays a refreshing sense of humor in a beer scene not known for having one.

accomplished by fermenting and conditioning ales at cooler temperatures (a blend of ale and lager yeasts sometimes is used), which kept fruity flavors and aromas in check—not unlike the kölsch. In *Radical Brewing*, author Randy Mosher posits that German immigrants familiar with brewing the cold-fermented ales of Cologne applied the techniques to American ales, resulting in the birth of the cream ale.

Just as in skinning a cat, there's more than one way to craft a cream ale. Some breweries opt for all malt, such as Narragansett Cream Ale, whereas Genesee Cream Ale employs adjuncts such as corn to add subtle sweetness. Sixpoint Brewery's Sweet Action ratchets up bitterness, helping make this one of the Brooklyn brewery's top sellers. Regardless of the ingredients, there's one commonality: cream ales are an ideal crossover beer that appeals to craft-beer converts and newcomers alike.

ALTBIER

In the nineteenth century, not every German brewery went gaga for pale

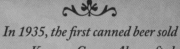

In 1935, the first canned beer sold was Krueger Cream Ale, crafted in Richmond, Virginia, by Kruger Brewing Company.

lagers. But some brewers stuck to their brew kettles, continuing to craft the same beers that had slaked drinkers' thirst for centuries. In the case of Düsseldorf, situated not far from where Germany abuts Holland and Belgium, that meant a copper-brown ale that would come to be known as the altbier.

The style is a marvel of genetic selection. The balanced dark ale is fermented with an unusual yeast strain adapted to cooler temperatures. It imparts the expected fruity flavors, but extended cold conditioning softens the fruitiness and contributes a crisp, clean profile and the smoothness for which lagers are loved. (Not coincidentally, Cologne, the birthplace of kölsch, is only about 30 miles away. The major difference between these dual cold-fermented styles is that the kölsch relies on pale malts.)

Until the nineteenth century, this Düsseldorf specialty had no official name. It was simply the local beer. That changed in 1838 when Mathias Schumacher, the founder of Düsseldorf's oldest brew-pub, Brauerei Ferdinand Schumacher, branded his beer an alt, which translates to "old," referencing the traditional ale-brewing techniques. It featured an amplified bitterness, a defining element of the Düsseldorf altbier. (Schumacher also aged his altbier in wooden casks, which is how it's traditionally served in Düsseldorf brewpubs.)

The name was picked up by other

TWO TO TASTE: ALTBIER

COPPER ALE
OTTER CREEK BREWING
ABV: 5%

To fashion its flagship altbier, Vermont's Otter Creek leans on a blend of six malts and a trio of hops that results in a copper-colored ale with caramel and toasted malts vying for your nose's attention. On the tongue, expect biscuits, toffee, and earthy and herbal bitterness touched by pine.

ORGANIC MÜNSTER ALT
BRAUEREI PINKUS MUELLER
ABV: 5.1%

Unlike the average darker-shaded alt, the Münster displays an atypical cloudy gold color. But the malt remains front and center, with a raw-dough aroma that mingles with lemons and straw. Taste-wise, expect honey-drizzled biscuits, tart fruit, and a dry finish.

BACKUP BEERS: *Alaskan Brewing Co. Amber, Bluegrass Brewing Co. Altbier, Long Trail Brewing Co. Ale, Ninkasi Brewing Company Sleigh'r Dark Double Alt Ale, Southampton Publick House Altbier, Tyranena Brewing Company Headless Man Amber*

German brewers. Also, two distinct offshoots of the alt emerged. First, there's the clean-drinking northern German altbier, which is less bitter than the Düsseldorf original and has become the dominant version of alt. (Don't worry too much about discerning the slight variations.) Second is the sticke alt (*sticke*, pronounced "shtick-uh," means "secret" in the local dialect), brewed just twice a year by Uerige in Düsseldorf. Also known as latzenbier, it's darker than the traditional altbier and boasts a boosted ABV and bitterness as well as rich, malty complexity. Sound delicious? It is. Now the bad news: the world's best sticke, from Düsseldorf's Uerige, is brewed only twice a year. Now the good news: you'll be able to happily drink these admirable altbiers all year.

Since 1838, Düsseldorf's Braueri Schumacher has brewed the city's famous altbier. Visit the brewpub for a taste of the house altbier served fresh from wooden casks, then bring a one-liter bottle of the beer back home. Much to my chagrin, the altbier is not sold in the United States.

CUT THROUGH THE HAZE

WITBIERS, HEFEWEIZENS, AND OTHER CLOUDY WHEAT BEERS

NE OF THE GREAT IRONIES of my life is that my wife is allergic to alcohol, especially in the form of beer. After a few pints of her favorite skunky IPA, she turns beet-red and hives bubble up, an intensely itchy sensation best approximated by wading through poison ivy in your birthday suit. After a night carousing with friends, a tomato complexion is a telltale sign of how much fun she's had—and how much hell there will be to pay the next day.

With beer, there's also an ingredient that can't hide, making its appearance known from 15 paces: wheat. As a brewing ingredient, wheat has a signature look and feel. The protein-rich grain provides a full body and mouthfeel, lively carbonation, a smoothness like freshly poured blacktop, and a head as creamy as, well, whipped cream. Most important, wheat makes a beer cloudier than a January morning in Seattle.

Used in small doses, wheat can add an intriguing complexity to just about every style of beer, from stouts to IPAs and even strong lagers. But I like wheat best when it's the star of the show, letting its smooth, hazy beauty shine in light and dark German weissbiers, spiced Belgian witbiers, and all manner of hop-mad American wheat ales. Read on to clear up these cloudy brews.

GERMAN WHEAT BEERS

For wheat-beer producers, 1516 was a very bad year. That was when William IV, Duke of Bavaria, instituted the Reinheitsgebot, which banned brewers from making beer with that grain.

This was a broadside against tradition. For centuries, wheat had been a crucial ingredient for brewers across central Europe, in particular Germany, where top-fermenting beer was broken down into two broad categories. Darker brews made with well-roasted barley were known as rotbier (*rot* is German for "red") and were probably precursors to lager. On the other end of the color spectrum there was weissbier, which translates to "white beer." (It's also known as weizenbier, aka "wheat beer.")

The term was a catchall for the comparatively lighter, paler-colored brews often made with raw wheat. They were an appealing counterpoint to the harsh, acrid flavors created by fire-dried barley malt. (The renowned beers of northern Germany's Einbeck were made with wheat and lightly roasted barley; see page 46.)

Although wheat beers were common across central Europe, where they were not subject to the restrictive Reinheitsgebot, royal privilege ensured that the style's production was tightly controlled in Bavaria. The noble Degenberger family, who are credited with crafting the first modern weissbier in the fifteenth century, were the sole legal producers of the style. (They owned a brewery in Schwarzach that still stands today.) The wheat-nixing Reinheitsgebot should have killed weissbier, but Duke Wilhelm—a member of the House of Wittelsbachs, Bavaria's ruling royal family—granted the Degenbergers the sole brewing exemption. The monopoly earned the noble clan barrels of bucks, though they had to pay a hefty tax for the privilege.

In 1602, the last Duke of Degenberg died without an heir. The rules of

ALL IS NOT WHITE IN THE WORLD

Popularity is forever fleeting. By the late 1700s, Bavarians had begun ditching weissbier in favor of the high-quality beer being produced in monasteries and, later, dark lagers and crisp and light pilsners. Weissbier was on a slow slide to irrelevance until a savior arrived in 1855, when the Munich brewer Georg Schneider leased Munich's Weisse Hofbräuhaus, keeping the weissbier tradition limping along while he trained his eyes on the real prize. In 1872, he struck a deal with King Ludwig II to relinquish the royal weissbier vise grip, allowing private breweries to craft the white stuff.

This decree did not instantly reverse the dwindling fortunes of wheat beer. The style was relegated to the fringes for much of the nineteenth and early twentieth centuries, and it was considered a health tonic fit for Grandma, Grandpa, and sickly souls. (Since weissbier was bursting with B-complex vitamins, German doctors often recommended it to cure vitamin deficiencies. Sure beats the socks off a multivitamin, eh?)

Sticking to its guns, the Schneider brewery kept making wheat beers, and by the second half of the twentieth century weissbier began swinging into fashion in northern Germany. Though weissbier had never before made inroads in that pilsner-dominated part

inheritance dictated that the family's assets reverted to the Wittelsbachs, including the privilege to brew weissbier. Did Duke Maximilian I, then the ruler of Bavaria, let the style succumb to a swift and painless death? Not when there was money to be made. Maximilian had a sudden change of heart, and in short order, a main weissbier brewery was built in Munich (the Degenberger family's Schwarzach brewer was imported to make beer) and innkeepers across Bavaria were ordered to purchase the Wittelsbachs' weissbier, nicely filling the royal coffers. In time a network of weissbier breweries blanketed Bavaria, and throughout the seventeenth and eighteenth centuries the light, lively, and elegant style was so popular that its sales reportedly provided the state with nearly one-third of its annual revenues.

of the country, younger drinkers were drawn to its appealingly fruity aromas, easy drinkability, and thirst-quenching character. G. Schneider & Sohn was ready to supply Germany, and soon the world, with a wide range of weissbiers. Let's take a look at the very many shades of white.

HEFEWEIZEN

If beer held a beauty contest, the runaway winner probably would be a Bavarian hefeweizen. Poured into a tall glass as curvaceous as a Victoria's Secret cover model, the wheat beer is a cloudy looker, all hazy gold and topped with a

Bavaria's Duke Albrecht V, of the Wittelsbach family reportedly declared that wheat beer was a "useless drink that neither nourishes nor provides strength and power, but only encourages drunkenness."

* * *

Looking to go pro with your homebrewing hobby? One of the world's top institutions to bone up on brewing knowledge is the Technical University of Munich at Weihenstephan, where you can earn a braumeister degree—if you speak German. The courses are not available in English.

TWO TO TASTE: HEFEWEIZEN

AYINGER BRÄU-WEISSE
BRAUEREI AYING
ABV: 5.1%
∽

King Kong would go gaga after his first sniff of this glowing, honey-colored German hefeweizen's intoxicating fragrance of ripe bananas sprinkled with spicy cloves. The full-bodied Bräu-Weisse drinks soft and spritzy, flaunting more fruit, peppery spice, and a moderately tart, citrusy finish. Pronouncing the brewery's name may be problematic, but remember this easy trick: say, "EYE-ing-gr."

FRANZISKANER HEFE-WEISSE
SPATEN-FRANZISKANER-BRÄU GMBH
ABV: 5%
∽

With roots stretching to the fourteenth century, Munich-based Franziskaner is one of Germany's oldest privately owned breweries (today it's a subsidiary of Anheuser-Busch InBev). Hefe-Weisse has an opaque, rusty gold color and a creamy, dreamy head. The archetypal aroma of bananas, light citrus, and bread is accompanied by a flavorful synergy of cloves, more bananas, and bubbles as far as the eye can see.

BACKUP BEERS: *Dry Dock Brewing Co. Dry Dock Hefeweizen, Erdinger Weissbräu Weissbier, Golden Road Brewing Hefeweizen, Live Oak Brewing Company HefeWeizen, Paulaner Hefe-Weissbier*

POUR YOU

Pouring a weissbier is sometimes a pain in the keister, as the highly carbonated style has a tendency to turn into a foamy monster. To decrease the risk, rinse the tall, curvy glass in cold water (do not dry it) and pour the beer down the side of the wet glass until only about an inch of beer remains in the bottle. Swirl it, stirring up the tasty yeast, and then dispense the blend on top of the poured brew. If you prefer a less cloudy beer, skip the last step. Either way, the beer will be delicious.

SLICE IS NICE?

To add a slice of citrus, or not to add a slice of citrus, that is the question. Personally, I don't like to add fruit to my beer, preferring to savor its natural flavors. In Germany, adding lemon to a hefeweizen is typically considered heresy, though adornment does occur on occasion (and there are historical documents chronicling lemon use at Munich's Hofbräuhaus in the nineteenth century). Furthermore, from a competing chemistry standpoint, citrus oils will destroy a handsome head. But really, there's no right or wrong answer. If you want to add lemon, go for it. This advice goes double for Belgian witbiers (see page 99).

foam tiara that's as thick and creamy as mousse. The aroma is an aphrodisiac, a beguiling swirl of bananas, citrus, cloves, green apples, and bubble gum that's mimicked in the beer's flavor. Silky smoothness, fabulous fizz, and bready and citrusy nuances ensure the beauty's place atop the podium. Either way, the beer will be delicious

The brewing behind the style's winning ways is a well-known secret. A hefeweizen is made with at least 50 percent wheat and is unfiltered, providing its baby smoothness, its cloudy appearance, and, thanks to the grain's proteins, a head like an angel's pillow. The flavor and aroma are supplied by

REPEAT AFTER ME: HEFEWEIZEN IS PRONOUNCED "HAY-FUH-VITE-ZEN."

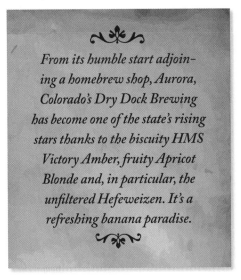

From its humble start adjoining a homebrew shop, Aurora, Colorado's Dry Dock Brewing has become one of the state's rising stars thanks to the biscuity HMS Victory Amber, fruity Apricot Blonde and, in particular, the unfiltered Hefeweizen. It's a refreshing banana paradise.

a singular yeast strain, *Torulaspora delbrueckii*, which imparts those distinctive characteristics of fruit, cloves, spice, and everything nice. (*Hefeweizen* means "yeast wheat.") Toss all those traits in a blender, add in an average ABV of about 5 percent, pour it into a tall glass to capture and display the copious foam, and you have a lovely low-alcohol German beer fit for long-haul hot-weather drinking.

You can hew to tradition with a German hefeweizen (any beer bar worth its salt has one on tap during the spring and summer). Or you could go for a great American alternative such as the Brooklyn Brewery's Brooklyner Weisse, Sierra Nevada's Kellerweis Hefeweizen, or Virginia's Starr Hill's Love. That'll handily describe how you'll feel after the first stimulating sip of hefeweizen.

A hefeweizen's clove-like aromas and flavors come courtesy of phenols, organic compounds that are naturally occurring by-products of fermentation; hefeweizen yeast causes a higher concentration of phenols.

* * *

For reasons that elude my feeble brain, a popular drink in Bavaria is Colaweizen, a blend of cola and weizenbier. No thank you.

ALL WHEAT, ALL THE TIME

Today, founding a wheat-beer brewery does not sound like a bonkers notion. In 1994, though, New Jersey's High Point Brewing seriously swam against the tide, focusing on hefeweizens, dunkelweizens, and weizenbocks released under the name Ramstein—a German town with a heavy population of expat Americans owing to its location near the Ramstein Air Base.

TWO TO TASTE: DUNKELWEIZEN

HACKER-PSCHORR DUNKLE WEISSE
HACKER-PSCHORR BRÄU GMBH
ABV: 5.3%

Although a standard-issue hefeweizen would get bowled over by rich food, darker wheat and barley malts give Dunkle Weisse the roasted malt sweetness required to stand up to hearty, even spicy fare. Yeah, bananas and dark fruits are in attendance, but the robust German ale also has a likable caramel complexity and a finish as dry as the day is long.

TUCHER DUNKLES HEFE WEIZEN
TUCHER BRÄU GMBH & CO.
ABV: 5.2%

Germany's Tucher may not nab the accolades of the Weihenstephan and Schneider breweries, but the Nürnberg-based brewery still makes several commendable weissbiers, namely, this handsome dark-brown dunkelweizen. It's creamy and just a bit sweet, drawing you in with caramel-covered bananas, yet the mouthfeel remains light. It's refreshing and repeatedly drinkable.

BACKUP BEERS: *Erdinger Weissbräu Weissbier Dunkel, High Point Brewing Company Ramstein Classic, Paulaner Hefe-Weissbier Dunkel, Weissbierbrauerei Hopf Dunkle Weisse*

DUNKELWEIZEN

In Bavaria, old-fashioned wheat beers were not as white as the driven snow. They were doubtlessly paler than the prevailing beers of the fifteenth and sixteenth centuries, but wheat beers were nothing like the golden, straw-colored hefeweizens of today. The old-timey wheat beers had a darker tinge, perhaps something along the color lines of Germany's rusty-red Schneider Weisse—itself a continuously brewed tradition since 1872.

These swarthy wheat beers did not die out. Instead, they were branded

A filtered hefeweizen is called a kristalweizen ("crystal wheat"). Minus the yeast and proteins from the wheat, the fruity aromas are subtler and more restrained. To me, it's about as much fun as drinking a light beer. A hefeweizen is all about the hazy pageantry.

★ ★ ★

To create its Kellerweis Hefeweizen, Sierra Nevada uses the traditional, time-consuming Bavarian technique of open fermentation. This encourages the production of fruity esters, creating a more flavorful, complex beer.

dunkelweizens ("dark wheat") and look like hefeweizens that have spent too much time at a tanning salon. A dunkelweizen is made with a proportion of highly kilned malt, which imparts the color, roasted complexity, and caramel sweetness typically found in a Munich dunkel (see page 44). However, except for the citrusy edge, the darker brew retains all the qualities that you (hopefully) enjoy in a hefeweizen. A dunkelweizen is creamy and fruity, bursting with bananas, bubble gum, cloves, apples, and all the other good things you've come to expect from a Bavarian wheat beer.

Though the regular ol' hefeweizen remains more popular, dunkelweizen is hardly endangered. Most of the major German brewers, including Weihenstephan, Hacker-Pschorr, and Franziskaner, have their own take on the style, and you can even find a dependable dark wheat beer in Trader Joe's house brand, Josephs Brau Dunkelweizen. Toss one in your shopping cart next time you're grocery shopping or go to the dark(er) side with an authentic German dunkelweizen.

WEIZENBOCK

In the early 1900s, Bavarian beer drinkers were atwitter over doppelbocks, the potent, bottom-fermented lagers that monks originally devised as a liquid meal (see page 49). Wheat-beer specialist G. Schneider & Sohn wanted in on the craze, too, but there was one snafu: the brewery cranked out top-fermented ales.

TWO TO TASTE: WEIZENBOCK

SCHNEIDER WEISSE TAP 6 UNSER AVENTINUS
PRIVATE WEISSBIERBRAUEREI
G. SCHNEIDER & SOHN GMBH
ABV: 8.2%

Ruby-colored Aventinus is one of those rare beers that'll give you pause, slamming on your sipping brakes so that you take your sweet time to unfold its algebra-complex layers of flavor. I'm talking plums, raisins, ripe bananas, cloves, and chocolate wrapped around a silky, negligee-like smoothness. The doppelbock will warm you like a wool coat, too.

WEIHENSTEPHANER VITUS
BAYERISCHE STAATSBRAUEREI
WEIHENSTEPHAN
ABV: 7.7%

Back in 1040, Weihenstephan was the house brewery for an order of Benedictine monks, reportedly making it the world's oldest continually operated brewery. Practice, it follows, makes perfection with this surprisingly straw-yellow potion that packs a hefeweizen's classic but far more intensified profile of cloves, banana bread, tangy citrus, and sweet malt. Vitus is like a hefeweizen that's been working out at the gym.

BACKUP BEERS: *Les Trois Mousquetaires Weizenbock Grande Cuvée, Victory Brewing Company Moonglow Weizenbock, Weissbierbrauerei Hopf Weisser Bock, Weyerbacher Brewing Co. Slam Dunkel*

ROGGEN THAT

One of Germany's rarer and more obscure beer styles is roggenbier (*roggen* is German for "rye"), a kissing cousin to the hefeweizen. Whereas hazy hefeweizens are wheat-driven, roggenbiers contain up to 50 percent rye. When fermented with hefeweizen yeast, roggenbiers end up with a smooth body that's as velvety as a smoking jacket. They also have a clove spiciness that's a great mate with spicy rye, creating a profile that recalls pumpkin pie. Don't go seeking out the style at your local beer store; roggenbiers mostly remain a draft-only niche. If you spot a roggenbier at your local brewpub, buy a pint on the double.

Where some beer makers might see a hurdle, Mathilde Schneider saw an opportunity. In 1907, he brewed a beer incorporating ingredients and techniques similar to those required for doppelbocks and then took a detour by using the house hefeweizen yeast. The crossbred brew was carbonated according to the *méthode champenoise*, in which effervescence is achieved through a secondary bottle fermentation. It was named Aventinus after a Bavarian historian. When tasted, Aventinus was nothing short of transcendent. The smooth, malt-forward beer was a royal rumpus of chocolate, bananas, cloves, and dark fruits such as dates, figs, and raisins.

Of late, Germany's G. Schneider & Sohn has been releasing experimental wheat beers that refuse to cave in to convention. *Meine Hopfenweisse* ("my white hop") is fruity, bitter, and totally tropical, and the fresh, gorgeously hopped, all-organic Schneider Weisse Tap 4 Mein Grunes relies on decidedly American Cascade hops. On a similar note, Weihenstephan also released a hoppy, one-off experiment called White Hoplosion.

Hello, world! The wheat-powered weizenbock was here to stay. The magnetic allure of this beefed-up dunkelweizen is easy to explain. A weizen is strong (usually 7 to 9 percent ABV) and warming, a bonfire for your belly that, thanks to softening and smoothing wheat, slides down easy. Awash in flavor, weizenbock offers aromatic twists and tasty, unexpected turns that don't always exist in its comrade in wintertime imbibing, barley wine (see page 198), which sometimes slides over the rails with caramel sweetness. It's a no-brainer that over the last century, the weizenbock has become a cold-weather go-to for German and American brewers alike.

SOUR GERMAN WHEAT ALES

More than 150 years ago, northern Germany made numerous spiced, fruit-flavored, or sour ales concocted with a hearty ration of wheat. Many of these styles have gone the way of the woolly mammoth, but two of my favorite wheat ales survived extinction. Meet the Berliner weisse and gose, two dusted-off styles that you'll soon pleasurably sour on.

BERLINER WEISSE

During their early nineteenth-century rampage across northern Germany, Napoleon's military forces made a mouth-puckering discovery. Among the numerous intoxicants that passed the

SOUR ON THE SUNSHINE STATE

Florida may be a long way from Berlin, but that has not stopped several Florida brewpubs from specializing in Berliner weisse. At Gulfport's Peg's Cantina, Doug Dozark (the son of the owner, Pam Wasserlink, and a production manager at Tampa's terrific Cigar City Brewing) makes Peg's G.O.O.D. (Gulfport Original On Draft) Berliner Weisse and several offbeat variants, including Ich Bin Ein Rainbow Jelly Donut and Jolly Green Rancher Berliner Weiss. Down at 7venth Sun Brewery in Dunedin, you'll find the Midnight Moonlight Berliner weisse and unusual, limited-edition variations spiced with everything from ginger to cherries, coconuts, kiwis, and Key limes. Both breweries are only about 25 miles apart.

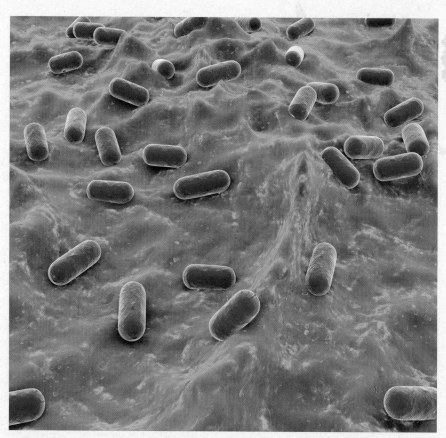

In food production, **Lactobacillus** *bacteria is crucial to the creation of everything from cheese to pickles, yogurt, and kimchi.*

TWO TO TASTE: BERLINER WEISSE

HOTTENROTH
BERLINER WEISSE
THE BRUERY
ABV: 3.1%

&

"The Berliner weisse is such a low-alcohol beer that it can appeal to the most hardcore beer geeks and to those who don't like beer," brewmaster Patrick Rue says of his Hottenroth, which is named after his grandparents. It's chock-full of *Lactobacillus* sour power, resulting in a shockingly pleasing citric tartness. It's as if lemonade and Champagne had a love child.

1809
PROFESSOR FRITZ BRIEM
ABV: 5%

&

Only with a Berliner weisse would a 5 percent ABV seem extreme. Though it's a touch stronger than I'd like, there's lots to love about 1809, which dedicates half its grain bill to wheat malt. A nose like lemon yogurt leads to a bright citric acidity, which is mixed with apples and apricots. The effervescence is crisper than cold seltzer.

BACKUP BEERS: *Bayerischer Bahnhof Brau & Gaststättenbetrieb Berliner-Style Weisse, Berliner Kindl Brauerei Weisse, 4 Hands Brewing Co. Prussia Berliner Style Weisse, Night Shift Brewing Somer Weisse*

soldiers' lips, one tart and effervescent ale left such an impression that it was nicknamed "Champagne of the north."

Of course a Frenchman would make a comparison to Champagne. Instead, I liken the cloudy Berliner weisse (born in Berlin, of course) to unsweetened lemonade, a beverage that's as immensely sour as it is refreshing—and low in alcohol, making it suitable for quaffing all summer.

To create the requisite tartness, the straw-pale wheat ale is concocted with warm-fermenting yeasts and *Lactobacillus* bacteria, which imparts the appealingly acidic flavor. Other breweries blend *Lactobacillus* with the wild yeast *Brettanomyces*, which is a vital ingredient in creating Belgium's sour and funky lambics. Those could be the bread crumbs that lead us back to the birth of the Berliner weisse.

The style does not have a clear-cut origin story and is subject to educated speculation. In *Classic Bottled Beers of the World*, British beer writer Roger Protz postulates that the style's roots lay with the Huguenots, Protestants from Belgium's Flanders region and France who favored sour red and brown ales. In the late seventeenth century, many fled religious persecution and migrated

IN GERMANY, ONLY BERLINER WEISSES BREWED IN BERLIN can use the name.

to, you guessed it, Germany. An alternative hypothesis is that Berliner weisse evolved out of Halberstädter Broihan, a darker-colored ale made out of barley and wheat that supposedly was popular in Berlin during the seventeenth century.

Though the origin of the sour ale is uncertain, its popularity was a no-brainer. During the nineteenth century, there were an estimated 250-plus brewers producing Berliner weisse, which was a uniquely customizable beer. Some Germans liked it acidic, and others watered it down or blended it with lager. A more classic way to curtail tartness was to serve Berliner weisse *mit Schuss*: with a sweetening hit of flavored syrup such as raspberry *Himbeersirup*, lemony *Zitronensirup*, or herbaceous woodruff (*Waldmeistersirup*). Traditionally in Germany, the sour ale is served in a large bowl-shaped glass with a straw, making Berliner weisse just about the only beer you can sip through a straw and not get laughed out of the bar.

That is, if you could find a bowlful of Berliner weisse. A growing taste for crisp and clear lagers meant that by the time the twentieth century was on its way out the door, only a handful of breweries producing Berliner weisse remained, including Weihenstephan and Berliner Kindl. But it was too early to write a eulogy. Buoyed by American brewers keen on crafting tart, quenching ales, the lemony Berliner weisse finds its vital signs improving.

Philadelphia's Nodding Head Brewery & Restaurant was the first American brewery to concoct a Berliner weisse, releasing its crisp and tangy Ich Bin Ein Berliner Weisse in 2000. More craft breweries followed suit with bottled versions of the sour stuff. Now Dogfish Head turns out the tart and peachy Festina Pêche. New Hampshire's White Birch Brewing has an invigorating Berliner Weisse, and California's Heretic Brewing makes the tangy Tartuffe. I don't think you will tire of these tart beers anytime soon.

GOSE

The first time I saw a man put salt in beer, I was bending elbows at a New Orleans bar. I was sipping Abita Jockamo, an agreeably bitter Louisiana-made IPA. To my right, a weather-beaten man with a face as lined as graph paper held an icy Dixie lager and a saltshaker. With a surgeon's precision, he sprinkled the salt into the bottle, swirled it, and took a long, satisfying gulp. *Sacrilege*, I thought, not knowing that for more than a millennium the seasoning has been the secret to one of Germany's odd, singular beer styles: gose (pronounced "goes-uh").

At first blush, the pale, top-fermented sour ale is the spitting image of the Berliner weisse. The sour ales both tout an ingredient bill of barley and wheat; the differences reside in gose's addition of salt and coriander, a spice that's associated with the Belgian witbier. (Gose and Berliner weisse were considered regional specialties and exempt from the Reinheitsgebot, the Bavarian purity law governing beer.)

There may be a deeper connection to Belgium. The style's name has some historians hypothesizing that gose is related to gueuze, a blend of sour aged lambics (see page 229). A more likely explanation of gose's name is the beer's origins in northwestern Germany, in Goslar, a mining town cut through by a river named the Gose.

The sour, salty stuff caught on, especially in Leipzig, about 100 miles to the east. Local brewers there began manufacturing gose, and as recently as 1900 there were more than 80 licensed *Gosenschenke*, or gose taverns, sprinkled throughout the town. Still, gose was never Leipzig's most dominant beer, and its difficult brewing process ensured that production remained limited.

Gose gradually declined from that peak of popularity, largely as a result of tastes changing to lagers, which decimated northern Germany's rustic top-fermenting beer specialists. Gose limped along until World War II, when German breweries were forced to cease production. After bombs stopped falling and treaties were signed, Leipzig found itself in the communist German Democratic Republic. In 1945, the last lingering

GAGA FOR GOSE

Ron Gansberg has a crush on the salty style. "One of the beauties of the style is that it's open to interpretation," says the Cascade Brewing brewmaster, who sometimes simultaneously releases his four seasons of gose as the "four goses of the apocalypse." Besides its quenching character, Gansberg sees another benefit to offering gose. Compared with other sour brews, "Gose is much more accessible because its acid level is much lower. We like to start people off with gose and transition them to the harder stuff," Gansberg says. "Gose is a gateway sour beer."

ONE TO TASTE: GOSE*

LEIPZIGER GOSE
GASTHAUS & GOSEBRAUEREI BAYERISCHER BAHNHOF
ABV: 4.5%

Perhaps I should let Matthias Neidhart, the president of the beer importers B. United International, describe his company's unpasteurized, bottle-conditioned gose: "You have the banana-y esters from the yeast and lactic character from the bacteria and a dry, salty finish that's not overpowering," he says. "It's refreshing and highly complex." I second that.

---

* *I'm not going to make you run around like a headless chicken to find a second gose. The style is not super-widespread, and any bottled versions are rather limited editions. For now, look to your local brewpub or keep your eyes peeled for one-off bottles appearing at your beer shop.*

gose brewery was confiscated. Leipzig's Friedrich Wurzler Braueri revived gose in 1949, but the owner's death in 1966 again spelled the style's end.

It refused to remain down for the count. In the 1980s, the bar owner Lothar Goldhahn began restoring one of Leipzig's most famous *Gosenschenke*, Ohne Bedenken. But what was a *Gosenschenke* without gose? He found a brewery in East Berlin to produce the odd, nearly forgotten beer and had a few old-timers try it. They approved. Though production has come in spurts and stops, gose once again has a pulse. It's regularly brewed by at least four German breweries, including Gasthaus & Gosebrauerei Bayerishcher Banhof in Leipzig's historic train station, and dozens of American breweries and brewpubs are also dabbling in the salty style.

In Oklahoma, Choc Beer Company turns out the tart, dry, summer-appropriate Gose, Widmer Brothers adds fruit and flowers to its Marionberry Hibiscus Gose, and Samuel Adams—yes, Sam Adams!—rotates in the soft, delicate Verloren Gose. In Portland, Oregon, Upright Brewing Company

Since gose is so great during the summertime, the German nickname for the beer is Sonnen-schirm, or "sun umbrella."

makes its Gose with a saison yeast strain and plenty of lactic acid, and its fellow Portland brewery Cascade Brewing creates a draft-only gose for each season.

Looks like that old man at the bar was not being a weird bird. He was merely ahead of the curve.

FROM BELGIUM, WITH HAZE

In Europe, Germany does not have an iron grip on brewing with wheat. Belgium, too, has a long history of making divine wheat ales with a nice amount of spice. It's time to meet the witbier.

Since gose and other classic styles from northern Germany were comparatively low in alcohol, drinkers seeking an extra kick often consumed them alongside spirits such as Kümmel, a liqueur spiced with cumin, caraway seeds, and fennel. If you ever find yourself in Leipzig, some bars serve gose mixed with everything from banana juice to white wine and Champagne.

THAT'S GREAT, SIR!

Europe's *grodziskie* was one bizarre beer. Made with 100 percent smoked wheat malt and hopped to the high heavens, the low-alcohol ale was for centuries one of the distinctive beers of a region that included Poland. It also was brewed in Germany, where the smoky beer was called *Grätzer*—Grätz was the German name for the city of Grodzisk, at one time a Polish brewing powerhouse. *Grätzer*, or *grodziskie*, stuck around longer than other rustic wheat beers, but by the mid-1990s the style was down for the count. But just like gose and Berliner weisse, modern brewers are agog over old-timey grätzer. Long Island's Blind Bat, which specializes in wood-smoked ales such as tart Old Walt Smoked Wit, makes the grätzer-inspired Vlad the Inhaler; Corvallis, Oregon's Flat Tail Brewing crafts Smokin' Wheat with a slight tang; and Professor Fritz Briem offers a smoky Grodziskie with a sour twist. The smoke is spreading around the world.

Professor Fritz Briem's historic re-creation of the Grodziskie is a smoky, wheat-driven delight. P.S. That's my dog, Sammy, in the background.

WITBIER

The last couple of decades have not been kind to the behemoths of global brewing. In the United States, they've watched their market share shrivel like a month-old lemon as beer drinkers ditch mass-produced lagers for more creative craft beer. It's the inevitable result of focusing less on flavor than on plumping a bank account.

As the saying goes, if you can't beat them, join them. Brewing conglomerates may have found a Trojan horse to infiltrate drinkers' taste buds and wallets: the Belgian-style witbier. MillerCoors makes Blue Moon, and Anheuser-Busch concocts Shock Top Belgian White. Despite an ongoing slump for megabrewers, Blue Moon remains MillerCoors's bright spot, spawning a range of year-round variations. And you know what? I can't bad-mouth Blue Moon. Cloudy, unfiltered, and kissed with oranges, it's as easy on the eyes as it is on the mouth.

If I were a MillerCoors employee, I would be thanking my lucky stars for Pierre Celis, a milkman who single-handedly saved the witbier from extinction. He lived in the Belgian village of Hoegaarden, about an hour east of Brussels. This region's specialty was smooth, elegant witbiers ("white beers"), which were made with oats and barley and spiced with dried orange peel and coriander. The style thrived for around four centuries, but by the mid-1950s the witbier could not withstand the hard-charging pilsners and lagers. Hoegaarden's last traditional witbier brewery, Brouwerij Tomsin, closed down in 1957.

Pierre Celis lamented the loss of witbier. Before becoming a milkman, he'd toiled a bit at Tomsin. Perhaps he could re-create the lost style. Celis did not possess a recipe, but he recalled the ingredients and unique spices. He brewed a batch at home, winning compliments for his homebrew. Encouraged, Celis left the cows behind and founded Brouwerij Celis in the stables beside his house, where he brewed his first commercial batch of Oud Hoegaards Bier. You may know it as Hoegaarden.

Demand soon outstripped production capacity. Celis relocated to a broken-down lemonade factory and upped his output. The witbier spread across Hoegaarden and then Belgium, France, and the Netherlands. The beer's atypical look was complemented by an unusual eight-sided serving mug that became the standard serving vessel. Nothing could stop Celis—except a fire. In 1985, an inferno destroyed his brewery. Since insurance would not cover rebuilding costs, Celis took an investment from Stella Artois. In a few years, the relationship soured like a bad batch of beer. Stella merged with another brewery to form Interbrew. It was the precursor to InBev, which later devoured Anheuser-Busch. Cost cutting led to diminished quality. Celis would not stand for subpar beer.

He sold his shares, bid Europe adieu, and moved to Austin, Texas, where he founded Celis Brewery. He made Celis White according to his original Hoegaarden recipe, finding fast success but not enough profit to satisfy his investors. To pay them off, he sold a share of his brewery to Miller. Cue déjà vu: corners were cut. The quality of ingredients suffered. Since the brewery was never wildly profitable, it was shuttered and the brand was sold to the highest bidder. (Until 2012, Celis White was made by Michigan Brewing Company.)

Although the business side of brewing was not kind to Pierre Celis, who passed away in 2011, the epitaph

Pierre Celis worked in conjunction with Belgium's Brouwerij St. Bernardus to develop the recipes for several beers. Grottenbier ("grotto beer") is a dark, effervescent ale that's aged for up to two months in limestone caves, receiving a weekly turning à la Champagne. Witbier is a top-shelf specimen of the style, with a billowy head and a perfume I wish I could bottle and sell.

to his career is the revival and enduring survival of an array of witbiers around the globe. In Quebec, Unibroue's Blanche de Chambly is riotously effervescent (*bière blanche* is French for witbier), and Long Island's Southampton Publick House kicks up the ABV (6.7 percent) without sacrificing drinkability in its Double White Ale. Austin's (512) Brewing Company keeps Texas's witbier tradition alive with its (512) Wit flavored with grapefruit peel, and South Carolina's Westbrook Brewing takes a trip to Southeast Asia for White Thai, which includes lemongrass and ginger.

As for Celis, there's a happy posthumous end to this tale. In 2012, his family purchased the trademark for Celis beers, and plans are afoot to use the brewer's recipes back in Texas. For the Celis family, it appears the clouds are finally clearing.

AMERICAN WHEAT ALES

When it comes to brewing, the United States does not have a long, sepia-tinted history with wheat. For much of the last century and a half, the preferred fermentable was barley, with perhaps corn or rice also tossed into the brew kettle. Wheat was reserved for baking or, occasionally, bourbon. Think back to your first taste of Maker's Mark. Compared with other bourbons, Maker's is softer and smoother, with a less spicy

TWO TO TASTE: WITBIER

WHITE
ALLAGASH BREWING COMPANY
ABV: 5%

When I first met my wife's mother, the only beer she drank was Miller 64. I bit my tongue and suggested that she try White, the flagship witbier from Portland, Maine's Allagash. She took a sip of the refreshing, cloudy blonde knockout, savoring its potpourri blend of coriander, Curaçao orange peel, and lemon zest, and it disappeared like water. You'll probably follow suit.

HITACHINO NEST WHITE ALE
KIUCHI BREWERY
ABV: 5.5%

In 2011, the Japanese earthquake temporarily knocked this brewery offline, but it's back crafting multifaceted ales such as this fabulously fragrant witbier. It packs no shortage of flavor with coriander, orange peel, nutmeg, and a splash of vitamin-packed orange juice. Hitachino Nest White is a great gulper on a hot afternoon.

BACKUP BEERS: *Brewery Ommegang Witte Wheat Ale, Brouwerij Bayik Wittekerke, Brouwerij van Hoegaarden Original White Ale, Clown Shoes Clementine White Ale, Lost Coast Brewery Great White, Microbrasserie Charlevoix Dominus Vobiscum Blanche*

TWO TO TASTE:
AMERICAN WHEAT ALE

GUMBALLHEAD
THREE FLOYDS BREWING CO.
ABV: 5.5%

I feel like I'm doing you a disservice by recommending Gumballhead, a beer that rarely escapes from the Midwest, much less Indiana, Illinois, and Ohio. But dagnabit, this straw-red wheat ale is just too good not to mention. The fragrant hops (pineapple, citrus) calibrate the lightly sweet malt with scientific precision, creating a refresher I could glug by the gallon. This Gum never loses its flavor.

EASY STREET
WHEAT BEER
ODELL BREWING CO.
ABV: 4.6%

Crafted in Fort Collins, Colorado, this wheat ale's name references the brewers taking the easy road and leaving the beer unfiltered. You'll find the laziness is to your benefit as you sip this smooth, moderately sweet treat with a light and appealing lemony profile. At such a skimpy ABV, you can drink Easy Street till the cows come home.

BACKUP BEERS: *Boulevard Brewing Company Unfiltered Wheat Beer, Firestone Walker Brewing Company Solace, Hangar 24 Brewery Orange Wheat, Harpoon Brewery UFO Hefeweizen, Southern Tier Brewing Company Hop Sun Summer Wheat Beer*

flavor. That's due to wheat, a not-so-secret ingredient for a rising tide of craft brewers.

AMERICAN PALE WHEAT ALE

Both the best thing and the worst thing about Bavarian hefeweizens is the yeast strain's gustatory assault of bananas and cloves. If you like these flavors and aromas, you're in luck: they're the limelight-hogging stars of the show, leaving little stage time for hops. And that's totally fine. Plenty of American and international brewers fabricate decidedly Chiquita-flavored, Bavarian-style hefeweizens.

However, a wave of American brewers is saying ixnay to the yeast strain. Instead, they're designing beers with a sizable percentage of wheat and fermenting them with ale or lager yeast strains that do not produce such an idiosyncratic flavor profile, giving hops and grains their time beneath the spotlight.

One of the first American breweries to embrace wheat wholeheartedly was Widmer Brothers, in Portland, Oregon. In 1986, sibling brewers Rob and Kurt Widmer were working at capacity with two beers, a German-style altbier and a filtered weizenbier ("wheat beer"). The owner of the local Dublin Pub, which carried both of the Widmer beers, wanted to sell a third. One problem: the brothers owned only two fermenters, leaving them no space to fiddle with experimentation.

BEYOND THE PALE

Wheat is not the exclusive domain of lighter-hued ales. One of the more interesting niches now being explored is the wheat stout, which marries dark-roasted malts with wheat. It's a smooth, roasty, and sometimes fruity ride worth taking. The style is still in its infancy, and commercial examples tend to be relegated to brewpubs or one-off experiments. A few commercially released wheat stouts include Maine-based Rising Tide Brewing Company's Ursa Minor and Dark Force from Norway's HaandBryggeriet, both of which are fermented with Bavarian yeast. Denver's Strange Brewing Company has taken this stylistic mash-up one step further and created the Cherry Bomb Belgian Stout. Booking a flight to Colorado to try a pint would not be a rash decision.

As a solution, they left a batch of the weizenbier unfiltered and appealingly cloudy, unwittingly giving birth to their flagship, Widmer Hefeweizen.

The Oregon ale is not a paint-by-numbers Bavarian hefe. Widmer Hefeweizen lacks an aromatic profile of bananas and cloves, instead trading on a floral, citrusy fragrance that has become a loose template for the slackly defined American pale wheat ale. Color-wise, these New World creations skew toward pale gold or perhaps apricot and, unless they're filtered, are as cloudy as their German forebears. The brews should have a plump, long-lasting head and a baby-smooth mouthfeel. And the aroma and taste? I'll let the hops do the talking.

Those little green flowers play a much more prominent role in these wheat ales. For example, Lagunitas Brewing Co.'s A Little Sumpin' Sumpin' Ale bursts with a juicy tropical-fruit bitterness and tips the scales at a robust 7.5 percent ABV (I drank cases of it while writing this book), and loads of Amarillo hops provide Peak Organic Summer Session Ale with a citrusy IPA-like aroma that's wedded to a crisp, lively body and 5 percent ABV. In contrast, Bell's Brewery's top-selling Oberon Ale is mildly fruity with a drop of citrus and a gentle twang. When a wheat ale is done so well, it's tough to beat.

Since siblings Kurt and Rob Widmer (left) founded their eponymous brewery in 1984, Oregon's Widmer Brothers has blossomed into one of the country's biggest craft breweries. Their Hefeweizen helped popularize the style in America, and they continue to innovate with a revolving collection of imperial stouts and IPAs, many of which are flavored with experimental or exotic hops.

BOULEVARD BREWING COMPANY
KANSAS CITY, MISSOURI

Boulevard brewmaster Steven Pauwels (left) and founder John McDonald (right) run one of America's best wheat-focused breweries.

John McDonald was not happy with his wheat beer. Sales of the filtered ale were so dismal that McDonald, the founder of the Boulevard Brewing Company in Kansas City, Missouri, considered discontinuing the brand. It was the early 1990s. Maybe America was not ready for wheat beer.

Before wielding his executioner's ax, McDonald and Boulevard fashioned a draft-only unfiltered version. It was as cloudy as London in winter. Kegs were delivered. Fingers were crossed. "The beer took off overnight," says Boulevard's brewmaster, Steven Pauwels. The success was a matter of perception. "It wasn't as clear as the mass-produced beer being offered," he adds. "Here was a locally produced beer that tasted great, and you could see that you were drinking something different."

Since that switch in 1994, Unfiltered Wheat Beer has become Boulevard's top-selling brand as well as the top-selling craft-beer brand in the Midwest. Moreover, wheat has become Boulevard's signature ingredient. The grain (much of it locally sourced) appears in a wide range of its bottle-conditioned beers, including the flowery and citrusy Single-Wide IPA; spicy Tank 7 Farmhouse Ale; fruity and fragrant ZŌN Belgian-Style Witbier; roasty, imperial Dark Truth Stout; and tropical Harvest Dance Wheat Wine. "Boulevard is a wheat-beer brewery," Pauwels says with pride.

WHEAT YOUR MATCH

Boulevard's story can be split into several acts. First, McDonald launched the brewery in 1989 in Kansas City's historic district. He cobbled together secondhand brewing equipment, some of it from the 1930s, and fired up a recipe that yielded the mellow and fruity Pale Ale. It was the brewery's first beer and remains an enduring favorite, though conquering customers took time.

Back then, the Midwest was monopolized by stomach sops such as Busch and Budweiser. One morning, McDonald went to a local tavern and tried to convert three drinkers to his Pale Ale. His sales guy bought the trio a round. One person refused to drink it. The other two took a tiny sip and pushed the beers aside, then went silent. "As I was walking out the door, one of the guys looked at me and said, 'Young man, that is absolutely the worst beer I have ever had in my life,'" McDonald told the *Heavy Table*. "I ran out of there thinking, *What have I done? I'm gonna go broke.*"

Boulevard did not go bankrupt, but the brewery did take a different turn in the late 1990s. Eager to get a handle on Belgian beers and bottle conditioning (the process of adding yeast and sugar to beer before bottling to stoke a secondary fermentation and naturally create carbonation), McDonald looked to import a brewer from Europe. He found Belgian brewing vet Steven Pauwels, who as a child spent his summers working in a regional brewery alongside his father. Impressed by Boulevard's commitment to quality and willingness to innovate, Pauwels crossed the Atlantic and became brewmaster, a post he has held since 1999.

"It's a great company to work for," he says. "The owner provides a lot of freedom, and there's never a dull moment." Or a dull beer.

NO SQUEEZE, PLEASE

Since assuming his perch, Pauwels has refused to operate on autopilot. Under the Smokestack Series banner, he engineers a range of complex, distinctive beers. They include the Love Child collection of sours; barrel-aged one-offs; and big, beautiful Belgians such as the strong The Sixth Glass Quadrupel, the golden and fruit-forward Long Strange Tripel, and Tank 7 Farmhouse Ale, which is one of the finest American saisons.

They're all excellent creations, but I must turn your attention to Harvest Dance Wheat Wine. The winter seasonal (see page 206 for more on the style) is inimitable because of Pauwels's literal translation of the style. "The idea was to get actual wine characteristics in a wheat wine," he says. "No one really understands the style, so we could do whatever we wanted."

Given free rein, Pauwels opted for 20 percent raw wheat, 25 percent wheat malts, a smidgen of oats, Belgian yeast, and tropical Citra hops as well as Hallertau. Harvest Dance is aged in American and French oak barrels, then bottle-conditioned with Muscat grape juice. The result is as if white wine went on a sweet, sticky vacation in the tropics with beer. You'll ask for seconds.

Just don't add any citrus fruit. A chief benefit of brewing with wheat is that it helps with head retention, creating long-lasting lids of foam. Adding a slice of lemon to a beer brewed with large percentages of wheat, such as a hefeweizen or witbier, may be aromatic and aesthetically pleasing, but the fruit's acids eradicate foam. "I never drink the Unfiltered Wheat with fruit, but the consumer rules," rues Pauwels, who notes that a lemon slice is often the norm, especially in Kansas City.

Unfiltered Wheat is still going gangbusters, but the cloudy beer's success has, oddly, not paved the road for its similarly overcast sibling, ZŌN (Flemish for "sun"), a summertime-release witbier spiced with coriander and orange peel. "Educating people about witbiers can be tough," Pauwels says. "Our Unfiltered Wheat is a little yellower, while ZŌN is a little cloudier and is more of a food beer."

Still, I'd wager that the witbier's success is not a matter of if, but when. After all, Pauwels takes his cues from Pierre Celis, the brewer responsible for witbier's revival (see page 99). "I used to know him really well," Pauwels says. "He always talked about making a beer that looks great, drinks different, and feels different." And for Boulevard, being different has made all the difference.

THE LIGHTER SIDE OF DRINKING

PALE ALES

BEFORE I WAS OLD ENOUGH TO DRINK, airport delays were such a drag. Eager to escape from my parents and siblings, I'd aimlessly wander a concourse, devouring minutes in the food court with an overpriced McDonald's hamburger or thumbing through enough magazines to get paper cuts on every finger. Waiting was most definitely the hardest part.

Not with a beer. With a cool pint in your palm, the minutes glide by as fast as a six-year-old on a Slip 'n Slide. Thus, after I passed through the pearly gates of legality, I'd spend airport delays bellied up to the bar, typically savoring an aromatic Sierra Nevada Pale Ale, the life preserver for craft beer fans staring at a sea of Bud, Coors, and Miller.

The fact that Sierra Nevada Pale has reached a state of national airport ubiquity is a testament to how far craft beer has come in the last three decades and to the enduring power of pale ale. Since it first filled mugs in England several centuries ago, pale ale has proved its worth as a most delightful middle ground of beer. The moderately boozy pale ale offers more heft and body than a pilsner or lager, as well as fruity and sometimes superhoppy flavors and aromas, but it remains effortlessly drinkable. Knock back two of 'em or, heck, three and you'll have little need to call a cab to shepherd you home.

In this chapter, we'll power through the history of the pale ale, from the environmental anomaly that led to its birth in Britain to the rise of the distinctly Belgian variant and finally to the American versions with their unbridled appreciation for the almighty hop. Although these brews may be clumped together beneath the pale ale banner, not every example is as fair as Victorian-era skin. Pale ales can run the gamut from golden to ruddy amber and may be fruity, bitter, or, in the case of Belgian strong pale ale, smashing enough to knock your socks clean off your feet.

It's time to go inside the pale.

ENGLISH PALE ALE

Despite being the single biggest ingredient in beer, water gets little respect. Hops, grains, and yeast steal every bit of buzz, leaving humble H_2O to wade in the shadows. But if you were to ask brewers, they'd happily give water its turn before the camera. Water's mineral content has a direct influence on a beer's flavor and profile. For instance, the soft water in the Czech Republic city of Plzeň is largely free of minerals and has a low concentration of bicarbonates, helping create the crisp, clean, trophy-gold pilsner.

Conversely, the hills surrounding Burton upon Trent, England, are filled with gypsum deposits, which add dissolved salts to the local water. The heightened levels of calcium and sulfates improve clarity and help accentuate hop bitterness, a quirk of chemistry that paved the path for the modern pale ale. Without a doubt, lighter-colored ales have existed for centuries, if not millennia. (It's hypothesized that the ancient Sumerians used sun-dried malt to make beer, doubtlessly providing a pale

Though Timothy Taylor & Co.'s Landlord has long been a legend in England, winning Champion Beer of Britain multiple times, the wonderful pale ale made with spring water and whole-leaf hops was not imported to the United States until 2012. Seek it out.

color.) In England, the manufacture of pale ales probably started sometime in the seventeenth century, when brewers ditched roaring fires and started drying malt in ovens fueled by coke. (It's a cleaner-burning form of coal created by heating the coal in the absence of oxygen, thus removing volatile gases and impurities.)

Although these ales were pale only when compared with the dark porters and brown beers common to that period, they proved to be a popular alternative, and one of the centers for brewing them was Burton upon Trent. Breweries such as Bass, which was founded in 1777, concocted pale ales that today probably would throw your brain for an oxymoronic loop: the Burton Pale Ale was considerably dark, somewhat sweet, and warming enough to ward off December's chill. For much of the eighteenth century, the Burton Pale Ale, or just the Burton Ale, was exported to Russia and the surrounding Baltic states and stuffed area breweries' coffers. However, an unfortunate gumbo of wars and trade embargoes—in 1822, Russia banned almost every British manufactured good, including cheese, umbrellas, and ale, but not porter—caused local brewers to seek a new cash cow.

At the time, a money-minting

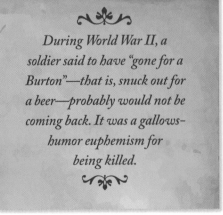

During World War II, a soldier said to have "gone for a Burton"—that is, snuck out for a beer—probably would not be coming back. It was a gallows-humor euphemism for being killed.

export was a hoppier pale ale that was being sent to India, most notably by a London brewer named George Hodgson. He supplied beer to the East India Company, which sent shipments to the subcontinent. Too bad Hodgson was greedy and tried to eliminate the middleman. The East India Company did not take kindly to that transgression and turned to the well-regarded brewers in Burton upon Trent to replicate this nicely bittered ale. Lo and behold, the local water allowed Burton's brewers to make a better bitter pale ale that in time came to be known as the India pale ale (for more on that style, see pages 128–151).

By the middle of the nineteenth century, those Burton beers with a bitter edge had gained a homeland toehold, and Burton upon Trent became one of the great brewing capitals of Britain and the world. Of course, every rise is met by a fall. Burton upon Trent's greatest asset was its water. In time, a chemist named C. W. Vincent cracked the water's mineral code and created a process called Burtonisation, which allowed brewers anywhere to mimic the Burton pale ales by adding gypsum.

The red triangle adorning every Bass label was Britain's first registered trademark.

TWO TO TASTE: ENGLISH PALE ALE

OLD SPECKLED HEN
GREENE KING PLC
ABV: 5.2%

Old Speckled Hen may be a bar stool stalwart, but the beer was born only in 1979 to commemorate the fiftieth anniversary of an MG car factory in Abingdon. (Old Speckled Hen was the name of the paint-covered automobile that workers used as the factory runaround—the "owld speckled un.") Despite nearly being killed off in favor of lager production, the Hen has endured to be a clear amber looker crowded with smooth flavors of caramel and toasted malt, plus fruity butterscotch aromas and a mild herbaceous hop profile. I recommend nabbing OSH in a nitro-pour can.

BASS PALE ALE
BASS BREWERS LIMITED
ABV: 5%

During the late nineteenth century Bass dominated the drinking landscape in Great Britain, becoming the country's most popular ale. Today it's an international icon shipped the world over (Bass was the first foreign beer sold in Japan, in 1860), owing its enduring success to its approachability. The glowing copper ale speaks of sweet malt, caramel, and the earth, featuring a mild fruity hop character and a speck of bitterness hanging out on the back end.

BACKUP BEERS: *Black Sheep Brewery Monty Python's Holy Grail Ale, Boddingtons Pub Ale, Cisco Brewers Whale's Tale Pale Ale, Firestone Walker Double Barrel Ale, Odell Brewing Company 5 Barrel Pale Ale, Samuel Smith's Old Brewery Pale Ale, Summit Brewing Company Extra Pale Ale*

TWO TO TASTE: STANDARD AND BEST BITTER

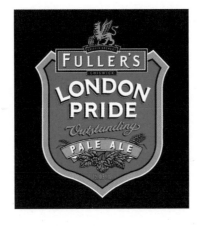

BITTER BREWER
SURLY BREWING CO.
ABV: 4.1%

A lifetime in the brewing trenches can leave some brewers feeling as bitter as a double IPA. To honor these tireless toilers and create a beer that can be glugged by the big gulp, Minnesota's Surly has crafted this tangerine-tinged standard bitter freighted with the aromas of toast and jam, partnered with an earthy bitterness and a lightweight ABV. Given the beer's summertime release in the 16-ounce cans, it's way too easy to drink a four-pack.

FULLER'S LONDON PRIDE
FULLER SMITH & TURNER PLC
ABV: 4.7%

One the fixtures of the British pub is London Pride, a best bitter with a complexity that far outweighs its gentle ABV. The tawny Pride draws you in with a scent of toffee and bread before taking you for a ride across smooth roads paved with earthy hops, biscuits, and caramel. P.S. On draft and cask in the United Kingdom, Fuller's Pride weighs in at a slightly lighter 4.1 percent ABV.

BACKUP BEERS: *Goose Island Beer Co. Honker's Ale, Drake's Brewing Alpha Session NorCal Bitter, Highland Brewing Company Black Mountain Bitter, Minneapolis Town Hall Brewery West Bank Pub Ale, Ridgeway Brewing Bitter, Tetley's English Ale*

Unlocking Burton's secret did not cause British brewers to engage in an arms race to create increasingly bitter beers. Some scaled back, creating what are now known as pale ales. They're earthy, fruity, and nicely malty, with just enough hop presence to give you a gentle static-electric jolt.

BEYOND THE PALE

As a style, the English pale ale plays it loosey-goosey, with numerous tributaries that go by the name of bitter. Originally, a bitter was a pale ale that was served on draft or as a naturally carbonated cask ale; the term *pale ale* referred to a bitter that was bottled. Today, bitters are both bottled and dispensed on draft, and these

The classic British drink the Black and Tan is made with a 50–50 mixture of Guinness and Bass Pale Ale. The darker yet lighter stout floats on top of the pale ale.

BEER IS MORE THAN 90 percent WATER.

> *Grand Teton Brewing Company's Bitch Creek ESB is in fact an extra special brown (and Bitch Creek is a real body of water). Still, it's worth sampling this sweetly malty, lightly bittered Idaho beer, which has won armloads of medals.*

COLD COMFORT

One of the most celebrated Burton upon Trent ales ever brewed was the rich heavyweight called Allsopp's Arctic Ale, which was created during the Victorian era for British explorers' expeditions to the Arctic Circle—the beer's strength prevented it from freezing. In 2010, homebrewer and adventurer Christopher Bowen and Fegley's Brew Works brewmaster Beau Baden set out to re-create the cold-weather ale during a motorcycle trip to the Arctic during which they brought along a portable brewery. A version of that brew, Fegley's Arctic Alchemy, won a bronze medal at the 2011 Great American Beer Festival.

Worthington's brewery was founded in Burton upon Trent in 1761 and utilized the prized local brewing water to great success. Today, the company (currently owned by MolsonCoors) is best known for White Shield, a classic English IPA, and Red Shield, a balanced English pale ale.

TWO TO TASTE:
EXTRA SPECIAL BITTER

ESB
REDHOOK BREWING
ABV: 5.8%

Since 1981, these Pacific Northwest brewing pioneers have been pumping out dependably excellent ales such as the piney and smooth Long Hammer IPA, the rich and malty Copper Hook, and the brewery's flagship, ESB. A malt-licked, caramel-sweet base serves as the launch pad for floral hops and a smooth, lightly bitter finish. The ESB is pretty simple, but simple can be pretty satisfying. A recent redesign has given Redhook's labels a fresh new look.

13 REBELS ESB
FRENCH BROAD BREWING CO.
ABV: 5.2%

When it comes to beer, Asheville, North Carolina, has an embarrassment of liquid riches, including this ESB named after the 13 original colonies. The vivid copper ale's got a grassy, herbal earthiness on the nose and palate. But there's also plenty of toast, a touch of caramel, and a dryness that, when combined with the moderate bitterness, makes this a surprisingly zesty easy drinker. At just 5.2 percent ABV, I could spend all night with this French Broad.

BACKUP BEERS: *Anderson Valley Brewing Company Boont ESB, Lakefront Brewery Organic ESB, McNeill's Brewery Extra Special Bitter Ale, No-Li Brewhouse Crystal Bitter, Ska Brewing Co. ESB Special Ale, Stoudt's Brewing Company Scarlet Lady ESB*

pale ales have been subdivided into three broad, overlapping categories:

STANDARD OR ORDINARY BITTER: Registering up to 4.1 percent ABV and often far below it, this barely boozy ale is the most commonly sold bitter in pubs; it is so light and drinkable, you can easily down several pints in an evening. In Britain, you'll find plenty of beers labeled as IPAs, though they're more accurately just a lower-alcohol pale ale, such as Greene King IPA.

BEST OR REGULAR BITTER: Like Goldilocks and her porridge, this bitter is not too strong and not too weak. It's usually between 4.2 and 4.7 percent ABV, and the category is a bit of a dying breed.

PREMIUM OR STRONG BITTER: Covering anything 4.8 percent and above, this maltier, hoppier brew is also called extra special bitter, aka ESB (but only in the United States; in the United Kingdom, ESB is a trademarked brand of Fuller Smith & Turner). Of late, the ESB has become a trendy style for American brewers looking to make an English-style ale with extra malt and hop oomph.

WATER, WATER EVERYWHERE*

FROM THE PILSNER TO THE DRY IRISH STOUT, H_2O'S VARYING MINERAL MAKEUP HAS BEEN INSTRUMENTAL IN CREATING SOME OF THE WORLD'S MOST ICONIC STYLES OF BEER. HERE'S WHY THE WATER IS SO SPECIAL.

DUBLIN, IRELAND: Its bicarbonate- and calcium-rich aquifers create hard water with high alkalinity. Brew a batch of beer with dark malts and the acidity they impart balances the pH, helping produce world-class stouts such as Guinness.

PLZEN, CZECH REPUBLIC: The crisp, golden, and nicely bittered pilsner probably would have been a very different beer if the local water used to make it were not so soft, or mineral-free.

MUNICH, GERMANY: Loads of carbonates require brewers to use darker malts to acidify the water, leading to sweeter, maltier, and somewhat darker lagers.

DORTMUND, GERMANY: Though it makes pilsners of the sort popularized in the Czech Republic, the city's mineral-rich hard water leads to a maltier flavor.

VIENNA, AUSTRIA: The city's mineral makeup is similar to that of Dortmund, but it has lower levels of calcium and chloride, and the equilibrium of calcium and bicarbonate is out of whack. The solution was to use a touch of toasted malts, leading to the birth of the amber-red Vienna lager.

LONDON: Low levels of calcium and high amounts of carbonates are the perfect blend for brewing porters, as the dark malts impart much-needed acidity for balance. Sodium and chloride in the water help smooth out the brews too.

* For more on the impact of brewing waters, check out John Palmer's indispensable How to Brew.

TWO TO TASTE: BELGIAN PALE ALE

TARAS BOULBA
BRASSERIE DE LA SENNE
ABV: 4.5%

Brasserie de la Senne makes beers that are low in alcohol, highly drinkable, and as bitter as old men. Zinnebir is a light, yeasty blonde ale with a pronounced hop bite, while Stouterik is a chocolaty, coffee-flavored dream. My favorite is Taras Boulba, a hazy-yellow stunner with a funky, fresh scent full of spicy yeast, lemons, and fruit. Boulba drinks dry, with malt sweetness that relents to grass, citrus, and hops, hops, hops.

LIQUID GOLD
CAPTAIN LAWRENCE BREWING COMPANY
ABV: 6%

A few years back, my buddy Aaron had a birthday BBQ for his wife, Meg. To celebrate, he bought a keg of Liquid Gold. For about 20 people. We took that as a challenge to drink as much of the spicy, peppery nectar as humanly possible. I abandoned count somewhere around pint number nine, lost in a thicket of bananas, cloves, oranges, and enough lively bubbles to lead me to pour yet another pint. Despite the next morning's skull-imploding hangover, I returned to help kick the keg.

BACKUP BEERS: *Big Boss Brewing Company Hell's Belle Belgian Style Ale, Brouwerij Kerkom Bink Blonde, Dieu du Ciel! Dernière Volonté, Harpoon Brewery Belgian Pale Ale, Omnipollo Leon*

BELGIAN PALE ALE

In the late nineteenth and early twentieth centuries, Germany was a terrible neighbor to its fellow European nations. In addition to instigating a number of wars, the country flooded the continent with its wildly popular light and elegant lagers. Combined with the crisp and herbaceous Czech pilsners, those beers provided a one–two punch that knocked Europe's brewing scene for a loop.

Though (comparatively) pale ale had been brewed in Belgium since the mid-1700s, the style had to be retrofitted to combat the pilsner and lager threat from both abroad and at home: one of the world's most ubiquitous lagers is Stella Artois, which was born in Belgium in 1926. To stave off the cold-fermented beers, Belgian brewers took inspiration from their British counterparts. They used pale malts, pilsner-appropriate noble hops from the likes of Germany and the Czech Republic, and indigenous Belgian yeast. The results tickled the fancy of the country's drinkers, and during World War I some beers were created to satisfy the palates of the British troops stationed in Belgium. After World War II, the Belgian pale took another twist, morphing into the style we recognize today: balanced beers with a delicate hop profile, a light hand with malt, moderate alcohol presence and bitterness, and Belgian yeast's trademark fruitiness and spice.

That's just the jumping-off point for Belgian pale ale. It inhabits a broad spectrum of flavors and hues, from the amber and pleasantly fruity De Koninck to the honey-hinted Palm and New York–based Brewery Ommegang's pale and cloudy BPA, which bursts with tropical fruit and loads of fragrant citrus. In fact, the American love affair with hops has led Belgian brewers to add ample hops to their pale ales, resulting in revelations such as the divinely dry De Ranke XX Bitter and Brouwerij Kerkom's way bitter, way drinkable Bink Blond.

BELGIAN GOLDEN STRONG ALE

It's been said that the devil is in the details, but in Belgium you can find Satan in the beer. It makes sense, I suppose, what with so many pious men pumping out heavenly brews (more on those on pages 152–171). Thus, it follows that one of the country's most well-known secular breweries, Moortgat, would craft a counterpoint to all that piety, Duvel— that is, Devil.

You might say that Duvel is devilishly strong. The pale ale is a prime example of my belief that you can't trust your eyes to tell you about a beer. Duvel is as golden as a wedding ring, a color that screams innocence. But that hue hides an 8.5 percent ABV. Such are the tricky pleasures of the Belgian strong

A LITTLE VISIT FROM BRETT

As the historian Ron Pattinson notes, many old-time British pale ales were matured for up to a year in wooden barrels, a favorite hiding place for the wild yeast *Brettanomyces* (see page 228 for more information). Given time, the yeast devours the beer's carbohydrates, creating unusual leathery flavors. When introduced unintentionally, *Brettanomyces* is an intruder, but it was standard operating procedure in the nineteenth century, and some British pale ales probably were infected with the wild yeast. That's no longer the case, but for a taste of the past, try Orval Trappist Ale. The monk-made elixir is generously hopped and when consumed fresh offers up spicy bitterness and a dry character. Given time, bitterness fades and *Brettanomyces* adds a funky, pleasing component and a dry finish.

DARK, STRONG . . . AND DECIDEDLY BELIGIAN

During my high school science class, I learned that for every action there's an equal and opposite reaction. That certainly explains the rise of the Belgian dark strong ale, a mirror image of the brawny golden ale. Whereas the golden is pale, fruity, and sweet, the darker strong ale (its ABV resides north of 8 percent) rides a rich and malty road paved with peppery spice, dark fruits, caramel, and toast. Dark strong ales largely reside in a category called quadrupels, which you'll learn about on page 171.

TWO TO TASTE: BELGIAN GOLDEN STRONG ALE

DUVEL
BROUWERIJ DUVEL MOORTGAT
ABV: 8.5%

Creating the style's gold standard requires a 90-day process featuring four different kinds of French barley, two different doses of sugar, additional yeast to spur a second fermentation in the bottle, and a lengthy stint in both warm and cold cellars. The end result is a dazzling blonde beauty that's spicy and strong, light and floral, and clean and compulsively drinkable. Be careful or that concealed alcohol will sneak up and take you by surprise.

DELIRIUM TREMENS
BROUWERIJ HUYGHE
ABV: 8.5%

You know life has taken a terrible turn for the worse when you have delirium tremens, the shaking frenzy that accompanies alcohol withdrawal. But life is going irrefutably right when you have a tulip glass full of Delirium Tremens. A trio of yeast strains creates a peppery, fruity, and clandestinely boozy treat with honeyed sweetness and a lingering bitterness on the back end. P.S. The Delirium range also includes dark Nocturnum and spiced Noël.

BACKUP BEERS: *Brasserie d'Achouffe La Chouffe, Brooklyn Brewery Local 1, Brouwerij Bosteels Pauwel Kwak, Brouwerij De Dolle Brouwers Stille Nacht, North Coast Brewing Co. Pranqster, Unibroue Don de Dieu*

pale ale, a category created by theft and changing tastes.

When Jan-Leonard Moortgat founded his eponymous brewery in 1871, it focused on the dark rustic ales of that era. When his sons, Albert and Victor, took the reins, they decided to rebel—no surprise there. They looked to Great Britain for inspiration, creating Victory Ale to commemorate the close of World War I. However, Victory was not a flawless winner. Seeking perfection, the sons fidgeted with the recipe, wanting their ale to have some of the same characteristics as the then-popular Scotch ale. Albert took a jaunt to Scotland and brought back a bottle of McEwan's Scotch ale, from which a brewing scientist harvested several promising yeast strains. One in particular could tolerate hotter fermentation temperatures without producing intensely

Duvel also makes the Maredsous range of abbey beers, which are licensed from the monks of Belgium's Maredsous Abbey.

* * *

For its Duvel Collection, the brewery commissions artists to create eye-catching, limited-edition artwork on its distinctive tulip glassware.

fruity flavors. (Usually, the warmer a fermentation temperature is, the fruitier a beer will be.)

New batches were brewed, resulting in a dark, strong, and uniquely fruit-forward ale. The response was vociferous. According to lore (and heavens, what is brewing without lore, conjecture, and hearsay?), a satisfied, or maybe just sauced, drinker proclaimed that the beer was a real devil. The name stuck. The beer's look did not. Duvel kept its dark tint until 1970, when, to keep pale lagers at bay (as well as monasteries' potent, newfangled tripel; see page 169), Duvel underwent another reformulation. The brewery designed a painstaking process of warm and cold fermentation, including adding extra fermentable sugars during bottling to increase body and alcohol content (more on that process in "Two to Taste" on page 117). The result was a potent beer with a trendy golden tint. The strong pale, or golden, ale had arrived, setting a benchmark for the burgeoning style.

During the winter of 1926, a Belgian brewery by the name of Artois decided to introduce an especially sparkling Christmas-time beer by the name of Stella— the Latin word for "star." And thus a legend was born.

Since that final tweak, Duvel has welcomed a host of imitators to its heathen club both in Belgium (Delirium Tremens, Lucifer) and in the United States (AleSmith Horny Devil, Lost Abbey Inferno Ale). As for commonalities, the beers, which are best enjoyed in the classic tulip glass, ride the color line from straw-pale to jewelry-store gold and come packing enough alcohol to cease rational thought after a single bottle. Sometimes the alcohol hits hard and hot, but other times it pulls a Houdini and disappears into a sweetly fruity, often nicely hoppy ale capped by a cloudy white head that an angel would be happy to call home.

The Devil, it most certainly seems, is in the details.

AMERICAN PALE ALE

In 1775, the American Revolution started with a single shot. More than 200 years later, America's craft-beer revolution started with a single hop. On November 15, 1980, Chico, California's Ken Grossman brewed a test batch of a complex, full-bodied pale ale that featured the unusual addition of copious amounts of the flowery, bright, and lightly spicy Cascade hop. The fragrant result was unlike anything the country's beer drinkers had ever tasted, a direct counterpoint to the crisp if cookie-cutter lagers crowding tap lines and

beer shelves at supermarkets. Grossman was on to something big, something different, even something revolutionary.

Confident in his creation, the following March he distributed the debut batches of Sierra Nevada Pale Ale, which has since become one of craft brewing's most successful and enduring brands and the aromatic template for American pale ale. Although its roots lay in British pale ale, the U.S. version is a most delicious deviation. Whereas English pale ales tend to be maltier and fruitier, with an emphasis on balance, the American take is crisper and hoppier, sometimes offering enough bitterness to make you wince—in a good way.

How does this differ from the IPA? To be honest, the line dividing the American pale ale and the IPA is as blurry as Vaseline-smudged glasses. For instance, Oskar Blues' Dale's Pale Ale is vigorously hopped to the tune of 65 international bittering units (IBUs) and boasts a 6.5 percent ABV—elevated numbers that should land that canned creation in the stronger, more hop-packed IPA camp. The same goes for Deschutes Brewery's Red Chair NWPA, a citrusy, 60-IBU sipper that has a decidedly unfeatherweight 6.2 percent ABV. Compare that with Chicago-based Half Acre's heavenly Daisy Cutter Pale Ale, an aromatic delight that despite being fashioned with five hops keeps the bitterness and booze in check. Daisy's got a dainty

TWO TO TASTE: AMERICAN PALE ALE

PEEPER ALE
MAINE BEER COMPANY
ABV: 5.5%

Launched by the brothers David and Daniel Kleban in a garage, the wind-powered Freeport brewery is committed to "do what's right." That means donating 1 percent of its sales to environmental groups, plus packaging its straightforward, balanced ales in elegant 16.9-ounce bottles decorated with clean and simple labels. My favorite is Peeper, a dry-drinking pale ale that is bursting with a sunny scent. If you like a hoppier pale ale, opt for the piney and citrusy MO.

SWEETWATER 420 EXTRA PALE ALE
SWEETWATER BREWING COMPANY
ABV: 5.4%

During the South's sticky, sauna-like summer (and most of the spring and fall, for that matter), few brews quench thirst quite like Atlanta-based SweetWater's flagship, a favorite since 1997. The key to the crisp West Coast–influenced pale ale's success is the combination of Cascade and Centennial hops, which provide plenty of citrusy pleasure harmonized by soft and sweet malt. It's the epitome of a six-pack beer.

BACKUP BEERS: *Abita Brewing Co. Restoration Pale Ale, Ale Asylum Hopalicious, The Brew Kettle Taproom & Smokehouse Four C's American Pale Ale, Firestone Walker Brewing Co. Pale 31 California Pale Ale, Real Ale Brewing Company Rio Blanco Pale Ale, 21st Amendment Brewery Bitter American, Yards Brewing Co. Philadelphia Pale Ale*

5.2 percent ABV, a number that'll ensure that you'll be able to pound one 16-ounce can after another.

Daisy embodies what I like best about the American pale ale: it offers ample hop fragrance and enough bitterness to enliven my palate without knocking my noggin clean off my shoulders, as is often the case with countless IPAs and imperial IPAs.

Although the Cascade hop is inextricably linked to Sierra Nevada Pale Ale, Anchor Brewing made extensive use of Cascade in its Anchor Liberty Ale, which was first brewed in 1975 to commemorate Paul Revere's late-night ride.

FIRESTONE WALKER BREWING CO.
PASO ROBLES, CALIFORNIA

Matt Brynildson (above) was not accustomed to brewing just one kind of beer. As head brewer at Chicago's Goose Island, he was exposed to dozens of different styles, working as part of a team that concocted 100 unique beers for the company's tenth anniversary. In 2000, when Brynildson headed west to central California's SLO Brewing Co., he continued to tinker with tons of recipes, winning Small Brewpub of the Year at the 2001 Great American Beer Festival.

As his star rose, SLO's fortunes sank. That year, Firestone Walker Brewing Co. bought SLO's Paso Robles production facility. Brynildson stayed on as brewmaster for Firestone, a company with a single-minded mission. "It was a pure pale ale brewery," he recalls. "Their mantra was that we want to do very few things very well."

The brewery's flagship was the rich and agreeably hoppy DBA, a British-style pale ale that sits for six days in an oak-barrel recirculating fermentation system inspired by the Burton Union (named for Burton upon Trent, the birthplace of pale ale), which was popular in nineteenth-century Britain. "The DBA was selling so well in the region that there was no reason to expand the portfolio," Brynildson recalls.

Since brothers-in-law Adam Firestone and British expat David Walker founded the company at Firestone Vineyards in 1996, the California concern has kept the spotlight on pale ales while broadening its mission, becoming one of the nation's most versatile and celebrated breweries. On the pale side, the DBA has been joined by the aromatic and easygoing Pale 31 and the liberally bittered Union Jack IPA. Dark brews get their due in the form of the creamy, coffee-scented Velvet Merlin Oatmeal Stout, plus robust Walker's Reserve Porter and rye-fueled black IPA Wookey Jack. The limited-release barrel-aged beers roost atop beer-ranking websites. You might say that most breweries' accomplishments pale by comparison.

A PERFECT 10

Brynildson's first chance to stamp his imprint on the brewery came when he attempted to reformulate the English-style Windsor Pale Ale, which was too similar to DBA. He altered the hop profile, relying heavily on floral, citrusy American hops such as Cascade, Centennial, and Chinook. "I morphed it into what we'd call a West Coast pale ale," Brynildson says of the fresh, bready revision now branded Pale 31 (California is the thirty-first state). In the year it was released, 2003, it won a gold medal at the World Beer Championships, the first of numerous awards Pale 31 has netted.

Accolades notwithstanding, the brewery largely slipped under the radar. "We were never the darlings of the beer-geek scene," Brynildson says. That changed in 2005. For Firestone Walker's tenth anniversary the next year, the owners let Brynildson off the leash. He brewed 10 different batches of beer, including a barley wine, an imperial oatmeal stout, and a wildly hoppy IPA. They aged in a blend of bourbon, brandy, and fresh-oak barrels for 10 months before, with area winemakers' input, the components were integrated like a liquid puzzle. The result was the intricate, uncommonly balanced, and port-like 10.

"I don't think anyone in our organization realized what a changing moment that would be," Brynildson recalls. "That beer's success really encouraged us to experiment."

RESEARCH AND DEVELOPMENT

The triumph of 10 gave Firestone Walker a green light to innovate. Each year, Brynildson mixes a new Anniversary Ale (13, 14, 15, etc.), drawing from a revolving and evolving collection of barrel-aged beers. Every blend is singular, as are the beers in Firestone's Proprietor's Reserve Series. Once a year, the brewery rolls out barrel-aged beers such as Parabola, an intense Russian imperial stout; Sucaba, a barley wine soaked with notes of vanilla, toffee, and caramel, and the souped-up Double DBA.

The brewery also is exploring pale ale's potent bigger brother, the IPA. In light of the achievements with Pale 31 and DBA, it's no surprise that Union Jack IPA "came out of the gate strong," Brynildson says of the abundantly hopped symphony of grapefruit, which won IPA gold at the Great American Beer Festival in 2008. It was followed by an imperial version dubbed Double Jack and most recently by Wookey Jack, an unfiltered black IPA.

If there's a negative, it's that these hoppy beers are not distributed nationwide. Instead, head to Trader Joe's and buy the grocery store's house brand, Mission St. Pale Ale and IPA, which are Firestone Walker beers by another name. When SLO Brewing was bought, Firestone inherited the Mission St. and Nectar Ales beers, which were contract-brewed at the facility. (Firestone has since sold Nectar Ales.) "Firestone Walker wanted nothing to do with the contract brewing side," Brynildson recalls. But Trader Joe's convinced the brewery to continue making the affordable Mission St. lineup, which also includes a hefeweizen, a blonde ale, and a brown ale.

Firestone, too, continues to expand. In 2013, it opened the Barrelworks in Buellton—it's about an hour south of Paso Robles, alongside Firestone's Taproom restaurant—to specialize in barrel-aged wild ales. (The risk of infecting the Union with unwanted bacteria and yeast is too great.) "We went from being a one-horse brewery to adding all sorts of different beers," says Brynildson, who was made a brewery partner on the tenth anniversary of his employment. And though Firestone Walker plans to add one to two beers to its portfolio every year, the brewery will never lose its focus on pale ales, barrel fermentation, and doing its job very, very well.

"We're a brewery that's living the art and process of brewing," Brynildson says, "and hopefully that's reflected in the beer."

AMBER ALE

When it comes to the American pale ale, the hops are the headlining act, with the malts serving as the crucial but hardly highlight-worthy supporting cast. Not so the pale ale's close relative, the amber, or red, ale, which derives its name from, you guessed it, an amber to nearly arterial tint. This category is an enormous umbrella that covers beers with similar hues that typically are supplied by crystal or darker specialty malts that add body, a rich caramel character, and a balance that's sometimes absent in the American pale ale.

Within this grouping, though, there's enough diversity to rival New York City. Some amber ales are biscuity and even-keel, such as New Belgium's flagship Fat Tire, or perhaps floral and low alcohol, such as Stone's copper-toned Levitation Ale. Others will wallop you with a two-by-four of bitterness, such as Ithaca's hulking Cascazilla and Terrapin's Big Hoppy Monster.

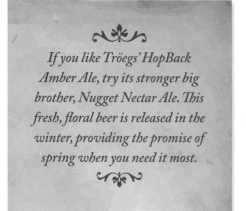

If you like Tröegs' HopBack Amber Ale, try its stronger big brother, Nugget Nectar Ale. This fresh, floral beer is released in the winter, providing the promise of spring when you need it most.

IN THE RED

One of the country's biggest cheerleaders of red ales is Denver's ambitious Black Shirt Brewing Company, which aims to expand the category into infinity. To date, its array of crimson-hued ales has included the Red IPA, Imperial Red Rye IPA, Pale Red, and both a Red Saison and a sour version. Color me impressed.

TWO TO TASTE: AMBER ALE

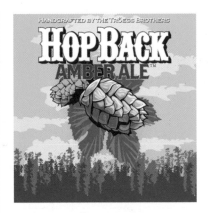

FAT TIRE AMBER ALE
New Belgium Brewing
ABV: 5.2%

Back in 1989, Colorado home-brewer Jeff Lebesch rode a fat-tired mountain bike through Belgium, sampling ales crafted with quirky yeasts, spices, and fruits—a lightbulb-lighting revelation. Upon flying home, the electrical engineer laid the groundwork for Fort Collins's New Belgium Brewing Company, launching in 1991 with the subtly fruity Abbey and the bready, slightly nutty amber ale he dubbed Fat Tire. Fresh and balanced, Fat Tire remains iconic two decades later.

HOPBACK AMBER ALE
Tröegs Brewing Company
ABV: 6%

For a moment, I'd like you to envision a handsome amber ale that glows like rubies glinting in sunlight. Next, take that amber ale and run it through a hopback vessel filled with the choicest whole-flower hops. With each pass, more of the garden-fresh, intense, and spicy aromatics infuse the ale, providing a fine foil to the sweet caramel malt. That's Tröegs HopBack, an amber ale fit for IPA junkies. It will always find a home in my refrigerator.

BACKUP BEERS: *Caldera Brewing Company Ashland Amber, Central Waters Brewing Company Ouisconsing Red Ale, Full Sail Brewery Amber, Magic Hat Brewing Company Roxy Rolles, Marble Brewery Red Ale, Nectar Ales Red Nectar, Speakeasy Ales and Lagers Prohibition Ale, Summit Brewing Company Horizon Red Ale*

(Color-wise, it's not uncommon for IPAs and amber ales to overlap.)

Whatever floats your flavorful boat, you'll probably find a fit within the amber realm. Sample several different brews to find out what tickles your fancy, then try a few more. In time, you may find you're better off red.

FRESH-HOP ALE

It could start in the middle of August or the first weekend in September. Whenever hops reach full maturity in the verdant fields of the Pacific Northwest, their full, ripe flowers filling the air with a sweet bouquet, farmers must bound into action. Harvest season has hit, and, sleep be damned, it's time to pluck the perennial plants' fragrant flowers.

Working around the clock, farmers and workers slice down towering bines and send them through machines that separate flat leaves (which are discarded) from round cones. Normally, the moist and resinous hops are sent directly to a kiln and dried, preserving them and saving them from the ravages of spoilage. That's done because recently harvested hops have a volatile nature, and their aromas and flavors rapidly fade, kind of like just-cut grass. Mowing the lawn releases an appealing perfume, a fresh scent that's equally beguiling and ephemeral. Soon, however, cut grass starts to rot, a putrefying path that also is taken by hops.

But during that brief window, ideally within the first 24 hours after plucking, brewers have a chance to use the moist hops to create fall's ephemeral embodiment of the season, the fresh-hop ale. Because the undried hops have a delicate, almost green character, they're best employed in pale ales (though pilsners and IPAs are also common), which serve as a perfect podium for the bounty of the harvest. Consider fresh-hop ales the beer-world equivalent of Beaujolais nouveau.

Like many advancements in the American pale ale, the style's creation can be credited to Sierra Nevada Brewing Co. Following a farmer's suggestion, in 1996 the brewery used farm-fresh Cascade and Centennial hops to craft its Harvest Ale. (Sierra Nevada now offers the Northern Hemisphere and Southern Hemisphere Harvest, using just-plucked hops from each half of the world.) From there, the fresh-hop movement was off and running, with the burgeoning style

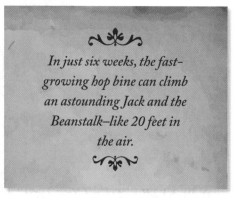

In just six weeks, the fast-growing hop bine can climb an astounding Jack and the Beanstalk–like 20 feet in the air.

championed by Pacific Northwest breweries such as Oregon's Deschutes, Full Sail, Hopworks Urban Brewery, Widmer Brothers, and Laurelwood. That was the case because the breweries are near the hops fields of Oregon and eastern Washington's Yakima Valley, where three-quarters of the American hop crop is grown. When harvest time hits, it's no hassle to take a field trip to a farm and return with burlap sacks crammed with sticky hops.

Still, this style is far from a provincial regional specialty. In Virginia, Blue Mountain Brewery uses the first 150 pounds of Cascade hops plucked from its own hop bines to make a celebratory batch of ale, and Pennsylvania's Weyerbacher Brewing Company uses Cascade hops picked from brewery president Dan Weirback's farm to fashion its annual Harvest Ale. Each fall, Minnesota's Brau Brothers Brewing Company makes its English-style Hundred Yard Dash Fresh Hop Ale with up to 11 different hop varieties harvested from its own hop yard, which is situated about a hundred yards from the brewery. No farm? No problem for Longmont, Colorado's Left Hand

TWO TO TASTE: FRESH-HOP ALE

HOP TRIP
DESCHUTES BREWERY
ABV: 5.4%

When the harvest day hits, brewers from Bend, Oregon's Deschutes clamber across the mountain pass to Salem, Oregon, to acquire farmer Doug Weather's aromatic crop. Within four hours of the hops being plucked from the bine, Deschutes tosses them into the brew kettle. Instead of overdosing on hoppy bitterness, this smooth pale ale mixes piney overtones and a bright garden smack with lovely malt sweetness. Deschutes also makes a fresh-hop version of its Mirror Pond Pale Ale and the Chasin' Freshies IPA.

FRESH HOP
GREAT DIVIDE BREWING CO.
ABV: VARIES

Though Denver's Great Divide is half a continent from the hop fields of the Pacific Northwest, the brewers do not let distance dissuade them from brewing fresh-hop ale. The brewery charters a truck with two drivers, having them drive whole-cone hops directly from a Washington farm to Great Divide, where an in-the-works batch of Fresh Hop is awaiting the fragrant flowers' arrival. The splendid results: grassy, citrusy hops set atop a balanced framework of malt, with a touch of pine thrown in for fun.

BACKUP BEERS: *Port Brewing Company High Tide Fresh Hop IPA, Thornbridge Hall Country House Brewing Company Halcyon Green Hop Harvest, Terrapin Beer Co. So Fresh & So Green, Green, Two Beers Brewing Co. Fresh Hop, Two Brothers Brewing Company Heavy-Handed IPA*

Though they may look mild-mannered, dried hops can be deadly. When tightly baled, the oily, resinous flowers have been known to combust spontaneously, sparking deadly fires like the one that destroyed a hops warehouse in Yakima, Washington, in 2006.

Brewing Co., which has hops flown in from western Colorado's Rising Sun Farms for the brewery's Warrior IPA.

Looking on a beer store's shelves for a bottle of fresh-hop ale is often a fool's errand. The majority of them are never bottled; rather, they're offered on tap at bars, brewpubs, and fests, such as Yakima's Fresh Hop Ale Festival (pictured on page 124) or the Willamette Valley Fresh Hops Fest, throughout the fall. Drink them on the double, as the fresh-hop flavors will diminish long before fall fades to frigid winter.

Until the 1960s, **MOST HOPS WERE** harvested painstakingly **BY HAND.**

THE BITTER TRUTH

IPAS

A S A KID, I WAS REALLY BONKERS FOR BLACK LICORICE. While some friends favored the comparatively sweet, mild flavor of Red Vines and Twizzlers, I preferred black licorice's uncompromisingly bitter assault, chewing the candy as if it were bubble gum—and likely causing that first cavity. From my perch of adulthood, I view licorice as the first bitter step in a lifelong culinary quest: fresh-pulled shots of espresso, tonic water laced with gin, broccoli rabe, and water spiked with a squeeze of lemon.

Thus, my favorite beer style is a no-brainer: I adore bitter India pale ales. Two or three times a week, under the guise of walking my dog, I sneak off to the corner store to score a sixer of Bear Republic Racer 5, Sierra Nevada Torpedo Extra, or other hoppy wonders packing a sweet and bitter smack matched by aromas of citrus, tropical fruits, or pine resin. My wife is addicted to chocolate. I'm a junkie for a fresh IPA.

And brewers are happy to give me another dose. The modern emblem of American craft brewing is the bitter, fragrant India pale ale. Though the style originated in England, stateside brewers have forever altered the formula, turning down malty caramel notes and cranking the hops to 11. The modern American IPA, especially pungent West Coast renditions, is a gateway craft beer, recalibrating palates accustomed to light lagers—that first ray of sunshine after years of rain. An IPA is often the first craft beer that people drink and think, *I never knew a beer could taste like that.*

IPAs have caught fire in craft brewing, with lip-pursing IPAs fathering double IPAs, each one boasting ever higher IBUs (the international bittering unit scale, which measures a beer's hop bitterness). Moreover, brewers have begun exploring what I like to call the "color spectrum of bitterness." Typically, IPAs range from sunset gold to amber. But recently a new breed of IPAs has emerged, displaying peculiar pigmentations: midnight black, rosy amber, snow-white.

In this class, the goal is to understand how different ratios and varieties of hops and malts combine to create a colorful, flavorful constellation of IPAs. When you taste them, pay close attention to the initial and lingering bitterness, malt sweetness, and the bouquet. Here's the lowdown on hopped-up brews.

GRUIT TO IT

Today, hops are considered nearly as crucial to beer as water. But if you were to time-travel back to the Middle Ages and become buddies with a monk brewer, you'd be surprised to find out that beer's recipe conspicuously lacked even a single hop leaf.

Beers were flavored with *gruit* (pronounced "grew-it"), which was a proprietary blend of bitter and astringent yarrow (a flowering plant), wild rosemary, and resinous, eucalyptus-like wild gale, along with various spices, such as cinnamon and caraway seeds. In large quantities, gruit was considered a euphoric stimulant and an aphrodisiac,

and many brewers often incorporated psychotropics such as henbane to enhance the effects. Whether because of public-health concerns or for religious reasons (those libidinous and inebriated heathens!), gruit was largely phased out by the 1700s in favor of hops.

Don't shed a tear for our departed friend gruit, which still flavors several seriously retro ales. A good gruit-style beer to try is Fraoch from Scotland's Williams Bros. It's based on the Scottish heather ale, which has been produced since 2000 BC, and counts bog myrtle (aka gale) as an ingredient, as does Posca Rustica from Brasserie Dupont. Also worth sampling is Cambridge Brewing Company's Weekapaug Gruit; in addition to gale, its ingredients include licorice, nettles, and wild rosemary.

An equally fascinating unhopped beer is sahti, Finland's traditional farmhouse beer that's bittered with berries and branches from the juniper bush. A nice interpretation is Dogfish Head's golden-brown Sah'tea. It recalls a banana-tinged wheat beer with an herbaceous quality like pine needles crossed with chai tea.

A HOP START

Hops are hardly a one-trick pony. In addition to imparting appealing bouquets and bitterness to balance sweet malts, hops serve as a preservative. This particular property was duly noted by the 1760s, when, according to *Amber, Gold and Black* author and historian Martyn Cornell, brewers were advised to add extra hops to beers being sent to hot climates, notably the Caribbean and, yes, India.

Throughout both the eighteenth and nineteenth centuries, the British Army and the East India Company had troops, officers, and civil servants stationed in India. To quench soldiers' thirst, Britain exported beer, mainly porter. This dark beer was the preferred beverage of the rank-and-file forces. By comparison, Cornell writes, middle- and upper-class Europeans living in India, civil servants, military officers, and trading-company toilers preferred pale ales generously fortified with hops.

So named because it was brewed with lightly roasted malts, the pale ale first appeared in the seventeenth century. The earliest incarnations were lightly hopped, but as the years passed and exports increased, Cornell explains, the lighter-hued ales grew hoppier and developed into "pale ales prepared for the India market." (They probably evolved out of October beer, a pale, heavily hopped beer brewed in the fall and intended to be matured for several years. In the eighteenth century, the style was popular with the landed gentry, who brewed and stored October beer on their country estates.) Around 1835, this highly hopped style was given a new, more lasting moniker: East India pale ale.

By the 1840s, the well-bittered, so-called East India pale ales began catching on across Britain, cementing a lasting place at the pub. Over the decades, English-style IPAs developed distinguishing characteristics. Generally, they possess earthy floral aromas backed by flavors of caramel and biscuits, a fruity underpinning, and a lingering bitterness. They are balanced ales with nuances worth savoring and a nice bitter zing—a lightly zippy punch to the taste buds.

AMERICAN EVOLUTION

Though the IPA was not invented in the United States, American brewers over the last three decades have assumed ownership of the style. Most breweries make at least one IPA and often many, many more; not doing so is almost like a diner refusing to serve hamburgers. But all IPAs are not equal. Unique blends of grains, yeast strains, and hops added at different times during the brewing process result in bitter brews as singular as a fingerprint. Broadly speaking, the American bitter beers are broken down into two loosely affiliated camps: East Coast and West Coast.

Consider them regional distinctions in much the same manner as North Carolina BBQ: eastern North Carolina specializes in a whole-hog style finished with a thin vinegar-based sauce; western North Carolina focuses on barbecued pork shoulder paired with a sweet and thick tomato-based sauce. They're both BBQ, but they differ by degrees. And don't even get me started on Texas, Memphis, and Kansas City 'cue.

EAST COAST IPA

The Beer Judge Certification Program, which creates ironclad standards for each style, does not divide American IPAs by geography. However, I feel

The long, warm, wave-smacked journey from England to India likely helped October beer age faster, creating a mature and complex beverage in months, instead of years.

TWO TO TASTE: ENGLISH IPA

INDIA ALE
SAMUEL SMITH
ABV: 5%

Since 1758, this British brewery (the oldest in Yorkshire) has cranked out balanced ales brewed with well water drawn from 85 feet underground and fermented in stone fermenting vessels known as Yorkshire squares, which help give its beers a fuller body. The golden India Ale boasts a sweet 'n' spicy scent, as well as a civilized flavor of toasted bread spread with fruity hops.

INDIA PALE ALE
MEANTIME BREWING COMPANY
ABV: 7.4%

London-based Meantime specializes in re-creating iconic British beers such as this tribute to the era of the British Raj. Mounds of fruity, earthy Fuggles and lightly sweet East Kent Golding hops help create this creamy ride that rolls across caramel, toffee, and bitter speed bumps, then detours to biscuits, tea, and a dry finish.

BACKUP BEERS: *Belhaven Brewery Twisted Thistle IPA, Fuller Smith & Turner PLC Fuller's India Pale Ale, Harviestoun Brewery Bitter & Twisted*

TWO TO TASTE: EAST COAST IPA

EAST INDIA PALE ALE
BROOKLYN BREWERY
ABV: 6.9%

Biscuity malts and herbal, lightly floral hops help this golden-amber, medium-bodied brew sing a tasty tune. Expect some caramel and a sharp bitterness too. Brooklyn Brewery now offers the East India Pale Ale in cans as well.

COMMODORE PERRY IPA
GREAT LAKES BREWING COMPANY
ABV: 7.5%

As a native Ohioan, I'm sworn to love this medium-bodied brew. You will, too, after one taste of this Cleveland ale with a big ol' malt backbone, fruity aroma, punchy bitterness, and smooth, dry finish.

BACKUP BEERS: *Dogfish Head Craft Brewery 60 Minute IPA, D.L. Geary Brewing Company Geary's IPA, Long Trail Brewing Company IPA, Magic Hat Brewing Company Blind Faith, Port City Brewing Company Monumental IPA, Shipyard Brewing Company IPA*

---

the same way about East Coast IPAs as Supreme Court justice Potter Stewart once felt about pornography. He opined that it was tough to define but "I know it when I see it." Based on endless, uh, research, I identify East Coast IPAs with balance, a strong backbone of malt sweetness (often caramel), a full body, a fair amount of fruity or citrusy hop character, and a moderately aggressive streak of bitterness to boot.

"Hold on," you say. "Isn't that kind of like a British IPA?" That's correct, astute drinker. Many of the East Coast's hoppy beers have a distinctly British

For another taste of vintage British IPA, try Southampton Publick House's Burton IPA. To replicate the classic beer, which is not wildly hopped, the brewery adds minerals such as calcium to the brewing water.

* * *

Hops have antibiotic qualities and are sometimes used as an alternative to antibiotics in animal feed.

* * *

Before the 1900s, brewers in the United States, Canada, and Australia crafted beers branded with the IPA moniker.

DNA, mutated by American verve and innovation. Partly, this is due to proximity. From New York, London and Los Angeles are about an equidistant flight. However, I have another hunch: at the dawn of the American beer boom in the 1980s and 1990s, the country's beer makers were inspired by the traditional lagers and ales of Germany, Belgium, and, yes, the United Kingdom.

For instance, Brooklyn Brewery devised the East India Pale Ale, and the IPA from Philadelphia's Yards Brewing proudly displays the Union Jack on its label. Another key factor was the British brewer Alan Pugsley, who was a sort of Johnny Appleseed of American beer. He set up breweries across Canada and New England, including Maine's Geary's and Shipyard and Boston's dearly departed Commonwealth Brewing. He brought

Stone tries to ensure the IPA is no more than 90 days old. Check the bottling date, and report expired beer via stonebrewing .com/freshbeer. *Also of note: Stone's Enjoy By series of double IPAs, which have their expiration date stamped on the label. After the date passes, unsold beers are supposed to be removed from the shelves.*

TWO TO TASTE: WEST COAST IPA

STONE IPA
STONE BREWING CO.
ABV: 6.9%

Considered the grand-daddy of the San Diego–style IPA, this hazy-gold stalwart has knocked drinkers for a bitter loop since 1997. It hasn't dulled with age, still bursting with grapefruit and a smidgen of harmonizing orange-juice sweetness, while maintaining a crisp mouthfeel.

SCULPIN IPA
BALLAST POINT BREWING
ABV: 7%

The Sculpin fish's fins contain venomous spines that, upon contact, result in redness and painful swelling. Sipping the creature's namesake beer will have far tastier consequences. A surprisingly light body serves as a platform for lush, juicy flavors and beguiling aromas of peaches, lemons, and apricots.

BACKUP BEERS: *Coronado Brewing Co. Islander IPA, Drake's Brewing Co. IPA, Fat Head's Brewery & Saloon Head Hunter IPA, Firestone Walker Brewing Co. Union Jack IPA, Green Flash Brewing Co. West Coast IPA, Lagunitas Brewing Company IPA, Port Brewing Company Wipeout I.P.A.*

BRITISH BOOK CLUB

Cornell's *Amber, Gold and Black* is an excellent historical read on the history of British brewing. Another worthwhile book is Pete Brown's rollicking *Hops and Glory: One Man's Search for the Beer That Built the British Empire*. The British beer writer traveled to India toting a keg of Burton IPA, brewed to specifications set in writing nearly 150 years earlier.

with him know-how and a decidedly British yeast strain known as Ringwood, which imparts a buttery flavor and notes of apple peel. It's a flavor that attracts as many as it turns away, but that's the point of beer: you won't—and should not—love everything that passes twixt your lips.

WEST COAST IPA

What is a West Coast IPA? Posing this question to craft-beer geeks is akin to asking politicians to a debate on a hot-button issue. One by one, die-hard hopheads will climb atop milk crates and, pints of piney beer in hand, begin preaching the bitter truth. This is to say, there's no widely held definition.

In fact, there are several factions worth discussing. First are the IPAs of California and, especially, San Diego. In this sunny stretch of the country, the IPAs tend to eschew sweet caramel malts for a lean, dry scaffolding designed to showcase hops' bow-down-before-me majesty. These potent beers tend to be as bitter as a widow's tears (packing IBUs creeping close to triple digits), with notes of biscuit and toast and aromas that recall a stroll through an upscale supermarket's fruit department: grapefruits, pineapples, oranges, lemons, mangos, lychees. These are fresh, vibrant beers that stampede across your palate, with a sticky bitterness that has as much staying power as a world-class bull rider.

GREEN FLASH BREWING COMPANY
SAN DIEGO, CALIFORNIA

Green Flash founders Mike and Lisa Hinkley specialize in hoppy beer.

Most brewery owners follow a familiar path. A passion for homebrewing leads to a professional brewing job in which kegs are cleaned, skills are honed, and recipes are polished. Eventually, a light bulb blazes: "Hey, I should start my own brewery." Mike Hinkley's career trajectory has been mighty different. "I've never had the patience to brew, but I can spend hours in a bottle shop reading labels," he says. "I'm a beer nerd."

Without once firing a brew kettle, Mike and his wife, Lisa, went from being pub owners pushing great craft beer to founding San Diego's Green Flash Brewing (he's CEO; she's vice president in charge of marketing). Since its debut in 2002, Green Flash (named after the quicksilver appearance of a green spot, or ray, right before sunrise or after sunset) has become a California, and national, trailblazer by focusing on hoppy ales,

Belgian beers, and the bitter middle ground where the two meet.

At first, the Hinkleys placed their bets on a decently hopped, lower-alcohol extra pale ale. The idea was to sell at grocery stores, a plan that appealed to Mike. "I fell in love with the idea of putting beer on the shelves and having my neighbors buy it," he says. Being a mainstream brewer proved problematic. Competition was intense. Carving out shelf space was tough, especially for an unknown brewery.

HARNESSING THE HOP

Salvation lay within the *Humulus lupulus* plant. Changing course, the Hinkleys set out to create "the benchmark of West Coast–style IPAs," Mike says. The brewers selected a yeast strain that fermented out dry, leaving little residual sweetness behind, and rounded out the recipe with Pacific Northwest hops, including grapefruit-like Simcoe, pungent Columbus, floral Cascade, and piney, citrusy Centennial. The result is an unrepentant and multifaceted bitterness (95 IBUs) matched to a lean and clean framework that closes out crazily crisp—especially for a 7.3 percent ABV beer.

In a nutshell, it's the quintessential West Coast IPA. "We're trying to make off the charts, exceptional beers that will enhance every occasion," Mike explains. Under brewmaster Chuck Silva, who joined the brewery in 2004, the last decade has seen Green Flash voyage to the far reaches of flavor aboard the almighty hop. The intense Imperial India Pale Ale smells like a marijuana apothecary. Hop Head Red IPA combines caramel sweetness with sticky, resinous hops and a floral aroma. Palate Wrecker lives up to its promise thanks to the unusual step of brewing with already hopped wort. Even the Barleywine Style Ale is crammed with hops galore.

Silva's bitter affinity is not confined to the United States. "We pulled aside 100 gallons of our Imperial IPA and fermented it with a Trappist yeast," Mike says of what became Le Freak, a zesty blend of a sweet and strong tripel with IPA aromatics—one of the first American-style Belgian IPAs. (It was inspired by Belgium's Houblon Chouffe Dobbelen IPA Tripel; see page 151.) Other Belgian successes include the funky spiced Saison Diego, the more classic fruity Trippel Ale, and Rayon Vert.

Green Flash's San Diego brewery is equipped with a 4,000-square-foot tasting room and beer garden, where you can pick and choose from 30 brews. Food trucks ensure you won't go home hungry.

"We started by asking ourselves, 'What would Green Flash be if we were brewing in Belgium 80 years ago?'" Mike says. The crew surmised that pre–World War II beers probably were infected with the wild yeast *Brettanomyces*. Four years were spent perfecting Brett-infected Rayon Vert—that is, Green Flash—a bone-dry, Champagne-bubbly elixir that faintly recalls a barnyard romp. Nailing the recipe was only the first hurdle. The bottle-conditioned beer created too much pressure for a standard 12-ounce bottle—it would explode—so the brewery reached out to manufacturers to create a sturdier bottle that could withstand higher pressure.

THE COLD TRUTH

"We go after a beer concept until we have it exactly the way we want," Mike says. That commitment continues after beer leaves the brewery. Since hoppier beers are very sensitive to heat and light, Green Flash created a comprehensive program to ensure freshness. They keep distributor inventories low (no beer is left to marinate in a sweltering warehouse), stamp beers with bottled-on dates, and ship every case in a refrigerated truck.

"We want every beer to taste as fresh as it does in our tasting room," he says. Which leads to the next point: in summer 2011, Green Flash expanded to a larger, modern facility in San Diego, but demand has been so great that the brewery will open an East Coast facility in 2015. "Forty percent of our beer goes to the East Coast," Mike explains.

Two breweries may seem like a handful, but the Hinkleys are no stranger to hard work, having raised two children while running a business together. The key, Mike says, is that "we have the same commitment and passion to what we're doing. Running a brewery is a 24/7 job, so it helps to be around your most important partner all the time." However, he hazards, "you have to put up your own boundaries"—but not with brewing.

"Every beer," Mike says, "should be an adventure."

PACIFIC NORTHWEST IPA

Up in the Pacific Northwest, the local brewers are no strangers to crafting profoundly hopped brews. That's partly a result of availability and convenience. Most American hops are grown in Washington and Oregon, providing a fragrant cornucopia for brewers to pluck (think back to the lesson on fresh-hop beers on page 123). In lieu of fashioning boozy and bitter behemoths, brewers in Oregon and Washington focus on intense aromatics—think pine trees and freshly cut flowers and grass— and rich, juicy flavors. At the same time, Northwest IPAs also angle for balance. They're perched at the edge of the diving board, whereas their Southern California compatriots have plunged into the bitter depths.

In the Pacific Northwest, I believe the next big star of the IPA scene will be Bend, Oregon's Boneyard Beer. Its RPM IPA, Hop Venom IPA, and Notorious Triple IPA are loving, bitter embraces to the hoppy bounty of Oregon and Washington. Boneyard is poised to be a big player.

TWO TO TASTE: PACIFIC NORTHWEST IPA

WORKHORSE IPA
LAURELWOOD PUBLIC HOUSE & BREWERY
ABV: 7.5%

One of the quintessential examples of a Pacific Northwest IPA, the copper-orange workhorse relies on a quintet of hops—Nugget, Simcoe, Amarillo, Columbus, and Cascade—to create its bright, punch-you-in-the-nose citrus aroma. It drinks as smooth as a summer lake, coating its flavors of tangerine, grapefruit, and pineapple in a slightly sticky sweetness.

INDIA PALE ALE
BRIDGEPORT BREWING CO.
ABV: 5.5%

One day, the crew at Portland, Oregon's BridgePort was hit by an in-your-face epiphany: We're situated in the heart of America's hop-growing region. We need to harness that bounty. In 1996, the brewers concocted this naturally carbonated, golden ale with a citrusy, floral perfume and an easygoing bitterness. You'll also dig the stronger, more bitter Hop Czar Imperial IPA.

BACKUP BEERS: *Big Al Brewing IPA, Deschutes Brewery Inversion IPA, Double Mountain Brewery Hop Lava, Full Sail Brewery Full Sail IPA, Ninkasi Brewing Company Total Domination IPA, Oakshire Brewing Watershed IPA, Pike Brewing Company IPA*

TWO TO TASTE: DOUBLE IPA

THE MAHARAJAH
AVERY BREWING CO.
ABV: 10.24%

Taking its name for the Sanskrit words for "great king," the Boulder, Colorado, royal double IPA, or DIPA, presents an intense scent of grapefruit and molasses. This late winter/early spring release slides down sweet and creamy, with 102 IBUs of regal, tongue-coating bitterness. Also divine: Avery's September-released duganA IPA, which the brewery deems a more drinkable version of Maharajah—well, as drinkable as a sticky, mercilessly bitter, piney 8.5 percent DIPA can be.

PLINY THE ELDER
RUSSIAN RIVER BREWING CO.
ABV: 8%

If double IPAs held a popularity contest, Pliny would win hands-down. Brewmaster Vinnie Cilurzo's cultishly beloved DIPA is a velvety, aromatic wonder packing a forest-fresh piney profile and a sweet-and-bitter balancing act. Whenever my friends visit from California, I beg them to line their bags with Pliny bottles, like a beer version of a drug mule. In certain parts of the country, Pliny the Elder can double as liquid currency.

BACKUP BEERS: *Alpine Beer Company Pure Hoppiness, Bell's Brewery Hopslam Ale, DC Brau Brewing Co. On the Wings of Armageddon Imperial IPA, Karl Strauss Brewing Company Big Barrel Double IPA, New England Brewing Co. Gandhi-Bot Double IPA, Smuttynose Brewing Company Big A IPA*

TIME OUT! GEOGRAPHY IS NOT THE END-ALL BE-ALL

Allow me to remind you that these regional differences are not definitive. Many breweries on the East Coast and in the Midwest make hop bombs that if you shut your eyes and took a big gulp you'd swear were brewed within spitting distance of the Pacific Ocean. (New York's Ithaca Flower Power, Florida's Cigar City Jai Alai IPA, and Michigan's Bell's Two Hearted IPA quickly come to mind.) And California breweries are no stranger to caramel-kissed IPAs. Styles and regional designations are mere starting points for describing beer.

DOUBLE IPA

I came of age in the 1980s and 1990s, my childhood marked by such cultural signifiers as Fruit Roll-Ups, Milli Vanilli, and a particularly catchy advertising jingle for Wrigley's Doublemint Gum. "A double pleasure is waiting for you," the tune began. "Double fresh, double smooth, double delicious to chew." Well, replace *chew* with *drink* and you'll have an inkling of what constitutes a double, or imperial, IPA.

Simply put, it's an IPA on steroids, loaded with heaps of the stinky green flowers to add extra bitterness, extra aroma, extra *everything*. Using gobs of hops has its drawbacks too. Bitterness requires a balancing measure of sweetness, meaning that brewers have to ratchet up their malt bill. More malts equals more sugars for the yeasts to wolf down, which in turn creates a higher alcohol content.

At their worst, double IPAs are an arms race gone awry. The beers are big, boozy, and unbalanced. But when brewers hit that ideal teeter-totter of balance, a double IPA is like the first runner-up at a beauty pageant: as beautiful as it is bitter. Russian River Brewing Company's Vinnie Cilurzo is credited with being the nation's first brewer to concoct a ludicrously hopped double IPA. While brewing at Temecula, California's Blind Pig Brewery in 1994, he debuted his Inaugural Ale. Though other IPAs of that time topped out at 50 or 60 IBUs, Cilurzo estimated that his registered a hair-raising 100 IBUs (the actual number was likely much lower). Doubling the hops was both a bold move and a calculated decision to compensate for the brewery's rustic equipment. If there were

Why are double IPAs sometimes called imperial? That's a nod to the royal pedigree of the Russian imperial stout, a class of beers so strong that they'll turn your legs to jelly. Learn more about them on page 193.

A STATE OF BEERVANA

Due to its crazy concentration of craft breweries and brewpubs, Portland, Oregon, often refers to itself as Beervana. My favorite time to visit the city is the end of July. The clouds have cleared. The sun is shining. And the last weekend of the month welcomes the Oregon Brewers Festival, a celebration of the best and buzziest West Coast brewers. The setting alongside the Willamette River can't be beat (*oregonbrewfest.com*).

MILE HIGH-PA

For decades, Colorado was Coors country, the land of "Rocky Mountain fresh" beer. Today, the state is one of the country's buzziest craft-brewing regions, and I'd be remiss if I didn't extol the pleasures of Colorado's excellent IPAs. To me, these Continental Divide brews reside on the middle ground between the East Coast and the West Coast. They're balanced and full-bodied, yet unrepentantly hoppy. I've happily spent countless afternoons sipping through Oskar Blues' dank and decadent Deviant Dale's IPA, bitter and fruity Odell India Pale Ale, and Ska Brewing's liquid marijuana–like Modus Hoperandi. If you get the chance, I recommend that you follow in my bitter footsteps.

Portland, Oregon's Pearl District is home to BridgePort BrewPub, which is located in the historic Portland Cordage Company Building. The soaring space is styled with brick and timber, and the fresh pale ales and IPAs are your best bets on tap.

TWO TO TASTE: TRIPLE IPA

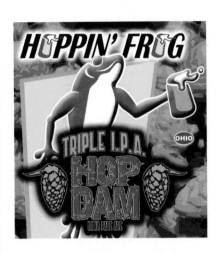

HOP DAM
HOPPIN' FROG BREWERY
ABV: 10%

To manufacture this bitter monster, the Ohio brewery specially built a stainless steel "dam" for the brew kettle to hold back the hops. Expect to be swept under by citrus and pine, with a caramel lifeboat to keep you afloat. As the brewery says, "It's like kissing a hop." If the triple IPA is too intense, give the Mean Manalishi Double IPA a spin.

DEVIL DANCER
FOUNDERS BREWING COMPANY
ABV: 12%

This struttin' Satanic IPA undergoes a lengthy 26-day stint of dry-hopping with a blend of 10 different hops. The sinus-clearing aroma smacks your sniffer with pine resin, citrus, flowers, and toasted malts. When sipped, the syrup-sticky, red Devil Dancer woozily spins you around toffee, caramel, and pine, before dropping you for a brutally bitter finish.

BACKUP BEERS: *Bierbrouwerij Emelisse Triple IPA, Fegley's BrewWorks Hop'solutely Triple IPA, Knee Deep Brewing Company Simtra Triple India Pale Ale, Moylan's Brewery Hopsickle Imperial India Pale Ale, Renegade Brewing Company Elevation, Speakeasy Ales & Lagers The Don*

off flavors in the beer, they'd be masked by the hoppy overload.

TRIPLE IPA

I'm all too happy to tout double and imperial IPAs, but a triple IPA goes one hop over the line. Like poker players tossing another stack of chips onto the pile, breweries have begun elevating the bitter stakes to ludicrous levels. At what point is it too much? A triple IPA is a palate-wrecking bomb to both your taste buds and your sobriety. Drink one if you're curious but make sure to share the triple with a friend. Or three. The technical limit for measuring IBUs is 100, so anything above that is as an educated guess—or a theoretical flight of fancy. The Danish brewery Mikkeller created the eye-popping 1000 IBU. The beer "tasted like chewing a hop field," wrote brewer Mikkel Borg Bjergsø. "I personally loved it." Would you?

Like really bitter beers? Each year, Hayward, California's The Bistro hosts a double IPA festival, as does Portland, Oregon's Sara-veza. You will not return with your palate intact (the-bstro. com; saraveza.com).

IPA HYBRIDS TO KNOW

Unlike Silly Bandz, planking, or tricking people into drinking Smirnoff Ice, the IPA trend shows no sign of slowing down. The bitter current is continuing to rage, branching out into tasty new tributaries worth exploring. Some are black, some are white, yet others are red. Each offshoot has a common thread, but these brothers in bitterness remain distinct—and distinctly delicious.

BLACK IPA

Typically, darker-hued brews saddle tongues and taste buds with rich, roasty flavors that flit from java to chocolate. They're terrific in a stomach-filling stout but tend to overpower a bracingly bitter tipple. Midnight-colored black IPAs, though, balance bitterness, citrus, tropical fruits, and maybe pine with a pinch of chocolate and roasted-coffee complexity. Since *black IPA* is a bit of an oxymoron, Cascadian dark ale—referencing the Cascade range in the Pacific Northwest, which many hop farmers and brewers call home—has been embraced as a substitute moniker. To me, though, this smacks of provincialism; black IPAs are made countrywide, which is why the Beer Judge Certification Program now brands the dark delight an American black ale.

No matter what you call the style, it's a delicate art to subdue dark malts'

TWO TO TASTE: BLACK IPA

PITCH BLACK IPA
WIDMER BROTHERS BREWING
ABV: 6.5%

BACK IN BLACK
21ST AMENDMENT BREWERY
ABV: 6.8%

Originally a one-off, Pitch Black was so beloved that the long-running Oregon brewers decided to elevate it to year-round status. You'll understand after one sip of the obsidian indulgence. Its scent is full of ripe fruit and nutty malt, with a bit of coffee that snuggles up nicely to hops. Also fun: Widmer's Rotator IPA series, which features new hop breeds and unique interpretations of the style.

San Francisco's 21st Amendment makes a number of canned bitter beers that make you rethink the aluminum container, including Brew Free! or Die IPA, Hop Crisis Imperial IPA (aged on spirals of oak designed to infuse flavor), and this ride on the dark side that decants a handsome mahogany. On the nose, there is a floral perfume of pine and citrus, with a bit of cocoa nibs. Don't let the color deceive you: it's a very easy drinker.

BACKUP BEERS: *Element Brewing Company Dark Element, Heavy Seas Beer Black Cannon Black IPA, North Peak Brewing Company Furry Black India Pale Ale, Otter Creek Brewing Black IPA, Peak Organic Brewing Company Hop Noir, Southern Tier Brewing Company Iniquity, Uinta Brewing Company Dubhe Imperial Black IPA*

BUILDING A BETTER BITTERNESS

BREWERS HAVE A BAGFUL OF TRICKS AND TOOLS FOR GOOSING BEER'S BITTERNESS AND IMPARTING SWOON-WORTHY AROMATICS. HERE ARE A HANDFUL OF TOOLSHED INVENTIONS AND TECHNIQUES THAT YOU SHOULD KNOW.

Dogfish Head's portable Randall Jr. is designed to instant-infuse flavors and aromatics into beer.

DRY HOPPING: *Hops are added to beer that has finished fermenting or is conditioning. This step creates an intensely aromatic brew that'll make hop lovers swoon.*

HOPBACK: *A sealed chamber linking the brewing kettle and the wort chiller is filled with hops. When the hot wort flows through the vessel, the liquid is infused with garden-fresh flavors and aromas that usually are lost during the brewing process. Instantly cooling the wort ensures that the hop compounds remain.*

HOP BURSTING: *To give IPAs a righteously aromatic profile, some breweries opt for this technique. Basically, heaps of hops are back-loaded to the end of the boiling process, resulting in a smooth bitterness.*

HOP TORPEDO: *Sierra Nevada invented this stainless steel cylinder, which harvests hops' oily resins and leaves bitterness behind. How? Envision an espresso machine. A basket is filled with plump, whole-cone hops and then loaded into the torpedo and pressure-sealed. The device is placed in a fermentation cellar, and beer courses through the torpedo to extract maximum aroma and flavor.*

RANDALL THE ENAMEL ANIMAL: *Delaware's Dogfish Head devised this device to make aftermarket alterations to an IPA's flavor. The brewery retrofitted a cylindrical water filter to attach to a keg's draft line. The filter is filled with a loosely packed flavoring agent such as whole-leaf hops or fresh mint. On the way to a glass, beer passes through Randall. Alcohol strips flavorful oils from the leaves, essentially instant-infusing the beer. The brewery also created the Randall Jr. for personal use.*

roasty astringency so that bitter hops can shine yet retain that trademark murky tint. To accomplish this, brewers rely on several brewing tricks. First, they use dehusked malt that, thanks to a process similar to rice polishing, offers less pronounced burnt, roasty flavors. Alternatively, brewers can borrow a technique used to concoct schwarzbiers, a superdrinkable German lager sporting an obsidian tint. Dark-roasted malts—the grains that are the building blocks of beer—are steeped in cold water, which dials back harsh flavors. (Compare this process to cold-brewed coffee, which lacks the stomach-roiling acidity of coffee made with hot water.) When this is done right, black IPAs balance a bright, fresh hop character with a rich, malty complexity that's suited for afternoon lounging or last call.

WHITE IPA

Come summer, the perfect beer to accompany your linen suit and sundress might just be this snow-hued brew. The white IPA is a hybrid ale that bridges

Deschutes is based in Bend, Oregon, which is known for outdoor sports such as hiking, mountain biking, skiing, and rafting.

WHAT'S OLD IS NEW AGAIN: GENEROUSLY HOPPED **DARK ALES WERE** BREWED IN THE **UNITED KINGDOM** MORE THAN A *century ago.*

EVERY MINUTE COUNTS

One of the strongest commercially available India pale ales is Dogfish Head's 120 Minute IPA. The limited-release beer possesses north of 100 IBUs and weighs in at 15 to 20 percent ABV. (Each batch is slightly different.) This high-butane brewski is boiled for two hours and continuously infused with aromatic American hops (the slow and steady technique imparts a deeper, richer flavor) before undergoing a months-long fermenting and aging process with additional hops. The result is a righteously bitter bombast that upon being opened floods the room with citrusy aromatics as strong as potpourri. It's as warming as any brown spirit.

144   CLASS FIVE

TWO TO TASTE: WHITE IPA

CHAINBREAKER WHITE IPA
DESCHUTES BREWING
ABV: 5.6%

Despite being named after a rugged mountain-bike race in central Oregon (Deschutes is based in Bend), Chainbreaker is an unabashedly smooth journey across a landscape of citrus, sweet orange peel, and coriander. Notes of fruity Belgian yeast help crank up the easy rider's complexity.

WHITE IPA
SARANAC BREWERY
ABV: 6%

From the foothills of New York's Adirondack Mountains comes this crossbreed. The opaque straw-colored ale has a luscious mouthfeel (thanks, wheat and oats!), fruity notes of orange peel, and tropical aromas on account of Citra hops. It's a hot-day beer with a twist.

BACKUP BEERS: *Anchorage Brewing Company Galaxy White IPA, Blue Point Brewing White IPA, Harpoon Brewery White IPA, NoDa Brewing Company Ghost Hop White IPA, Samuel Adams Whitewater IPA*

the divide between a hoppy IPA and a cloudy, wheat-driven witbier (see page 99 for more information on the style).

Typically, an unfiltered Belgian witbier is crafted with orange peel and coriander, which add appealing notes of citrus and spice. Witbier is a gentle, graceful beer perfectly suited for sipping as lazy, sun-soaked afternoons slide into evening. Brewers build on the perfection by adding citrusy hops that cozy up to a witbier's fruity flavors. The result is a lightly bitter, easy-drinking aromatic delight that'll be right at home in your backyard cooler. This hybrid has just started bubbling up, but its drinkability ensures that it'll fast become a warm-weather favorite.

RED IPA

This style is pretty simple to understand. A red IPA opts for a grain bill heavy on caramel malt. The grain gives beer a rich, sweet flavor and a hue straight out of Satan's wardrobe. Combine that with the brewers' preferred hop profile—

Scientists believe that bitterness played a role in evolution. Since many toxic plants taste bitter, tasting one trips an internal alarm: do not eat. Ignore that and open another IPA.

pine, citrus—and plenty of resinous flavors and you have a luscious, full-bodied brew that's catnip for bitter-beer fiends. To me, it's more filling than your everyday IPA, but a red IPA remains a beer that you can still effortlessly drink by the six-pack. These days, seeing red is a very good thing.

Most beers are made with a hodgepodge of hops, the flowers that add bitterness, aroma, and flavor. Some hops are ideal for imparting fragrance, while other varieties are better suited for adding bitterness. Matching hops' strengths and weaknesses helps brewers' create singular flavor profiles. The process is akin to cooks using different ratios and proportions of spices. Lately, brewers have stopped mixing hops. Instead, they're dosing beers with a single variety, allowing drinkers to discern each hop's unique characteristics. Each beer doesn't stay in circulation long, but look for continuing releases from Mikkeller, Hill Farmstead, Flying Dog, and Yazoo Brewing Company, which operates the ongoing Hop Project.

TWO TO TASTE: RED IPA

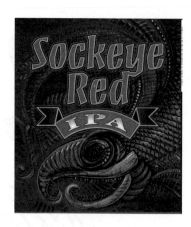

SOCKEYE RED IPA
MIDNIGHT SUN BREWING CO.
ABV: 5.7%

HOP HEAD RED
GREEN FLASH BREWING CO.
ABV: 7%

Anchorage, Alaska's marvelous Midnight Sun offers the lights-out Sockeye, named after a salmon breed. Mimicking the fish's flesh, Sockeye has a reddish-amber hue, along with a pungent whiff of pine resin, ripe citrus, and biscuits rising in the background. Resin reappears in the flavor alongside grapefruit, but they're ironed out by sweet caramel.

The color tone comes courtesy of caramel malts, which give the crimson IPA a rich base. From that springboard, the beer leaps into a bitter sea bobbing with pine trees and grapefruit before surfacing for a slick finish. P.S. There's an overpowering floral perfume because the brewers dry-hop the dickens out of Head.

BACKUP BEERS: *Lakefront Brewery Fixed Gear, Oskar Blues G'Knight Imperial Red Ale, Samuel Adams Tasman Red, SanTan Brewing Company Count Hopula Blood Red IPA*

Located alongside the banks of the Milwaukee River, Wisconsin's Lakefront Brewery has, since 1987, been ahead of the curve. The Milwaukee beer maker released the country's first certified organic beer, Organic E.S.B., and it places a premium on using native ingredients; Local Acre Lager and Wisconsinite wheat beer are made with grains and hops grown in the state. Additionally, the brewery tour is a hoot.

REMEMBER: FRESH IS BEST

Drink an IPA as soon as possible. Let Russian River's aromatic Pliny the Elder be your guide. The label reads, DOES NOT IMPROVE WITH AGE! HOPPY BEERS ARE NOT MEANT TO BE AGED! These beers are best fresh, with the in-your-face aromatics diminishing over time. Make sure to check the date on each bottle and try to avoid IPAs that have been marinating in unrefrigerated spaces. And please, always store your IPAs in a fridge.

RYE IPA

This is one of my favorite stylistic mash-ups. Since I could legally drink (and a year or two before that blessed date), I've savored a nice bolt of rye whiskey such as Old Overholt or Rittenhouse. These whiskeys pack a dry, spicy taste that is a refreshing contrast to the sweetness of a bourbon such as Maker's Mark. When rye is used in beer, the grain can add complexity, sharpness, subtle spiciness, and a refreshing dry finish. In other words, the grain's profile is the perfect complement to a nicely bittered IPA.

California's Bear Republic Brewing uses rye as its muse in many beers.

TWO TO TASTE: RYE IPA

HE'BREW BITTERSWEET LENNY'S R.I.P.A.
SHMALTZ BREWING COMPANY
ABV: 10%

Named after the potty-mouthed funnyman Lenny Bruce, this coppery double IPA is capped by a beige head, with a scent that calls to mind caramel, citrus, pine, and a thick slice of rye bread. Sip it to explore a world of honey, biscuits, and citrus bitterness. The R.I.P.A. on Rye variant is aged in oak barrels that once held rye whiskey.

HOP ROD RYE
BEAR REPUBLIC BREWING CO.
ABV: 8%

Bear Republic often experiments with rye, most notably in the aggressive Hop Rod. It zooms from the bottle a deep amber, its unabashedly floral fumes—citrus, pine—laced with traces of caramel and spice. Taste-wise, bitterness is balanced by a sweet-spicy profile and a peppery finish rooted in earth. (If you spot the Ryevalry Belgian-style IPA on draft at your local bar, I'd advise you to order a pint.)

BACKUP BEERS: *Barrier Brewing Company Evil Giant IPA, Harpoon Brewery Rich & Dan's Rye IPA, Laughing Dog Brewing Rocket Dog Rye IPA, Sierra Nevada Brewing Co. Ruthless Rye IPA, SweetWater Brewing Company LowRYEder IPA*

KNOW YOUR STRENGTH

When I have bits and bobs and odds and ends—rubber bands, beer cozies, bumper stickers—that have no particular place to go in my apartment, I throw everything into my kitchen drawer, the repository of ephemera. That's the idea behind the American strong ale, a vaguely defined style that's a storehouse for any beer that tops, oh, let's say 7 percent ABV. A double IPA could be classified as a strong ale or even a barley wine. So let's not put these burly brews in a box. Just know that when you see the words *strong ale*, the beer will not be a weak wallflower. Fittingly, the style's poster child is Stone Brewing's aggressively flavored and appropriately named Arrogant Bastard Ale.

In 2012, social-media mavens Ashley Routson (@TheBeerWench) and Ryan Ross (@RyanARoss) founded IPA Day, a virtual lupulin-lovers meet-up built around the hash tag #IPADay. The event usually occurs in August.

TWO TO TASTE: BELGIAN IPA*

RAGING BITCH
BELGIAN-STYLE IPA
FLYING DOG BREWERY
ABV: 8.3%

HOUBLON CHOUFFE
DOBBELEN IPA TRIPEL
BRASSERIE D'ACHOUFFE
ABV: 9%

Brewed to commemorate Flying Dog's twentieth anniversary, Raging was such a success that it joined the year-round lineup. A trio of American hops—Columbus, Amarillo, Warrior—provide a citrusy bouquet that plays well with the fruity yeast. Sweet malts and grapefruit steer you to a pleasingly spicy finish.

On the label, a happy little elf harvesting hops gives a clue to the aromas and flavors that await you inside. First brewed in 2006, the bottle-conditioned, unfiltered brew drinks dry and lively, with an earthy, zesty nose and a pleasantly fruity, peppery profile backed by plenty of bitterness. It expertly blends a double IPA and a Belgian tripel.

BACKUP BEERS: *Ale Asylum Bedlam (U.S.), Clown Shoes Muffin Top (U.S.), New Belgium Brewing Belgo IPA (U.S.), Stone Brewing Company Cali-Belgique IPA (U.S.), Terrapin Beer Company Monk's Revenge (U.S.), Urthel Hop-It (Belgium), Duvel Tripel Hop (Belgium)*

* *Try one beer from the United States and one from Belgium.*

BELGIAN IPA

Inspiration is a two-way street, and in no field is this more apparent than in brewing. Sparked by the rise of abundantly hopped American ales, Belgian brewers have begun releasing their own bitter pale-hued beers. Upon returning from the Great Alaska Beer & Barley Wine Festival in 2005, Hildegard van Ostaden, brewmaster at Ruiselede, Belgium's Urthel, devised the Hop-It double IPA dosed with European noble hops, and Belgium's Brasserie d'Achouffe Houblon Chouffe Dobbelen IPA Tripel blends citrus aromas with fruity esters—a trademark of Belgian yeast.

Across the Atlantic, American brewers also have cottoned to this fusion brew. They're using Belgian yeast strains to create dry beers with a yeasty, fruity profile, a curiously appealing funk, pillowy heads, and a beguiling American-hop bouquet. It's like the United States had a baby with Belgium.

IN SUPERMARKETS, **IPAS** *are the* SECOND-MOST POPULAR CRAFT-BEER STYLE BEING SOLD.

TOASTING TO A HIGHER POWER

TRAPPIST AND ABBEY-STYLE ALES

DURING MY JUDAIC UPBRINGING, I devoured numerous affronts to good taste. From gelatinous gefilte fish to matzo that recalled baked cardboard, piety did not translate to a pleasing dinner plate and, more pointedly, an enjoyable glass of wine. I am speaking of Manischewitz, that molar-achingly sweet wine that I choked down during the Passover holiday. How I hated that kosher wine, which tasted as if the grapes had been dragged through a Domino Sugar factory. Religious booze left a bad taste in my mouth, a problem that's foreign to monks in Austria, France, the Netherlands, and Belgium.

Many of those pious men are members of the world's most exclusive brewing club, one with a guest list that few breweries can crack: Trappist beer. Brewing is largely a democratic endeavor. With enough resources and time, any skilled brewer can craft a bitter IPA or a stout the color of chimney soot, but it takes more than talent to create Trappist beer. Globally, there are more than 170 Trappist monasteries. To earn money for their orders, the monks make and sell goods such as clothing, cheese, and, at a handful of approved abbeys, some of the world's rarest, most revered beer.

As an adjective, *Trappist* is a designation of origin that covers a wide swath of the beer cooler. Some Trappist ales are straw-toned thirst quenchers, whereas others are dry, bitter, and funkier than James Brown. Trappist ales can be golden and candy-sweet or opulent, intricate, and dark with fragrances of baking spices and dark fruit. Above all, many Trappist ales, along with their growing ranks of secular equivalents, are belly warmers, boasting elevated booze levels (they typically range somewhere between 6 and 12 percent alcohol by volume) that ensure you'll sip them at a snail's pace.

A note of caution: the fact that a beer is brewed by monks or someone who has taken a shine to their styles does not ensure that it will be delicious. Drain pours do abound. However, there is ample transcendence as well. Find the right beer and drinking it could well qualify as a religious experience.

A RELIGIOUS REBELLION

In 1664, Armand-Jean le Bouthillier de Rancé, the abbot at La Trappe Abbey in Normandy, France, began a reform movement to restore the original rules of the Roman Catholic Cistercian order, as well as add additional orders. This movement swept Europe, creating the Order of Cistercians of the Strict Observance, whose followers took their name from a breakaway abbey: the Trappists.

Trappist monks, like their fellow Cistercian monks of the Common Order, follow a set of communal-living precepts called the Rule of Saint Benedict. Beyond an abiding belief in serving God, the Cistercians are guided by a dedication to peace, prayer, and manual labor (the Trappist motto is *Ora et labora*, "prayer and work"). In addition, Trappists abstain from meat. This combination led them to embrace agricultural practices and brewing. (Remember, back then drinking water often was contaminated, and brewing beer ensured that pathogen-riddled H_2O did not send you six feet under.)

During the Middle Ages, breweries at monasteries were commonplace, nowhere more so than with the Trappists. They used brewing to support the monasteries as they sprouted throughout Europe, ensuring self-sufficiency—well, when they weren't being destroyed during the anti-Catholic French Revolution and World Wars I and II. (Many monasteries also left France during Napoleon's rocky, cannonball- and gunfire-filled reign.) Numerous breweries bit the bullet, reduced to cinders or ravaged for copper and other valuable metals. Those that survived were rewarded after World War II, when Trappist beers—a term popularized sometime between the two tussles by the brothers brewing Belgium's Chimay—began to gain in popularity, buoyed by the monks' reputation as peerless craftsmen and the desire to rebuild decimated local economies. (In particular, Chimay rapidly ramped up operations, a decision that helped make it one of the world's most renowned Trappist breweries.)

FLATTERED, I'M SURE

If imitation is the sincerest form of flattery, Trappist brewers are awash in adulation. To capitalize on the popularity of these monk-made beers, secular breweries began calling their beers Trappist and adorning them with ecclesiastical imagery and names. Though the monks were tolerant men, they could not forgive copyright in-

fringement. Lawsuits were filed. And litigation ensued. The end result: in 1997, eight Trappist monasteries founded the International Trappist Association. The purpose of the organization is to prevent businesses from piggybacking on the monks' reputation for quality goods, namely, liqueur, cheese, bread, biscuits and cookies, chocolates, and beer. Concerning beer, the hexagon-shaped logo bearing the Authentic Trappist Product logo is granted only if breweries meet four criteria:

1. The brewery has to be within the monastery, and the beer must be brewed by the monks or under their supervision. (Secular workers are acceptable, though.)
2. Brewing should never be the monks' primary focus.
3. Brewing income should cover the monks' living expenses and maintenance of the monastery and its grounds; any profits above and beyond that must be donated to charity.
4. To ensure impeccable quality, Trappist beers must be monitored constantly by the association.

The women's branch of the Order of Cistercians of the Strict Observance often is referred to as the Trappistines.

The term Cistercian *derives from* Cistercium, *the Latin name for the French village of Cîteaux. The Cîteaux Abbey was founded there in 1098 by the Benedictine abbot Saint Robert of Molesme so that he and fellow monks could follow the strictest interpretation of Saint Benedict's Rule, marking the beginning of the Cistercian order.*

The nearly 170 Trappist monasteries are scattered across the globe, from Argentina to Australia, Brazil, the Czech Republic, Chile, Taiwan, Indonesia, and even Israel.

EIGHT IS ENOUGH:
MEET THE ABBEYS PRODUCING TRAPPIST BEER

Trappist beer is one of the most exclusive brewing cliques in the world. Currently, only eight monasteries are legally allowed to brand their beers with the Authentic Trappist Product logo. These eight breweries make the cut.

This postcard-perfect setting is southern Belgium's Notre-Dame de Scourmont Abbey, better known as the birthplace of Chimay beer. While the beers are produced at the abbey, they're pumped into tanker trucks and transported to a nearby bottling plant for packaging.

BIÈRES DE CHIMAY

At southern Belgium's Notre-Dame de Scourmont Abbey, the brothers began brewing in 1862, starting a tradition that has made Chimay one of the wold's most recognized Trappist brands. The monastery's well water serves as the base for a trio of beers: the dark and fruity Chimay Rouge (red cap), the strong and lightly roasty Chimay Bleue (blue cap), and the golden Chimay Tripel. (Sold in 750-ml bottles, the Rouge is called Première; Bleue goes by the moniker Grande Réserve; and Tripel is called Cinq Cents.) The spent brewing grains are fed to the brothers' herd of cattle, which produce milk used to create Chimay's four superb cheeses, including one that has a beer-soaked rind.

BRASSERIE D'ORVAL

In Belgium's deeply southern region of Gaume you'll find the Abbaye Notre-Dame d'Orval, which, since its founding some 900 years ago, has been knocked down and rebuilt several times, most recently in 1931. Orval (the name means "valley of gold") began distributing its beers the following year, becoming the first abbey to ship its beers around Belgium. The abbey's trademark bowling pin–shaped bottle contains its sole product: the crisp, hoppy, and lightly funky Orval pale ale (for more on pale ales, see p. 115). The brewery is open to visitors only two days a year, typically in September.

BRASSERIE DE ROCHEFORT

An aura of mystery surrounds the brewery at the Abbaye Notre-Dame de Saint-Rémy, where the brothers have been

making beer in secrecy since 1595. The abbey currently produces just three beers: the fruity, caramel-focused Rochefort 6 (red bottle cap); the stronger, more intensely fruity Rochefort 8 (green cap); and the figgy, creamy, and richly boozy Rochefort 10 (blue cap).

BROUWERIJ DER TRAPPISTEN VAN WESTMALLE

Though it was founded in 1794, Westmalle did not become a Trappist abbey until 1836. That year, the newly minted brothers decided to toss their robes into the brewing ring, devising a light and sweet beer. A few decades later, they added a dark, strong beer that laid the groundwork for the dubbel and, in the next century, a strong pale ale that bore the label of Tripel—the first of its kind. Westmalle's two main products are Westmalle Dubbel and Westmalle Tripel.

BROUWERIJ WESTVLETEREN

Some of the world's most sought-after beers—Trappist or otherwise—are brewed at Belgium's Abbey of Saint Sixtus of Westvleteren near the hops-growing city of Poperinge. The brothers began brewing in 1838 but did not start selling to the public until 1931. Except for rare occasions, the limited-quantity, label-free offerings are sold only at the abbey. They include the green-capped Westvleteren Blonde, the stronger blue-capped Westvleteren 8, and the potent, cultishly beloved yellow-capped Westvleteren 12, which is consistently rated one of the world's best.

BROUWERIJ DER SINT-BENEDICTUSABDIJ DE ACHELSE KLUIS/ACHEL

Though the brothers of the Abbey of Saint Benedict have brewed only since 1998, their history dates to 1648, when Dutch monks built a chapel in Achel, Belgium. It was lost to the French Revolution before the ruins were rebuilt, and, in 1871, the building became a Trappist monastery. Brewing was commonplace until World War I, when the monks fled the abbey and the Germans ransacked the copper brewing

These hay bales dot the picturesque, forest-encircled property at Belgium's Abbaye Notre-Dame d'Orval. At the abbey, the brothers produce the Orval pale ale, as well as cheese made with milk collected from local farms.

equipment. The brothers returned to brewing in 1998 and in 2001 began offering the now widely available Trappist Achel 8° Bruin, a dubbel; Trappist Achel 8° Blond, a tripel; and Achel Trappist Extra, a strong dark ale.

BROUWERIJ DE KONINGSHOEVEN/ LA TRAPPE

In 1999, the Dutch Trappist brewery based in the Onze Lieve Vrouw van Koningshoeven abbey ran afoul of the International Trappist Association. The association did not take kindly to the fact that the abbey—which was founded in 1884—was bought by Bavaria, a massive lager brewer. Since then the discord has been smoothed over, and in 2005 the abbey regained its Trappist designation. The

brewery's lineup includes La Trappe Blond, the Isid'or pale ale, a dubbel, a tripel, a quadrupel, and the only available Trappist witbier.

STIFT ENGELSZELL

A hair more than 120 miles east of Munich sits northwestern Austria's Stift Engelszell, that country's sole Trappist monastery. The abbey was founded in 1293 but did not start brewing until 2012 to pay for the restoration of its frescoes and paintings. (The monks previously had made Trappist-approved liqueur.) The inaugural release was a dark, strapping ale known as Gregory, named after the order's revered abbot Gregory Eisvogel. Stift Engelszell also produces Benno, a strong pale ale named after another abbot.

GO WEST, BELGIAN BEER DRINKER

The monks of Saint Sixtus of Westvleteren make it tough to acquire their rich, dark fruit–drenched quadrupel, which is rated regularly as one of the world's best beers. (It's nice, but not worth trading for your firstborn.) Customers must call to make a reservation—overcoming the endless busy signals—provide their license plate numbers, and swear they will not resell the beer. In 2012, importers Shelton Brothers and Manneken-Brussels made obtaining 12 a bit easier by selling Westvleteren gift packs, the proceeds of which will fund the abbey's restoration.

MONASTIC FLAVORS, SECULAR MANUFACTURING

Although only a tightly controlled cabal of monasteries is legally permitted to manufacture Trappist beers, there's no law against producing monastic-style beer. Countless commercial Belgian and American breweries offer riffs on religious beer, decorating labels with images of jolly friars and saints, names of fictitious abbeys, or words such as brother and monk.

The standard labeling line is that these are abbey beers, *bières d'abbaye*, or even Belgian-style beers. The designation covers offerings from secular, Belgian-inspired breweries in the United States such as Maine's Allagash and New York's Brewery Ommegang as well as beers produced by non-Trappist monasteries and commercial breweries in partnerships with monasteries.

Here's where the logic gets a little muddy: in 1999, in response to the International Trappist Association crackdown, the Union of Belgian Brewers introduced the Certified Belgian Abbey Beer trademark, which identifies beers linked to an existing or abandoned abbey (this includes non-Trappist abbeys as well). For the beer to bear the logo, the brewery must pay royalties to the abbey and/or order, and those funds must be used to support the order's charitable activities or activities dedicated to the cultural preservation of the abbey.

IS IT A TRAP?
MORE MONASTIC BREWERIES AROUND THE WORLD

In northern France right by the Belgian border, on a small hill near the town of Godewaersvelde ("God's plain"), you'll find the Abbaye du Mont des Cats. Here, the monks are known for producing a cow's-milk cheese using dairy products from local farms. While the monastery no longer has an operational brewery, the Chimay brewery produces a Mont des Cats beer for the abbey.

SAINT JOSEPH'S ABBEY

After this Trappist order's founding as Petite Clairvaux in Nova Scotia in the early 1800s, several devastating fires forced it to relocate to Rhode Island and, finally, Spencer, Massachusetts, where the monks settled in 1950. They've long specialized in making preserves and jellies but now are building a brewery and branching out into brewing. With the assistance of monks from

Chimay, the brothers had hoped to start producing beer by fall 2013.

MONT DES CATS

The monks behind France's Mont des Cats produce a wonderful amber beer touched by caramel sweetness and a spot of bitterness, but their Bière Trappiste is not an official Trappist beer. The beer is brewed at Belgium's Chimay, breaking the rule that Trappist beer must be created within the walls of an abbey.

ABBEY OF MARIA TOEVLUCHT

The Netherlands may soon receive its second official Trappist brewery in Klein-Zundert, where the monks of Maria Toevlucht are toiling hard to set up shop inside their abbey. The brothers see brewing as a way to entice new members to join the monastery.

In the days before labeling, the Trappist breweries used different colored bottle caps to tell their beers apart. The tradition endures today.

During the world wars, most Trappist breweries were raided for their copper kettles, which the Germans confiscated for their war production. Westvleteren was the only brewery to keep its kettles.

ABBEY OF NEW CLAIRVAUX

In 1931, the newspaper magnate William Randolph Hearst purchased a medieval chapterhouse—Santa Maria de Ovila, which was started in 1190 around the village of Trillo, Spain—and shipped it to northern California, where his plans to rebuild the abbey crumbled and he bequeathed the stones to the city of San Francisco. In 1994, the Trappist monks of the Abbey of New Clairvaux (founded in 1955) gained possession of the chapter house ruins and began reconstructing it stone by stone. To aid them, the nearby Sierra Nevada Brewing Company partnered with the brothers to produce the Ovila line of Trappist-style abbey ales, and a portion of the proceeds is earmarked for the order.

MONASTERY OF CHRIST IN THE DESERT

These Benedictine monks in New Mexico operate the Abbey Beverage Co., which produces Monks' Ale, Monks' Tripel, and Monks' Wit at their monastery and a local brewery. The brothers proclaim that they develop their beers "with care and prayer."

BEFORE WE TASTE, A NOTE ON STRENGTH

In a minute, we'll delve into the styles of Trappist beer identified as single (or enkel), dubbel, tripel, and quadrupel. Our brains digest these words, and the rational result is that we think that a dubbel (the Flemish word for "double") should be twice as strong as a single and a quadrupel will outweigh a single by the power of 4. Once again, logic fails. These beers are each a step up the ladder of alcohol potency, but they grow gradually stronger and do not require the use of multiplication tables to pinpoint their alcoholic percentage. However, you can roughly estimate that a dubbel uses twice the malt of a single and a tripel relies on three times the standard malt bill. Got that? Now, onward!

SINGLE

In an ideal world, I'd pour samples of all four Trappist beer styles and take you on a sometimes golden, sometimes dark, and altogether besotted journey through the category of monk-made ales. My plan makes perfect sense, but there's one very good reason this can't happen: there's no longer a beer known as the single.

When the Trappists started brewing in the early nineteenth century, they focused on low-alcohol beers (often 3 percent ABV or even lower). They were known as enkel, aka single, and referred to a monastery's basic, no-frills recipe. These lightweight beers were never distributed widely, being reserved for the brothers, abbey guests, and the needy. As the years passed and the brothers started brewing stronger beers and selling them to the public, the enkel slowly rode off into the sunset.

In their stead, we find the equally exclusive patersbier. Less a style than a general frame of mind, patersbier ("father's beer") is a weaker beer that the monks brew for their personal consumption or perhaps for celebrations. These beers rarely leave the monasteries' walls, though they're occasionally offered to the public in the monasteries' tasting rooms.

Today, there's no all-purpose phrase to describe a Trappist brewery's lightest beer. Instead, look to the lowest number in the brewery's beer portfolio (e.g., Achel 5°) or perhaps the adjective *blond* or *blonde*. Even then, these "light" beers are as different as the days of the week. The Trappistes Rochefort 6 is strong and dark, clock-ing in with a 7.5 percent ABV and touched by toffee and dark fruit. In contrast, Koningshoeven's La Trappe Blond is hazy, fruity, and redolent of cloves, and the Westvleteren Blonde drinks dry, effervescent, and crisp with a grassy bitterness.

These "light" beers have about as much in common as cats and dogs, and they're best appraised on their own.

GET A DEGREE

Instead of names, many Belgian beers are plainly identified by a number, such as Rochefort 6, 8, or 10. This hearkens back to Belgium's old-time system of measuring a beer's strength in degrees. In a nutshell, taking a beer's specific gravity—its density in relation to water after fermentation is finished—subtracting 1, and multiplying by 100 allows one to calculate the number. For example, a beer with a final gravity of 1.080 would be 8 degrees. The higher the number is, the stronger the beer will be, but degrees are not an equal correlation to alcohol percentage. A Rochefort 8 will weigh in at a robust 9.2 percent ABV.

Cistercian monks may be mostly quiet, but they do not take a vow of silence. In fact, there are three main times when talking is permitted: work, spiritual exchanges, and "spontaneous conversation on special occasions," according to the Order of Cistercians of the Strict Observance.

LIGHT BEERS, LONG JOURNEYS

PACK YOUR BAGS AND BOOK A FLIGHT TO BELGIUM TO TRY THESE ABBEYS' RARE, EASYGOING BEERS.

WESTVLETEREN BLOND (ABBEY OF SAINT SIXTUS OF WESTVLETEREN)

As with all the Westvleteren beers, purchasing this 5.8 percent blonde ale requires you to take a trip to the monastery in Belgium.

ACHEL BLONDE 5° AND ACHEL BRUIN 5° (BROUWERIJ DER SINT-BENEDICTUSADIJ DE ACHELSE KLUIS)

For a taste of either the draft-only golden or the brown ale (both 5 percent ABV), you must travel to the abbey. The stronger Achel Extra Blonde also is sold only at the abbey.

CHIMAY DORÉE (NOTRE-DAME DE SCOURMONT ABBEY)

Translating as "Chimay Golden," this pale 4.8 percent treat is solely available at the abbey or its associated area inn, Auberge de Poteaupré. If you've come this far, you might as well spend the night.

PETITE ORVAL (ABBAYE D'ORVAL)

Incredibly crisp and dry, the 3.5 percent Petite Orval is sometimes available at the monastery and at A l'Ange Gardien, a tavern owned by the monastery.

WESTMALLE EXTRA (ABDIJ DER TRAPPISTEN VAN WESTMALLE)

Brewed only twice a year, this 5 percent beer is reserved for monks and abbey guests to drink during lunch.

DUBBEL

For a beer writer wading through the muck of half-truths and muddled history, it's refreshing to uncover a style's story of origin that does not cause historians to contemplate combat in a boxing ring. Hence, the tidy tale of the dubbel, a beer traced back to an abbey known as Our Lady of the Sacred Heart in Belgium's Kansas-flat

Koningshoeven is translated as "the king's gardens" because the Dutch king donated the land to the monks, who had relocated from the La Trappe monastery in Normandy.

In 1946, the Abbey of Saint Sixtus, brewers of the lusted-after Westvleteren ales, licensed Belgium's St. Bernardus brewery to make beers bearing the St. Sixtus name. The agreement ended in 1992, but the secular brewery's abbey beers remain a close ringer for Westvleteren's tough-to-acquire ales.

WESTMALLE DUBBEL
BROUWERIJ WESTMALLE
ABV: 7%

No journey into the decadent world of dubbels is complete without Westmalle's iconic ale. Since the brothers boosted the original brown ale's potency in 1926, it has inspired legions of imitators. Many are good, but few are better than this ruddy-brown malt bomb that creamily sashays across your palate. There's a nose of nuts, raisins, and bananas, which jibe well with rich, indulgent flavors of caramel and malt. One important note: the dubbel matures differently in the larger 750-ml bottle. The aftertaste is slightly subtler.

PATER DUBBEL
BROUWERIJ CORSENDONK
ABV: 7.5%

Founded in the late fourteenth century, northern Belgium's Priory of Corsendonk once contained a sizable brewery, which cranked out beer from the 1600s until the priory was shut down by the Austrian emperor Joseph II in 1784. Fast-forward 200 years, and Corsendonk beers were once again being produced—minus the monks. Nonetheless, you'll find monastery-influenced releases that include the dubbel-style Abbey Brown Ale. The lively ruby release has a spicy nose and tastes of brown sugar and toasted bread chunked with dried plums and raisins. It's delightful.

BACKUP BEERS: *Brasserie St. Feuillien Brune, Bierbrouwerij De Koningshoeven La Trappe Dubbel, Brouwerij Duvel Moortgat Maredsous 8, Brouwerij St. Bernardus Prior 8, Chimay Première (Red Cap or Rouge)*

Westmalle TRIPEL DUBBEL trappist

countryside near Westmalle, just east of Antwerp. Within the abbey's walls you'll find Westmalle, one of Belgium's most revolutionary Trappist breweries.

One day in 1856, the brothers decided to brew something new. Instead of the light, somewhat sweet witbier they'd manufactured for several decades, they dialed up a dark brown ale that was strong and had a decidedly fruity edge. Perhaps word of the brown ale would have spread sooner, but the monks did not dive deeply into commerce until 1921, when they started selling their brews to commercial traders. A few years later, in 1926, the Westmalle monks turbocharged the brown beer's recipe, making it stronger still and creating the model for what became known as the dubbel.

It's a reasonably beefy beer, weighing in at 6 to 8 percent ABV and displaying a color like freshly tilled soil mixed with red clay. The dubbel's body should be heavy—there's no mistaking that—and the flavors will be tilted toward sweet, rich, dark fruit complemented by an aroma that evokes raisins, plums, and perhaps bananas or chocolate as well. The hops will be inconspicuous, like wallflowers at a school dance: present but unnoticed.

To try an archetypal dubbel, buy just about any one brewed by a Belgian monastery or, to be honest, any brewery that lists Belgium as an address: fierce competition ensures that a shoddy dubbel will die a fast, lonely death. On this side of the Atlantic, I do not believe that the quality of American dubbels is quite up to snuff. Brewers are too concerned with imitating the style's standard-bearers, abandoning their instinctual tendency to innovate. Still, there are standouts to be found, such as the dubbel from Ohio's farm-based Rockmill Brewery; Lost Abbey's California-crafted Lost & Found Abbey Ale; and Goose Island Beer Co.'s Pere Jacques, a malty and fruity marvel named after a Belgian abbot who gave the Chicago brewers a brewery tour.

Phew. That's enough info to digest. Find a goblet and get a drink on the double.

FOUR FABULOUS BELGIUM-INSPIRED BREWERIES IN THE UNITED STATES

Order a beer from any of these breweries and you will not be disappointed.

1. **BREWERY OMMEGANG:** Blended with Liefmans Kriek, Three Philosophers is a most curious cherry-accented quadrupel.

2. **THE BRUERY:** The inventive 12 Days/Years of Christmas series finds inspiration in strong, Belgian-style dark ales.

3. **THE LOST ABBEY:** Made with raisin purée, Lost & Found Abbey Ale ranks high on the list of all-time great dubbels.

4. **BREWERY VIVANT:** The Belgium-influenced brewery's outstanding beers include the abbey-style Solitude dark ale and the Triomphe Belgian IPA.

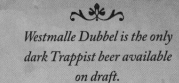

Westmalle Dubbel is the only dark Trappist beer available on draft.

ALLAGASH BREWING COMPANY

PORTLAND, MAINE

Allagash Brewing founder Rob Tod pouring a glass of his iconic White.

Like countless recent grads, Rob Tod had a fuzzy future. After grabbing a geology degree from Vermont's Middlebury College, he odd jobbed around Colorado before returning to Middlebury, his sights somewhat set on graduate school. To pay the bills, he began washing kegs at the local Otter Creek Brewing Company. Within days his plans to earn a doctorate disappeared. "I fell in love with brewing," says Tod, who, despite no formal brewing training, soon decided to open a brewery with an atypical focus: Belgian-style beers.

The notion was planted by happenstance. One day, Tod randomly bought Celis White, the Belgian witbier brewed by the style savior Pierre Celis (see page 99). He initially thought the beer tasted strange, even bad, but a few more bottles changed his opinion. He hoped to provide beer drinkers a similar road to enlightenment. "If

I spent a year of my life building and running a brewery, it was important to give drinkers something unique," Tod says. By summer 1995, a year after he washed his first keg, Tod had relocated to Portland, Maine, and opened Allagash Brewing Company (named after a town in northern Maine). Tod's lightly cloudy launch brew was spiced with coriander and Curaçao orange peel, his personal take on the classic witbier that, quite simply, was called White.

Since White's debut, Allagash has become one of the preeminent American Belgian-inspired breweries. Name a classic Belgian style and Allagash probably has made a version. The core lineup includes the nutty, malty Dubbel; the dry and deceptively potent Tripel; and Four, a quadrupel saturated with flavors of dark fruit. Additionally, Allagash extensively dabbles in oak aging. Most impressively, it operates a coolship (see the picture on page 232), allowing the brewers to create spontaneously fermented beers.

It's Belgian technique blended with American improvisation and Maine terroir.

THE WHITE STUFF

White is Allagash's category killer, constituting nearly 80 percent of the brewery's sales. It's one of the most commonly found draft beers in the Northeast (the witbier is a natural fit for seafood) and graces tap lines from coast to coast. But ubiquity did not occur overnight. "When we first came out with White, it was considered an experimental beer," Tod recalls. "People would say, 'Why is this beer cloudy? Why does it look weird? Why does it taste strange?'"

Was Tod brewing the beer wrong? With few peers making witbiers and able to offer advice, he was forced to learn through trial and error, figuring out how to manage yeast properly and, more important, get White into people's hands. "For the first twelve years, we couldn't give it away," says Tod, who frequently led educational events and beer dinners. "We were banging our heads against the wall." A turning point was the national success of MillerCoors's Blue Moon, which sank advertising dollars and resources into making a cloudy beer both acceptable and commonplace.

Another way that Allagash distinguished itself was the four-pack. The smaller serving size (the six-pack is standard) allowed customers to take a less costly chance on White and its follow-up, the Trappist-inspired Dubbel. Novel packaging took another step in 2001, when Tod decided to embrace another Belgian tradition by capping beers with a cork and a cage, à la Champagne, and bottle conditioning them. Though pricey ("The cork alone costs as much as a 12-ounce glass bottle," Tod says), the presentation and the extra step created a complex and elegant product from the outside in.

Allagash's barrels are filled with Curieux, the Belgian Tripel that's aged in Jim Beam barrels.

THE BIRTH OF COOL

Allagash is in an enviable position. With White providing steady income, the brewers are able, and encouraged, to explore the outer boundaries of brewing. Their creativity has been expressed in beers such as Odyssey, a dark wheat beer aged in heavily toasted American oak barrels; Victoria Ale, a Belgian strong ale made with Chardonnay grapes; and Gargamel, a Belgian-style sour ale aged in French oak alongside local raspberries and a house-cultivated strain of *Brettanomyces*.

Wild yeast is a favorite ingredient for Allagash. In addition to appearing in Confluence Ale and Victor Francenstein (made with Cabernet Franc grapes and souring *Lactobacillus* bacteria and aged in French oak wine barrels), the brewery built a coolship in 2008—essentially a large shallow pan that allows yeast to inoculate the cooling wort naturally—to create some of the nation's first spontaneously fermented beers, a centuries-old tradition in Belgium.

Whereas White is readily available, Coolship releases are rare and exceedingly limited. Flavored with fruits such as cherries and raspberries, the beers spend years in oak barrels, allowing the native yeast and bacteria to revise the flavor profile, creating funky ales not unlike the finest lambics of Belgium. When the brews do debut, the brewery-only releases are so eagerly anticipated that the hundreds of bottles vanish in days, if not hours.

As for the future, Tod sees no end to innovations at Allagash. "With the Belgian brewing tradition, there's an emphasis on experimentation and an unlimited palate of ingredients," Tod says. "It's my personality and the culture of a brewery to always do new things."

Soon it was common to find dinner tables crowned with corked beers such as the smooth, fluffy, and strong Tripel and its accidental fraternal twin. That beer was born in 2004, when a delayed bottle shipment forced Tod to store a portion of Tripel in empty Jim Beam barrels. When the golden ale was tasted a couple of days later, the beer was so wholly transformed that it became a new beer, christened Curieux.

TWO TO TASTE: TRIPEL

TRIPEL
BIÈRES DE CHIMAY
ABV: 8%

LA FIN DU MONDE
UNIBROUE
ABV: 9%

Crack this tripel's trademark snow-white cap and you'll unleash a yeasty, hop-forward aroma with notes of juniper, apricots, and candied orange peel. Poured into a chalice, the tripel presents a cloudy golden body and a head that calls to mind cotton blossoms. Tripel drinks dry and gently bitter with a great grassy aspect and just enough sweetness to make you lick your lips in anticipation of another sip. Remember that in 750-ml bottles the Tripel is known as Cinq Cents. Buy it and share with friends.

I was first introduced to this tripel about eight years ago at a beer festival, where an enthusiastic, and plainly pickled, brewery rep kept screaming, "It's the end of the world, but you keep coming back for more!" Curious, I inched over, finding the Quebec-brewed La Fin du Monde—French for "the end of the world." The creamy ale is Canada's most medal-laden beer owing to its seamless blend of Champagne fizz, yeasty and floral aromatics, and a dry drinkability that's smoother than a French pickup artist.

BACKUP BEERS: *Brouwerij Bosteels Tripel Karmeliet, Brouwerij de Ranke Guldenberg, Brouwerij der St. Benedictusabdij de Achelse Trappist Achel 8° Blond, Brouwerij Westmalle Trappist Tripel, Pisgah Brewing Co. Solstice*

TRIPEL

Around the world, 1919 was a terrible year for alcohol. Finland enacted the *kieltolaki* ("ban law"); the United States passed the Volstead Act, which soon would usher in Prohibition; and Belgium passed the Vandervelde Act. To curtail rampant liquor abuse, minister of justice Émile Vandervelde forbade cafés, bars, and other public places to serve distilled spirits and allowed imbibers to buy the hard stuff only if they purchased two liters at a time—an outlay that most workers could not afford.

Although Vandervelde was successful in passing his nanny-state act (it remained on the books until 1983), he left open a gaping loophole: wine and beer were not included. Just because the government made it tough to drink liquor, that did not mean that Belgians lost a taste for the hard stuff. To capitalize on the thirst for potent beverages, brewers looked to amplify their beers' alcohol content.

Hot on the heels of the success of their heady dubbel, the monks at Westmalle went back to the brew kettle. For a few years the brothers had, off and on, brewed a blonde ale. They decided to roughly triple the amount of malt used in the standard recipe, resulting in 1934's strong, golden "superbier." Admittedly, that is an awesome name for a beer, but the designation and the recipe did not stick. Over the next 22 years, the brewers tinkered with the

TRIPEL, TAKE TWO

With the cloudy nature of brewing history, it's not surprising that there's debate about the first brewery to make a tripel. Brewing expert Michael Jackson believed that Hendrik Verlinden of Belgium's secular De Drie Linden first developed the golden style in the early 1930s to compete with Czech pilsners. Since Verlinden often helped the Westmalle monks with brewing, this story does have some logical heft. No matter: Verlinder's lasting mark in history is that he trademarked the name *Witkap Pater = Trappistenbier*, becoming the first secular brewery to piggyback on the monks' good name. Though the Witkap-Pater brand (now brewed by Brewery Slaghmuylder) no longer carries the Trappistenbier designation, it continues to focus on abbey-style ales, including a fairly flavorful and commendable tripel.

Before Westmalle's final tinkering with the recipe for its golden-hued tripel in 1956, some tripel-style beers displayed a darker tint.

ingredients, adding more hops, and in 1956 they renamed the beer the Westmalle Tripel.

It is the style's supremely balanced keystone: a spicy, hazy-gold symphony of citrus and herbal bitterness, hay, and fruit that drinks surprisingly, somewhat precariously dry considering its 9.5 percent ABV. (The trick is adding special forms of sugar that provide the yeast with extra sustenance, increasing the alcohol content without affecting the beer's body.) In the last half century, the tripel has grown into one of the most popular Trappist-style ales, lending its name to a bevy of imitators and differentiating itself from the golden strong ale with a slightly darker tint, fuller body, and rounded mouthfeel.

It's tough to toss a rock in Belgium without knocking over a tripel, such as Brouwerij Het Anker's Champagne- and apricot-like Gouden Carolus Tripel. In light of the American market's affinity for strong ales, it's not surprising that the style has grown as fast as grass after a late-spring rain. You'll delight in uncapping Boulevard Brewing's Long Strange Tripel, Green Flash's Trippel Ale, or Midnight Sun's cheekily named Panty Peeler. They're tripels that balance strength with drinkability, brightening your mood without coating your tongue in cavity-causing sweetness.

Grab a tulip glass. It's time to take a trip.

QUADRUPEL (QUAD)

Consider for a moment the humble Kleenex: when the facial tissue arrived on the American market in 1924, it was a radical development, ushering in the new era of disposable products. But over the course of the twentieth century, the trademarked brand became a generic term used to describe any old facial tissue, much in the same way that *Xerox* came to be a catchall term for "photocopy."

In that light, let's look at the similar case of the quadrupel. In 1991, the Koningshoeven monastery in the Netherlands created the distinctive La Trappe Quadrupel. It was a sweet beast, a dark mahogany 10 percenter packed with flavors of figs, cherries, and raisins with enough alcohol to help you endure a cold European winter. Indeed, the Quadrupel originally was brewed only during the winter, but its popularity led the monks to make it a year-round release. Success breeds imitation, and the Quadrupel was not immune to brewers capitalizing on the Koningshoeven beer's good name. The quadrupel lost its capital letter, and in Belgium you'll find De Halve Maan's Straffe Hendrik Quadrupel and Brouwerij Van Steenberge's Gulden Draak 9000 Quadruple.

Here's the curious part: Trappist breweries long produced strapping beers that were too weighty to be

TWO TO TASTE: QUADRUPEL

TRAPPISTES ROCHEFORT 10
Brasserie de Rochefort
ABV: 11.3%

Among the abbey's trio of
numbered beers (including the
strong, dark 6 and the dubbel 8),
the blue-capped 10 is the monks'
unquestioned masterpiece. The
boozy quadruple (is there any other
kind?) pours a leathery brown
with ruby highlights and tastes
of caramel, figs, and Christmas
fruitcake, with a creaminess that
coats your mouth like the world's
tastiest paint. Fresh, 10 is terrific,
but to experience transcendence,
try it aged.

LA TRAPPE QUADRUPEL
Bierbrouwerij De Koningshoeven
ABV: 10%

Being first does not always
mean you do something best, but
Koningshoeven remains at the top
of its game with this beer that kick-
started the quadrupel crave when it
debuted in 1991. The amber-orange
beer is all about dark fruit and
bananas, an interplay of sweet and
spicy, with big bubbles, all of which
conceal its colossal alcohol content.
If you pay a visit to the brewery,
you can buy oak-aged quadrupel,
which will have spent some
quality time in port, white wine,
or bourbon barrels.

BACKUP BEERS: *Avery Brewing Company The Reverend, Brouwerij St.
Bernardus Abt 12, De Leyerth Brouwerijen Urthel Samaranth, De Struise
Brouwers Pannepot, Karl Strauss Brewing Company Two Tortugas
Holiday Quadruple Ale, Southampton Publick House Abbot 12*

called dubbels and too dark to fall
under the tripel umbrella, in particular
Chimay Blue (or Grand Reserve),
Trappist Westvleteren 12, and Trappistes
Rochefort 10. These beers were never
categorized collectively except perhaps
to be called a dark strong ale—a useful,
if vague descriptor. Today these dark
and strong ales, in Belgium and abroad,
are collectively known as quadrupels,
or just quads. (These strapping beers
are also sometimes referred to as an
Abt. It's the Dutch word for "abbot,"
the leader of an abbey.)

Retroactively labeling an existing
beer does seem silly, especially in
light of the fluidity of brewing. Look
at the lean and bitter American IPA:
in 30 years, it's done a 180 from its
malty, earthy English ancestor. So take
the quadrupel with a grain of salt,
preferably in a goblet. These hearty ales
are not bashful about their alcohol and
malty sweetness, filled with enough
chocolate, caramel, and flavors of dark
dried fruit to fill a hiker's backpack.

Savor quads as Koningshoeven
originally intended: on a frigid winter
night, surrounded by a few friends
with whom you wouldn't mind being
stranded during a snowstorm.

TURN ON THE DARK

STOUTS, PORTERS, AND ADDITIONAL INKY DELIGHTS

HEN I STILL WAS USING my drinking training wheels, swilling cheap and frosty lagers until sunrise destroyed the night, I rarely stepped outside my intoxicating comfort zone. Cost and quantity were my double-headed masters, keeping my beer choices strictly bottom shelf. But whenever extra quarters jingled in my jeans, I'd escape my Queens apartment—a hellhole where cockroaches doubled as carpeting—take a jaunt across the street to the local Irish pub, and order a pint of Guinness that was poured with glacial slowness by a bartender who had eyebrows that looked like friendly white caterpillars.

"Cheers, lad," the bartender would toast, one of the rare times I didn't mind being called a little boy. I took my time sipping the ebony-hued beer, savoring the creamy crown and roasty complexity. My first forays into the world of stout were nothing but memorable.

If it were not for the mass-produced, delicious ubiquity of Guinness, millions of beer drinkers most likely would not take their first baby steps away from light, crisp lagers and dabble in the dark side of beer. But though Guinness is grand, the Irish ale is hardly the final proper noun on stouts and their precursors, the porter. A couple of hundred years ago, this lightly sour blended ale was the preferred beverage of Britain's working class, eventually spawning a collection of equally delectable offspring such as

the luscious milk stout, the briny oyster stout, the smooth oatmeal stout, the turbo-boosted Russian imperial stout, and the Baltic porter later reconceived by Scandinavians and Russians as a native quaff. When tasting these brews, I beg you to suspend any preconceived notions of what they might taste like on the basis of their appearance. Though these beers may look like used motor oil, many drink feather light.

It's time to try some black magic.

THE ROAST WITH THE MOST

The thread binding stouts and porters together is color. These brews inhabit the darker end of the color spectrum: the deep, dark brown of a farmer's muddy

boots or the dyed black locks of a Goth. These after-dark colors and the cocoa- and coffee-like flavors that accompany them are the result of roasted malt and roasted barley, which hail from two different sides of the grain silo.

use it in conjunction with other dark-roasted malts, or they steer clear of roasted barley and rely solely on roasted malts to supply color and flavor. You'll recognize these brews by their darker head and, often, more pronounced flavors of espresso, a charred profile, or notes of cocoa and nuts.

Black may denote the absence of all color, but in porters and stouts that particular hue symbolizes a riot of aroma and flavor.

Malt, if you remember, is barley that has been soaked in hot water, jump-starting germination and creating the enzymes required to convert proteins and starches into fermentable sugars. Skip germination and barley's sugars are kept under lock and key. There are benefits to using roasted unmalted barley in beer, especially roasted barley. The dark-brown grain is great for creating a lustrous, lasting bone-white head as well as imparting a midnight tint and a sharp and bitter, verging on astringent, flavor—a cup of dark-roasted coffee, if you will.

Roasted barley does not stand on a pedestal by its lonesome. Brewers

WHERE IT ALL BEGAN: BRITISH PORTER

In the beer-stained, hops-scented annals of brewing history, few styles have been as bastardized, misinterpreted, tweaked, and all-around adulterated as Great Britain's porter, the launching pad for every dark brew you'll read about in this chapter. The story starts with the simply named brown beer. In London during the late seventeenth and early eighteenth centuries, the heavy, treacly beer was the city's dominant style. Its reputation was not sterling, leaving the door open for new beer to steal market share.

During the early eighteenth century, the lighter-colored new-fangled pale ales started catching on in London. To create a product that was competitive, brewers tweaked

their recipes and concocted a decently hopped brown beer that, thanks to a long fermentation, was less sweet. The beer was placed into barrels and matured for months, a process that helped mellow out the stuff. As a result of the sanitary (or, rather, unsanitary) conditions of that era's breweries, bacteria and the wild yeast *Brettanomyces* doubtlessly loitered inside the wood; given time, they gave the beer a tart, lightly lactic character. Londoners lapped it up, especially the hardworking

For another terrific read on the history of porter, peruse Ron Pattinson's aptly named Porter!

In Britain, ales and beers were not always one and the same. Beer signified brews that were appreciably hoppier than ales. This distinction drew to a close in the nineteenth century with the rise of that hopped-up favorite of today, the India pale ale. P.S. Porter originally was considered a beer.

porters who hoofed heavy freight off ships and ferried parcels and merchants' goods around town.

Portering was truly back-breaking, calorie-draining labor that demanded steady refueling. According to the historian Martyn Cornell, the pack-mule men got an energizing boost of carbohydrates and calories from the beer that they sipped at local pubs outfitted with outdoor benches and tables for storing their loads while they imbibed. The beer was associated so closely with the workers that by 1721 it began to appear in writing bearing their profession's name: porter.

So began the reign of porter. Breweries grew from small companies to massive operations, producing porter on a major scale, creating a proud product of the Industrial Revolution—and fuel for its tireless toilers. In addition to winning over British drinkers, the brew was soon shipped out to colonies and across the prevailing trade routes, landing in Ireland, Denmark, Russia, Scandinavia, and India (for more on the intertwined history of porters and IPAs, see page 129). To meet demand, coopers crafted ever more massive vats for aging, flooding the marketplace—and occasionally London, too. In 1814, at Meux's Brewery, a vat's corroded hoops suddenly broke free, sending more than 200,000 gallons of porter gushing out, destroying homes and killing eight people.

TWO TO TASTE: BRITISH PORTER

LONDON PORTER
MEANTIME BREWING COMPANY
ABV: 6.5%

FULLER'S LONDON PORTER
FULLER SMITH & TURNER PLC
ABV: 5.4%

Meantime is one of London's newer breweries, but these beersmiths dig deep into the past to fabricate their lineup of historically influenced lagers and ales, such as their London Stout (formulated without roasted barley) and this porter packed with seven malts and a slew of earthy Fuggles hops. The deep brown beer's aroma of lightly roasted malt and cocoa leads to zigzagging flavors of coffee, toffee, and peat smoke. London Porter starts smooth and creamy and concludes with a dry, somewhat bitter finish.

"Rich, dark and complex" is the slogan for this admired British brew made with crystal, chocolate, and brown malts as well as fruity and vegetal Fuggles hops. The snazzy dark-brown brew is streaked with ruby highlights, and its nose shouts, "Get your malt here! And your pipe tobacco and toffee candy too!" There's some sweetness in the sipping as well as enough chocolate and bread to thrill those who like to start their day with Nutella on toast.

BACKUP BEERS: *D.L. Geary Brewing Company Geary's London Porter, Greenport Harbor Brewing Company Black Duck Porter, Salopian Brewery Entire Butt English Porter, Samuel Smith Old Brewery The Famous Taddy Porter, St. Peter's Brewery Old-Style Porter, Williams Bros. Brewing Co. Midnight Sun*

FUNGUS AMONG US

Around 1903, the Danish brewing scientist Niels Hjelte Claussen, the director of the laboratory of the Carlsberg Brewery in Copenhagen, examined a sample of English "stock beer" (a strong aged beer used for blending with young beer) and made a most interesting discovery: the beer, which was stored in breweries and blended with younger beers to give them an aged flavor, contained an unusual yeast strain that he named *Brettanomyces*—Greek for "British fungus." This was no knock against the Brits. The name of the customary brewing yeast, *Saccharomyces*, translates to "sugar fungus." For more on feral, insatiably hungry *Brettanomyces* and its funky flavor contributions to lambics and other sour or wild ales, check out Class 10 beginning on page 225.

UNITED STATES PATENT OFFICE.

NIELS HJELTE CLAUSSEN, OF COPENHAGEN, DENMARK.

MANUFACTURE OF ENGLISH BEERS OR MALT LIQUORS.

No. 813,199.　　Specification of Letters Patent.　　Patented Feb. 20, 1906.

Application filed May 17, 1904. Serial No. 208,464.

To all whom it may concern:

Be it known that I, NIELS HJELTE CLAUSSEN, a subject of the King of Denmark, residing at Copenhagen, Denmark, (having a post-office address at 40 Rahbeks Alle, Copenhagen, aforesaid,) have invented new and useful Improvements in the Manufacture of English Beers or Malt Liquors, of which the following is a specification.

It is well known that Hansen's researches have given rise to a far-reaching reform in the practice of brewing, both on the continent of Europe and in America, and that in accordance with this reform a single and systematically-selected species of *saccharomyces* is now almost exclusively used as pitching-yeast instead of accidental mixtures, as was formerly the case; but a like reform has not been introduced into English breweries and in spite of numerous trials which have been made. The fermentation has been commenced either by means of a single pure cultivated species of *saccharomyces* or with a mixture of several species, according to the method formulated by Van Lehr, (*Transactions of the Institute of Brewing,* VII;) but neither in the one nor in the other case has it been possible to carry on a continuous manufacture, and the attempts have ultimately always had to be abandoned in consequence of the unsatisfactory results, the cause of which has not been ascertained. An explanation of this fact was sought by many authors in the supposition that a special secondary yeast was necessary for assuring the secondary fermentation of English beers; but the supposition was never positively proved, and it has always met with decided opponents, (Jörgensen and Riley, *Allgemeine Brauer und Hopfenzeitung* No. 257, page 2,817.) The authors who wrote more precisely stated what was supposed to be the hypothetic secondary yeast always called it a "*saccharomyces*," (Sykes, *The Principles and Practice of Brewing,* second edition, London, 1902, page 483.) From the same point of view Van Laer made the only attempt which has hitherto been made to isolate the secondary yeast and use it in the practice of brewing. He isolated ten different species of *saccharomyces,* (*Sacch. pastorianus* and *Sacch. ellipsoideus,*) and he supposed to have found the secondary yeast among these. (*Transactions of the Inst. of Brewing,* VII, page 55.)

My present invention is based on the discovery that the fine flavor and condition characterizing and peculiar to English beer is not essentially due to the yeast (*saccharomyces*) nor to the raw materials employed, but is due to a particular group of micro-organisms, which have hitherto not been isolated or described. The group in question belongs to the fungi, but is distinctly different from the *saccharomycetes*. According to what has been hitherto ascertained this group should be placed in the species "*Torula,*" but until the position of the group in the botanic system has been determined by exact scientific investigation I propose to call it "*brettanomyces*" (*βρεττανός=Briton,* and *μυκης= fungus.*) I have, for example, isolated *brettanomyces* from English beers old in bottle in the following manner—that is to say, I have distributed an adequate quantity of the deposit of a bottle of English ale or stout—as, for instance, Bass's India pale ale, Guiness's Dublin stout, &c.—in melted wort-gelatin and allowed the same to stiffen, and after the lapse of about three days there were formed visible specks of vegetation by the *saccharomyces* cells contained in the wort-gelatin whether or not they belonged to the cultivated or to the wild species of yeasts. These specks may often attain a considerable size. Only after several days does a fresh set of specks appear. These grow slowly and on the whole remain comparatively small. These specks (apart from any colonies of bacteria) consist of *brettanomyces* and can afterward be produced in absolutely pure cultures in the usual way, assuming a round oval elongated thread or irregular form.

The characteristics which distinguish *brettanomyces* from the other fermentation-producing budding fungi are the following:

First. The cells of *brettanomyces* are smaller in size than the cells of *saccharomyces-cerevisiae,* and they are quite varying in shape, assuming a round oval elongated thread or irregular form.

Second. When permitted to stand for months, the culture of *brettanomyces* in wort or sugar solutions produce a flocculent growth of thread-formed mycelium floating above the deposit first formed.

Third. No endospores are formed.

Fourth. Glucose, fructose, and maltose are fermented, but saccharose is not attacked, as *brettanomyces* contain no invertase.

Fifth. *During the fermentation the acidity of the fluids is considerably increased,* and

AND THEN CAME STOUT

As the decades stacked into centuries, porter slowly slipped from its perch. Pale ales climbed in popularity, as did sweeter brews. Porter's progeny, the dry Irish stout, in time overtook its sire—a further insult, since stout porter was originally a description for a very strong porter. Recipes changed with the years, then cheapened. By the mid-twentieth century, porter was considered a déclassé drink, a cheap quaff fit for pence-pinching old men, and became all but extinct. The style seemed destined for the dustbin, and in some respects that's where it still resides. Few breweries today make sour porter in the time-intensive, purposely infectious manner of brewers bygone.

Today, the style has so deviated from its origins that, like old married couples whose characteristics and quirks end up

One of the few remaining breweries that employ the blended-porter technique is England's Greene King, which creates Strong Suffolk Vintage Ale by blending Old 5X—a tart 12 percent ABV ale aged in oak vats for at least two years— with young, dark BPA.

blurring together, porter is pretty much indistinguishable from stout. According to the official style guidelines for the Beer Judge Certification Program, the only appreciable difference is that stouts use roasted barley—which is not always the case. In fact, as the brewing historian Ron Pattinson notes, many British porters and brown stouts in the early nineteenth century used identical recipes. The sole difference: less water was used in the making of stout to create a stronger beer.

A NEW PORT: AMERICAN PORTER

So where do we stand today? Unless you're nipping a slightly tart, dark-colored beer, you're not sipping a historically accurate porter. Plenty of modern porter interpretations do exist, though, and you'll usually find them to be a touch lighter than stouts, displaying a dark-brownish hue and a less astringent, categorically roasty profile. British porters tend to play their cards closer to their chest, with sweet flavors of caramel

Porter originally was aged in butts, wooden casks that held 108 gallons of beer. Get your mind out of the gutter.

THE POWER OF THREE

One of the enduring legends about porter's origin is that the beer was invented by a gent named Ralph Harwood, who tried to replicate a brew dubbed three-threads: an equal blend of styles known as ale, highly hopped beer, and twopenny, a potent pale ale. This tale has proved to be pure claptrap.

TWO TO TASTE: AMERICAN PORTER

DUCK-RABBIT PORTER
DUCK-RABBIT CRAFT BREWERY
ABV: 5.7%

Dark beer is the modus operandi for North Carolina's Duck-Rabbit. I've never sipped a subpar Duck-Rabbit brew, and that's why I think you'll dig this handsome robust porter. It tastes like a dark chocolate truffle encasing a core of cold-brewed coffee, and a few scoops of oats make for smooth and silky sipping. In other words, it might be your new favorite beer.

BLACK BUTTE PORTER
DESCHUTES BREWERY
ABV: 5.2%

Deschutes did not take the easy route. When the Oregon brewery was founded in 1988, it made the bold move to launch with the boldly dark Black Butte Porter. That might have been the smartest decision it ever made. The chocolaty porter has since become Deschutes's flagship brew, in large part because of its smooth wheat-driven mouthfeel and a lingering peck of hop bitterness on the finish.

BACKUP BEERS: *Denver Beer Co. Graham Cracker Porter, Great Lakes Brewing Company Edmund Fitzgerald Porter, Hill Farmstead Brewery Everett, Lonerider Brewing DeadEye Jack Porter, Narragansett Porter, Speakeasy Ales & Lagers Payback Porter*

or toffee, reserved alcohol, and a mild hint of roasted malt.

American porters, which were some of the most popular beers of the first-wave craft-beer movement in the late 1970s and 1980s, are more imaginative and off the cuff, employing smoked malts, serious hops, fruits, chocolate, coffee—everything but the kitchen sink. In Hawaii, Maui Brewing Co. uses hand-toasted coconut in its CoCoNut PorTeR, creating a silky, chocolaty treat with a tropical edge. Clown Shoes re-creates a favorite fall dessert in its Pecan Pie Porter. The Funky Buddha Lounge & Brewery in Boca Raton, Florida, goes even further into food infatuation, having devised Maple Bacon Coffee Porter, which, in the best way possible, tastes like breakfast in a bottle.

Like the porters of yore, you've already done some hefty lifting with this reading. It's time to drink your reward.

Possibly the strangest, tastiest porter I've ever tried is the Michigan-based Right Brain Brewery's Mangalitsa Pig Porter. Each batch includes four cold-smoked Mangalitsa pig heads—brains removed— and there are several bags of bones in each batch. The result is a smoky curiosity.

THE DUCK-RABBIT CRAFT BREWERY
FARMVILLE, NORTH CAROLINA

Summers in eastern North Carolina's Farmville can melt a Popsicle in a minute flat. In this tiny town of tobacco-ringed farmland outside Greenville, the average summertime highs verge on 90°F, with enough humidity to drench a shirt on a short stroll. To the point, it's the kind of weather that forces beer drinkers to daydream about killing thirst with an icy pilsner, cold kölsch, or canned lager.

The Duck-Rabbit Craft Brewery does not offer any of the above. Since Paul C. Philippon (pictured) founded his brewery in August 2004, Duck-Rabbit has focused squarely on the darker side of beer drinking. The lineup includes a silky oatmeal-powered porter, an enchantingly hoppy and bitter brown ale, a crisp and roasty schwarzbier, a gently sweet and smooth milk stout, and the immense Rabid Duck Russian Imperial Stout.

Common sense dictates that these beers are best for a blizzard-socked winter eve, but "it's a misconception that dark beers fail to be thirst-quenching," Philippon says. "Our best-selling beer is Milk Stout. This is true twelve months out of the year, even in the hottest part of the summer." Think about it. A lager or pilsner is best cold. Ever sipped a Budweiser that's been sun-baked until lukewarm? It's pretty unpleasant. By comparison, a dark beer can benefit from increased temperatures, which allow aromas and flavors to unfold like origami in reverse. "I think wet and refreshing is wet and refreshing," he says. "If you approach dark beers with an open mind, there's nothing to be afraid of."

GETTING SCHOOLED

That Philippon delights in debunking prevailing beliefs is no accident. In a previous life, he was a philosophy

professor, toiling at colleges such as Eastern Michigan University. But academia is a tough career that is built on the long slog of securing a tenured position. "I was pursuing a profession in which long-term job prospects weren't as great as I thought they'd be," he says. It was time to choose a second career.

Philippon had been a passionate homebrewer since 1987, a journey that began with a summer job at a research farm. One day after work, his supervisor mentioned that he had to go home and bottle beer. "Sirens went off in my head," Philippon says. "That was

the first time I heard of making beer at home." Soon afterward, he bought homebrewing supplies and started an increasingly obsessive hobby that accompanied him through his whistle-stops on the academic train.

Seeking an out, Philippon enrolled at Chicago's renowned Siebel Institute of Technology to polish his brewing process. After graduating, he mailed résumés to breweries and landed a job at a brewpub in Cincinnati. Of his career change, "My colleagues were not surprised," he says, laughing. "They partook of my homebrew quite frequently." The Ohio brewpub led to a gig at Louisville, Kentucky's Pipkin Brewery (it was later bought by Bluegrass Brewing). In 2000 he was recruited to start Williamsville Brewery in Farmville. By the end of 2003, Williamsville's owners wanted to quit the business.

"That's when the stars aligned and I went to a bank to ask for a ton of money," says Philippon, who bought the brewery but not its recipes, rebranding it the Duck-Rabbit Craft Brewery. Its name and optical-illusion logo (it recalls a duck or a rabbit) are drawn from Ludwig Wittgenstein's *Philosophical Investigations*. It's the intersection of philosophy and beer, Philippon's past and dark, delicious future.

A GRAIN OF THOUGHT

Understanding that the most successful American craft breweries create beers with a common thread (the Belgians of Allagash, the aggressively hoppy ales of Stone), Philippon decided that his brewery's hook would be his longtime fascination: dark beer.

"I love the range of flavors available in dark beers," he says. "The fun is to imagine a particular flavor profile and then to work with various malts and techniques to come up with a recipe that will achieve that profile." Since launching the brewery, Philippon has won a clutch of medals for his inky creations, including both a gold for Baltic Porter (an annual fall release) and a bronze for milk stout at the 2009 Great American Beer Festival. However, getting consumers to try his dark brews could be trying.

At first, the brown ale did not catch fire. The "American-style" brown ale, as Philippon calls it, has a citrusy bitterness and flowery aroma from its Amarillo and Saaz hops. "We got comments like, 'I think it's delicious, but it doesn't taste like a brown ale,'" the brewer says. Though it was slow to catch on, Brown is now doing whiz-bang business and has been joined by the deceptively bitter Hoppy Bunny American Black Ale.

Today Philippon's biggest challenge is brewing enough beer to meet demand, especially for the milk stout. To manage, the brewery recently expanded, a satisfying step for a brewer who relishes contradicting the status quo. "It wasn't lost on me that brewing dark beers in North Carolina was a little bit crazy," Philippon says, "but I feel at home swimming against the stream."

DRY IRISH STOUT

We can learn much about beer drinking from Ivan Pavlov's drooling dogs. The Russian physiologist used whistles, tuning forks, and bells to make canines salivate in anticipation of eating. A similar conditioned response occurs every March 17. On Saint Patrick's Day, drinkers worldwide don green attire and reach for a cool glass of inky Guinness. Let's call it pack behavior.

Although millions of creamy pints of Guinness have been glugged over the centuries (I'm sure you've sipped several of them), few people pause to ponder the origins of the dry stout. Back in the early eighteenth century, the popularity of porter had swept across Great Britain

One of the earliest written references to a stout beer is in a 1677 letter found in the Egerton Manuscripts, a collection of texts that deal mainly with the history and literature of Italy and France (they were bequeathed to the British Museum by Francis Henry Egerton, the eighth Earl of Bridgewater). The sentence reads: "We will drink to your health both in stout and best wine."

THE RECORDS START

The Guinness World Records franchise does in fact refer to the brewery. The idea for a compendium of records and minutiae sprang forth from a hunting trip in Ireland in 1951. Guinness's managing director at that time, Sir Hugh Beaver, was enmeshed in an argument about the fastest game bird in Europe: the grouse or the koshin golden plover. Unable to find a suitable answer and realizing that there were likely countless other debates occurring every night, he decided that there was probably a market for a fact-filled book. In 1955, *The Guinness Book of Records* was published, becoming the ultimate barroom debate settler—at least until the advent of the smartphone.

AW, SHUCKS: OYSTER STOUTS

Classically, oysters have been an ideal pairing with dry stouts, with their briny profile complementing the full-bodied, creamy brew. To underscore the excellence of that pairing, brewers have begun tossing freshly shucked oysters and their liquor into brew kettles, creating beguiling ales with one foot in the ocean and the other behind the bar. Drink an oyster stout while downing an oyster and you'll experience creamy magic, with the smooth, sweetly chocolaty notes of the stout melding with the bivalves, which impart a lingering oceanic tang: the beer draws out the oyster's sweetness, and the bivalve brings out the brine in the beer.

If you swing by Asheville, North Carolina, the Oyster House Brewing Company's oyster-infused Moonstone Stout is on tap at the Lobster Trap restaurant and around town. There are also several laudable bottled versions, such as Porterhouse Brewing Co.'s silky Oyster Stout and Flying Dog Brewery's Pearl Necklace Oyster Stout, but in breweries the delicious coupling usually is crafted as a one-off experiment. Brewers, here's my plea: I love oysters. I doubly love oyster stouts. Please make more of them.

TWO TO TASTE: DRY IRISH STOUT

GUINNESS DRAUGHT
GUINNESS LTD.
ABV: 4.2%

There's not much else I can add to the Guinness mythology. It's a creamy delight from night to morning—try dropping a few depth charges of espresso into your next brunch pint. The cagey Guinness cats will not fess up to this fact, but the beer's signature twang allegedly comes from blending in about 3 percent sour beer aged in ancient oaken vats crawling with all manner of flora and fauna. Fact? Fiction? Who cares, if the beer tastes great?

DARK STARR STOUT
STARR HILL BREWERY
ABV: 4.2%

If you ever find yourself cruising along the Virginia coast, I heartily recommend that you seek out the closest beer store and buy as much Starr Hill as you can find. Brewmaster Mark Thompson navigates the lower depths of alcohol with flavorful aplomb, devising sub–5 percent ABV delights that include Dark Starr, which has won nearly as many medals as Michael Phelps. Starr drinks like cashmere coated in coffee grounds (in a good way) and crushed dark chocolate.

BACKUP BEERS: *Christian Moerlein Brewing Company Friend of an Irishman Stout, Furthermore Beer Three Feet Deep, Gritty McDuff's Brewing Company Black Fly Stout, Mendocino Brewing Company Black Hawk Stout, Sly Fox Brewing Company O'Reilly's Irish Stout*

and Ireland, leading to a black-gold rush for brewers such as the Irishman Arthur Guinness, who in 1759 commandeered an unused brewery at Dublin's St. James's Gate.

Initially, he brewed his version of the era's popular British porters, which were sometimes called stout to describe their potency. By the early nineteenth century, new techniques had been discovered to blacken barley malt, creating so-called patent malt. Brewers were able to create dark beers by mixing patent malt with pale malt; doing that also imparted a subtle roastiness to the beer and left behind less sweetness after fermentation than did the standard brown malts, resulting in essentially a drier beer. Taking advantage of these advancements, in 1821 Arthur Guinness II used the darker grains to formulate a recipe that evolved into the *leann dubh*—Irish for "black beer"—adored every Saint Patrick's Day and the remaining 364 days of the year too. (Halfway through the twentieth century, Guinness began phasing out patent malt for roasted unmalted barley, which can add a dry, bitter taste.)

The dry Irish stout is a counter-intuitive brew. Though it's the color of La Brea tar pits, dry stout is sneakily light-bodied, offering an appealing bitterness (courtesy of roasted barley), coffee-like nuances, and, if dispensed using nitrogen (see page 28), a nice creaminess like frosting on a birthday cake. (To spur draft sales in the late 1950s and 1960s, the company perfected the technique of nitrogenation—introducing nitrogen to a liquid—to create a more consistent, longer-lasting head.) Besides Guinness, the classic examples of the style are Ireland's Murphy's and Beamish Irish Stout, which usually are served via nitrogen when on draft, but they hardly have a monopoly on the style. Great American versions are available nationwide, from Maine-based Shipyard Brewing's Blue Fin Stout to the Old No. 38 Stout from North Coast Brewing in Fort Bragg, California. The luck of the Irish is everywhere you look.

BROWN ALE

Though porter and stouts supplanted brown beer in London, that style did not remain in its grave forever. It merely went into hiding and then underwent radical plastic surgery, emerging around

Until the late 1950s, a single pint of draft Guinness came from the combination of two different casks: one older and matured and one younger, fresher, and more carbonated.

TWO TO TASTE: BROWN ALE

NEWCASTLE BROWN ALE
THE CALEDONIAN BREWERY COMPANY LIMITED
ABV: 4.7%

I was 19 years old and living in London for the summer, which meant I could drink legally. I fondly remember one night at a cheery pub where I bumped into two kids my age. They were on a spending spree financed by the theft and sale of electronic goods. In celebration, they bought me a pint of Newcastle and then another. I spent the night savoring the lovely, light-bodied ale that tasted of caramel, sweet malt, and, given the company, a subtle nuttiness as well.

KOKO BROWN
KONA BREWING CO.
ABV: 5.5%

In elementary school I was addicted to Almond Joy, that coconut candy bar coated in chocolate. One sip of Hawaii-based Kona Brewing's Koko Brown returns me to my childhood candy compulsion. The brown ale's biscuit-like flavors are complemented by a tidal wave of nutty toasted coconut, which washes over your tongue without overwhelming it with sweetness. It's like giving your taste buds a beach vacation.

BACKUP BEERS: *Big Sky Brewing Company Moose Drool Brown Ale, Good People Brewing Company Brown Ale, Ithaca Beer Company Nut Brown Ale, Long Trail Brewing Co. Harvest, Sixpoint Brewery Brownstone, Tommyknocker Brewery Maple Nut Brown Ale*

the turn of the twentieth century sporting a brand-new look. A brewer named Thomas Wells Thorpe revised the brown ale, creating the dark, sweet, and low-alcohol (just 2.7 percent ABV) Mann's Brown Ale.

Its success took nearly two decades. To save raw ingredients during World War I (and perhaps to decrease drunkenness), the British government began a push toward weaker beers, limiting their strength. The policy had unintended consequences. Strong beers tend to stay fresher longer, whereas lower-strength beers are more prone to spoilage. Draft beer at the pubs was going off, especially the dominant dark mild ale, which took its flavor and hue from roasted malt. ("Mild" merely meant it was fresh and unaged.) To mask the shoddy quality of dark mild, it was mixed with a shelf-stable, unspoiled bottled beer—namely, its natural mate, the brown ale.

Drinkers across the country took to knocking back glasses of "brown and mild," and the rush to brew brown beers was officially afoot. The style's fortunes rose alongside the mild ale for much of the middle stretch of the twentieth century until mild sales started falling in the 1960s. Today, mild sales are merely a blip on Britain's beer radar, but the brown ale soldiers on. In Britain, the style tends to take on a maltier, sweeter, and nuttier edge, as exemplified by Samuel Smith's Nut Brown Ale and,

in the United States, by Fat Gary's Nut Brown Ale from Pittsburgh's East End Brewing Company.

By and large, though, innovation is the hallmark of American brewers' infatuation with brown ales. Stateside examples tend to scale back on malt sweetness, up the hops, and perhaps incorporate some nuts, spices, fruit, or coffee, as in Lost Coast Brewery's Raspberry Brown; Surly Brewing's a.m.-p.m. mash-up, Coffee Bender; and Mississippi's Lazy Magnolia, which adds whole-roasted pecans to its Southern Pecan Nut Brown Ale.

A few pints of these beers and brown could soon be your favorite color.

BALTIC PORTER

Back in the late eighteenth century, the brewers of Great Britain were an industrious, enterprising lot. In addition to keeping their countrymen in the cups with porter, they shipped their dark brews to India and across the chilly Baltic Sea to Scandinavia, Eastern Europe, and Russia. The rich, robust ales (and a stronger version known as Russian stout) were a perfect fit for those dwelling in a cold, snow-covered climate, and porter became so popular in the export markets that brewers there decided to make their own indigenous versions. And here is where Britain is left behind.

During that era, most British breweries embraced top-fermenting ale yeast, which fashions a trademark fruity character. But on the Continent, there was a preference for cold-loving bottom-fermenting lager yeast. Therefore, when brewers in Finland and Russia began to formulate their versions of the import from London, they decided to use lager yeast, and thus was Baltic porter born. (Unintentionally, when porter was being exported to these areas, its journey over the frigid Baltic Sea may have mimicked the cold-conditioning process crucial to making smooth, crisp beer. Today, some breweries still use the ale yeast and ferment the beer at cooler temperatures à la kölsch; see page 79.)

In these modern times, the style still thrives in Baltic Sea–bordering countries such as Poland, Russia, Latvia, and Finland. The brews often display

In the United Kingdom, Newcastle Brown Ale is affectionately nicknamed the Dog. It's a euphemism that comes from a classic excuse in Newcastle for sliding down to a pub to sip a pint of the brown ale: walking the dog.

a lush hue ranging from ruby to dark brown; a malty-sweet scent that recalls toffee, dried fruit, and chocolate; and a smooth roasted flavor dominated by dark malt and a lip-smacking sweetness. The harsh, burned character that sometimes plagues porters should be as restrained as a spy under interrogation in a Baltic porter.

Intrigued by this hybrid style, American brewers have begun to dabble in Baltic porter. You'll find virtuoso performances in Smuttynose Baltic Porter, Flying Dog Brewery Gonzo Imperial Porter, and Ska Brewing Nefarious Ten Pin Imperial Porter, but for your first trip to the Baltic Sea, opt for a European porter.

TWO TO TASTE: BALTIC PORTER

NO. 6 PORTER
BALTIKA BREWERIES
ABV: 7%

SINEBRYCHOFF PORTER
OY SINEBRYCHOFF AB
ABV: 7.2%

One of the pleasures of living in New York City is proximity to ethnic enclaves such as the Russian neighborhood of Atlantic Ocean–fronting Brighton Beach. When the summer sun beats down, bright and blistering, I book it to the beach and cool off with Baltika brews, especially the porter. This may seem counterintuitive, but lagers become less appealing as they warm up. Baltika No. 6 remains sweet and slick, offering black cherries, cocoa, and enough warming alcohol to make me fling myself into the crashing waves.

As you now know, the Baltic porter goes both ways: lager and ale yeast. This Finnish brewery founded by a Russian colonist opts for the top-fermenting route, using the Guinness yeast strain to produce its porter. (The brewery's original yeast strain died during Finland's 1919–1932 Prohibition.) The unfiltered result is blacker than a busted Bic pen, flaunting its opulent chocolate cake aroma and flavors of raisins, figs, and coffee-splashed bittersweet chocolate. The ample booze conceals itself like a chameleon.

BACKUP BEERS: *Flossmoor Station Restaurant & Brewery Killer Kapowski (on draft, it's called Killer Kowalski), Foothills Brewing Company Baltic Porter, Les Trois Mousquetaires Porter Baltique, Lightning Brewery Black Lightning Porter, Uncommon Brewers Baltic Porter, Żywiec Breweries Porter*

WHAT'S OLD IS NEW AGAIN

SHEPHERDING BEER TO A RIPE OLD AGE TAKES TIME AND PATIENCE. BRINGING AN OLD BEER BACK FROM THE DEAD, WELL, THAT'S A MAGIC TRICK WORTH DISCUSSING. BEER STYLES, LIKE CLOTHES AND MUSIC, ARE ALWAYS SLIDING IN AND OUT OF FASHION, TELLING A STORY OF A TIME AND PLACE. SINCE THERE'S NOT A STOREHOUSE STOCKED WITH EXAMPLES OF EVERY BEER EVER MADE, INTREPID SCIENTISTS, RESEARCHERS, AND BREWERS HAVE TAKEN IT UPON THEMSELVES TO FILL EMPTY BOTTLES WITH A TASTE OF THE PAST. HERE ARE A FEW FAVORITE TIME-TRAVELING TIPPLES.

Pretty Things's brewmaster Dann Paquette (right) and rep Jim Barnes get dressed in period-appropriate garb for a Once Upon a Time release.

ONCE UPON A TIME

Beer historian Ron Pattinson digs up bygone recipes and collaborates with husband-wife brewery Pretty Things Beer & Ale Project to revive beers such as the 1832 XXXX Mild Ale and the dry, dark, and happy 1901 KK (*oldbeers.com*). Pattinson also partners with breweries such as Brouwerij de Molen in the Netherlands to create beers such as the London-style 1914 Porter and 1914 Triple Stout SSS.

ANCIENT ALES

In 1999, Delaware's Dogfish Head began working with Dr. Patrick McGovern, an expert in ancient beverages, to breathe new life into dead drinks. The series has included the lightly sweet and fruity Chateau Jiahu, which was based on traces found on 9,000-year-old Chinese pottery. Drinking vessels from King Midas's tomb inspired the floral and graceful Midas Touch. And the Aztec cocoa powder, cocoa nibs, honey, chilis, and annatto seeds of Theobrama ("food of the gods") came about after scientists analyzed shards of Honduran pottery and discovered a chocolate-based alcoholic potion.

PAST MASTERS

Since 1845, the venerable British brewery Fuller's has jotted down every recipe in a brewing book. Today, Fuller's has begun reviving the vintage formulations with its Past Masters series, which has featured the rich and warming XX Strong Ale (first brewed on September 2, 1891) and the creamy, fruity, and chocolaty Double Stout, whose inception dates back to August 4, 1893.

MILK STOUT

If you like a slightly sweeter stout, look toward a category dubbed milk stouts (also called sweet or cream stouts). Instead of half-and-half, the milk in question is lactose, an unfermentable sugar typically found in the dairy product. When added to beer, lactose creates a fuller body and imparts a sweetness that balances out the roasted characteristics.

Milk stout got its start as a literal blending of stout porter (as the stronger stuff was then known) with a healthy pour of milk, which served as a lunchtime reviver to help laborers get through the rest of the day—kind of like the 5-Hour Energy shots of its era. In time, brewers began adding milk directly to the beer during fermentation before nixing it from the formula in favor of lactose. (Since it is unfermentable, it does not provide the yeast with any fuel.)

Milk stout rose to popularity in Great Britain in the early half of the twentieth century, when brewers touted

One of the earliest mentions of milk stout dates to 1875, when a brewer named John Henry Johnson applied for a patent for a beer containing whey, hops, and lactose.

TWO TO TASTE: MILK STOUT

MILK STOUT NITRO
LEFT HAND BREWING CO.
ABV: 6%

Capped under pressure with nitrogen (the gas that gives draft Guinness its creaminess), this stout charges from the bottle with masses of microscopic bubbles that cascade into a thick head that's as sumptuous as an angel's pillow. Expect a luscious creaminess and flavors of roast and milk chocolate. Pro tip: turn the bottle upside down and pour the beer like you're shaking ketchup from a Heinz 57 bottle. I promise you that the beer will rarely foam over.

YOUNG'S DOUBLE CHOCOLATE STOUT
WELLS & YOUNG'S BREWING COMPANY
ABV: 5.2%

Break out the brownies and ice cream when uncapping this British stout with a chocolate flavor so nice they named it twice. A healthy measure of chocolate malt joins forces with bona fide dark chocolate, chocolate essence, and a "special blend of sugars" (shh . . . it's lactose) to create a voluptuous pitch-black potion that surprisingly doesn't taste as sweet as a candy shop. It's silken perfection—if you like chocolate, I mean.

BACKUP BEERS: *Butternuts Beer & Ale Moo Thunder Stout, Hardywood Park Craft Brewery Gingerbread Stout, Keegan Ales Mother's Milk Stout, Lancaster Brewing Company Milk Stout, Tallgrass Brewing Company Buffalo Sweat Stout, Three Floyds Brewing Co. Moloko*

the beer as a nutritious—and sometimes doctor-prescribed—tonic suitable for nursing mothers. (Guinness also was given to breast-feeding moms, hence the stout's nickname: mother's milk.) "Each pint contains the energising carbohydrates of 10 ounces of pure dairy milk," boasted the original label for Mackeson Milk Stout. First brewed in 1907, it was one of the earliest and most enduring examples of milk stout. (The brand now is owned by Anheuser-Busch InBev; a 4.9 percent ABV version brewed in Trinidad and Tobago is known as Mackeson Triple XXX Stout, whereas the Mackeson Stout brewed in the United Kingdom is about 3 percent ABV.)

As the century chugged on, milk stout slowly waned in popularity and in time even lost its descriptive moniker. After a stretch of rationing following World War II, the British government allegedly banned brewers from using the word *milk* in advertisements and labels and hyping stout's healthful properties. The Mackeson brand soon ceased using overt dairy imagery (a famous illustrated advertisement features a manly beer barrel snuggling up to a cooing milk churn), and milk stout simply went under the generalized mantle of sweet stout.

The United States has less rigid restrictions on labeling. Milk stout in the States proudly boasts its dairy-case designation, and brewers have gone

bonkers with the style by adding their own offbeat twists. In Georgia, Terrapin Beer makes Moo-Hoo Chocolate Milk Stout. Mississippi's Lazy Magnolia puts sweet potatoes in its draft-only Jefferson Stout. New Jersey's River Horse adds oats to the mix for its Oatmeal Milk Stout. It's so good, I won't bat an eye if you pour a glass for breakfast.

OATMEAL STOUT

Not long after we're presented with dessert menus at a restaurant, my wife likes to point out my supposed birth defect: "I can't believe you were born without a sweet tooth," she says, her eyes lingering on the double-chocolate volcano cakes I'll never order. Dear readers, it's true: I favor savory eats over sweets, a DNA-programmed preference that also influences my beer-drinking decisions and could explain why I so dearly adore oatmeal stout.

The beer's name is one of those no-duh descriptions. It's a standard-issue stout made special with the addition of oats, which turn a magic trick by creating a creamy and full-bodied lingerie-silky brew without the extra sweetness of lactose. An oatmeal stout is like strong black coffee with a quick shot of half-and-half, hold the sugar. Though oats have always been a key crop in northern England and Scotland—they're a major ingredient in haggis—brewers did not start adding

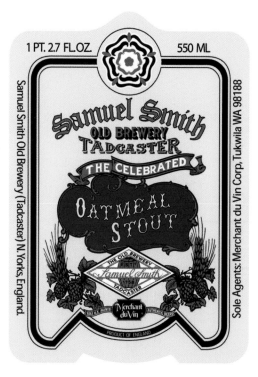

oats to stouts en masse until the early twentieth century in response to the rise in popularity of milk stout.

Catering to the changing consumer palate, oats added a tinge of appealing sweetness, but their primary role was to massage mouthfeel and add

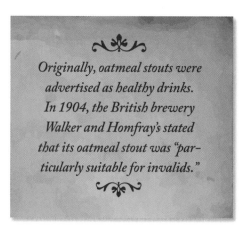

Originally, oatmeal stouts were advertised as healthy drinks. In 1904, the British brewery Walker and Homfray's stated that its oatmeal stout was "particularly suitable for invalids."

layers of complexity. Like milk stout, the oatmeal variant was a popular British quaff through World War II, when its popularity fell off the deep end. By the disco-loving 1970s, the style was as good as dead, but in 1980, Samuel Smith dug it up from the grave. The brewery released Oatmeal Stout, giving the style a new heartbeat and spurring other British brewers, and in time American brewers, to play with the breakfast-friendly grain.

Today, it's tough to toss a rock at a beer store and not hit an oatmeal stout. From California, you'll find Lost Coast Brewery's 8 Ball Stout and Firestone Walker's Velvet Merlin (see box below), and Saint Louis Brewery serves up Schlafly Oatmeal Stout and Massachusetts's Ipswich Ale Brewery makes the velvety Oatmeal Stout. Thanks to this revival, sowing your oats has taken on a delicious new meaning.

At first, Firestone Walker called its oatmeal stout the Velvet Merkin, referencing the pubic wig that prostitutes once wore after shaving off all their hair, well, down there. A slight case of moralistic outrage led the brewery to change the name to Velvet Merlin.

TWO TO TASTE: OATMEAL STOUT

WOLAVER'S OATMEAL STOUT
WOLAVER'S FINE ORGANIC ALES
ABV: 5.9%

Here's my spiel on organic beer. All the ecologically appropriate, sustainably raised ingredients in the world won't amount to bupkis if a brewer makes crappy beer. Vermont-based Wolaver's does not. The oatmeal stout, the brewery's first foray into dark beer, is blacker than an Exxon oil spill and is anointed with a creamy head seemingly dispensed from a Reddi-wip can. The taste: smooth sailing across a sea of nuts, espresso, and bittersweet chocolate.

OATIS OATMEAL STOUT
NINKASI BREWING COMPANY
ABV: 7.2%

Named after the Sumerian beer goddess, Ninkasi is the proud product of Eugene, Oregon, and, thanks to brewer Jamie Floyd's no-hops-spared approach, one of the fastest growing breweries on the West Coast. The Total Domination IPA and Tricerahops Double IPA are already classics, but I dig Oatis, a creamy oatmeal stout that's as smooth as silk sheets in a honeymoon suite. It's bigger than most oatmeal stouts, with a nice bitter ballast and plenty of roast and chocolate to lead you to a dry finish line.

BACKUP BEERS: *Anderson Valley Brewing Company Barney Flats Oatmeal Stout, McAuslan Brewing St-Ambroise Oatmeal Stout, Oakshire Brewing Company Overcast Espresso Stout, Samuel Smith Old Brewery Oatmeal Stout, Short's Brewing Company Short's Brew Über Goober Imperial Oatmeal Stout*

TWO TO TASTE: FOREIGN EXTRA STOUT

LION STOUT
LION BREWERY LIMITED
ABV: 8%

Lion's outsize strength doesn't disrupt its nimble balance. The Sri Lankan–born king of the jungle pours out like liquefied obsidian, flaunting a healthy brown head with a nose of creamy mocha coffee. The flavor calls to mind rich chocolate milk—full fat, none of this skim nonsense—with notes of figs and licorice and a smooth, medium-bodied drinkability that hides the beer's boozy depth charge. This Lion may roar, but it won't bite.

EXTRA EXPORT STOUT
BROUWERIJ DE DOLLE BROUWERS
ABV: 9%

Brewers usually march to their own drumbeat, but this export stout was created upon the request of B. United International, the importers for this rustic Belgian brewery. De Dolle's small-batch pleasures include the Dulle Teve tripel, the strong and dark Oerbier, and this well-fizzed, extra-strong export stout. It's tart, dry, and as bitter as a traitor's kiss, with appealing flavors of black licorice and deeply roasted coffee.

BACKUP BEERS: *Alameda Brewing Co. Black Bear XX Stout, Coopers Brewery Best Extra Stout, Desnoes & Geddes Limited Dragon Stout, Guinness Foreign Extra Stout, Snake River Brewing Zonker Stout*

FOREIGN EXTRA STOUT

A couple years back, I found myself at a Ghanaian restaurant in Brooklyn called Meytex Lounge. Beyond fufu, fish, and plenty of stews, the spot's specialty was black-market African beer such as South African Breweries' sweet, coffee-accented Castle Milk Stout and gluggable Gulder Lager. But the brew I liked best was the Guinness Foreign Extra Stout.

What's the difference between FES and the pint you can get at an Irish pub? Unlike rich, creamy classic Guinness, the FES was created for export to hot tropical countries. To survive the journey, the stronger, more potent FES (7.5 percent ABV) is highly hopped and packs an emphatically roasty character. If regular Guinness were a cup of diner coffee, FES would be a double shot of espresso. It's not for fainthearted drinkers. It pours brownish black with a thick tan head. On the nose, the aroma recalls a coffee-roasting plant, and the full-bodied flavor is a bit like biting into a chunk

Guinness Foreign Export Stout was exported to the United States from 1817 to 1920, when Prohibition put the kibosh on it. Shipments resumed only in 2010.

of bittersweet chocolate. It's intense yet smooth, packing a hoppy bitterness that lingers like the finest tongue-coating IPA. (Much like the Baltic porter, the export countries exposed to the FES eventually started making their own versions, especially in the Caribbean.)

To my palate, the foreign extra stout (or export stout, if that floats your boat) treads a pretty fine line alongside the massive Russian imperial stout. But when pressed for a distinction, I'd say foreign export stouts are like turbocharged versions of milk stout or dry stout or maybe a less hop-aromatic imperial stout. The ones sold in tropical countries, such as Sri Lanka's Lion Stout and Jamaica's Dragon Stout, tend to lean toward the sweeter side of the conversation, whereas other versions, such as Seattle's Pike Street XXXXX Stout, tend to be drier and a bit more assertively bitter.

One taste of these brews, and what's foreign will soon be familiar.

AMERICAN STOUT

American stout is the end result of evolution and inspiration. Just as England's slightly sour porter begat Ireland's dry stout, American brewers use the Irish invention as a stepping-stone to create stouts that disobey easy categorization.

American stouts usually share a roasted character, perhaps recalling coffee or bittersweet chocolate, plus a pitch-black tint that could verge on dark brown like

TWO TO TASTE: AMERICAN STOUT

ORGANIC SURVIVAL 7-GRAIN STOUT
HOPWORKS URBAN BREWERY
ABV: 5.3%
~

Hewn from barley, wheat, oats, amaranth, quinoa, spelt, and kamut (the namesake seven grains), Survival pours as black as a funeral shroud, offset by creamy mocha foam. It smells of cocoa and strong, dark-roasted coffee—the beer is finished with cold-pressed organic Holler Mountain coffee from the cult roaster Stumptown. There's ample roasted java piloting the flavor profile, but Survival remains as rich and as silky as an angel's robe, with hops providing a nicely bittersweet close. I could happily live on Survival for days.

TRES BLUEBERRY STOUT
DARK HORSE BREWING CO.
ABV: VARIES
~

I was reared in the Midwest, a land of hot summers and brutal, unrelenting winters for which the only salve is sipping mass quantities of beer as dark as the December sky. To combat seasonal depression, Michigan's Dark Horse devised a quintet of stouts, each of which I recommend. There's an oatmeal stout, a cream stout, a smoked stout, an imperial stout, and, most deliciously, a blueberry stout. Like a DNA experiment gone deliciously right, the fruit intertwines with flavors of chocolate and roast malt, resulting in a most unusual, most wonderful hybrid.

BACKUP BEERS: *Avery Brewing Company Out of Bounds Stout, Bar Harbor Brewing Company Cadillac Mountain Stout, Mad River Brewing Company Steelhead Extra Stout, Maine Beer Company Mean Old Tom, Sierra Nevada Brewing Co. Stout*

a well-loved football. (A handy rule of thumb for telling a stout from a porter is the pronounced presence of roasted barley's trademark dry, assertive, coffee-like bitterness.) The alcohol content may skyrocket up to 6 or 7 percent ABV, but it also can hover around 4 or 5 percent. There's no target brewers are trying to hit. Instead, it's as if they've been given carte blanche and told simply, "Make a dark and delicious beer."

To answer that directive, brewers have opened up an arsenal of additives. For its Chicory Stout, Dogfish Head relies on Mexican coffee, roasted chicory, licorice root, and even the supposedly mood-improving herb Saint-John's-wort, and Twisted Pine Brewing Company in Colorado and Lakefront Brewery in Milwaukee amp up the style's inherent coffee qualities in their respective offerings, Big Shot Espresso Stout and Fuel Cafe. (Coffee-infused stouts are a particularly eye-opening trend.) In Michigan, Bell's Brewery composes Cherry Stout from locally grown Montmorency cherries. Like chocolate? You're in luck with California-based Bison Brewing's Organic Chocolate Stout and Brooklyn Brewery's Black Chocolate Stout. Heck, even hopheads can find their favorite floral, citrus aroma profile in Rise American Stout from Chicago's Revolution Brewing.

Name a favorite flavor and you're likely to find it highlighted in a stout. The two at the left can get you started.

IMPERIAL STOUT

In modern craft brewing, one of the most popular adjectives bandied about is *imperial*. Whether attached to a hoppy IPA, a crisp pilsner, or a malty red ale, the descriptor's presence announces that a beer is brawny, a beefcake bursting at the bottle cap with extra alcohol and flavor. Bigger is better, an imperial ale seems to imply, a sentiment echoed on best-of beer lists that are often disproportionately weighted toward brews that'll get you drunk on the double.

To pinpoint this trend's inception, we must turn our bleary eyes back to the eighteenth century, an era in which British brewers earned scads of shillings selling porters to the thirsty citizens of Russia. Among the fans of this darker ale was the Russian royal court. As is often the case with the wealthy and powerful, the Russian royalty demanded the finest brew, with *best* equated with *strongest*. In the 1760s, London's Anchor Brewery (owned by the noted Thrale brewing family) obliged, sending over a stout—the term used to describe the most potent porters—of dizzying strength. According to legend, Catherine the Great adored this beefed-up brew, and it continued to be exported to Russia. (Thrale's later was bought by the British brewery Barclay, Perkins & Co., which eventually merged with the Courage Brewery. Until production ceased in 1993, the brewery continued to make what was known as Courage Russian Imperial Stout. Happily, the British brewer Wells & Young's revived the brand in 2011.)

Since the birth of the Russian imperial stout, or just the imperial stout (though some may say otherwise, to me they're one and the same), the style has seen its star wax and wane. As the twentieth century began creaking to a close, the imperial stout was seemingly a goner, another ale relegated to the history books. But in the 1980s, at Yakima Brewing and Malting Co., Pacific Northwest brewing pioneer Bert Grant developed an imperial stout that sent drinkers into a tizzy. Though the dark brew tipped the scales at a relatively diminutive 6 percent ABV, the stout's significant bitterness helped create the template for the American-style imperial stout, one of the signature sips of the extreme-beer movement.

Today's imperial stout is a thoroughly American creature. It's a massive work of art, as dark as a lunar eclipse

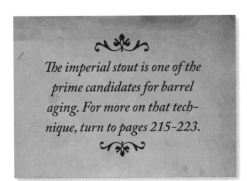

The imperial stout is one of the prime candidates for barrel aging. For more on that technique, turn to pages 215–223.

and more often than not offering a double-barreled blast of bitterness to complement and balance the roasted accents, the chocolaty flavors, and an ABV that often floats above the 10 percent ceiling. Come snowman season, the imperial stout is a linchpin in breweries' lineups, and picking just one to taste is as tough as parents picking their favorite kids. (Hey, Mom and Dad, it's me, right?) And truth be told, you'll probably be equally thrilled if you crack open a readily available Bear Republic Brewing Co. Big Bear Black Stout or a rare bottle of Three Floyds Dark Lord Imperial Stout, a beer so revered that its release demands a daylong celebration (see the box below). Go on, give in to the dark side.

Once a year, Indiana's Three Floyds opens up its brewery to throw Dark Lord Day, a bands-and-beer bash celebrating the release of its cultish Dark Lord Imperial Stout. Some of America's most lusted-after craft beers are imperial stouts. Raucous, highly attended release parties surround the annual debut of Surly Brewing Co.'s Darkness, The Bruery's Black Tuesday, Cigar City Brewing's Hunahpu's Imperial Stout, and Foothills Brewing's Sexual Chocolate Imperial Stout.

TWO TO TASTE: IMPERIAL STOUT

OLD RASPUTIN RUSSIAN IMPERIAL STOUT
NORTH COAST BREWING CO.
ABV: 9%

I'll bet anyone a hot bowl of borscht that ruble for ruble, you won't find a more delectable, affordable Russian imperial stout than Old Rasputin. Rasputin is blacker than a raven lost in a coal mine and smells like Raisinets doing the backstroke in a double espresso. There's more bitterness than you'd expect, and you'll gladly, and greedily, drain every inky drop. Seriously, it's one of the best bargains in craft beer.

YETI IMPERIAL STOUT
GREAT DIVIDE BREWING COMPANY
ABV: 9.5%

Let me tell you about the yeti, the ape-like Abominable Snowman supposed to prowl the Himalayas. That's a lie. It's found in snowy Denver, Colorado, where the beast is actually an imperial stout that'll climb atop your tongue and pummel it with roast malt, caramel, and toffee before unleashing its hop bite. P.S. If you like the Yeti, try the different variations Great Divide offers— Belgian-Style Yeti, Oak Aged Yeti, Barrel Aged Yeti, Espresso Oak Aged Yeti, and Chocolate Oak Aged Yeti. All are tremendous.

BACKUP BEERS: *AleSmith Brewing Company Speedway Stout, Kern River Brewing Company Class V Stout, Ölvisholt Brugghús Lava, Oskar Blues Brewery Ten Fidy Imperial Stout, Stone Brewing Co. Imperial Russian Stout, Thirsty Dog Brewing Company Siberian Night Imperial Stout*

STOUT CELEBRATION

SOMETIMES THE MERE PRESENCE OF THESE DARK BEERS IS REASON ENOUGH TO CELEBRATE. HERE ARE SEVERAL STOUT BASHES WORTH YOUR TIME.

INTERNATIONAL STOUT DAY

stoutday.com

On a single day in November, bars, breweries, and restaurants around the globe join forces to fete the stout, featuring events ranging from beer-and-chocolate pairings to rare cask ale tappings and special stout releases.

STOUT MONTH AT FORT GEORGE BREWERY & PUBLIC HOUSE

Astoria, Oregon

fortgeorgebrewery.com

For this well-regarded brewery, dark and dreary February marks a "celebration of a beer style that is not just a strong porter." Each year, the brewers cook up stouts with offbeat ingredients such as hot peppers, smoked black walnuts, and butternut and acorn squash.

THE ABYSS RELEASE AT DESCHUTES BREWERY

Portland and Bend, Oregon

deschutesbrewery.com

To celebrate the fall debut of this imperial stout brewed with licorice and molasses and partly aged in oak and bourbon barrels, Deschutes holds rollicking daylong parties at its pubs in Bend and

Portland. Expect Abyss-infused food and rare vintage vertical tastings. For once, blacking out is encouraged.

STOUT MONTH AT MOUNTAIN SUN PUB & BREWERY

Boulder and Denver, Colorado

mountainsunpub.com

Since 1994, Colorado's medal-winning Mountain Sun has marked February as its annual stout month. At the brewery's trio of pubs, you'll find oodles of ebony elixirs such as the Cherry Dip Stout, the hoppy Trickster Stout, and scads of imperial stouts. The celebration also features its Stout Homebrew Competition.

JOHNNY BRENDA'S ANNUAL STOUT BRUNCH

Philadelphia, Pennsylvania

johnnybrendas.com

Every March, the combination rocker dive, restaurant, craft-beer bar, and concert venue opens its doors at 11 a.m. and rolls out a roster of dark, luscious stouts partnered with oysters and a full Irish breakfast.

IMPERIAL STOUT FESTIVAL AT BEER REVOLUTION

Oakland, California

beer-revolution.com

It's all punk rock all the time at Oakland's finest sticker-covered craft beer bar, which for its March fest dedicates most of its 47 meticulously curated drafts to the sobriety-alleviating pleasures of imperial stouts. A word to the wise: arrive via mass transit, not in an automobile.

NEW HOLLAND BREWING

PILGRIM'S DOLE
WHEATWINE ALE
ALE AGED IN BOURBON BARRELS
The High Gravity Series from
NEW HOLLAND
BREWING

HAIR OF THE DOG
BREWING COMPANY
FAMILY · CRAFT · FRIENDS
PORTLAND OREGON

1 PINT 6 FL

SMUTTYNOSE Co.
BREWING

- The Smuttynose Big
Beer Series: big beers
in big bottles, released
seasonally in very
limited qu...

...ND CA

...NDERBUSS
BARLEYWINE

CBC

D. & BOTTLED BY SMUTTYNOSE B...
...TSMOUTH, NH · WWW...

The Smuttynose BIG BEER Ser

Wheat Wine Ale

MALT BEVERAGE BREWED FROM 53% WHEAT, 47% BARLEY

...MENT WARNING: (1) ACCORDING TO THE SURGEON GENE...
...ES DURING PREGNANCY BECAUSE OF TH...
...S IMPAIRS YOUR ABILIT...

J.W. LEES
MANCHESTER
BREWERS SINCE 1828

HARVEST
ALE 2006
VINTAGE LIMITED EDITION

11.5% vol

THE ORKNEY BREWERY

Skull Splitter

THE AUTHENTIC ORCADIAN ALE
HAND CRAFTED IN SMALL BATCHES

THE ORKNEY BREWERY

GEBRAUT NACH DEM BAYR. REINHEITSGEBOT
WEIZEN-EISBOCK

AVENTINUS
WEIZEN
EISBOCK

APPEARANCE
A crystal-clear, rich tawny-red colour beer; a tight,
smooth head with hints of red and amber colour

AROMA
Juicy, almost fruity malt character, together with a
medley of fresh and dried fruits, dates and figs, hints
of ginger and cinnamon spice, hints of vanilla

PALATE
A rich, fruity, wine-like complexity on the palate
includes fresh and dried fruits, warm exotic spices,
and light summer citrus fruits

KEY INGREDIENTS
Very best pale ale malt – and plenty of it – together
with crystal and chocolate malts provide a rich, fruity
backbone which is perfectly balanced by the spicy
herbal character of East Kent Goldings hops

Bottle UPC - 7 98100 50012 3

SKULL SPLITTER IS OUR STRONGEST ALE, WHICH IS NAMED AFTER THORFINN EINARSSON WHO WAS THE
7TH VIKING EARL OF ORKNEY. SOPHISTICATED, SATINY SMOOTH WITH A DECEPTIVELY LIGHT CHARACTER,
IT IS A TRIBUTE TO OUR COLOURFUL FORBEAR. ON THE NOSE, THIS STRONG BEER HAS A FRUITY MALT
CHARACTER, WITH HINTS OF DARK FRUIT, SPICY HOP, DATES AND FIGS. ON THE PALATE, RICH AND COMPLEX
WITH SWEET TOASTED MALT, MOLASSES, FRESH AND DRIED FRUIT AND HINTS OF WARMING SPICES.

ST KILLIAN
IMPORTING
WORLD CLASS ALES & LAGERS
EST. 1983

CURE FOR THE COLD

BARLEY WINES AND OTHER
WINTER WARMERS

THE PLEASURES OF WINTER TEND to lessen as childhood leaves you in the rearview mirror. A blustery blizzard is no longer a day off from school but instead is a backbreaking date with a shovel. Cold snaps are not an excuse to recline on a couch with bad TV but a reason to fret about the furnace. Yes, hot chocolate is a wintertime tradition that cuts across all ages, but sometimes—pardon me, *often*—we require something stronger to survive this subfreezing season. For this, I look to the belly-heating pleasures of barley wine, which may be the English language's most delicious oxymoron.

Trust me: this barley wine will warm you up.

People park in the driveway. They drive on the parkway. To this list, I'll add barley wine, which contains no grapes. In fact, this type of ale shares few attributes with fermented grape juice save for an alcohol percentage that typically climbs into double digits. Barley wines match that brawn with big flavors. Some are fruity. Some are bitter. Others are aged in oak. Above all, these beers are thick and warming, providing the liquid courage to dig out the driveway yet again.

Like IPA, barley wine was born centuries ago in Britain. Over time the beer lost its luster and started sliding into irrelevance. Following the same script as they did with hoppy ale, American brewers took a shine to the style and tweaked the ratios and ingredients. They gave this potent British ale an appealingly bitter edge, a new lease on carbonated life, and a crucial wintertime role: the beer world's Saint Bernard. When you sip a barley wine, pay close attention to the complex flavors and the way they evolve as the beer warms up. Here's the scoop on this fine (not) wine.

A BRITISH BEGINNING

Grab a cold beer, climb into my time machine, and travel with me to eighteenth- and nineteenth-century Britain. During that era, the British Isles and Europe were filled with farmhouse breweries that crammed their brew kettles with barley malt and, in a process called parti-gyle brewing, made multiple beers from the same

TRADEMARK

grains. (The technique has since fallen out of favor, and modern breweries use unique grain bills for each separate beer.) It might be helpful to think of parti-gyle brewing as a penny-pinching grandma reusing a tea bag: the first batch is the strongest, and each subsequent hot-water plunge creates a progressively weaker beverage.

The first running, or wort, contained the lion's share of fermentable sugars, which yeasts convert into alcohol. The second batch resulted in a "common beer," and if enough residual sugars remained, a third running resulted in what was called "small."

The less-potent beers were consumed first, as they spoiled faster. But the stronger first runnings had staying power. They were socked away for a later date, as their elevated ABVs prevented spoilage.

Now comes a bit of conjecture: in either a game of one-upmanship with fellow brewers or perhaps to safeguard the ales against spoiling, British beer makers kept enhancing their beers' alcohol levels.

Achieving that was no easy shakes. Just like people, yeast loses its ability to function properly in high levels of alcohol. To shake the fungi from their drunken slumber, the brewing staff would roll beer barrels around the brewery or even pump oxygen through the liquid. Thus awakened, the yeast continued to work its slow and steady microscopic magic. The extended fermentation and aging process worked wonders, mellowing out barley wines—crucial for a high-alcohol beer—and creating layers of intricate, multifaceted flavors as fine as anything fermented from a grapevine.

If you strolled into a bar in the 1800s and asked for a barley wine, you'd be met by a puzzled look. These beefy brews (which occasionally were mixed with weaker beers to impart complexity) went by several wine-averse aliases—strong ales, winter warmers, stock ales, old ales—or, quite commonly, they simply were marked by multiple Xs branded into a wooden barrel. Were all these examples of what we today consider to be barley wines? Not at all, but they were strong enough to make your eyes spin. In fact, the term *barley wine* wasn't used commercially until at least 1903, when what is now Bass Brewers Limited released its Bass No. 1 Barley Wine. In advertisements in medical journals, Bass deemed its "royal tonic" suitable for nursing mothers and diseases ranging from indigestion to insomnia, anemia, and "leanness."

Anchor Brewing uses the second runnings from its Old Foghorn barley wine to make the lighter, low-alcohol Anchor Small.

BASS STOPPED *producing barley wine* IN 1995.

For a deep dive into the style, try reading Fai Allen and Dick Cantwell's terrific Barley Wine: History, Brewing Techniques, Recipes. *FYI: Cantwell is cofounder and head brewer at Seattle's excellent Elysian Brewing Company.*

ENGLISH-STYLE BARLEY WINE

Over time, barley wines in Britain lost their luster. Much like today's malt liquor, barley wines were marketed more for their booziness than for their flavor, and even the iconic Bass No. 1 was discontinued. It's understandable. Barley wines' heavy malt bill makes them more expensive to brew, and British beers are taxed on alcohol content, dissuading breweries from devising stronger beers. Despite these obstacles, the brawny style endures, albeit with diminished popularity, in British breweries such as J.W. Lees and Ridgeway, and American breweries such as Pennsylvania's Weyerbacher (Blithering Idiot) and Oregon's Pelican Pub & Brewery (Mother of All Storms) also follow the malty English model.

Generally speaking, snifter-fit English barley wines range in hue from copper pennies to shoe-polish brown, and they present fruity aromas and, typically, scaled-back bitterness. British barley wines are rounded and balanced, and they may be less boozy and bitter than their Yankee counterparts. No surprise there: the United States does brash and bold best.

AMERICAN-STYLE BARLEY WINE

In the United States, few beer drinkers had laid their paws on a barley wine until 1975, when San Francisco's Anchor

TWO TO TASTE: ENGLISH-STYLE BARLEY WINE

VINTAGE HARVEST ALE
J.W. LEES & CO.
ABV: 11.5%

What comes once a year? Your birthday and the December 1 release of J.W. Lees's Vintage Harvest Ale. The annual elixir is hewn from that season's barley and hops yield, resulting in an ale as smooth as a silk tie with a flavor profile that calls to mind whiskey topped off with toffee, brown sugar, and maple syrup.

CRIMINALLY BAD ELF
RIDGEWAY BREWING
ABV: 10.5%

There's no shortage of Christmas cheer—or is it jeer?—at this British brewery, which turns out mischievous holiday ales such as Pickled Santa, Reindeer's Revolt, and Criminally Bad Elf. This naughty copper-colored barley wine has a nice nose of apples and roasted caramel as well as a creamy texture touched by honey, plums, and a hot hit of booze.

BACKUP BEERS: *Arcadia Ales Cereal Killer Barleywine Ale, Flat Earth Brewing Co. Winter Warlock Golden English Barley-Wine Ale, Fuller, Smith & Turner P.L.C. Fuller's Vintage Ale, Heavy Seas Beer Below Decks Barleywine Style Ale, Olde Hickory Brewery Irish Walker Barley-Wine Style Ale, Pretty Things Beer & Ale Project Our Finest Regards*

TWO TO TASTE: AMERICAN-STYLE BARLEY WINE

BIGFOOT BARLEYWINE-STYLE ALE
Sierra Nevada Brewing Co.
ABV: 9.6%

Unlike its stealthy and mythical namesake, Sierra's Bigfoot is a common, uncommonly elegant creature. The rust-tinged brew presents a fruity perfume and a malt sweetness that is cinched in restraints by an emphatically bitter streak. When aged, the beer grows more balanced as the hops recede into the background. Its ubiquity makes it a cellaring favorite.

XS OLD CRUSTACEAN BARLEYWINE
Rogue Ales
ABV: 11.5%

This ruby-tinged ale's aromatic catnip consists of caramel, toffee, and lovely citrus—no surprise considering how it is IBU'd to the nines with Chinook, Perle, and Centennial hops. Luscious currents of raisins and brown sugar balance Crustacean's bitterness. P.S. The swing-top bottle is a keeper, too.

BACKUP BEERS: *Avery Brewing Co. Hog Heaven Dry-Hopped Barleywine Style Ale, Boulder Beer Killer Penguin Barleywine, Rock Art Brewery The Vermonster, Santa Fe Brewing Co. Chicken Killer Barley Wine Ale, Uinta Brewing Company Anniversary Barley Wine Ale, Victory Brewing Company Old Horizontal Barleywine Style Ale*

Brewing released Old Foghorn Barleywine Style Ale. It explored new territory, relying on a large load of flowery Cascade hops, one of the defining flavors of American pale ales and IPAs. And there the fence was built. American and some Canadian brewers' heavy hand with hops—while keeping the klieg lights on malt, unlike an imperial IPA—became the defining element of the Stateside style, which has caught fire like kindling in a hearth.

For example, Hair of the Dog Brewing Co.'s Doggie Claws displays 70 IBUs and an 11.5 percent ABV, Rogue Ales's XS Old Crustacean registers more than 100 IBUs and an 11.5 percent ABV, and Full Sail Brewing's Old Boardhead Barleywine Ale flaunts 91 IBUs and 9 percent ABV. Take down a 22-ounce bottle and it's lights out for you and your taste buds. (To be fair, lofty ABVs require scads of hops to make the sweetness even–steven.)

Owing to the inclusion of Pacific Northwest–grown Simcoe and Centennial hops, Hair of the Dog says Doggie Claws is made in the "West Coast style." Don't worry about splitting hairs to distinguish between East Coast and West Coast barley wines.

Nonetheless, you can't categorize North American barley wines as hulking hops monsters. Some have spicy aspects, such as Real Ale Brewing Company's rye-driven Sisyphus Barleywine Style Ale. For its Corps Mort, Quebec's Microbrasserie À l'abri de la Tempête uses smoked barley that provides that caramel-sticky ale with a Scotch-like complexity. In its Odd Beers for Odd Years program, Stone Brewing tweaks the recipe for its Old Guardian Barley Wine (and the Imperial Russian Stout). The 2011 release, Old Guardian Belgo, was made with a Belgian yeast strain that imparted banana notes that quirkily complemented the toffee flavors, bitterness, and warming 12 percent ABV. Like Bass's barley wine of yore, consider it a royal tonic to help you greet Old Man Winter with a grin.

On American bottles the beer is labeled as "barley wine–style ale." That's because the Alcohol and Tobacco Tax and Trade Bureau does not want to mislead retailers or consumers into believing they're buying wine.

* * *

Barley wines are usually released only in the winter, but if you see one sitting in a cooler, buy it. This style is tamed by the ravages of time (see page 291).

A MATTER OF AGE

As a teenager, I was a bitter hothead with rough edges that would take years to sand down—kind of like a barley wine. Let me clarify. Every barley wine you pluck from a shelf is ready to drink; no brewery releases a beer that does not meet its exacting standards. In fact, some breweries *demand* that you drink them on the double. "We make our barley wine with the intention that it should be enjoyed right away," says Paul Philippon, the philosophy professor turned founder of Farmville, North Carolina's Duck-Rabbit Craft Brewery (see page 180 for more on Duck-Rabbit). "I always feel like beer is for drinking, not saving."

Nonetheless, some barley wines do well given time to mature. Take the Flying Mouflan from Pennsylvania's Tröegs Brewing Company. Instead of in the dead of winter, this ruby-brown brew that's bazooka-blasted with Chinook, Warrior, and Simcoe hops is released in the spring. The brewers recommend cellaring the barley wine for at least four months, letting the alcohol heat and the hops calm down (aromatic intensity will diminish over time). On bottles of Deschutes Brewery's Mirror Mirror barley wine, as with all its Reserve Series releases, there's a "best after" date recommending that you wait before cracking the wax-sealed cap. My advice: buy several bottles of your favorite barley wine and consign them to your cellar for several months or even years. Good things come to those who wait. (For more information on aging, see page 287.)

(For more information on aging, see page 287.)

GOING GRAPE

Barley and grapes aren't mortal enemies. I like to think of them as unlikely lovers, sort of like the chihuahua and the corgi that were parents to my handsome mutt, Sammy. Brewers have begun adding grapes to their ingredient list, creating hybrids with new dimensions of flavor that may appeal to both beer lovers and wine diehards. Unlike brewers using oak barrels that once contained, say, Syrah or Chardonnay, grapes are an integral part of the brewing process, serving as fermentable fuel for yeast and bridging the gap between a vine and a bine. Blue Moon Vintage Blonde Ale is made with Chardonnay juice, and Cascade Brewing's tangy The Vine Northwest Style Sour Ale is refermented with the juice of white wine grapes. Muscat grapes have made appearances in Avery Brewing's one-off Muscat d'Amour Barrel-Aged Wild Ale and Cantillon's rare Vigneronne, and Dogfish Head's Noble Rot gets two infusions of unfermented grape juice, including viognier grapes infected with botrytis fungus. If you stumble across a bottle, I suggest sipping it from a wineglass.

HAIR OF THE DOG BREWING COMPANY
PORTLAND, OREGON

Most breweries launch with three, four, or even five different styles of beer, such as a bitter IPA, a roasty stout, a crisp lager, and a mellow pale ale. Present drinkers with enough options and perhaps they'll find a beer that tickles their taste buds, drawing them back for another pint.

Alan Sprints did not care for variety. He debuted Hair of the Dog in November 1993 with a single beer that even today would seem eccentric: Adam, a historic re-creation of an ale popular in Dortmund, Germany— in the nineteenth century (see page 67). Weighing in at 10 percent ABV, Adam was dark, bitter, and opulent, with wisps of cocoa, smoke, and leather. This was an all-in bet on an oddball.

"Only having one beer made it more difficult," Sprints admits, "but Adam remains one of our most popular beers today." Building on the success of Adam, Sprints has over several decades created a lineup of new, unusual, rather strong, or barrel-aged styles of bottle-conditioned beer, many of which are linked

to people in his life. Beer writer and historian Fred Eckhardt inspired Fred, a strong golden ale made with rye and 10 different hop varieties. Sprints's mother was the namesake for Lila the lager, and his grandma Ruth became an aromatic American pale ale. Celebrated beer writer Michael Jackson was reborn as a sour Flanders red-style ale that naps for 30 months in oak and sherry casks. Blue Dot is an appealingly pungent unfiltered double IPA named after our planet and brewed in honor of Earth Day. Then there's Doggie Claws, a barley wine with a canine-worthy bite.

A FOREIGN EDUCATION

Sprints came of beer-drinking age in the 1970s, a light and fizzy time for American imbibers. In search of character, he turned to European imports before furthering his liquid education in the 1980s with Sierra Nevada and Anchor Steam. But it wasn't until he moved to Oregon in 1988 to attend Portland's Western Culinary Institute (now Le Cordon Bleu College of Culinary Arts) that a beer career seemed plausible.

That year marked the first annual Oregon Brewers Festival, an imagination-igniting event that led Sprints to join the Oregon Brew Crew (a local homebrew club), where he eventually served as its three-time president. During that stint, Sprints met a number of brewing pioneers, later landing a job at Portland's Widmer Brothers Brewing. He toiled there from 1991 until 1993, when his Hair of the Dog journey began.

Though Sprints brews beautiful pale ales and double IPAs, it's his stronger beers that have earned him loads of laurels. In 1995, he created Eve, a version of Adam that was frozen, resulting in a stronger, richer elixir with hefty sweetness and alcohol.

"Adam and Eve were made to educate people about the possibility of beer," Sprints says. "We had

people try them after they sampled our other beers. They blur the line between beer and cordials."

The next year Sprints debuted Dave, which was frozen three times, with the ice removed until the ABV reached a robust 29 percent. Dave proved so popular that in 1998 it won first place at San Francisco's vaunted Toronado Barleywine Festival (see page 213), and it eventually was bottled in ultrasmall batches. (At an online auction in 2008, five bottles sold for $2,838.30.) Sprints did not enter Dave in 1999. "It's not really a barley wine, but an eisbock" he explains of the beer.

To fix that, in 2000 Sprints dialed up draft-only Fido, a West Coast barley wine employing piney Simcoe and intensely citrusy Amarillo hops, plus wildflower honey from Mount Hood. It did not win first place at the Toronado festival, but Sprints sensed he had a winner. The next year, he changed its name to Doggie Claws, bottled it, and created an annual wintertime tradition. (The label features a bulldog clad in a Santa cap

surrounded by menorahs.) Doggie is grand fresh but should improve with age—if you can buy a bottle.

THERE'S A LIMIT

Sprints brews only about 500 cases of Doggie Claws annually, and his other libations are also limited. Using the brewery's first—and only—brew kettle, Sprints and his sole assistant pump out 120 gallons of beer at a time, to the tune of about 600 barrels a year. Considering that many craft breweries brew *thousands* of barrels of a single beer, that's an incredibly minute amount. "I'm one of the few breweries not intent on expanding," says Sprints, who still writes label copy and decides on bottle artwork. "If we can be profitable and pay our employees a good wage, then we're doing well."

Sprints accomplishes this by running a tasting room that offers draft-only beers, such as the Little Dog series of beers made from the second, or weaker, runnings of strong beers, including Adam, Doggie Claws, and Fred. Plus, Sprints slices out the middleman and does an annual direct-to-consumer anniversary dock sale every November, releasing rare barrel-aged and vintage beers.

"I make more money on the beer I produce instead of producing more beer," Sprints says of the sales, which also underscore his other Hair of the Dog mission statement: aging beers. Sprints regularly sets aside 40 cases of certain releases and has more than 1,000 cases of vintage beers, encompassing hundreds of batches, in reserve. "I'm able to prove that for beers, aging 10 or 20 years is not a long time," he says. "Our beers have staying power."

My advice: Buy Adam, Fred, or Doggie Claws and in a decade make a bottle a holiday present to yourself.

Hair of the Dog's founder and brewmaster Alan Sprints specializes in strong, bottle-conditioned beer.

MORE STOMACH-STOKING BEERS WORTH SAMPLING

Barley wines do not have a lockdown on wintertime drinking. From concentrated eisbocks to smoky Scotch ales, here are several more brawny styles to seek out when the mercury takes a nosedive.

WHEAT WINE

Barley wines are not immune to brewer experimentation. One of my favorite twists is the relatively recently created wheat wine. Barley wine's heady richness is cut with a large percentage of wheat, which imparts a softer, rounder mouthfeel to the ale as well as a touch of tartness. Wheat wines often are finished with a healthy measure of hops, imparting a bright flavor punch not traditionally found in the standard caramel-heavy barley wine.

The style's inception was the fortuitous result of a homebrewing mishap. In the late 1980s, Phil Moeller was brewing a batch of barley wine with a friend, and they added too much wheat. "As all brewers do, they drank their mistakes and they found it delicious," says Glynn Phillips, the owner of Rubicon Brewing Company in Sacramento, California, where Moeller was the original brewmaster.

In 1988, to celebrate Rubicon's first anniversary, Moeller made the strong, smooth, and surprisingly drinkable Winter

TWO TO TASTE: WHEAT WINE

WHEAT WINE ALE
Smuttynose Brewing Co.
ABV varies: 10–12%

This medal-nabbing wheat wine has a hazy, nearly golden hue. Its scent is an equally winning mix of citrus and vanilla perfume thanks to more than a month of aging on a blend of Centennial hops and oak. On the palate there's a pinch of caramel sweetness, but crisp bitterness and smooth oak balance out this luscious slow sipper. Buy a couple of bottles to sit on for several years, until the wheat wine reaches its prime.

PILGRIM'S DOLE WHEATWINE
New Holland Brewing Company
ABV: 11.4%

Released every November, this Michigan beer's name describes the bread and ale rationed out to travelers on holy pilgrimages. Drinking Dole may not a religious experience make, but loads of wheat malt (50 percent of the grain bill) and a layover in used bourbon barrels will take you on a lush journey across caramel, vanilla, and sugar-sprinkled buttered toast. Beware: the booze is sneaky strong.

BACKUP BEERS: *Boulevard Brewing Co. Harvest Dance Wheat Wine, DuClaw Brewing Company Misery Wheat Wine-Style Ale, Fort Collins Brewery Wheat Wine Ale, Mystic Brewery Old Powderhouse Wheat Wine, Short's Brewing Company Anniversary Ale*

Wheat Wine—the first commercially brewed example of the hybrid. Since then, the style has begun appearing in the lineups at brewpubs and breweries looking for a unique wintertime offering or perhaps a celebratory ale. In California, Marin Brewing Company cooks up Star Brew Triple Wheat Ale (giving Moeller credit on the label), and St. Louis's Perennial Artisan Ales makes the fluffy, fruity Heart of Gold Wheat Wine Style Ale.

Despite wheat wine's growing popularity, brewers were not allowed to brand their bottled releases with the words *wheat wine* until 2005, when Portsmouth, New Hampshire's Smuttynose released its Wheat Wine Ale after an eight-month tug-of-war with federal regulators over using *wine* in the beer's name. Accolades were almost instant: Wheat Wine Ale won a gold at that year's Great American Beer Festival. It's complex, full-bodied, and full of flavor without diving into the deep end of sweetness.

With these wheat wines, there will be no whining.

EISBOCK

It's easy to curse winter's endless snow and ice, but remember that the freezing temperatures do supply one joyous blessing: the eisbock. This German beer, which ranges in color from light black to burnt sienna, is an example of better drinking through science. In a process called freeze distillation or fractional freezing, brewers send a strong lager dubbed a *bock* into deep freeze. The water freezes, leaving behind the alcohol (alcohol solidifies at −173°F, compared with water's 32°F). Removing the ice crystals creates a more concentrated beer with a thicker body, an amplified malty flavor that can be sweet or fruity, and a lofty alcohol level. Consider this process the opposite of watering down booze.

In the United States, the government deems this process a form of distillation, with the end product considered hard liquor. (To make eisbock, breweries must have a separate distillation license; spirits also are taxed at a higher rate.) Several small U.S. breweries skirt the issue and play with the style, such as Michigan's Kuhnhenn Brewing Co., but there are no such legal roadblocks in Europe, where the eisbock was created by accident more than a century ago.

A wooden barrel filled with the German brewery Kulmbacher's bock was mistakenly left outside during a cold snap. The beer mostly froze, and when it was discovered, the brewers

The "ice" category for cheap lagers is a glorified gimmick. They're frozen, yes, but water is added to return the alcohol content back to normal—and satisfy the federal government.

TWO TO TASTE: EISBOCK

AVENTINUS WEIZEN-EISBOCK
G. SCHNEIDER & SOHN
ABV: 12%

This German brewery's standard weizenbock (weizen is German for "wheat") is a superb banana-nuanced delight. Freezing it creates this snifter-worthy treat. The chestnut-hued eisbock's complex aroma slinks from raisins to cloves and butterscotch, with a creamy, cashmere-smooth mouthfeel. Flavors of honey and dried fruits dominate. Bananas and cloves ride shotgun.

HOFSTETTNER GRANITBOCK ICE
BRAUEREI HOFSTETTEN
ABV: 11.5%

This Austrian brewery creates its base bock by caramelizing the wort with white-hot rocks and then fermenting the beer in granite troughs. The process gives the toffee-scented, burgundy-brown eisbock intensified flavors of caramel, which are evened out by herbal undertones. The syrupy beer flows like lava across the tongue, with a sweetness that stops just short of saccharine.

BACKUP BEERS: *Kuhnhenn Brewing Company Raspberry Eisbock (primarily distributed in Michigan), Kulmbacher Reichelbräu Eisbock*

chipped away the ice, leaving behind a surprisingly opulent brew. (The process can be repeated, creating an increasingly richer and stronger beer.) Germany and Austria still create eisbocks of uncommon complexity and strength that are best savored in a snifter. These are potent, sip-them-slowly beers made of the winter and for winter drinking.

SCOTCH ALE/ WEE HEAVY

If I'm roasting beside a fireplace, I crave a drink that tastes and warms like a roaring fire. Sometimes I'll sip several fingers of fine peaty Scotch,

Dark Horse Brewing Company's Scotty Karate Scotch Ale is named after a honky-tonkin', punk-rockin' Michigan musician prone to wearing a taxidermied buffalo head as a hat. He writes that his Scotch ale tastes like "a smoky chocolate-chip cookie, wild roadside cherry-asparagus, woody, crispy leaf on a fall day."

but more often than not I'll opt for a Scotch ale. Also known as the wee heavy, strong (6 to 10 percent ABV), dark-toned Scotch ale is identified by its profoundly malty profile, often calling to mind caramel, dark fruits, or butterscotch with perhaps a bit of smoke bathing the mix.

Scotch ale's roots reach back to the nineteenth century, when brewers in Edinburgh were producing strong pale ales that were the equivalent of England's dark, sweetish Burton Ale. They were commonly concocted with pale barley malt and just a handful of bittering hops, largely in line with today's sweet, brawny English-style barley wines. But branding flexed its marketing muscle, and soon Scotch ales bore the name of their birthplace.

Historically, brewers in Scotland did not make their beers smoky by design. But over the last decade or two, largely in the hands of American brewers, peaty and smoky aromas and flavors have become intertwined with the style, which features almost no hop bitterness.

In the United States, you'll find fabulous versions from San Diego's AleSmith Brewing Company, which makes the smoke-smooched Wee Heavy; Founders Brewing Company ages its Backwoods Bastard in bourbon barrels. North Carolina's Highland Brewing

SCOTCHING CONFUSION

As you peruse beer shops and bar drinks list, you may come across a beer style known as Scottish ale. Do not confuse this with Scotch ale. Though Scottish ale still shines a spotlight on malt (and sometimes has smoky notes too), the sibling style skews lighter and less sweet. It's for drinking by the pint, not sipping in a thistle glass, and makes a great accompaniment to the first cool twinges of fall. Estimable examples of the category include Innis & Gunn Original, Three Floyds Robert the Bruce, Belhaven Scottish Ale, and Four Peaks Kilt Lifter.

Scotland's Traquair House (above) is reportedly the oldest continually inhabited home in that country. The property's history stretches back to the twelfth century, when it contained a hunting lodge for the country's kings. Traquair House once had a brewery that produced beer for its residents and workers on the estate, before falling into disuse in the nineteenth century. In 1965, the brewing equipment was discovered, giving rise to the Traquair House brewery, which still uses traditional oak fermentation vessels (left).

TWO TO TASTE:
SCOTTISH ALE/WEE HEAVY

OLD CHUB
OSKAR BLUES BREWERY
ABV: 8%

Lurking inside the can is a Coke-colored treat with a rich, grain-sweet aroma mixed with alcohol and a wisp of smoke; Chub is made with a touch of beech wood–smoked malt. It drinks lightly sweet, detouring to coffee, caramel, and a dash of smoldering wood—like your clothes after sitting downwind from a campfire. The can makes Old Chub criminally easy to drink.

SKULL SPLITTER
THE ORKNEY BREWERY
ABV: 8.5%

Situated on an archipelago in northern Scotland, the Orkney Brewery produces a range of dark and fruity ales, sumptuous stouts, biscuity low-alcohol bitters, and this Scotch ale. Named after a noggin-knockin' Orkney Viking, Skull Splitter serves up an aromatic assault of plums and toffee, leading to flavors of molasses, dried figs, and smoke reminiscent of a single-malt Scotch. Warms like one, too.

BACKUP BEERS: *Great Divide Brewing Company Claymore Scotch Ale, Middle Ages Brewing Co. Ye Olde Kilt Tilter, Moylan's Brewery Kilt Lifter Scotch Ale, Sprecher Brewing Company Pipers Scotch-Style Ale*

gooses the formula by adding extra hops and chocolate malt to its Tasgall Ale.

Still, Scotland has not forsaken the style. A delightfully drinkable introduction is the Belhaven Wee Heavy, and some of the most classic examples are found at Traquair House Brewery. At an estate inhabited by the same family for more than five centuries, copper kettles and wooden fermenting vessels are used to turn out the silky, toffee-tinged House Ale and coriander-spiced Jacobite.

No matter which sweet, muscular, and full-bodied Scotch ale you select, I recommend that you drink it in an aroma-intensifying thistle glass, which resembles the blossom of a thistle—Scotland's national flower. (A tulip glass or snifter is an appropriate alternative.) A Scotch ale is an ideal after-dinner drink to savor as the clock ticks late and the fire's embers turn red and die.

SEVEN GREAT BARLEY WINE FESTIVALS TO ATTEND

THESE BIG BEERS DESERVE A BIG-TIME CELEBRATION. FROM VIRGINIA TO ALASKA, HERE'S WHERE TO GO TO BE A BARLEY WINO.

CAMBRIDGE BREWING CO. BARLEYWINE FESTIVAL

Cambridge Brewing Co., Cambridge, Massachusetts

cambrew.com

The Boston area's finest brewpub digs deep into its cellar, pulling out nearly a dozen different versions of its Blunderbuss and Arquebus barley wines, including versions aged in Chardonnay, Sazerac rye, or port barrels.

HARD LIVER BARLEYWINE FEST

Brouwer's Café, Seattle, Washington

hardliver.com

Eat a big breakfast before arriving at this Belgian bar's annual sobriety-bludgeoning shindig. It features more than 60 primarily West Coast barley wines, many of which have been aged several years for this event.

THE GREAT ALASKA BEER & BARLEY WINE FESTIVAL

William A. Egan Civic & Convention Center, Anchorage, Alaska

auroraproductions.net/beer-barley.html

This festival provides frostbitten locals and fearless travelers with tastes from both Pacific Northwest and Alaskan standouts such as Kenai River Brewing Co., Midnight Sun Brewing Company, and Silver Gulch Brewing & Bottling Co., the northernmost American brewery.

LUCKY LABRADOR BARLEYWINE & BIG BEER TASTIVAL

Lucky Labrador Beer Hall, Portland, Oregon

luckylab.com

An annual fixture for more than a decade, Lucky Labrador's fest features more than 40 high-alcohol heavyweights from Portland and farther afield. Expect plenty of vertical tastings and aged rarities.

MAD FOX BARLEYWINE FESTIVAL

Mad Fox Brewing Co., Falls Church, Virginia

madfoxbrewing.com/barleywinefest

Excellent East Coast barley wines from the likes of North Carolina's Duck-Rabbit Craft Brewery, New York's Blue Point Brewing Co., and Maryland's Heavy Seas Beer and

Held in January, Anchorage's Great Alaska Beer & Barley Wine Festival features many heady beers that never reach the rest of the United States.

DuClaw Brewing Co. get their due at this high-gravity hullabaloo. Mad Fox's barley wines also ain't shabby.

TORONADO BARLEYWINE FESTIVAL

Toronado Pub, San Francisco, California

toronado.com

Since 1994, this lovably scuzzy, sticker-strewn San Francisco dive has hosted California's most prestigious liver-pummeling festival. Bring an empty six-pack holder to tote around samples of skull splitters from breweries both local (Speakeasy, Firestone Walker, Triple Rock) and national.

SPLIT THY BROOKLYN SKULL

Mugs Alehouse, Brooklyn, New York

mugsalehouse.com

For nearly 15 years, this venerable good-beer stronghold—it began pouring brews in 1992—has hosted this multiday celebration devoted to barley wines and additional brain blasters. (The festival is based on Philadelphia's longer-running Split Thy Skull.) Expect heavy hitters from breweries such as Weyerbacher, Arcadia, Shipyard, and Brooklyn Brewery, which is located down the block.

BOURBON COUNTY

BRAND STOUT

STOUT AGED IN BOURBON BARRELS

SINCE 1992

ORIGINAL BOURBON   BARREL AGED STOUT

13% ALCOHOL BY VOLUME • 355ML - 12 FL OZ

ECLIPSE

IMPERIAL

STOUT

.com

Founders
Brewing Co.
Since 1997
GRAND RAPIDS, MICHIGAN

HIGHLY ACCLAIMED

KBS

A STOUT ALE
N OAK BOURBON BARRELS
EF FROM: rheumatism, neuralgia, sciatica, lame back, lumbago,
toothache, sprains, swellings, and all manner of distress.

WHITE OAK
India Pale Ale

CIGAR CITY
BREWING

1 23456 78901 2

OK+

IA-DR-VT-CT-MA-HI-ME-DE-NY-
CA CASH REFUND

OVER A BARREL

AGING BEER IN WOOD

F ROM FOREHEAD TO FEET, I'm a beer man to my marrow. I'll choose beer over wine every day of the week, and a cocktail best be special to make me pass on a perfectly calibrated pale ale. But my drinking regimen is hardly rigid. At the end of a night, beer takes a backseat to an inch or two of bourbon or whiskey with a couple of cubes of ice to ensure that I'll sip the spirit.

My tastes lean toward dry and spicy rye whiskeys such as Rittenhouse, and Sazerac, and soft, sweet wheated bourbons from W. L. Weller, Old Fitzgerald, and Pappy Van Winkle. Though each spirit has distinct merits, they all share a key trait: each one is aged in newly charred oak barrels. Inside the wood, a clear spirit undergoes a lengthy, mysterious process encompassing chemical reactions, oxidation, and flavor extraction from the wood. When a distiller deems the aging complete, the finished product is entirely dissimilar to the original spirit. I consider bourbon and whiskey proof that alchemy is real.

This process is not exclusive to liquor. Brewers also are tapping into the transformative magic of aging beer in oak barrels that once contained bourbon, though they're just as likely to use a Chardonnay or rum barrel if it's available. Wood is becoming another crucial ingredient in brewers' bulging kitchen cabinets. On their endless mission for quirky new flavors, they're using wooden barrels to season and spice their beers with a nuanced touch usually reserved for Michelin-starred chefs. Given time, barrels soften and revise beer, adding appealing notes of oak and extracting flavors left behind by the cask's former inhabitant, which ranges from bourbon to sherry, Pinot Noir to aquavit.

When done right, barrel aging contributes complementary flavors that elevate beer to flavorful new heights. Read on to find out when bourbon and imperial stout became inseparable pals.

WOOD YOU KNOW?

Back when the telephone and the light bulb were barely a twinkle in people's eyes, every ounce of beer in the United States and Europe was fermented and transported in wooden barrels. They were imperfect vessels. Although wood was excellent for containing liquid and could impart mellowing notes of vanilla and oak, it often harbored unwelcome colonies of bacteria and yeast that sometimes led to spoiled beer. (In Class 10, you'll find that some brewers do want microbes to infect their beer; see page 226.)

The issue of infection was solved when brewers began modernizing, swapping wood for stainless steel. In many respects, stainless steel is an ideal material. It adds no unwanted flavors to beer, and it's largely nonreactive. Breweries can use chemicals and cleaners to scrub-a-dub-dub away undesirable microbes. If protocol is followed, beer should ferment according to plan. Stainless steel blazed the path for consistent mass-produced beer.

Now, however, brewers are turning their backs on progress and casting their eyes to a simpler, more unpredictable time. In every sense, this technique is a barrel of fun.

BOURBON, MEET BEER

A primary reason for this trend taking off is the hidebound bourbon industry.

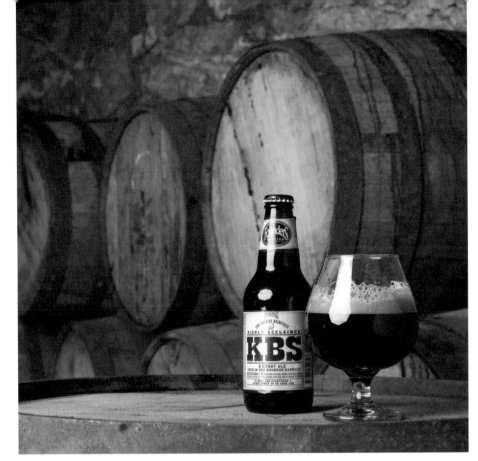

Founders Brewing's bourbon barrel-aged KBS is regularly ranked one of the country's best imperial stouts. Look for its release every April.

seashells by the seashore. In Louisville, Kentucky, it's a no-brainer that Bluegrass Brewing matures its silky, smoky Bourbon Barrel Stout in spirit-soaked oak for 60 to 90 days. Founders Brewing consigns its chocolaty, coffee-infused KBS (Kentucky Breakfast Stout) to bourbon barrels and cave ages the concoction for a year. Adapting the formula to Scotland's specialty, Harviestoun Brewery ages its Ola Dubh Special Reserve (aka "black oil") in retired Highland Park single-malt Scotch whisky oak casks that are 12, 16, 30, or even 40 years old.

One of the first breweries to take

Legally, bourbon distilleries can use a new, freshly charred white-oak barrel only once. After the brown spirit is emptied out, the barrel is dumped onto the open market. Traditionally, many Maker's Mark, Jim Beam, and Evan Williams barrels were exported to other distilleries, which used them to age tequila, rum, and even Scotch. Over the last several decades, breweries have begun buying used bourbon barrels. A few months or sometimes just a few weeks is all beer requires to ensnare the lush vanilla notes found in bourbon (and if the barrel was recently emptied, perhaps an alcohol boost as well).

Not every beer is ripe for renovation. Lighter styles such as lager, pilsner, and kölsch will be dominated by the flavors of bourbon and oak. A better candidate for transformation is a stronger beer such as the heady tripel that Allagash ages in Jim Beam barrels until it becomes the Curieux. More commonly, bourbon and whiskey barrels are used for darker beers such as a brawny barley wine or a strapping imperial stout.

Today the coupling of bourbon barrels and beer is as commonplace as

Looking for a boozy breakfast treat? BLiS ages maple syrup in bourbon barrels, and Mikuni's Noble Tonic 01 maple syrup slumbers in used barrels from New York's Tuthilltown Spirits.

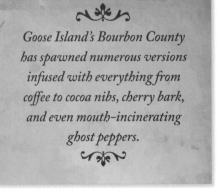

Goose Island's Bourbon County has spawned numerous versions infused with everything from coffee to cocoa nibs, cherry bark, and even mouth-incinerating ghost peppers.

advantage of this pairing was Chicago's Goose Island. In 1992, that brewery was nearing its thousandth batch. To commemorate that milestone, head brewer Greg Hall dialed up a heavy-duty stout. It was dumped into used Jim Beam barrels and 100 days later was christened Bourbon County Stout. The inky, boozy potion defied categorization. Literally. At the 1992 Great American Beer Festival, the beer was disqualified for not adhering to any existing style. But what was once an anomaly has become a lauded style, spurring the creation of four distinct GABF categories: wood- and barrel-aged beer, sour beer, strong beer, and strong stout. Brewers' ability to experiment with bourbon-drenched oak is as endless as the brown rivers of bourbon flowing from Kentucky.

THE WIDE WORLD OF WOOD

Whiskey and bourbon barrels may dominate the barrel-aging sector, but they're not the only available timber. Barrels used to season Chardonnay, brandy, rum, port, and Pinot Noir also have a built-in expiration date. As the flavors of vanilla and oak diminish each time a barrel is filled, a winery or distillery eventually must discard casks that have been drained of the desired essence. But a wine- or liquor-saturated cask could be the key breweries need to unlock a beer's full potential.

For its Window Pane series, North Carolina's Mother Earth Brewing ferments a beer with local fruit (blackberries, figs, raspberries, peaches) and ages it for up to three months in used brandy, Chardonnay, or Pinot Noir barrels. In particular, Pinot Noir barrels have become a favorite of Oregon's Oakshire Brewing, which makes one-offs such

In 2012, the beer recommendation website Pintley launched one of the country's more compelling barrel-aging projects. Called Oncemade, it tasks two Massachusetts breweries to produce a limited-run barrel-aged beer; the beers are packaged together in a hand-numbered wooden box along with two handmade wooden coasters, a signed letter from the brewers, and a piece of one of the barrels (oncemadebeer.com).

California's Anderson Valley Brewing Company partnered with the bourbon makers at Wild Turkey Distillery to create an exclusive line of bourbon barrel–aged beers. The first release was the Barney Flats Oatmeal Stout aged for three months in a Wild Turkey barrel. Look for releases in bottles and on draft.

Instead of going through the back-wrenching labor of filling barrels, some breweries use oak chips (occasionally soaked in a liquor of their choosing) or even spirals of unlikely woods such as cedar.

as the cherry-infused Cerise Noir and the scrumptiously tart Skookumchuck Wild Ale. (As you'll learn in Class 10, breweries that dabble in wild or sour ales prefer old barrels because they're perfect for cultivating colonies of microflora.) Care for some brandy? Try California-based Coronado Brewing's honeyed Barrel-Aged Barley Wine or Captain Lawrence's Golden Delicious tripel, which is aged in apple brandy barrels. Across the Atlantic Ocean in Norway, Haandbryggeriet (the "hand brewery") finishes its Norwegian Porter in aquavit barrels.

Whatever your poison, you're sure to find it soaked in oak.

THAT'S THE SPIRIT

Whiskey starts life as a distiller's beer, or wash, that's made with malted barley, water, and yeast and then distilled and usually aged; hops are the only missing ingredient. Beer and whiskey cross paths again only atop a bar. Lately, though, brewers have begun pulling double duty as distillers and distillers have begun acting like brewers. In California, Anchor Brewing specializes in re-creations of vintage whiskeys. Michigan's New Holland Brewing doses distillates with hops and offers a line of beer-inspired Brewers' Whiskeys. Flipping the script, Nashville's Corsair Artisan Distillery releases spirits based on recipes for imperial stouts, pumpkin ales, and even a witbier, and Sierra Nevada Brewing supplies the smoky brown ale that St. George Spirits of Alameda, California, transforms into single-malt whiskey.

Another tasty tributary of this trend involves distilleries sending bottle-ready beer through a still, putting a beer and a shot inside a single bottle. Germany's G. Schneider & Sohn has its banana-noted Schneider Aventinus doppelbock distilled into Edelster Aventinus by the Schraml distillery. Japan's Kiuchi Brewery turns Hitachino Nest White Ale into Kiuchi No Shizuku. The German brewery Uerige distills its strong brown ales Sticke and Dopplesticke, respectively, into Stickum and Stickum Plus. California's Charbay distillery creates one of my favorite examples of this burgeoning category. Charbay sources Bear Republic's Racer 5 IPA—one of my desert-island IPAs—and transforms the beer into Doubled & Twisted Light Whiskey and the aged R5 Hop-Flavored Whiskey. It's heaven for hopheads looking to hit the hard stuff.

Each barrel is as unique as a fingerprint and will create different characteristics. For the sake of uniformity, many breweries blend together different batches.

Tequila barrels are particularly tough to come by because distilleries in Mexico use them until they fall apart.

NINE KNOCKOUT WOOD-AGED
BEERS TO TASTE

RESERVE SERIES
HOP GOD

Nebraska Brewing Company
ABV: 10.1%

A hazard of aging beer in bourbon barrels is that oak and booze become the major players in the flavor game, overpowering the beer as easily as a pro wrestler does his fixed opponent. That's hardly the case with this special version of Hop God, a citrusy Belgian IPA that spends six months sleeping in French oak Chardonnay barrels. The wooden slumber gives God luscious tannins, a tropical complexity, and a complementary vinous character. It's heavenly.

DARK APPARITION

Jackie O's Pub & Brewery
ABV: 10.5%

When I attended Ohio University in Athens in the late 1990s, O'Hooley's was a ho-hum brewpub. But since then it has been rebooted as Jackie O's, and brewmaster Brad Clark has made a national splash with his sour ales and barrel-aged behemoths, namely, the limited-edition versions of the chewy Dark Apparition Russian imperial stout aged in bourbon barrels. Clark regularly releases loads of other barrel-aged gems at the brewpub. A great time to visit is during Ohio Brew Week (see page 301).

ECLIPSE

Fifty Fifty Brewing Co.
ABV: 9.5%

To facilitate the outsize demand for its imperial stout, this Truckee, California, brewery runs the Eclipse Futures program. It allows customers to place a 50 percent down payment to reserve a bottle—before the beer is bottled. Every batch of Eclipse, which debuts each December, is aged for at least six months in oak barrels that previously contained the likes of bourbons and whiskeys such as Rittenhouse Rye, Four Roses, Elijah Craig, and Buffalo Trace.

WOODCUT SERIES

Odell Brewing Company
ABV: Varies

In 2007, this Fort Collins, Colorado, brewery bought brand-new lightly charred oak casks from Canton Cooperage in Kentucky, kicking off its Woodcut Series. The focus is on drawing out the barrels' natural tannins and subtle notes of vanilla. To date, Odell has debuted six Woodcuts, including a golden ale, a crimson ale, a double-strength märzen lager (the classic Oktoberfest beer), and a Belgian-style quadrupel.

BOXER'S REVENGE

Jester King Craft Brewery
ABV: 10.2%

Because of a handful of handcuffing laws, Texas fell behind the craft-beer curve. But a new crop of innovative breweries is catching up quickly, none more than the Austin-area Jester King. It makes excellent rustic ales such as the barrel-aged sour saison Das Wunderkind! and the farmhouse-style Black Metal imperial stout. Then there's pugilistic Boxer's Revenge: a potent "provision" ale (a specialty of farmhouse breweries near the Franco-Belgian border) aged in French oak wine barrels alongside multiple strains of *Brettanomyces* and fragrant Cascade, Columbus, and East Kent Goldings hops.

J SERIES

Two Brothers Brewing Co.
ABV: Varies

For its J Series, Illinois's Two Brothers (Jim and Jason Ebel, the namesake Js) age their beers for four weeks in French-oak foudres—essentially, enormous wooden tanks. They add deep, complex flavors of vanilla and oak to two terrific offerings. The Long Haul Session Ale is a lightly malty all-day drinker (just 4.2 percent ABV), and the crisp honeyed Resistance IPA is suffused with pine, citrus, and oak that hangs out on the back end.

PALO SANTO MARRON

Dogfish Head Craft Brewed Ales
ABV: 12%

Never known to ride the easy route, Delaware's Dogfish Head built a 10,000-gallon fermentation vessel from Paraguayan palo santo wood—the largest wooden tank built since Prohibition. The wood, which often is used by South American winemakers, adds scads of caramel and vanilla to this sweet, sticky, and roasty mahogany ale that glides down like maple syrup.

JAI ALAI AGED ON WHITE OAK

Cigar City Brewing
ABV: 7.5%

Wayne Wambles is wild for wood. The brewer at Tampa, Florida's top brewery loves to experiment with unlikely lumber such as Spanish cedar and lemon and grapefruit wood, which can impart tart, sour characteristics. I dig the Jai Alai, a resinous and tropical IPA that's altered by a brief but fruitful affair with white oak. It contributes a touch of drying tannic complexity, plus a hit of vanilla that harmonizes with the hop bitterness and, oddly, dill.

BIG WOODY BARLEYWINE

Glacier BrewHouse
ABV: 10.75%

If the Glacier BrewHouse were anywhere but Anchorage, Alaska, drinkers would write hymns to the glory of the brewery's barrel-aged beers. Secreted beneath Glacier is a chilled vault housing "the Wall of Wood," with oak casks from around the world containing at least 50 special-release beers, including tart lambic-style ales, oatmeal stouts, double IPAs, and Big Woody. Made with massive amounts of English barley, the deeply fruity and malty barley wine rests for at least a year in Jim Beam bourbon and Napa Valley wine barrels. It's worth booking a flight to Alaska.

SIX FANTASTIC BARREL-AGED BEER FESTIVALS

WOOD WILL WIN YOU OVER AT THESE TOP OAK-SOAKED CELEBRATIONS.

FROM THE BARREL

Santa Margarita, California

firestonebeer.com

To celebrate the anniversary of Prohibition's end, Firestone Walker helps put on an event featuring tapas paired with the best American barrel-aged libations: Kentucky bourbon, wine from California's Central Coast, and rare beers from the likes of The Bruery, New Belgium, and Ballast Point.

WEST COAST BARREL AGED BEER FESTIVAL

Hayward, California

the-bistro.com

Each fall, the Bistro (the self-proclaimed "home of extreme beer and live music") hosts this celebration centered on BBQ, bands, and more than 60 barrel-aged beers. Bring friends so you can try them all.

FESTIVAL OF WOOD AND BARREL AGED BEER

Chicago, Illinois

illinoisbeer.com

Since 2003, the Illinois Craft Brewers Guild has hosted one of the largest American festivals dedicated to beer and wood. Expect more than 150 beers from coast to coast, with awards given in categories such as fruit beers, wild acidic beers, and strong porter/stout.

THE LITTLE WOODY BARREL-AGED BREW & WHISKEY FESTIVAL

Bend, Oregon

thelittlewoody.com

At this annual end-of-summer fest a roll call of Oregon's finest brewers, including Deschutes, 10 Barrel Brewing, Ninkasi, and Oakshire, offer up one-off barrel-aged beers. For those that prefer the even stronger stuff, the festival offers a curated collection of small-batch spirits.

EXTREME BEER FEST

Boston, Massachusetts

beeradvocate.com/ebf

The most popular session during the Beer Advocate crew's annual ode to over-the-top beers is the Night of the Barrels, featuring more than 60 oak-aged rarities and a "wood panel" of renowned brewers.

STONE OAKQUINOX

Escondido, California

stoneworldbistro.com/oakquinox

Beer expert "Dr." Bill Sysak curates this ludicrous collection of 100-plus rare beers from cultish breweries such as Kern River, The Lost Abbey, and Belgium's 3 Fonteinen. The fun—gulp—starts at 10 a.m. You won't find a more extravagant collection of barrel-aged beers in America.

PUCKER UP

SOUR AND WILD ALES

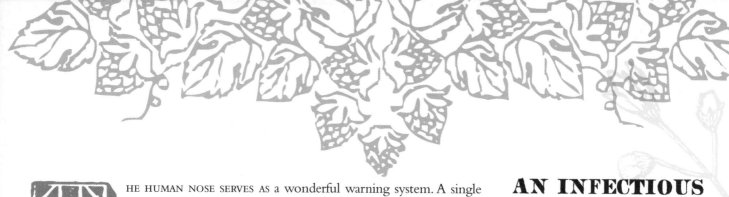

THE HUMAN NOSE SERVES AS a wonderful warning system. A single pungent whiff of expired milk will make you dump it down the drain, and the moldy scent from last week's meat loaf consigns it to a trash can. Your snout also tells you when a beer breaks bad. I've opened countless light-struck, past-their-prime lagers and ales that were skunkier than Pepé Le Pew. (Drinking an off beer does not cause intestinal distress, but your taste buds definitely will revolt.) However, there's one odor that will confuse even the finest-tuned sniffer: sour. Though it typically signifies rotten, in a brewer's practiced hands, sour ales can be as complex and sublime as the finest wine.

As a category, sour ale stretches its arms around a wide, offbeat range of beer styles and brewing techniques. For centuries, sour ales have been equated with Belgian beers such as tart lambics and cherry-infused krieks as well as Germany's lesser-known Berliner weisse and gose (see pages 94-98). Now American brewers also are earnestly channeling their inner mad scientists, dosing beers with wild, unruly yeasts such as *Brettanomyces* and bacteria such as *Pediococcus* and *Lactobacillus* during fermentation or the aging process and then sending them to slumber in wooden barrels, giving them time to perform their acidic magic.

Within the dark and damp wood, the microscopic critters start devouring sugars and carbohydrates. Over months, often years, they tweak the DNA of beer, altering pH levels and slowly creating a mouth-puckering tartness and earthy, offbeat flavors that in the best way possible recall a barnyard romp. Like stinky cheese, these ales are as challenging as they are charming. Stick around past the initial shock and you'll be treated to beguiling undertones: Champagne-like effervescence, a refreshing tang, palate-cleaning acidity, and perhaps natural sweetness from the fresh fruits (including peaches, raspberries, and cherries) that brewers can use to complement and round out the sourness.

Here's the sweet science on sour beer.

AN INFECTIOUS DRINK

Sour ales are a product of time, patience, and intentional contagion. This contradicts the standard brewing protocol. By and large, brewers require that their equipment be as sterile as a surgeon's operating room, allowing yeast strains to perform a lockstep fermentation march toward the expected flavor profile. When the brewing environment and processes are spot-on, yeast does its work as automatically as a worker on an assembly line. But if errant bacteria or fungi enter the fray, they can throw a wrench into the liquid works. Flavors and aromas skitter in tart, funky directions: those are the telltale symptoms of infection.

Yet in a balanced, well-crafted beer, these often unwanted flavors can add desired complexity. The trick is to administer these microscopic magicians in the right ratios, fostering the right environment (usually a wooden barrel), and waiting. Then waiting some more. Unlike normal beers, which can be bottle-ready in as little as two or three weeks, sour beers often age for a year, sometimes two or three, before they're ready for consumption.

THE WILD JOURNEY

The path to sourness is not a straight line. One route to ride is lactic acid bacteria. The members of this family of microbes, which includes *Lactobacillus* and *Pediococcus*, convert lactose and other sugars into lactic acid, the sour key to a cavalcade of fermented foods. With lactic acid, cabbage becomes sauerkraut. Cucumbers proceed to pickles. Milk morphs into yogurt, kefir, sour cream, and cheese. When it comes to beer, the presence of lactic acid generally is considered a defect and a sign of spoilage; you'll taste that telltale sour twang.

Lactic acid bacteria—specifically *Lactobacillus*—can also be a welcome friend. The bacteria's fermentation creates a dry, tangy profile that's a signature flavor in German ales such as salt-kissed gose and Berliner weisse, along with Belgium-born Flanders red and brown ales (read further for more about these). Given time, *Lactobacillus* bacteria create sour ales that'll shock your palate but never knot up your tongue. That's the case because the bacteria cease reproducing when the beer reaches a certain pH level. It's the symbolic 5 p.m. work whistle.

In contrast, *Brettanomyces* is the tireless workhorse of the yeast universe, unwilling to take a siesta. Though Brett, as it's sometimes called, is a slow worker, taking months to make its appearance known, it never ceases toiling. The yeast continuously devours lingering carbohydrates and sugars, like Pac-Man presented with endless pellets to munch. Given too much time, Brett beer may thin out and become aggressively undrinkable, like something sucked up from a puddle in a horse stable.

When it is carefully monitored, though, *Brettanomyces* is a marvel, imparting enticingly musty, earthy accent notes often described as "barnyard" or, more generally, "funky." This wild yeast strain is not best suited as the star of the flavorful show but rather as an intriguing, unforgettable supporting actor. (Sometimes brewers use *Brettanomyces* in conjunction with *Lactobacillus* and perhaps *Pediococcus*, resulting in a sour, funky tour de force.) *Brettanomyces* may be pitched directly into the beer during fermentation or when bottling, but often beer is infected when it's sent to snooze in Brett-infested oak barrels. The yeast adores dark, wet oxygen-permeable wood, and once it has infiltrated timber, it'll linger like the world's worst houseguest.

COURTING DISASTER

Besides persuading consumers to buy offbeat wild ales and sour beers, one of brewers' biggest challenges—and fears—is infection. *Brettanomyces* is a hardy bugger that's not easily assassinated, especially after it hunkers down in the moist crevices of a cask or inside a bottling line. An errant spore could spell doom for a batch of standard beer; this is why brewers' fanatical cleaning procedures must border on obsessive-compulsive disorder.

FOR A GREAT DEEP DIVE
INTO THE WORLD OF
WILD ALES AND SOUR BREWS,
PICK UP
JEFF SPARROW'S *Wild Brews*.

SAY HELLO TO MY LITTLE FRIENDS

MEET THE BACTERIA AND YEAST RESPONSIBLE FOR CREATING SOUR AND WILD ALES.

LACTOBACILLUS: This bacteria (which sours milk, thus creating yogurt) often is used to make sour German ales such as Berliner weisse and salt-kissed gose as well as Belgian-style Flanders red and brown ales. Its fermentation results in the production of lactic acid, which creates a dry, tangy profile in a brew.

PEDIOCOCCUS: This anaerobic bacteria (it survives without oxygen) creates a by-product called diacetyl, which generates flavors such as butterscotch and butter (it's used to manufacture butter substitutes). However, over time the diacetyl is reabsorbed (often with the assistance of hungry *Brettanomyces*), resulting in a refreshing acidity. *Pediococcus* produces plenty of lactic acid.

BRETTANOMYCES: This slow-growing, hard-to-kill wild yeast has an insatiable hunger, devouring complex sugars and carbohydrates that other yeasts find unpalatable—it will eat just about everything except a glass bottle.. It's behind that earthy, horsey, leather-like scent. Brewers both fear and revere this yeast, whose presence is considered a defect in wine. The yeast lives on the skin of fruit. *Brettanomyces* can be present in a sour beer, but it is not responsible for creating a sour profile.

Roughly translated from Latin, the sign above the barrel room at Southern California's Lost Abbey reads "in the wild yeast we believe." Those barrels contain some of the country's finest wild ales.

BELGIAN SOUR AND WILD ALES

If you wish to pucker your pout, perhaps you should book a trip to Belgium. It is the motherland of sour and wild ales and continued to nurture them long after other brewers turned their backs on infected beer. Let's meet the complexly flavored clan.

LAMBIC

The beating heart of every beer is its yeast strain, that great driver of aroma and flavor. Today breweries depend on pure, cultured yeast strains that can deliver replicable flavor profiles, the lingering legacy of Denmark's Dr. Emil Christian Hansen, who worked at the Carlsberg Laboratory in Copenhagen. Hansen built upon the research of Louis Pasteur, which showed that brewing yeast often was riddled with bacteria and mold. Hansen discovered that there were only a few types of yeast that were useful in brewing and developed the technique for separating them out and propagating them. This technique first was put into use at the Carlsberg breweries in 1883.

Yeast finally was tamed. However, not every brewer decided to forgo unpredictability. One of the last lingering remnants of that Wild West era of brewing, when all beers were aged in wood and often unintentionally infected with unruly yeasts and souring bacteria, is

Belgium's lambic. A specialty of Brussels and the mainly rural Senne Valley to the west, lambics are spontaneously fermented ales whose roots extend back centuries before Hansen and Pasteur. Born on the region's farms and brewed with their agricultural bounty, lambics have existed for around 500 years, a stretch that has seen the style remain largely unchanged. Then as now, the rustic ales are concocted from at least 30 percent unmalted wheat, with the remainder consisting of barley malt.

The initial steps in making lambic follow the standard brewing script. Grains are boiled to create the wort (the sugar-rich broth that becomes beer), and hops are added. Whereas brewers typically favor fresh and pungent hops, lambic brewers rely on aged, stale hops that have lost their bitterness and aromas but retain their preservative prowess.

Ordinarily, hot wort is cooled quickly to the appropriate temperature and yeast is pitched. With lambics, the steaming wort is pumped into large, shallow trays called coolships, where the liquid is allowed to cool down overnight. Windows are flung open. Catching a ride on air currents, microscopic yeasts and bacteria flutter into the coolships, settling into the broth. (Lambics are brewed only from roughly October to May because of the threat of inviting the wrong kind of infection during the sweltering summer.) The wild critters may help jump-start fermentation, but they're not usually enough to

shepherd the beer on its journey to your mouth. The inoculated wort is transferred to wooden barrels teeming with souring bacteria and colonies of Brett famished for a sugary banquet.

Next, brewers twiddle their thumbs. Lambics take their sweet time to finish fermenting and develop their intricate, supremely acidic flavor profile. By and large, most lambics are not served straight, an experience that would be somewhat like slurping a shot of vinegar. Instead, lambics are fermented with fruits such as cherries, raspberries, black currants,

WORD UP

The term *lambic* probably is derived from Lembeek, which is a lambic-brewing municipality near Brussels. Alternatively, the word may stem from a type of still called an *alambic* or perhaps from *lambere*, a Latin term that means "to sip."

In Belgium, one of the top places to try lambics is at Brussels's beloved Moeder Lambic (moederlambic.com), which has two locations in town and cellars stocked with the country's tartest treasures.

and peaches, which sweetly temper the acidity. Alternatively, batches of one-, two, and three-year-old lambics are blended together, bottled, and allowed to continue aging and fermenting. Called gueuze, the result is a dry, somewhat fruity elixir with a lip-scrunching sourness. Do not sip one soon after brushing your teeth.

Like Champagne in France, a true lambic can be produced only in this

SMARTEN UP ON SOUR TERMINOLOGY

Look closely at that label. These phrases will clue you into the flavors lurking inside each bottle.

CASSIS: A lambic fermented with black currants.

FARO: A blended lambic sweetened with sugar and pasteurized, preventing the beer from continuing fermentation; relatively rare.

FRAMBOISE: A lambic or Flanders ale fermented with raspberries.

KRIEK: A lambic or Flanders ale fermented with sour cherries.

PÊCHE: A lambic fermented with peaches.

POMME: A lambic fermented with apples.

TWO TO TASTE: FRUIT LAMBIC

LINDEMANS CASSIS
Brouwerij Lindemans
ABV 4%

Back in 1809, the farming Lindemans clan—wheat and barley growers, the lot of 'em—began spending the long chilly winters brewing lambic. By 1930, brewing was more important than farming, and beer became the family business. Smart move. Lindemans makes superb fruited lambics, including a lovely kriek, a fine framboise, and this stunning cassis. Black currants create a showstopping violet-red shade and a sweet mixed-berry nose, which is echoed in the flavor. But the lactic tartness does a bang-up job balancing the sweetness; give Cassis a spot on the dessert tray.

ROSÉ DE GAMBRINUS
Brasserie Cantillon Brouwerij
ABV: 5%

Mention the word *lambic* to the average beer geek, and he'll sing hosannas about Brussels-based Cantillon, where microbe maestro Jean-Pierre Van Roy makes some of Belgium's most revered spontaneously fermented potables. I really want you to try Rosé, a framboise fermented in oak casks with whole fresh raspberries, resulting in a dry, tart foxtrot of berries and earthy funk. Can't find this Cantillon? Just nab any other bottle from this brewery. Each one's a crack lambic.

BACKUP BEERS: *Brouwerij Boon Kriek, Brouwerij De Ranke Kriek De Ranke, Brouwerij Oud Beersel Oude Kriek Vieille, Brouwerij Van Honsebrouck N.V. St. Louis Framboise, Hanssens Artisanaal Oude Kriek*

TWO TO TASTE: GUEUZE

OUDE GEUZE VIEILLE
BROUWERIJ OUD BEERSEL
ABV: 6%
~

Though persnickety regulations nix Oud Beersel from cooking wort in its brewery, a steady supply of fermentable broth (brewed by Brouwerij Boon according to Beersel's recipes) ensure that the circa-1892 lambic producer can still fashion the funky stuff. The brewery packs the wort into its bug-infested oak barrels, where the sands of time—and occasionally fruit—transform the liquid into a framboise, a kriek, and this rustic gold gueuze with reckless carbonation. Oude's got a grassy, leathery scent, loads of lemon flavor, a tingly acidity as sharp as shattered glass, and, for smooth drinkability, a spoonful of sweetness. More, please.

GEUZE MARIAGE PARFAIT
BROUWERIJ BOON
ABV: 8%
~

Since 1975, brewer Frank Boon has been a key figure in lambic's survival and revival, tending to this timeworn brewery in the town of Lembeek. Boon is a consummate artisan, adhering to age-old techniques and working with local farmers to source sour cherries for his krieks. But I like Mariage Parfait. It's made mainly with lambic that's at least three years old, a stretch that allows the straw-gold, Champagne-bubbly brew to develop an oaky aroma drenched in barnyard funk. Surprisingly full-bodied Parfait packs a full-bore bitterness cut with acidic fruit and, thanks to the barrels, a lick of vanilla.

BACKUP BEERS: *Brasserie Cantillon Brouwerij Gueuze 100% Lambic, Brouwerij 3 Fonteinen Oude Geuze, Brouwerij Girardin Gueuze 1882 (black label), Brouwerij Lindemans Gueuze Cuvée René*

Belgian region, and there are precious few of the traditional lambic breweries remaining. The most revered is Brasserie Cantillon Brouwerij, which has made the tart stuff since 1900. Brouwerij Boon, Lindemans, and 3 Fonteinen also craft exceptional lambics; Oud Beersel sources wort from elsewhere and infects with it in the brewery's barrels. Additionally, some breweries, such as Hanssens Artisanaal and Gueuzerie Tilquin, do not brew but instead source an assortment of aged lambics and then blend them into finished products. It's a dwindling, if delicious, art form.

SPREADING SPONTANEITY

The concept of spontaneous fermentation is not exclusive to Belgium. Following the lead of lambic producers, brewers around the globe, especially in the United States, are inoculating their wort with native microbes. Although the sour, funky brews can't be branded lambics, they offer some of the same characteristics that make the Belgian ales so peculiarly pleasing.

At California's Russian River Brewing Company, brewmaster Vinnie Cilurzo (also a master of the double IPA; see page 139) slings the dry and sharply citric Beatification, a spontaneously fermented "Sonambic"—a Sonoma-made lambic. The barrel-aging experts at Cambridge Brewing Company in Massachusetts often tinker with spontaneous fermentation. Upland Brewing Company in Bloomington, Indiana (which operates a dedicated sour brewery), uses traditional lambic-brewing techniques to create a range of sour beers infused with fruits both expected (cherries, raspberries) and unexpected (kiwi, persimmon).

Coolships, too, have gained in popularity—well, a little bit. The Allagash Brewing Company based in Portland, Maine, outfitted its brewhouse with an authentic coolship (see page 166 for more on the brewery). It was the first step in creating its barrel-aged Coolship series, which includes the pink-tinted Cerise, aged with tart cherries, and the blended, gueuze-like Resurgam. Block 15 Restaurant & Brewery in Corvallis, Oregon, installed a coolship in fall 2010 and dedicates half its cellar to wild ales. Elsewhere, Vermont's Hill Farmstead Brewery uses its coolship to create a range of spontaneously fermented ales, and a coolship is crucial to the beers made at Washington, D.C.'s Bluejacket.

Now comes the question: Where can I try these beers? The answer: finding them will take some serious luck or planning. Storing barrels require tons of square footage, multiplied by the months and years it takes to age the beer—with no guarantee that the liquid inside will be suitable for consumption. When the spontaneously fermented beers are released, the quantities are so limited and the demand so rabid that many breweries presell their ales long before they can grace the shelves. One of the most widely distributed spontaneously fermented beers, New Glarus's fresh, clean, and fruit-forward Raspberry Tart, is sold only in Wisconsin. Sigh. If you stumble across a spontaneously fermented ale, snag it. If I sent you out to buy one, it might leave a sour taste in your mouth.

Allagash Brewing has equipped its brewery in Portland, Maine, with a traditional coolship, which it uses to create a lineup of lambic-style sour beers.

THE SOUR ALES OF FLANDERS

The Dutch-speaking region of northern Belgium known as Flanders has no shortage of indigenous beers doctored with bacteria and wild yeast.

Combining lambic with kombucha, a fermented tea, may seem like a crazy idea, but the otherwise disparate live-yeast drinks do have a common thread: *Brettanomyces*. After sampling kombucha, Don Feinberg of the Chicago-based importers Vanberg & DeWulf had a blending brainstorm. He enlisted a lambic brewer from Belgium's Brouwerij De Troch, a scientist, and an organic kombucha producer, and the crackerjack team created a harmonious convergence called Lambrucha. It's low in alcohol (just 3.5 percent ABV) with a bright citric tartness and a touch of earthy funk. Seek it out.

In addition to lambic, Flanders is renowned for its red ales and brown ales, many of which sport the same infections as lambic—minus the poetic serendipity. Here's how to tell these siblings apart.

FLANDERS RED ALE

The origin story of this crimson-colored ale starts with the dark porters of England, which in the eighteenth and nineteenth centuries were one of that country's most popular beers. Porter was made by blending freshly brewed beer with older, tarter beer that probably was infected with *Brettanomyces* by chance (see page 175). Seeing the popularity of that style, Belgian brewers began to try their hand at it, most prominently Brouwerij Rodenbach, which was founded in West Flanders in 1821.

Today, Belgian brewers do not leave the tartness up to luck or lax hygiene. Flanders red ale is made using a mixture of lighter and darker barley malts (often corn is added to supply a smooth, rich character), which combine to create the classic

Want a taste of a tarter Rodenbach? Try the Grand Cru, which bumps up the ratio to two-thirds old oak-matured beer. Brewers use the phrase "Grand Cru" to describe a limited beer that's often stronger or more elaborate.

reddish-brown hue. After the wort is inoculated with the brewery's house blend of yeast and bacteria, which includes a healthy colony of *Lactobacillus*, the beer is aged for upward of two years, catnapping in gargantuan oak tanks called *foudres*. When deemed ready, the soured ale often is blended with a younger beer for consistency and balance.

Uncap the classic Rodenbach or Duchesse de Bourgogne and you'll instantly understand why the Flanders reds sometimes are called the "Burgundies of Belgium." The complex ale boasts a touch of oaky tannins, alongside fruity flavors and a sharp, red wine–like astringency complemented by a dry finish that lasts until your next lightly puckering sip.

FLANDERS OUD BRUIN

West Flanders is linked to the red ale, but its eastern neighbors favor the homegrown brown ale, more evocatively known as the *oud bruin*, or "old brown." Compared with the more acetic red, oud bruin relies on comparatively darker malts, which supply rich flavors of toffee, plums, figs, and caramel. It's a sweet and malty delicacy with a moderately tart, appealingly acidic edge—something like Sour Patch Kids candy in liquid form. The style's lineage stretches back to the 1600s, when old brown was brewed as a provision beer, a stronger brew designed for keeping. All that sitting around gave

TWO TO TASTE: FLANDERS RED ALE

DUCHESSE DE BOURGOGNE
BROUWERIJ VERHAEGHE
ABV: 6%

The duchesse in question is Mary of Burgundy, who died after a horse-riding mishap in 1482. The Flanders red ale is a fitting tribute, a blend of two ales aged in oak for 8 months and 18 months, respectively. The young-old marriage (apt for a duchesse who received her first matrimonial proposal when she was five) is a marvel, providing a tart, sour cherry–like punch partnered with a sprinkling of chocolate, sweet caramel, and a wine-like acidity.

RODENBACH CLASSIC
BROUWERIJ RODENBACH
ABV: 5.2%

I like to think of Rodenbach Classic as a Belgian sour wearing training wheels. Each bottle is made of one part older oak-ripened ale— upward of two years old—and three parts fresh ale fermented in stainless steel. The three-to-one ratio produces a ruddy-brown stunner with raspberry-tinted foam and a bouquet like sour cherries bathed in brown sugar. Ripe red fruits reveal themselves on first sip, with a wisp of oak and just enough tangy sourness to make Rodenbach a first-order thirst slayer.

BACKUP BEERS: *Brouwerij Bockor N.V. Cuvée des Jacobins Rouge, Brouwerij Strubbe Ichtegem Grand Cru Flemish Red Ale, Brouwerij Verhaeghe Vichtenaar*

TWO TO TASTE:
FLANDERS OUD BRUIN

GOUDENBAND
BROUWERIJ LIEFMANS
ABV: 8%
∞

Although beer itself might be considered a gift (especially at the end of another grizzly bear workday), Liefmans underscores the point with its tissue paper–wrapped line of adult presents, including the cherry-infused Cuvée-Brut and Goudenband. The classic, world-class oud bruin is as intricate as a puzzle, crammed with caramel, a splash of vinegar, and dark fruit—a rich, tart-sweet seesaw.

PETRUS OUD BRUIN
BROUWERIJ BAVIK
ABV: 5.5%
∞

Belgium's Bavik dabbles in an impressive array of beverages, from flavored lemonades to sparkling water, the Wittekerke witbier, Bavik pilsner, and Petrus Oud Bruin. Petrus ripens for 24 months in oak barrels, creating a gently sour charm that jibes with the malty date-like sweetness, woody tones, and moderate ABV. You could drink two and happily reach for a third—or try Oud Bruin's lighter, equally twangy relative, Petrus Aged Pale.

BACKUP BEERS: *Brouwerij Bockor Bellegems Bruin, Brouwerij Van Honsebrouck Bacchus, Brouwerij Van Steenberge Monk's Café Flemish Sour Ale*

---

the bacteria time to toil, creating the trademark sour trait.

Over the centuries, old brown has lost a bit of alcoholic heft, and its production methods have evolved from a fluke to a well-oiled machine. Eschewing microbe-infested wood, old brown often is fermented in spic-and-span stainless steel at warmer temperatures (around 60°F), giving the bacteria a kick in the can to convert the sugars into lactic acid and mellow out. (Oud bruins are aged in wood, highlighting the overlap with the Flanders red and the styles' elasticity.) The most prominent producer of oud bruin is Liefmans, which lets its brown ale age for four to eight months before different vats of beer are blended together with younger brew to create its Oud Bruin and stronger, more widely available Goudenband.

A few bold American brewers have attempted to re-create and tweak oud bruin. In New York, Brewery Ommegang collaborated with Liefmans to craft the cherry-infused Zuur (Dutch for "sour"). Captain Lawrence

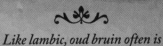

Like lambic, oud bruin often is used as a platform for blending cherries and raspberries, creating alternative takes on kriek and framboise, respectively.

Brewing Company released the award-winning Rosse e Marone, and Oregon's Deschutes Brewery devised the fruity, partly wine barrel–aged The Dissident, sold under its Reserve Series. They're all delicious, but I recommend that you begin your brown journey with a few of these old Flanders faves.

AMERICAN WILD AND SOUR ALES

I like to think of American brewers as magpies. They scan the globe, spotting shiny brewing techniques and glittering, appealing ingredients, and then incorporate them into their nest—er, brewery. Beside hops, some of the buzziest tools in American brewers' sheds are wild yeasts and bacteria, ingredients so popular that they require their own categories at the Great American Beer Festival (GABF): American-Style Sour Ale and American-Style Brett Ale.

These funky, sometimes sour, sometimes challenging, but always interesting ales do not strictly follow the tart tradition of Belgium or that of Germany (with its gose and Berliner weisse). Instead, the American brewers use recipes as a launch pad to create something thrillingly novel, wholly their own. One of the first Stateside sour ales to capture the country's attention was concocted by the Belgian native Peter Bouckaert, a veteran brewer from Rodenbach who had taken the reins at,

DO THE MASH

Though purposely inoculating ales with *Lactobacillus* is a surefire ticket to sour flavors, breweries need not mess with microorganisms to create a puckering profile. Instead, they can add lactic acid, use acidulated malt, or employ the sour mash method. For the last approach, after mixing grains with water and boiling the mixture to create wort—the sugary broth that becomes beer—brewers top the liquid with raw grain, which contains natural souring bacteria. The brewing vessel is sealed, and CO_2 is pumped in to form an anaerobic environment and keep out unwanted microorganisms; the grain's natural bacteria are now primed to munch the sugars and create sourness.

AN UNCOMMON ALE

One of the more fascinating footnotes to American brewing is the Kentucky Common, a nearly extinct style that once was popular around Louisville. Unsurprisingly in bourbon country, the dark beer was made with plenty of corn as well as a sour mash, a technique used by distillers. The result was a refreshing beer with a lightly acidic edge. Today, several Midwestern breweries are dabbling in the style, including the New Albanian Brewing Company in Indiana which makes the Phoenix Kentucky Komon, and Chicago's Local Option, which offers the plainly named Kentucky Common.

Local Option's sour, roasty Kentucky Common is a peculiar taste of the past.

TWO TO TASTE: AMERICAN-STYLE BRETT ALE

SANCTIFICATION
RUSSIAN RIVER BREWING COMPANY
ABV: 6.75%

∽

No *Saccharomyces* was used to ferment this beer, reads the label on this . . . ale? Or is it a lager? Sanctification is a category-defying quaff fully fermented with Brett, giving the radiant, wedding ring–gold brew scant sourness but plenty of tart Granny Smith apples, lemon zest, and a crisply dry conclusion. Sanctification is a weirdly refreshing beer that would be my summertime go-to—if it weren't so expensive. Alas.

WHITEOUT WIT BIER
ANCHORAGE BREWING COMPANY
ABV: 6.5%

∽

Every one of Alaskan Gabe Fletcher's releases is inoculated with wild *Brettanomyces* yeast and aged in French oak barrels, resulting in distinctive ales such as this lightly tart take on the classic Belgian witbier. Indian coriander and black peppercorns provide a zesty kick, and lemon peel and equally lemony Sorachi Ace hops provide a bright citrus punch that jibes with the mellow vanilla that is supplied by a siesta in Chardonnay barrels.

BACKUP BEERS: *Allagash Brewing Company Interlude, Boulevard Brewing Co. Saison-Brett, Crooked Stave Artisan Beer Project (anything; all their beers include* Brettanomyces*), Green Flash Brewing Co. Rayon Vert Belgian-Style Pale Ale, Mikkeller Yeast Series (either Brettanomyces Bruxellensis Pale Ale or Brettanomyces Lambicus Pale Ale)*

---

fittingly, Fort Collins, Colorado's New Belgium Brewing Company.

After a failed oud bruin experiment, the brewery invested in a serious stock of oak barrels. In 1999, the investment paid dividends when Bouckaert concocted La Folie Sour Brown Ale (The Folly), an earthy, face-contorting treat with sour-apple flavors and a bright, acidic body. The feedback was an avalanche of positivity: La Folie won gold at 2001's GABF.

Since then, the country has gone wild for funky ales. The leader of the pack might be California's Russian River (see "Spreading Spontaneity" on page 232), where brewmaster Vinnie Cilurzo tends to a flock of bugs that deliciously infect his offbeat array of Belgian-inspired, barrel-aged ales. Also stupendous is Michigan's Jolly Pumpkin Artisan Ales, where Ron Jeffries specializes in rustic, 100 percent oak-aged, unpasteurized sour ales that rival fine wines for nuance. Elsewhere, Avery Brewing Company in Boulder, Colorado, runs the experimental, limited-release Barrel-Aged Series, devising curiosities such as the Brett-dosed Dépuceleuse ale made with sour cherries and aged in Zinfandel barrels.

In Southern California, Lost Abbey brewmaster Tomme Arthur is such a nut for wild yeasts that above the entrance to the brewery's barrel room hangs a sign proclaiming IN ILLA BRETTANOMYCES, NOS FIDES: roughly translated from Latin, the phrase means "in the wild yeast we believe." One taste of the bourbon barrel–aged Cuvèe de Tomme, infected with Brett and crafted with sour cherries, and you'll be a convert too.

While *Brettanomyces* may be the muse of Arthur at Lost Abbey, Ron Gansberg, the brewmaster at Cascade Brewing in Portland, Oregon, shuns yeast in favor of *Lactobacillus*. He exclusively uses the bacteria to create blended, barrel-matured sour ales that he often infuses with fruit. His Kriek Ale gets its kick from six months of sitting in oak in the company of Bing and sour pie cherries, whereas his Bourbonic Plague is a blend of potent porters aged in oak, wine, and bourbon barrels (plus one flavored with vanilla beans and cinnamon), then aged on dates for *another* 14 months. Each year's batch is a bit different, which is one of the pleasures of sipping wild or sour ales: they're the products of living organisms that march to their own weird, wonderful drumbeats.

For years, one of the big jokes about Jolly Pumpkin Artisan Ales was that the brewery did not make a single pumpkin beer. In 2010, the brewery finally embraced its name, releasing the gourd-packed La Parcela No. 1 Pumpkin Ale.

TWO TO TASTE: AMERICAN-STYLE SOUR ALE

APRICOT ALE
Cascade Brewing
ABV: 8.5%

Apricot Ale is constructed by fermenting a sweet Belgian tripel for up to 16 months in French-oak wine barrels with ripe apricots. The golden-orange elixir smells strongly of ripe, fragrant fruit, with a tinge of oak. Sometimes fruit beers can be too syrupy, but this one embodies balance: sweet and sour, creamy yet medium-bodied, and as tart and refreshing as fresh-squeezed lemonade on a summer afternoon. P.S. Cascade will ship its beer to most states. Visit cascadebrewingbarrelhouse .com for details.

LA ROJA ARTISAN AMBER ALE
Jolly Pumpkin Artisan Ales
ABV: 7.2%

This Belgian-style amber ale (reminiscent of a Flanders red) is constructed by blending sour beers matured in oak barrels for 2 to 10 months (younger, rawer batches balance older, oakier lots), resulting in an earthy, ruby-hued revelation. Swirl La Roja slowly, sniffing the musty aromas of dark fruit and hay, before taking an exploratory sip. A gentle tide of dry, sweet sourness soon reveals raisins and caramel, ending with assertive woodsy warmth that lingers like whiskey.

BACKUP BEERS: *Cisco Brewers Monomoy Kriek (part of The Woods series), Goose Island Beer Company Juliet, New Belgium Brewing Company La Folie, New Holland Brewing Blue Sunday Sour, Samuel Adams Stony Brook Red (part of the Barrel Room Collection), The Bruery Tart of Darkness*

WOMEN IN BREWING

New Belgium takes its souring program so seriously that it employs a "sensory specialist" who is in charge of blending beers and managing the wood cellar. Her name is Lauren Salazar, and she's part of the changing face of craft beer. Although the brewing industry is dominated by men, increasing ranks of women have been entering the craft beer field. The Pink Boots Society, which is only open to women in brewing, counts nearly 1,000 members, from CEOs to writers, sales representatives, publicans, and brewers. This is no novelty. These women are making some of the country's best beer.

In Oregon, Tonya Cornett brews beers such as Hop-Head Imperial IPA and Cherry Baltic Porter for Bend Brewing Co., as well as the sublime ISA (a hoppy "India session ale") and S1NIST0R Black Ale at 10 Barrel Brewing Co. (She works for both breweries.) Since 1987, Carol Stoudt has been the brewmaster at Pennsylvania's Stoudt's Brewing Company, crafting winners like their dry and bitter Pils and immense Fat Dog Stout. Barbara Groom is the brewmaster and owner of Lost Coast Brewery in Eureka, California, which makes the wonderful 8-Ball Stout. Across the Atlantic in Belgium, Brouwerij Dilewyns' Anne-Catherine Dilewyns (pictured below) brews first-class beers such as Vicaris Tripel and spiced Vicaris Winter. Try it, and you'll be tickled pink.

If you're ever driving through central Illinois, stop in Normal or Champaign to visit Destihl, which is quietly making some of America's most interesting wild and sour ales. Its rotating, evolving Saint Dekkera Reserve Sour Ale series of barrel-aged, spontaneously fermented beers is brilliant (destihlbrewery .com). Same goes for Texas's Freetail Brewing (freetailbrewing.com), which is building a world-class souring program in San Antonio. Sour heads, keep tabs on both of these breweries.

Saint Dekkera

RESERVE SOUR ALE

SINGLE BARREL AGED, SPONTANEOUSLY FERMENTED, WILD ACIDIC SOUR ALE

Brewed by DESTIHL.

CROOKED STAVE ARTISAN BEER PROJECT
DENVER, COLORADO

Crooked Stave founder Chad Yakobson focuses on beers fermented with the wild yeast **Brettanomyces.**

Chad Yakobson's was working toward a future in winemaking when things went sour. At Colorado State University in Fort Collins, he was studying horticultural science, focusing on grape growing, when he tried New Belgium's La Folie, the local brewery's acclaimed sour ale. "The first sip was shock and awe," Yakobson recalls. "At first, I thought it tasted like sauerkraut." La Folie grew on him, though its flavorful science remained a mystery until he moved to New Zealand to study winemaking, where he learned about the wild yeast *Brettanomyces.* In wine, it's a defect. In beer, it can bring beautiful funk.

"From that day forward, I sought out sour beers," says Yakobson, who embarked on a globetrotting odyssey. In London he worked as a sommelier, sampling Belgian lambics and gueuzes after work, before touching down in Australia, Africa, and Asia. During a bus trip through Thailand, he began formulating a plan to return to Colorado and launch a perception-shifting brewery powered by *Brettanomyces.* He enrolled at the International Centre for Brewing and Distilling in Edinburgh, Scotland, and began his master's degree dissertation, which became an open-source website dubbed the Brettanomyces Project.

Yakobson's research led him in early 2011 to establish Denver's Crooked Stave Artisan Beer Project. Instead of brewing, he sources wort from Prost Brewing and, in a sparse, barrel-filled facility that recalls a winery, inoculates the liquid with *Brettanomyces* and, occasionally, souring bacteria, creating beers that defy categorization. "They're not ales or lagers," he says. "It's an entirely new family of beers, a very broad grouping that I term *wild*."

BLAME IT ON THE STRAIN

Wild implies unpredictability, something untamable. Yakobson seeks to harness, or at least deeply understand, *Brettanomyces*, approaching it with scientific rigor and an explorer's curiosity about the unknown. That's because *Brettanomyces* is a little-understood organism, with only a few commercially produced strains.

There's a plethora of *Saccharomyces* strains (the standard brewing yeast), he says, but with *Brettanomyces* there are more distinct species, including *bruxellensis*, *claussenii*, and *custersianus*. "There's more genetic variation in *bruxellensis* than in all of *Saccharomyces*," he says. "The ability to have 200 to 300 Brett strains is a possibility."

To identify suitable strains, Yakobson began collecting beers from breweries that do not rely on lab-pure cultures, such as Belgium's Cantillon and 3 Fonteinen, and cultivating the strains. "I keep every strain, whether I like them or not," he says. "Some that don't start off nice become beautiful after nine months."

Yakobson's experiments have included a tart, low-alcohol take on tafelbier, or table beer, a light-bodied Belgian brew traditionally served with meals; called Petite Sour, it's sometimes flavored with fruit. The *Brettanomyces*-fermented Hop Savant experiments with hops in each batch. And Wild Wild Brett is an R&D series based on the seven colors of the rainbow.

"Using the color wheel was a way to incorporate different strains of Brett into different recipes," he explains. The fully Brett-fermented releases include Yellow, an homage to South Indian cuisine flavored with mango and turmeric. Rouge counted hibiscus flowers, rose hips, and hawthorn berries among its ingredients. The unfiltered

Orange was a witbier riff spiced with coriander, Minneola tangelos, and bitter orange peel, a combination that, much to Yakobson's surprise, had universal appeal.

"This was the ultimate beer-geek beer, but non–beer drinkers and women were telling me how approachable and delicate it was," he says. This contradicts the common belief that wild-yeast beers should smell and taste like an amble through a barnyard.

MONEY FOR SOMETHING

Starting a brewery specializing in funky barrel-aged beers might seem like commercial suicide. *Brettanomyces* takes time to develop its flavors, time a money-crunched fledgling brewery may not have. In late 2011, when Yakobson needed funds to relocate Crooked Stave from Fort Collins to Denver, he imitated a winery.

Wineries commonly sell memberships that ensure a bottle allotment, in turn receiving cash up front. Following their lead, Yakobson launched the Cellar Reserve membership, selling 400 slots for $300 apiece. Purchasers received exclusive glasses, T-shirts, and releases such as the Blackberry Petite Sour and the cognac barrel–aged Sour Quad, as well as future beer discounts. "We are grateful of the extreme faith that people have in our beers," he says.

In Denver, Yakobson is continuing his experiments. He opened a coolship-equipped brewery and taproom in a foundry turned open market called the Source, and he's been turning his attention to rustic, early-twentieth-century saisons, specifically the Surette (the name for saison in several regions of Wallonia). It's a firmly bitter, lightly carbonated, wood-aged farmhouse beer with a tart, complex profile—almost like a young lambic. That it is a decidedly different saison is precisely the point for Yakobson. "A crooked stave is the one in a barrel that's different, which portrays our brewery's central theme," he says. "We're progressing fermentation science by using a yeast that people said was incompatible with brewing."

AROUND THE WORLD IN 80 PINTS

INTERNATIONAL BEER STYLES

IT'S COMMON TO LIVE IN a beer cocoon. Surround yourself with friends who love bitter IPAs or imperial stouts, only hit bars that serve craft brews, and it's easy to believe that everyone drinks the good-beer Kool-Aid. Alternatively, if someone only visits saloons where "variety" is Bud, Miller, and Coors, offered in both regular and light, and takes his or her beer-buying cues from ads during football games, that person might believe the beer revolution never occurred.

The reality is a combination of column A and column B. Today, there's more interesting and higher-quality beer being brewed than at any time during U.S. history, but craft beer is still a long way from reaching critical mass. Fewer than 10 percent of Americans deviate from mainstream belly soakers. The battle is far from over. And it's being waged the world over. In Italy, France, Japan, and Scandinavia, risk-taking craft brewers also have begun cranking up brew kettles and, pint by pint, changing their countries' brewing landscapes.

Whether it's a Norwegian brewery fighting the pervasiveness of lagers or a French brewery competing against wineries for space on the dinner table, the story is the same around the world: brewers are engaged in David-and-Goliath struggles to bring drinkers better beer at any cost.

In this chapter, you'll learn how Japanese breweries such as Baird Brewing are providing an alternative to Sapporo and Asahi and read about the singular French style dubbed *bière de garde*. You'll be taken to Belgium, where a nineteenth-century farmer's humble summertime beer has become a worldwide phenomenon and then travel back in time to Colonial America to see the origins of contemporary brewers' new infatuation, pumpkin beers.

It's time to pack your bags. A world of beer is waiting.

CANADA

A few years ago I exited La Banquise, Montreal's 24-hour poutine specialist, with the kind of thirst that accompanies an afternoon spent devouring fries crowned with cheese curds and salty gravy. Needing a beverage, I pedaled my bike down Rue Rachel, away from downtown, and spotted the squat Dépanneur Peluso convenience store.

I locked up and entered, expecting standard-issue sodas and Molson beer. Yet as I strolled past the coolers, I noticed a rear room filled with more than 300 varieties of Quebec-brewed beers, neatly shelved by style. It was like entering a thrift store and finding rows of haute couture.

But which beers were worth my Canadian dollar? Well versed in U.S. craft brews, I was a blank slate on the 75-plus Quebec breweries, most of which don't sell their beers beyond the border. I aimlessly wandered the aisles until Alain Thibault, the shop's former beer expert, offered to be my guide. The brewing traditions of France, Belgium, and Great Britain, he explained, have influenced Quebec. Commercial production commenced in the late seventeenth century under the French, and the British industrialized brewing a century later. As in the United States, the microbrew craze percolated in the late 1980s, leading to today's boom. He pointed out standouts such as Charlevoix's creamy,

Montreal's Dépanneur Peluso is stocked with just about every beer that's brewed in Quebec.

lemony Dominus Vobiscum Blanche; Dieu du Ciel!'s coffee-infused Péché Mortel imperial stout; and Hopfenstark's piney Postcolonial IPA.

From that day forward, I paid closer attention to the rich and varied brewing scene of Canada, In British Columbia, breweries such as Central City Brewing are influenced by the Pacific Northwest, whereas Russell Brewing Company looks to England for unfiltered creations such as the toffee-accented IP'eh and Bloody Alley Bitter. (Also exemplary is Driftwood Brewery, maker of Fat Tug IPA and Farmhand Ale.) In Toronto, Mill St. Brewery turns heads with selections such as Coffee Porter and Lemon Tea Ale, and Spearhead Brewing Company makes the pineapple-infused Hawaiian Style Pale Ale.

Sorry, Molson and Labatt Blue: the outlook for Canadian beer is looking mighty flavorful, eh?

GET TO KNOW FOUR GREAT CANADIAN BREWERIES

L'ABRI DE LA TEMPÊTE

Terroir takes a starring turn in these ales crafted on the Iles-de-la-Madeleine archipelago in the Gulf of Saint Lawrence north of Prince Edward Island. Ocean breezes impart a salty nuance to the locally harvested barley, which head brewer Jean-Sébastien Bernier uses in winning creations such as the silky toffee-tinged Corne de Brume ("fog horn") Scotch ale, the rustic and lightly salinic Écume, and the delicate Belle Saison, made with foraged herbs.

DIEU DU CIEL!

I once spent part of a summer living in Montreal, an experience enriched by my apartment's proximity to Dieu du Ciel!, a brewery whose name loosely translates to "Oh, my God." That's what I exclaimed as I drank the brewery's ingenious ales. The Équinoxe du Printemps Scotch ale is made with maple syrup. Rosée d'Hibiscus witbier gets its pink tint and floral nuance from hibiscus flowers. And Route des Épices is packed with peppercorns and rye, a lightning bolt of spicy ingenuity.

CENTRAL CITY BREWING COMPANY

This British Columbia brewery's commitment to crafting high-quality unpasteurized ales paid off in 2012, when it was named Brewery of the Year at the Canadian Brewing Awards. That's largely due to its canned lineup of Red Betty brews (Red Racer in Canada), including the refreshing coriander-spiced Classic White Ale, the crisp Classic Lager, and the terrifically aromatic Classic Pale Ale and IPA, which could go toe to toe with anything brewed on the West Coast.

HOPFENSTARK

Less than a half hour north of Montreal you'll find quirky Hopfenstark, where brewer Fred Cormier fashions some of Canada's most eccentric and engaging ales. Whether he's brewing a tart Berliner weisse such as Berlin Alexanderplatz or the *Brettanomyces*-infected Boson de Higgs, a smoky, low-alcohol ale named after a hypothetical particle in physics, Cormier's beers are guaranteed to spark a discussion. Keep an eye out for the seasonally rotating Saison Station series.

FRANCE:
Bière de Garde

Several springs back, my wife and I flew to Paris, France, to visit friends. She was psyched. "Finally," she said, "we're going to a country that celebrates all the things I like: good bread, good cheese, good dessert, and great wines." I shuddered. Not that I have a vendetta against wine. I've nipped my fair share of Syrahs and Rieslings. It's just that France's beer scene leaves much to be desired unless you savor light lagers such as Kronenbourg 1664.

I did not have to submit myself to that indignity thanks to a serendipitous stroll near the Centre Pompidou, a renowned arts complex in the Fourth Arrondissement. A block away, down a side street, I spotted Cave à Bulles, the Bubble Cave, a store dedicated to craft beer. Over several hours, the proprietor Simon Thillou talked me through beers culled from all corners of France and Belgium. There were blondes, saisons, barley wines, fragrant pale ales, and plenty of examples of France's proud indigenous brew.

It was conceived in northern France's Nord-Pas de Calais region, which adjoins the English Channel, the North Sea, and, most critically, beer-mad Belgium. In the border-straddling land known as French Flanders, the climate is cooler, not suited for growing grapes. Fortuitously, the

MEET A WORLD OF BEER IN MONTREAL

For an excellent immersion in the world of Canadian beer, I suggest you attend Montreal's wonderful annual festival Mondial de la Bière (*festivalmondialbiere.qc.ca*). You'll be able to sample hundreds of beers from Quebec and around the world that are never sold in the United States.

weather is suitable for cultivating barley and hops, which the local brewers use to create strong, rustic farmhouse ales dubbed *bières de garde*, aka "beers for keeping." (Traditionally, *bières de garde* were brewed in early spring and kept in chilly cellars for sipping through the warmer summer months; they're now made year-round.)

Broadly defined, *bières de garde* register a fairly strong 6 to 8 percent ABV. The brews' hues can range from blonde to light brown to rich amber, with a sweet aroma displaying a musty complexity, fruit, and perhaps spicy herbal bitterness. The rich, medium-bodied beer typically drinks smooth,

> *In America, Central City's Red Betty beers were called } Red Racer until a lawsuit by Bear Republic Brewing forced the name change. The California brewery makes Red Rocket Ale and Racer 5 IPA.*

with lively carbonation and a malt-forward flavor accompanied by a balanced bready or caramel sweetness.

Though northern France's brewing industry was decimated during World Wars I and II, numerous traditional *bières de garde* endure today. In Bavay, a few miles from the Belgian border, Brasserie Theillier makes the rich and bubbly La Bavaisienne, which tastes of caramel, bread, and the earth. In contrast, Brasserie Saint-Germain's honey-colored Page 24 Bière de Printemps is moderately fruity, spicy, and sweet.

American craft brewers have taken to the style too, with terrific examples that include Two Brothers Brewing Company's Domaine DuPage and Garde Dog, which is Flying Dog Brewery's spring seasonal.

It's a taste of the French countryside from afar.

WATCH OUT, WINE

As recently as the 1890s, France was home to more than 2,000 breweries, a number that dropped to less than two dozen after World War II. Today, brewing in France is making a slow, steady comeback, aided by organizations such as French Craft Brewers (take a peek at *frenchcraftbrewers.com*).

TWO TO TASTE: BIÈRE DE GARDE

3 MONTS
BRASSERIE DE SAINT-SYLVESTRE
ABV: 8.5%

Saint-Sylvestre relies on locally grown hops and roasted malts to manufacture its lagers and ales. My pick of their litter is this straw-gold master stroke with fruity aromas backed by bread, cloves, and a bit of barnyard funk. It is vigorously carbonated, with flavors of apples, pears, and honey and an earthy bitterness. Additionally, the brewery makes the bottle-conditioned Gavroche, a malty red ale with a fair amount of fruitiness and earth.

BLOND BIERE DE GARDE
BRASSERIE CASTELAIN
ABV: 6.4%

One of France's few independent artisanal breweries, Castelain is helmed by Annick Castelain, the granddaughter of the brewery's founder. Under her stewardship, Castelain crafts sterling rustic ales, including this exquisite Champagne-corked *bière de garde*. It's a gorgeous gold, packing a sweet and fruity perfume, herbal complexity, and bitterness as appealing as a sunny spring afternoon.

BACKUP BEERS: *Brasserie La Choulette Les Bière Des Sans Culottes, Les Brasseurs de Gavant La Goudale, Lost Abbey Avant Garde, Schlafly Beer Bière De Garde*

GET TO KNOW FIVE GREAT FRENCH BREWERIES

BRASSERIE DUYCK

Four generations of the Duyck family have brewed in Nord-Pas de Calais, specializing in *bières de garde* sold in Champagne bottles, including the toasty, caramel-like Jenlain Ambrée and its sparkling sibling, Blonde. In recent years, Duyck has expanded its line to include the flowery and refreshing Jenlain Or and the full-bodied Blonde d'Abbaye.

BRASSERIE THIRIEZ

In that blurry region of French Flanders, Daniel Thiriez focuses on Belgian-influenced ales that are a little bit earthy, a little bit rustic, and all enjoyable. The Blonde is a fresh and spicy number with an alluring hop bouquet, which is cranked up in the dry, low-alcohol Extra—a superb little session beer. I can't speak highly enough of the beers from Brasserie Thiriez.

BRASSERIE BOURGANEL

By the tail end of the twentieth century, traditional brewing in the south of France had all but died. To bring it back from the brink, Christian Bourganel launched his namesake brewery in Vals-les-Bains, a spa town famed for its lush flora and fauna. Local terroir is displayed in the chestnut-filled Bourganel Bière aux Marrons and the Bourganel Au Nougat, which contains nougat cream.

BRASSERIE DU MONT BLANC

For nearly 200 years, Mont Blanc has used glacier water to brew its line of beers that leans on exotic and unlikely spicing. The malty award-winning La Rousse amber ale is a blend of barley, oats, and wheat that's spiced with hibiscus and elderberry; La Blonde is finely flavored with licorice and coriander; and La Violette leans on violets.

BRASSERIE SAINT-GERMAIN

Since its inception in 2003, the northern France brewery has released some of France's most lauded *bières de garde*, which are sold under the Page 24 banner. The unpasteurized, bottle-conditioned creations include the grassy, bitter, and earthy Réserve Hildegarde and its toasty sibling, the Ambrée. Also tremendous: the tangy, citrusy Blanche witbier.

BELGIUM AND FRANCE: *Bière de Champagne*

From time to time, I appreciate a fine glass of French Champagne or sparkling wine. And that time is usually between 11 p.m. and midnight on December 31, when bottles are popped and bubbles fly willy-nilly. For me, the effervescent elixir is best suited for wintertime celebrations, though a strong case can be made for lazy, hazy summer days sprawled atop a picnic blanket.

No matter. Next New Year's Eve, I suggest that you bypass the bubbly and instead select a bottle of one of brewing's newest and most intriguing categories of beer, *bière de Champagne*. Also known as *bière brut*, many of these hybrid beers follow the same painstaking protocol used in Champagne production. The beer undergoes lengthy multiple fermentations, the bottle is turned slowly so that yeast collects in its neck (*remuage*), and then the neck is frozen and pressure drives out the yeast bung in a process called *dégorgement*.

The payoff is best experienced in a flute. Like its namesake, the delicate *bière de Champagne* should be bone-dry and display berserk bubbles, with an elevated alcohol content and a color that can be paler than peach fuzz or as dark as rye bread. The Belgian breweries Bosteels and De Landtsheer pioneered this labor-intensive technique, but variations (although without *remuage* and *dégorgement*) are now being produced by

---

TWO TO TASTE: BIÈRE DE CHAMPAGNE

DEUS BRUT DES FLANDRES
BROUWERIJ BOSTEELS
ABV: 11.5%

Shaking up and spraying DeuS (pronounced "DAY-ews") would be a disservice to this *bière brut*, which is fermented in Belgium but finished in France's Champagne region. (In Belgium, brewers are not allowed to use the term bière de Champagne.) The net result: a bone-dry surprise with plenty of citrus, a fab touch of funk, and nose-tickling bubbles that stick around until the last prickly sip.

KRAIT PRESTIGE
COBRA BEER PARTNERSHIP LIMITED
ABV: 8%

Starting with a lager brewed in Poland, this beer is injected with ale yeast harvested from Belgium's Rodenbach brewery and then allowed to condition for several weeks. The corked, toasty result drinks smooth and lightly floral, sliding down at a gentle 8 percent ABV—well, gentle for a sparkling wine, at least. A word of caution: Krait might be sweeter than you would like.

BACKUP BEERS: *Brouwerij De Landtsheer Malheur Bière Brut, Microbrasserie Charlevoix Dominus Vobiscum Brut, Mikkeller Nelson Sauvignon, Samuel Adams Infinium*

A TRIP TO MARS

A close relative of *bière de garde* is *bière de Mars*, which is released in March (*Mars* in French). These beers are best fresh, not for keeping, and serve as a seasonal bridge between winter and spring. *Bières de Mars* do not share a unifying flavor profile, but they traditionally were brewed in late winter, when the fermentation cellars were coolest. Chilly temperatures give the ale smoothness and a crisp, lager-like complexity. You'll find fine modern interpretations produced by Southhampton Publick House and Bayou Teche (try the Courir de Mardi Gras), while Jolly Pumpkin Artisan Ale doctors its version with wild yeast for a funky farmhouse edge.

A STATE OF ENLIGHTENMENT

Several years ago, Massachusetts's Ben Howe splurged on a pricey bottle of *bière de Champagne* imported from Belgium. The high cost, coupled with the lack of American brewers experimenting with the style, led Howe (a former assistant brewer at Cambridge Brewing Company) to launch Enlightenment Ales. He uses the labor-intensive techniques of Champagne production to create intensely carbonated beers like Enlightenment Brut. Additionally, he makes "urban farmhouse" creations such as the dry, tropical Illumination IPA.

Sam Adams, which makes the Infinium in conjunction with Germany's Weihenstephan, and Denmark's Mikkeller, which doctors its Nelson Sauvignon (a *bière de Champagne* made with Nelson Sauvin hops) with *Brettanomyces* and ages it for three months in barrels that once held Austrian Sauvignon Blanc.

These beers are not exactly commonplace. But if you find a bottle, that's reason enough to celebrate.

BELGIUM: SAISON

Drinking water was once like playing Russian roulette: Did this glass contain the contagion that would finally kill you? To nix the risk for cholera and other intestinal assassins, people relied on hygienic fermented beverages such as cider, mead, and, chiefly, beer.

Beer was lifeblood, especially for the French-speaking Wallonia region of southern Belgium. Centuries ago, as now, grain farms covered the countryside like a patchwork quilt. Armed with the fruits of their labor, farmers often pulled double duty as brewers, using their excess harvest grains to brew strong beers that were suited for saving. But before the age of refrigeration, brew kettles were not fired up during the summer—hot weather was an open invitation for unruly yeast and microbes to befoul beer.

Instead, farmers spent the winter brewing batches of *saison* (French for "season") that were stored until summer.

During the harvest, the dry, earthy, thirst-quenching beers were dispensed to hardworking field hands to ensure that they did not keel over from dehydration or to serve as a buzzy restorative. As fellow beer writer William Bostwick dubs it, the saison was the Gatorade of the 1800s.

Over the last several centuries, the rustic saison has remained as open to interpretation as a Rorschach blot, with no right or wrong answers. Saisons can be as blonde as Barbie's hair, or maybe they'll take a turn to the dark side like Stillwater Artisanal Ales's A Saison Darkly, Goose Island's peppercorn-spiced Pepe Nero, or Brasserie Fantôme's Black Ghost. (Belgium's Fantôme makes a particularly diverse line of saisons, including a chocolate version.) Some saisons ride a dry and prickly road, such as the archetypal Saison Dupont and Pretty Things's Jack D'Or. Others incorporate

For more on Belgian (and French) farmhouse beers, read Phil Markowski's Farmhouse Ales: Culture and Craftsmanship in the Belgian Tradition. *(Formerly the brewmaster at Southampton Publick House, Markowski now works at Connecticut's Two Roads Brewing Co.)*

ALL MINE

Fieldhands were hardly the only hardworking laborers with their own restorative beverage. In southern Belgium's Hainaut province, local miners slaked their thirst with *grisette* ("little gray"), a refreshing low-alcohol ale that was lighter than a saison and, more often than not, blended barley malt with wheat. (The name may reference the color of the mined rocks or the working-class women who served the men their liquid rations; they were known as grisettes after the cheap gray dresses they originally wore.) Over time the style faded into obscurity, but it's making a small, steady resurgence in the United States. You'll find modern interpretations from Pennsylvania's Sly Fox Brewing Company and McKenzie Brew House, and Belgium's Brasserie St. Feuillien makes a range of grisettes that, sadly, are not imported to the United States.

AN UPRIGHT CITIZEN

If you have a hankering for farmhouse-inspired Belgian and French beers and find yourself in Portland, Oregon, I recommend that you beeline it to Upright Brewing. Founder Alex Ganum relies on locally sourced grains and hops, a saison yeast strain, and open fermentation (the vessels are not sealed shut) to create a collection of rustic, multifaceted, and sometimes sour or *Brettanomyces*-infected barrel-aged beers.

TWO TO TASTE: SAISON

SAISON DUPONT
BRASSERIE DUPONT
ABV: 6.5%

The style's unquestioned king is
Saison Dupont, the benchmark
by which all other contenders are
judged. Brewed on the same farm
since 1844, Brasserie Dupont relies
on spring water and its proprietary
yeast strains to fashion the snappy,
lively saison. It's sublimely citrusy,
with hints of pepper and a tinder-
dry finish that makes Dupont an
eternal revelation. The farmhouse
brewery's collection of seek-them-
out saisons also counts the dry,
herbal Forêt and Avec les Bons
Vœux, a spicy, zesty release for the
holiday season.

SAISON ATHENE
SAINT SOMEWHERE BREWING
COMPANY
ABV: 7.5%

When it comes to brewing, Tarpon
Springs, Florida, is not on the tip of
anyone's tongue. Saint Somewhere
aims to change that with its
inspired, boredom-deficient
Belgian-style ales, whether it's the
dubbel-saison hybrid Lectio Divina
(spiked with wild yeast for good
measure), the sweet and sour Pays
du Soleil dubbel, or Saison Athene.
Chamomile, rosemary, and black
pepper supply the hazy, tarnished-
gold saison with a zesty herbal
complexity that cuddles with citrus
and an effervescence that'll tickle
the back of your throat as you
savor the last Sahara-dry sip.

herbs, spices, or fruit, such as Cigar City's
Guava Grove Saison and Southampton
Publick House's Cuvée des Fleurs, which
is made with edible flowers.

Still, some of my favorite saisons
feature funky flavors courtesy of the wild
yeast *Brettanomyces* or maybe a measure
of puckering complexity provided by
souring bacteria. This may seem to fly
against the original intentions of the
brewers. Weren't they trying *not* to make
infected beers? Indeed, but think about
where the farmer-brewers probably
stored their beer: the barn. Packed with
animals and feed, a barn is a breeding
ground for wild bugs. Winter and spring
lasted long enough for them to find a
comfortable home inside beer.

Hence, I have a sweet spot for
Boulevard Brewing's dry, earthy Saison-
Brett, The Bruery's Saison de Lente,
and Seizoen Bretta from Logsdon
Farmhouse Ales in Oregon. They're
thirst-quenching creations suited to
summer—or any other month that
strikes your fancy. With beer, it's always
drinking season.

BACKUP BEERS: *Brasserie St. Feuillien Saison, Brooklyn Brewery
Sorachi Ace, Funkwerks Saison, Jolly Pumpkin Artisan Ales Bam Bière,
McKenzie Brew House Saison Vautour, Stillwater Artisanal
Ales Stateside Saison*

SAISONS OFTEN ARE LUMPED INTO THE loose category of FARMHOUSE ALES.

GET TO KNOW FIVE GREAT AMERICAN FARMHOUSE BREWERIES

HILL FARMSTEAD BREWERY
GREENSBORO, VERMONT

For eight generations Shaun Hill's family has laid claim to this farm in Greensboro Bend, a town of around 600 in the state's lush and leafy Northeast Kingdom. Armed with well water and a healthy appreciation for hops, Hill generates complex saisons, wild ales, stouts, IPAs, and the Ancestral Series of offerings that bear the forenames of family members. I'm partial to Ephraim, a resinous imperial pale ale named after his great-great-grandfather. Each summer, the brewery hosts the Festival of Farmhouse Ales. Bring a tent and a hankering for saisons.

WEEPING RADISH FARM BREWERY
GRANDY, NORTH CAROLINA

In 1986, Uli Bennewitz opened North Carolina's first brewery, an operation that over the last three decades has grown to encompass a 14-acre farm and butchery in the Outer Banks. Benneweitz's Bavarian roots mean that the Reinheitsgebot shapes his beers, including the kölsch-style OBX Beer and Black Radish schwarzbier. Pop by the farm to pound beers and snack on kielbasa and bratwurst made by the brewery's German master butcher.

ROCKMILL BREWERY
LANCASTER, OHIO

Southeastern Ohio's rural Lancaster might be a world away from Belgium's Wallonia, but Matthew Barbee's farm shares one important trait with the famed brewing region: a nearly perfect match to the water's mineral and bicarbonate makeup. In a converted horse barn, he crafts a quartet of hand-corked, bottle-conditioned organic beers: a dubbel, a tripel, a witbier, and a farm-appropriate saison.

LOGSDON ORGANIC FARMHOUSE ALES
HOOD RIVER, OREGON

After several decades wrangling brewing yeast, Wyeast Laboratories cofounder David Logsdon debuted his eponymous brewery in 2011, earning instant acclaim for his all-organic lineup of saisons, witbiers, and Belgian-inspired sour ales made with locally grown hops. Even more exciting, the farm currently is growing Schaerbeekse kriek trees brought over from East Flanders—the traditional cherries used in kriek production (see more on page 229).

OXBOW BREWING COMPANY
NEWCASTLE, MAINE

With the brewery's location in a renovated barn on an 18-acre farm, it's fitting that head brewer and owner Tim Adams focuses on farmhouse-inspired beers with a Belgian bent. Saison yeast drives the flavor the rustic Space Cowboy Country Ale and the dry and citrusy Farmhouse Pale Ale, and the addition of *Brettanomyces* fuels the sake-like Sasuga Saison and the spicy, pungent Funkhaus. In the coming years, you'll want to keep a close eye on Oxbow.

UNITED STATES: PUMPKIN BEERS

Autumn beer drinking is deliciously intertwined with Germany's malty märzen, the subtly sweet lager that's coupled to Oktoberfest (see more on page 51). Although that style is well and good—and sometimes *really* good—American brewers have begun exploring fall-appropriate beers made with an indigenous vegetable: the pumpkin.

Consider it a return to roots. Back when America was still under England's thumb, Colonial brewers relied on expensive malted barley imported from the mother country. To stretch out the costly grain, crafty brewers grabbed anything and everything that contained fermentable sugars and flavor, such as Jerusalem artichokes, persimmons, spruce tips, molasses, corn, and pumpkins.

I must tip my hat to those resourceful colonists who re-created the luxuries (or was that necessities?) of home far from it, but these were rough, inelegant ales cherished more for alcohol content than for flavor. Understandably, when Americans learned to grow barley, pumpkin- and persimmon-fueled beers faded from tavern taps.

For much of the nineteenth and twentieth centuries American brewers ignored the gourd, leaving it to pie bakers and kids to carve into grinning jack-o'-lanterns. The fruit

began reappearing in the brew kettle in the 1980s, most notably at Buffalo Bill's Brewery in Hayward, California. While thumbing through a brewing book, founder Bill Owens stumbled upon the factoid that George Washington once brewed a beer starring squash. (The nation's first president was also an avid distiller.) In 1986, that lightbulb moment led Owens to use pumpkin pie spices such as cinnamon, cloves, and nutmeg to create Pumpkin Ale. (Today, the stronger Imperial Pumpkin Ale contains actual pumpkin.)

The gourd revolution was officially off the ground and galloping as fast as Ichabod Crane's horse. Nearly three decades later, there are

Every fall, Seattle's Elysian Brewing hosts the Great Pumpkin Beer Festival. The two-day celebration features dozens of ingenious pumpkin brews, such as the gourd-based PK-47 malt liquor and beer dispensed directly from a massive scooped-out pumpkin, where it has undergone a secondary fermentation.

enough different pumpkin beers to populate a patch, with many versions popping up in late summer to meet the outsize demand, seasonality be damned. Plenty are like liquefied pie, sweet and spiced with ginger, nutmeg, clove, and cinnamon. Some are bitter and dark as squid ink, such as the Pumpkin Imperial Spruce Stout from Vermont's Rock Art Brewery. Other breweries opt to incorporate pumpkin into a saison or a sour ale or even age a burly version in freshly emptied rum barrels, such as Avery Brewing's Rumpkin.

Name the style, and breweries can add pumpkin to it. It's a neat trick for a gourd to create beers that are a total treat.

LET'S GO NUTS

What's the next big foodstuff in craft brewing? Call me nuts, but I believe it'll be peanuts. Hazelnuts, pecans, and chestnuts are commonplace beer ingredients, but it's peanut butter that makes Americans swoon. With that in mind, Ohio's Willoughby Brewing makes the Peanut Butter Cup Coffee Porter and Maryland's DuClaw Brewing cooks up Sweet Baby Jesus! It's a porter that tastes like a Reese's Peanut Butter Cup on a bender, which also ably describes Terrapin's Liquid Bliss. The Georgians age the beer with boiled green peanuts —a nutty take on dry hopping.

TWO TO TASTE: PUMPKIN BEER

SMASHED PUMPKIN
Shipyard Brewing Co.
ABV: 9%
～

This Maine brewery's nutmeg-and-cinnamon-spiced Pumpkinhead Ale is so beloved that Shipyard starts pumping it out in the summer. Better still is Pumpkinhead's stronger big brother, Smashed Pumpkin. It smells of yanked-from-the-oven pumpkin pie, with nice notes of baking spices and enough booze to make you knock-kneed. It drinks lightly sweet, spicy, and luscious, rocking a bitter load.

DARK O' THE MOON PUMPKIN STOUT
Elysian Brewing Company
ABV: 6.5%
～

Dick Cantwell is dedicated to pumpkins. Over the last decade, the cofounder of and head brewer at Seattle's Elysian Brewing Company has devised dozens of different gourd beers, including this full-bodied stout made with roasted pumpkin seeds, pumpkin flesh, and a sprinkling of cinnamon. The result is a creamy, chocolaty indulgence with a roasty finish that lasts long past the witching hour.

BACKUP BEERS: *Big Boss Brewing Harvest Time Pumpkin Ale, Cape Ann Brewing Company Fisherman's Pumpkin Stout, Heavy Seas Beer The Great Pumpkin, New Holland Brewing Company Ichabod Ale, Southern Tier Brewing Company Pumking, Weyerbacher Brewing Co. Imperial Pumpkin Ale*

FIVE FANTASTIC FRUIT BEERS

WHY SHOULD PUMPKINS HAVE ALL THE FUN? THESE BEERS GIVE FRUIT A GOOD NAME.

WISCONSIN BELGIAN RED

New Glarus Brewing Company
ABV: 4%

New Glarus is one of the nation's most cultishly revered breweries, no doubt as a result of genius creations such as Wisconsin Red. State-grown Montmorency cherries and wheat join forces with Belgian barley and Hallertau hops, then spend a year aging in oak tanks. Time transforms the ingredients into a spritzy, ruby-hued restorative that smells like a stroll through a cherry orchard. It's summer in a glass.

BAR HARBOR BLUEBERRY ALE

Atlantic Brewing Company
ABV: 5.2%

One of the prettiest cities in the Northeast is Bar Harbor, Maine, which is near Acadia National Park. The town is a summertime favorite, as is this mellow, light-bodied ale that harnesses the state's beloved berry. Don't be afraid: the blueberry appears only in the aroma, and there's none of that syrupy, cloying character that besmirches fruit beers' good name.

FALLEN APPLE

Furthermore Beer
ABV: 6.2%

Although the brewery is no stranger to strange beer (Knot Stock pale ale is spiced with black pepper, and Thermo Refur sour ale contains organic red beets), brewer and owner Aran Madden outdoes himself with his autumn specialty, Fallen Apple. He blends fresh-pressed cider with a cream ale made with lactose (milk sugar), which adds a touch of sweetness. It tastes like an apple that eloped with a bottle of Champagne.

BRAINLESS ON PEACHES

Epic Brewing Co.
ABV: 10.7%

Utah is overlooked on the national brewing landscape, an oversight that'll change once word spreads about Epic (no relation to the New Zealand brewery). The Salt Lake City crew crafts brain-flash brews such as Sour-Apple Saison, Scotch-like Smoked & Oaked, Hop Syndrome Lager, and a big ol' Belgian-style golden ale called Brainless on Peaches. Organic peach purée and a lie-down in French Chardonnay casks make Brainless a fruity, wine-like pleasure.

KEY LIME PIE

Short's Brewing Company
ABV: 5.5%

At first blush, the beers from Short's Brewing seem like a high-concept joke conceived after a couple of tokes. What else can one think about Pistachio Cream Ale, PB&J Stout, and Strawberry Short's Cake? But I'm here to tell you these weirdos work, dear drinker, none more than Key Lime Pie. Graham crackers, Marshmallow Fluff, and fresh limes conspire to create a tart-and-sweet treat that won gold at 2010's Great American Beer Festival.

257

GREAT BRITAIN AND SCOTLAND

British beer gets a bad rap as being boring. The country is best known for its milds and bitters and an affinity for mass-produced lagers, beer styles whose nuanced pleasures and restrained ABVs seem quaint to American craft-beer drinkers who are conditioned by hoppy, boozy beers.

It's time to toss that generalization into the trash bin. Over the last decade the beer scene in Britain and Scotland has blossomed, shaking off the confining shackles of cask ale and creating brews every bit as inventive as those crafted across the Atlantic Ocean.

One of the first breweries to break out in a big way and blaze a path for fellow U.K. brewers was Scotland's BrewDog. Inspired by a trip to the West Coast and its rule-breaking, hop-mad breweries such as Stone, in 2007 BrewDog began forging a new U.K. identity with ales such as pungent Hardcore IPA, Tokyo★ imperial stout crafted with cranberries and jasmine and aged with toasted French oak chips, and Dogma Scotch ale, infused with guarana, honey, kola nuts, and poppy seeds. These were not the average bloke's pint of bitter at the pub.

Today, the British brewing landscape has begun to look as varied and inventive as its counterparts across the pond. In London, Kernel Brewery has made waves with its bold, citrusy American-inspired pale ales and IPAs as well as throwbacks to the nineteenth century such as the lusciously oily, espresso-like Export Stout. Also in London, Brodie's Beers whips out bang-up IPAs and Camden Town Brewery does spot-on spins on foreign styles such as the supremely drinkable American-style Camden Pale (insanely aromatic but just 4 percent ABV) and Ink, a hop-blasted nitrogenated stout that's every bit as creamy as Ireland's favorite quaff.

Elsewhere in the country, Thornbridge Brewery is adept at both classic styles such as the hefeweizen-style Versa and new-breed delights such as the Raven black IPA and Kipling, which they describe as a tropical South Pacific pale ale made with New Zealand's Nelson Sauvin hops that packs the flavors of passion fruit and kiwi. Want another IPA? Situated about 45 minutes from London in Henly-on-Thames, Lovibonds Brewery makes the lasciviously named 69 IPA—6.9 percent ABV, that is. U.S.-bred Centennial and Columbus hops give the golden brew a citrusy nose as well as a clean bitterness.

Besides BrewDog, Scotland's craft-brewing ranks include the archaic beers of Williams Bros. Brewing Company (the dark elderberry-flavored Ebulum is based on a sixteenth-century recipe), the oak-aged ales of Innis & Gunn, and, in the scenic Scottish Highlands, the progressive beers of Black Isle Brewing Co. Equipped with a couple of cows, a handful of horses, a bounty of sheep, and loads of farm equipment, the environmentally focused brewery grows 120 acres of organic barley that it turns into the malty Red Kite Ale, the complex and balanced Porter, and the smooth Hibernator Export Oatmeal Stout. These beers are anything but boring.

BrewDog has begun opening branded pubs across the United Kingdom, serving both modern European brews and imported American craft beers.

GET TO KNOW FOUR GREAT BRITISH BREWERIES

SUMMER WINE BREWERY

This Yorkshire brewery sets itself apart by focusing on unfiltered, unpasteurized, and above all flavor-forward ales such as Barista Espresso Stout, the berry-like Rouge-Hop, and the devilish Diablo. The IPA is heavily dosed with American hop varieties such as tropical Citra, which lend notes of lychee, mango, and plenty of sticky pine. As their website says, "We plan to tear up the rule book and brew beers that demand you sit up and take note by shaking up your senses and thus redefining how Yorkshire beer is perceived."

DARK STAR BREWING CO.

Since 1994, this West Sussex outfit has won over legions of drinkers with uncommonly balanced and always inventive ales such as Black Coffee Pilsner, Milk Chocolate Stout, Summer Meltdown (made with Chinese stem ginger), and Hophead. Instead of socking drinkers over the head with bitterness, this 3.8 percent ABV golden ale is an easy sipper with a fantastic floral aroma courtesy of Cascade hops.

OTLEY BREWING COMPANY

This Wales brewery focuses on modern unfiltered, naturally carbonated cask ales and bottle-conditioned brews that shatter "the woolly cardigan and beard syndrome." To that end, there are hoppy O4 Columbo, robust O6 Porter, and O-Garden, a whimsical riff on the classic Belgian witbier Hoegaarden. Otley's hazy take on the wheat-beer style is dosed with coriander, cloves, and orange peel, resulting in a dry, citrusy delight.

MAGIC ROCK BREWING

Compelled by a love of American craft beer, brothers Richard and Jonny Burhouse and head brewer Stuart Ross launched Magic Rock in 2011. The team's focus on unabashedly hoppy ales manifests itself in West Coast–style ales such as grapefruit- and mango-drenched, sticky tropical Cannonball IPA and Clown Juice "India wit ale." Yup, it's a hoppy witbier.

NEW ZEALAND

During wartime, nations ask their citizens to make sacrifices in the name of patriotic duty. In New Zealand during the throes of World War I, that sacrifice took the form of closing the pubs at 6 p.m.

As the reasoning went, cutting drinkers off at 6 p.m. meant they would be more productive the next day—hangover legislation at its finest. More than 160,000 New Zealanders signed a petition demanding the 6 p.m. closure, which became a temporary measure in 1917. The next year the nanny-state law became permanent.

On the surface, this law seemed full of upside. Since the pubs closed at 6 p.m., men could spend more quality time with their families. Perhaps they did, but Dad was probably pie-eyed. When the work whistle blew at 5 p.m., there was a mad stampede to the pub. Every minute counted. Every beer was pounded. The preferred beers for mass consumption were light and crisp lagers, the kind that college kids consume by the case. Instead of lessening consumption, the government measure merely taught multiple generations of New Zealanders how to binge drink. The "six o'clock swill," as the tradition became known, lasted until 1967. Kiwis' preference for mild, gulpable lagers lingered like the hangover the government was trying to avoid.

Thankfully, the long national nightmare is coming to a close. In the last decade, New Zealand has begun embracing the sort of bold, inventive ales that have become synonymous with the modern American brewing scene. Epic Beer makes fragrant, uncompromisingly bitter IPAs, such as Armageddon and Hop Zombie, that would be right at home on the West Coast. The brash Yeastie Boys toy with conventions in beers, as in their smoky, Scotch whiskey–like Rex Attitude strong ale, which is made with 100 percent peated malt. The team at 8 Wired specializes in modern interpretations of classic styles, such as the hoppy Haywired wheat beer and the surprisingly strong Saison Sauvin. Kaimai Brewing focuses on a range of rye-driven beers, any of which you would be happy to swill at 6 p.m.—and all night long as well.

Why didn't the liquor companies and breweries put up a fight? The 6 p.m. closure was a preferable alternative to Prohibition, a measure that barely came up short in New Zealand's 1919 national election.

Hops grown in New Zealand (Motueka, Riwaka, Nelson Sauvin) have become increasingly popular in the United States thanks to their unique flavors and aromas as well as the fact that the country has zero natural pests. By default, no pesticides are needed.

GET TO KNOW FOUR GREAT NEW ZEALAND BREWERIES

8 WIRED BREWING CO.

After his wife, Monique, gave him a homebrew kit, the biochemist Søren Eriksen decided to ditch his research career (last project: sea urchins) and open a brewery in New Zealand. A road trip across the United States provided all the inspiration he needed to open 8 Wired, named after a gauge of wire used for electronic fencing. Ericksen's beers are equally shocking: Hopwired IPA made with New Zealand malt and hops, campfire-nuanced The Big Smoke porter, and the strong Belgian-style The Sultan made with sultana raisins.

EPIC BEER

Back in the 1990s New Zealand's Luke Nicholas studied in California, where he acquired a hankering for hoppy ales and a talent for brewing them. Fast-forward to 2006 and after a few brewing stops elsewhere, he at last launched Epic Beer, a hop-first collection of pale ales, IPAs, and even a lager that's undergone serious dry hopping.

YEASTIE BOYS

New Zealand's pop culture–inspired Yeastie Boys buck brewing conventions with beers such as Gunnamatta IPA made with Earl Grey Blue Flower tea and Digital IPA concocted with New Zealand–grown Pacific Jade, Nelson Sauvin, Pacifica, and Cascade hops that deliver pungent tropical-fruit notes. (Scan the bottle's code with your smartphone to get the recipe.) Also terrific: the roasty, smoky, and fresh-smelling Pot Kettle Black IPA.

TUATARA BREWERY

It's named after a New Zealand reptile whose ancestors (as they say on their website) "used to smoke behind bike sheds with stegosaurus 200 million years ago." Founded in 2001, Tuatara focuses on clean, spot-on modern interpretations of international styles, including the Bavarian Hefe, Munich Helles, London Porter, and American Pale Ale.

One of Sweden's only indigenous styles of beer is gotlandsdricke, *a strong and smoky ale made with rye and juniper. It originated on the farm breweries of Gotland, an island adrift in the Baltic Sea.*

Come Christmastime, many Norwegian breweries make a strong, dark, and sometimes spiced beer called juleøl. *In Denmark, a similar holiday beer is known as* julebryg.

Until January 1, 1995, SWEDEN FORBADE **any beer stronger** THAN 5.6% ABV.

In Norway, special beers once were crafted to honor the deceased, and a body could not be buried until the beer was brewed.

SCANDINAVIA

Twenty years ago, I'd have had a hard time choosing the worse fate: endure a Scandinavian winter without heat or spend three months drinking only the region's pale and weak lagers. Brewing was not the strong suit of Sweden, Norway, and Denmark, a triumvirate dominated by lagers such as Ringnes, Carlsberg, and Tuborg.

Part of the ubiquity stems from taxation. Stronger beers are saddled with a higher tax rate, which penalizes brewers for traveling to the far fringes of flavor. (In Denmark, beers below 2.8 percent ABV are not taxed.) Then there's the issue of buying beer. In Sweden, only government-run Systembolaget ("system company") stores can sell beers stronger than 3.5 percent ABV, and in Norway beers stronger than 4.75 percent ABV can be sold only at specially licensed shops or the state-run chain Vinmonopol—in other words, "wine monopoly."

The dominance of lagers seemed absolute, with the roadblocks cemented in place. But year after year, beer after inventive beer, Scandinavia has begun rewiring its brewing culture. In Norway, a land where the government once decreed that farmers had to grow barley and hops and brew a specific amount of beer lest they be fined or lose their land, Nøgne Ø and Haandbryggeriet specialize in screwy formulations incorporating everything from West Coast hops to Colombian coffee and juniper branches.

Sweden has also seen a similar explosion. Under the stewardship of head brewer and rock-band drummer Mattias Hammenlind, Sigtuna Brygghus has experienced meteoric growth with hop-influenced ales such as its East Coast IPA, Summer IPA, South Pacific Pale Ale, and East River Spring Lager, which is "produced with AC/DC in the speakers at the brewery to ensure the perfect quality." Based on a family farm that's more than 250 years old, Oppigårds

ITINERANT ALES

Gypsy brewer is a term used to describe a nomadic brewer who does not own a brewery but instead brews by using other people's equipment on a temporary basis. In legalese, this arrangement is known as an alternating proprietorship. The prominent ranks of gypsy brewers include numerous Danish breweries such as Mikkeller, Evil Twin, To Øl, and Kissmeyer as well as America's Stillwater Artisanal Ales and California's sour-focused The Rare Barrel, which specializes in sour beers brewed elsewhere but fermented and aged in its own facility.

Bryggeri has garnered global plaudits for the aromatic Amarillo and the dark and divine Starkporter. Situated on the Nynäshamn archipelago, Nynäshamns Ångbryggeri's unpasteurized ales, such as the Fatlagrad Smörpundet Porter and Bedarö Bitter, are named after the local geography. Nils Oscar makes a barley wine and an imperial stout that'll cause your eyes to swirl like peppermint candy. (Finland is still lagging behind, but breweries such as Plevna and its Severin Extra IPA and Siperia imperial stout are showing drinkers the flavorful light.)

As for Denmark, what that country's breweries have accomplished is nothing short of stunning. Since the nonprofit organization Danske Ølentusiaster ("Danish Beer Enthusiasts") was founded in 1998, educating consumers and bar owners alike, the nation has seen breweries spring up like mushrooms after an April rainstorm. Mikkeller is ranked regularly as one of the world's best breweries thanks to gonzo recipes such as Texas Ranger chipotle porter, a series of spontaneously fermented fruit beers, and smoky, bacon-like Rauch Geek Breakfast imperial stout. Nørrebro Bryghus has double IPAs and coffee stouts that'll make you do a double take to check the label. A legend at the trailblazing Ølfabrikken brewery, madcap brewer Christian Skovdal Andersen has resurfaced at Beer Here,

making the commendable Dark Hops black IPA and Mørke, a porter modeled after pumpernickel bread.

The list of avant-garde breweries stretches on and on. Nowadays, being stranded in Scandinavia all winter might be a blessing.

INTERESTINGLY, ONE OF **SWEDENS TOP-SELLING BEER BRANDS IS** Brooklyn Brewery.

GET TO KNOW FOUR GREAT SCANDINAVIAN BREWERIES

NØGNE Ø

Smitten by the American craft breweries he encountered while flying, Norwegian pilot Kjetil Jikiun purchased a homebrew kit, developed his brewing prowess, and, inspired by the Washington breweries Elysian and Hood Canal, launched Norway's inaugural craft brewery. Nøgne Ø focused on hoppy beers before turning its attention to subtle saisons, lightly smoky tripels, thirst-quenching witbiers, and even a Christmas ale inspired by Norway's winter-warming spiced wine gløgg. Nøgne Ø also makes sake, the first European brewery to create the traditional Japanese rice beverage.

MIKKELLER

Like a nomad, the Danish brewer Mikkel Borg Bjergsø (above) sets up in breweries across the United States and Europe to formulate brain-bending ales such as his "educational" ales concocted with different hops and yeast strains and the Beer Geek Brunch Weasel coffee stout made with Vietnamese beans "harvested" from civet cat droppings. (Mikkel's identical-twin brother also runs a top-notch wandering brewery that's called Evil Twin. I recommend his odd ales as well.)

HAANDBRYGGERIET

For inspiration, the former homebrewers behind Norway's Haandbryggeriet ("hand brewery," referring to their small-scale production) turns to Norwegian heritage and Norse mythology to brew intriguing beers such as smoky Norwegian Wood, a traditional farmhouse ale flavored with juniper berries and twigs; Hesjeøl, a harvest ale made with barley, oats, and rye; and Dark Force, a potent wheat stout with a hoppy edge.

NØRREBRO BRYGHUS/ KISSMEYER BEER AND BREWING

Tired of cranking out like-water lagers for Carlsberg, Anders Kissmeyer cofounded Denmark's Nørrebro Bryghus brewpub in 2003. He focused on curating a diverse, flavorful portfolio with beers such as La Granja Espresso Stout, North Bridge Extreme imperial IPA, and the barley wine–style Little Korkny Ale. Though Kissmeyer remains a consultant at Nørrebro, he also launched Kissmeyer Beer and Brewing in 2010, crafting hits such as zingy PilNZer packed with New Zealand hops and silky, roasty Honey Porter, which is flavored with Danish heather honey.

ITALY

I used to get so angry at Italian restaurants. Although they served crunchy crostini, al dente pasta, and mozzarella-swaddled pizzas with fire-licked crusts, one crucial category was missing from menus: great beer. I'd be presented with a wine list as long as my arm, but the beer selections were limited to insipid lagers such as Peroni and Moretti. Food and wine had flavor to spare. Beer was an alternative to sparkling water.

Finally, I'm happy to report, that boot-shaped nation is making beer a big priority, using herbs, spices, and ingenuity to create quaffs that complement the dinner table—and sometimes become the centerpiece. It's a massive turnabout. In the mid-1990s, there was virtually no craft beer commercially produced in Italy; today, there are around 400 breweries, 140 of which were established between 2008 and 2010.

The brewing scene really started gathering steam in 1995, when the Italian parliament legalized home-brewing and also made running a brewpub much easier. That was the kick in the pants that brewers and entrepreneurs needed. Much like the United States at the dawn of its brewing revival in the 1980s, Italy had no beer tradition. With no history books to follow and zero expectations from the public, early breweries such as Le Baladin and Birrificio Italiano let their creativity and whims run willy-nilly, finding a receptive audience eager to give flavorful lower-alcohol beers—that is, in comparison to wine—a go.

Like the American brewing landscape, Italy's is much too varied to sum up in a single sentence. The U.S. influence can be seen in the hop-forward ales of Almond '22 and Birra del Borgo, but there's also a wild experimental streak. For example, Le Baladin has used smoked lapsang souchong tea and whiskey yeasts and purposely oxidized its barrel-aged beers, and Birrificio Torrechiara cooks up sour ales that would make Belgium proud.

What excites me most is that Italian brewers are using local ingredients to give their beers a unique twist. Grado Plato's Strada San Felice amber lager gets an earthy, nutty kick from chestnuts, as does Birrificio Amiata's Bastarda Rossa. Fresh basil from the Liguria Riviera is the secret addition to Birrificio La Superba's Genova lager. Wormwood (absinthe's key ingredient) appears in Piccolo Birrificio's Chiostro, and local Timorasso grapes star in Birrificio Montegioco's sparkling, fruity Tibir.

It's a nod to Italy's past with an eye toward a most refreshing, flavorful future.

SKY-HIGH BEER

One of the more novel U.S. brewpubs is New York City's Birreria, which is perched like a cherry atop the Italian food emporium Eataly. The brewpub specializes in house-made sausages and seasonally influenced, cask-conditioned artisanal ales created by a trio of American and Italian breweries, including Dogfish Head and Italy's Del Borgo and Baladin. The chestnut-flavored Wanda and the peppercorn-spiked Sofia are lovely to savor when the retractable roof opens up. Rome's Eataly also has a Birreria.

LET THE CAT OUT

Brasserie 4:20 is one of Rome's top spots to sample craft beer, dispensing selections from Italy and around the globe—and not a single drop of wine. (The collection of lambics and vintage bottles is particularly jaw dropping.) If you pop in, try the restaurant's house line of experimental and barrel-aged beers, Revelation Cat. They're also distributed in the United States, in case you can't catch a flight to Rome.

GET TO KNOW FIVE GREAT ITALIAN BREWERIES

BIRRIFICIO LE BALADIN

If one person embodies modern craft brewing in Italy, it is Matterino "Teo" Musso, the Renaissance man behind Le Baladin. In a small village outside Torino, the eccentric Musseo (he plays music to his beer, supposedly to help the yeast grow) invents most peculiar ales such as Egyptian-style Nora, made with ginger, myrrh, orange peel, and the nutty grain kamut; the elegant and intense oxidized barley wine Xyauyù; and dry, effervescent Al-iksir, which is fermented with Scottish whiskey yeasts. Besides brewing, Musso has devised beer-infused cheeses and chocolates as well as beer jelly. As if that's not enough, in Essaouira, Morocco, he runs a guesthouse (a *riad*) where Baladin beer is served.

BIRRIFICIO TORRECHIARA

Sour heads, take note: under the Panil brand, Dr. Renzo Losi has perfected puckering beers such as the tart, earthy unpasteurized Barriquée. The Flanders red ale undergoes a triple fermentation in stainless steel, in Cognac barrels from Bordeaux for three months, and in the bottle. Rarer yet is the Barriquée Riserva, which spends a total of 15 months in Cognac barrels for extra oaky, wine-like complexity. Bonus brewery: another great Italian sour specialist is Birrificio Loverbeer.

BIRRIFICIO DEL DUCATO

The Parma region of Italy is the birthplace of prosciutto, Parmesan cheese, fizzy Lambrusco, and Birrificio del Ducato, where onetime homebrewer Giovanni Campari offers revisionary takes on conventional styles. The dry-hopped lager Via Emilia and the Nuova Mattina (New Morning) saison spiced with coriander, ginger, licorice, and chamomile are both prime, but I think you'll dig Verdi, an imperial stout brewed with chili peppers. The stout decants the color of crisp bacon, and its flavor recalls cocoa and coffee, with a tingly tongue burn that builds with every sip.

BIRRIFICIO ITALIANO

Founded in 1997 outside Como, Birrificio Italiano has been instrumental in leading Italian drinkers out of the Peroni doldrums. Amber Shock is a fruity, caramel-influenced pleasure, and the refreshingly acidic Fleurette is seasoned with the likes of roses, violets, honey, and black pepper. Still, the standout is Tipopils, a dry and decadently bittered pilsner that is as good as, if not better than, anything coming from Germany or the Czech Republic.

BIRRA DEL BORGO

Biochemist Leonardo di Vincenzo's out-of-control homebrew hobby led him to switch career paths and in 2005 open this brewery about an hour northwest of Rome. Inspired by English and Belgian traditions, di Vincenzo brews balanced beers such as the ReAle Extra American-style pale ale given aromatic heft with the addition of Amarillo and Cascade hops, the spelt-driven Duchessa saison (a version blended with Cantillon lambic was called Duchessic), and the hefty, winter-friendly 25 Dodici spiced with bitter orange peel.

Birra del Borgo brewmaster Leonardo di Vincenzo.

JAPAN

Let's play a game of free association. If I say "Japanese beer," what crops up in your gray matter? Probably, your mind will wander to sushi restaurants and karaoke bars where lagers such as Asahi, Sapporo, and Kirin reign supreme. On the surface, I have nothing against these brands. They're fine, crisp quaffs suited for a night spent belting out tone-deaf renditions of Bon Jovi tunes (um, maybe that's just me) or tucking into a tuna roll. But apart from exotic names, these Japanese beers are barely distinguishable from Miller Lite and other Stars and Stripes lagers—except for their elevated price tags.

Japan does have its fair share of craft breweries cropping up across the islands, but their arrival is a rather recent development, even when judged against the still-budding American movement. A large part of the blame goes to the government. Until 1994, the only licenses were granted to breweries that produced at least 2 million liters (more than 500,000 gallons) of beer each year. That's almost enough beer to fill an Olympic-size swimming pool. No bootstrapping brewer could produce and sell that much beer right off the bat. The going got a little bit easier in 1994, when Japan loosened its laws and licensed smaller breweries that produced at least 60,000 liters (about 15,000 gallons) of beer annually.

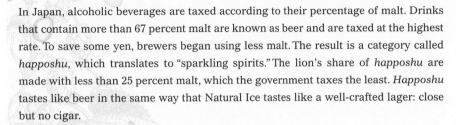

A SPARKLING TAX DODGE

In Japan, alcoholic beverages are taxed according to their percentage of malt. Drinks that contain more than 67 percent malt are known as beer and are taxed at the highest rate. To save some yen, brewers began using less malt. The result is a category called *happoshu*, which translates to "sparkling spirits." The lion's share of *happoshu* are made with less than 25 percent malt, which the government taxes the least. *Happoshu* tastes like beer in the same way that Natural Ice tastes like a well-crafted lager: close but no cigar.

For an American nanobrewer starting on a single-barrel system (see page 268), that's still an insane number, but it was just the break Japanese brewers needed. Now, in the United States, tomorrow's brewery owners are today's homebrewers. That transition is a tad rarer in Japan because of a law that bans homebrewers from brewing beer that's stronger than 1 percent ABV (not that the cops will break your door down for making a double IPA). Instead, much of Japan's craft beer comes from the practiced hands of sake brewers, who are well versed in the arts of fermentation and sanitation—two of brewing's most important skills. A crash course in malt and hops was all it took for sake specialists such as Kiuchi Brewery and Oze No Yukidoke to leap across the brewing kettle into beer.

Beyond sake brewers, the Japanese craft-brewing scene has been aided by risk takers such as the American Bryan Baird. After finishing grad school, the beer aficionado moved to Japan in 1995, a time when brewpubs and microbreweries were springing up nationwide there. Dissatisfied with his job, he decided to combine his two great passions: craft beer and Japanese culture. He returned to the United States to study at California's American Brewers Guild, apprenticed at Seattle's Redhook Ale, and drove up

IN JAPAN, CRAFT BEER IS commonly called *ji-bīru, which means* "LOCAL BEER."

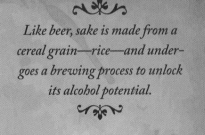

Like beer, sake is made from a cereal grain—rice—and undergoes a brewing process to unlock its alcohol potential.

NANO, NANO

When it comes to brewing great beer, size does not matter. Since starting a full-bore production brewery can easily cost millions of dollars, many homebrewers eager to go pro but not drown in debt are opting to open small-scale nanobreweries. There's no Merriam-Webster–approved definition, but I consider a nanobrewery to be a pipsqueak outfit typically run on a bare-bones budget by one or two do-it-all brewers—that means handling brewing, packaging, and distribution. My cutoff: a three-barrel system or smaller. You'll find nanobreweries in just about every state, and their diminutive size allows brewers to experiment with unusual fruits, wild yeast strains, and wackadoodle formulations. In Hillsboro, Oregon, Ambacht Ales spikes all its beers with Pacific Northwest honey, which adds an alluring sweetness, and Vermont-based Lawson's Finest Liquids relies on maple sap in lieu of water to make the potent Maple Tripple and employs cinnamon and sprigs from red spruce trees for its winter seasonal. Some nanobreweries start small to get off the ground, such as Long Island's hop-focused Barrier Brewing and New Hampshire's inventive, barrel-mad White Birch, before outsize demand allows them to expand. Today's nanobrewery may in time become the next big thing. (Lawson's recently graduated to a slightly bigger set-up.)

In recent years, Hill Farmstead, The Alchemist, and former nanobrewery Lawson's Finest Liquids have helped Vermont blossom into a must–visit for craft-beer pilgrims.

and down the West Coast researching hundreds of breweries and brewpubs. In 2000, Baird moved to Japan's coastal Numazu and cofounded Baird Beer with his wife, Sayuri.

Entering Japan's beer market can be dicey. The country's traditional culture places stigmas on business failure; modern craft brewing is a risky business known for goosing tradition. As an outsider, Baird did not have a mortal fear of failure. Flying in the face of the country's dominant lagers, Baird made one of his first year-round beers the balanced, gently malty Teikoku IPA. To everyone's surprise, the square peg fit into a round hole.

Although Baird crafts many hop-driven beers, the brewery is distinguished by his equation that blends Japanese sensibilities and American brewing: character = balance + complexity. The formula applies to all of Baird's beers (adorned with woodblock-print labels), whether a bittersweet porter or a seasonal ale made with locally harvested fruits. It's pinpoint craftsmanship married to innovation, the hallmark of many of my favorite Japanese breweries.

GET TO KNOW FOUR GREAT JAPANESE BREWERIES

FUJIZAKURA HEIGHTS BREWERY

It sounds like the setup for a bad joke: What happens when a Japanese brewery makes traditional German beers? Well, the brewery wins armloads of medals at international brewing competitions. Fujizakura's great German-influenced brews include the smoky Rauch, brisk Pils, and sublimely banana-accented Weizen.

KIUCHI BREWERY

The most widely available Japanese craft beers come from traditional sake producer Kiuchi, which creates the Hitachino Nest family of ales. The cloudy, fragrant White Ale is a perennial favorite (see page 100), but the Espresso Stout and the sake-like Red Rice Ale are also superb.

ISE KADOYA MICROBREWERY

For more than 400 years, the Kadoya café has earned its keep selling tea and mochi, a glutinous rice cake traditionally eaten on Japanese New Year. But in 1997, the family-run operation (which also makes soy sauce and miso paste) branched out into brewing, crafting flavorful American-inspired beers such as Triple Hop Ale, the well-roasted Stout, and crisp Genmai Ale, made with roasted brown rice.

YO-HO BREWING COMPANY

To ensure the quality of the beer on its trans-Pacific trip, Nagano-based Yo-Ho packages its brews in cans. Seek out American-inspired selections such as malty, grapefruit-driven Aooni India Pale Ale, Tokyo Black Porter, and aromatic Yona Yona Ale. Former Yo-Ho brewer Toshi Ishii, who sharped his skills at California's Stone Brewing, now runs Ishii Brewing in Guam.

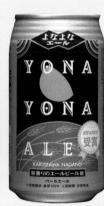

BRING IT ON HOME

CELLARING BEER AND PAIRING BREWS WITH FOOD

ONE OF THE MOST ICONIC moments of 1980s cinema took place in a summer resort in New York's Catskills Mountains. In 1963-set *Dirty Dancing*, Jennifer Grey plays shy young Frances "Baby" Houseman, who has a blossoming romance with dance instructor Johnny Castle, played by Patrick Swayze. After plot twists, pregnancy turns, and plenty of 1960s tunes, the flick culminates with Castle declaring, "Nobody puts Baby in a corner," and a show-stopping dance scene.

I feel much the same way about beer. For decades, beer was boxed into a corner, allowed out only during deemed-appropriate occasions: sporting events, bars, backyard BBQs. Restaurants offered beer that was about as exciting as anything on tap at a gas station. "Vintage beer" was a euphemism for a forgotten six-pack left to gather dust. In short, wine had a mixed martial arts stranglehold on fine-dining and fine-drinking occasions. Beer was the beverage of the parched, chicken wing–eating proletariat.

Slowly and steadily, beer is coming out of its corner and assuming a spot atop the dinner table or slinking into cool basements and spending a few years getting older and, ideally, better. In short, beer is becoming wine without the pretension. As you'll learn in this chapter, beer is a splendid sidekick for food, everything from nibbles previously considered cocktail fare to anything that might cross your dinner plate at home or when dining out. You'll also be given the lowdown on aging beer, which can build new flavors while whittling others down and encouraging appealing elements to mingle. With beer, your home is the final—and most fun—frontier.

WHEN BEER MET FOOD

When it comes to food, wine can be a finicky partner. Perfect pairings can be a pleasure, but finding the right match requires skill and finesse, like parallel parking with only a couple of inches to spare. By contrast, beer is a more forgiving mate. Its scope of ingredients, styles, and easily understood flavors (bitter, sweet, chocolaty, etc.), combined with a general lack of acidity, means that finding the right mealtime companion is a snap.

Although I'll provide general pairing guidelines, don't limit yourself to them. This is all about opening your mouth and experimenting, finding flavors and combinations that harmonize with your palate. There is no right or wrong. There are only different degrees of deliciousness.

GUIDELINES FOR BETTER BEER PAIRINGS

As the chef and co-owner at San Francisco's well-regarded The Monk's Kettle and The Abbot's Cellar, Culinary Institute of America–trained Adam Dulye focuses on coupling fresh, seasonal American fare with the best of American and international beer. His pairings are so spot-on that Dulye has been tapped to devise the beer-food combinations at SAVOR (see sidebar on page 277) and the Farm to Table Pavilion at Denver's Great American Beer Festival. Here are Dulye's top 10 tips for pairing food and beer.

1. **KNOW THE THREE C'S.** There are three basic principles: comparing, cutting, and contrasting.

   "The first, and simplest, pairing technique is comparing," Dulye says. "For example, that would mean pairing the citrus notes of hops with a dish accented with lemon juice or lemon zest, or an imperial stout with chocolate cake. You're looking for similarities. Right out of the gate, most people go after 'compare.' It's a comfort zone and a word that's been built up. Once people have one really good experience with beer and food, that a-ha moment, they're hungry for more."

   "A second basic pairing technique is cutting," Dulye says. "It's flipping the idea of comparing." That means using crisp, effervescent pilsners to cleanse your palate after eating fatty food or a robust porter to cut through the richness of a cheeseburger.

   "The third, and toughest, technique is contrasting. You want a beer to reflect something different in food, to fill in missing flavors," Dulye says. A classic example is contrasting oysters with a dry Irish stout, a delicious example that flies counter to common sense (see page 182 for more on oyster stouts). "People always tell me, 'Oh, you want it to taste bad? 'Contrast' does not mean it will taste bad."

2. **DECISIONS, DECISIONS.** "When you're thinking about a pairing, whether at home or at a restaurant, you should decide what food you'd like to eat or what style of beer you'd like to drink. It's easier to create a pairing if you have a specific food or beer style in mind."

3. **KNOW YOUR NOSE.** "Don't ignore your initial impression of what you taste or smell. Your beer perceptions are your own. Go with them. If you try and taste and smell someone else's thoughts on what a beer is, you'll end up missing your own."

4. **NO COLD SHOULDER.** "Temperature can adversely impact a pairing. Putting bottles of beer in the freezer or ice chest can be great for BBQs, but serving beer too cold can affect its sensory profile. Proper temperature is important, but you don't have to get too snobby."

5. **SAVOR THE SEASONS.** Dulye embraces cooking with seasonal ingredients, which can be matched to seasonal beers. Those rib-sticking stews and braised meats are great with rich beers such as Scotch ales, and light summer salads may find their match in a gentle witbier or a cheery little kölsch.

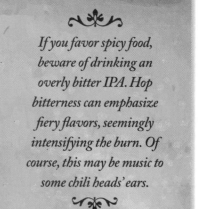

If you favor spicy food, beware of drinking an overly bitter IPA. Hop bitterness can emphasize fiery flavors, seemingly intensifying the burn. Of course, this may be music to some chili heads' ears.

To boost your beer-pairing skill set, I recommend two fantastic books: Brewmaster's Table from Brooklyn Brewery head brewer Garrett Oliver and Lucy Saunders's The Best of American Beer and Food: Pairing & Cooking with Craft Beer.

Generally speaking, Belgian ales are among the most food-friendly styles. At dinner, it's tough to go off track with a Belgian saison, dubbel, or tripel.

I ♥ NY

If you're ever road tripping through New York's Hudson Valley, plug Peekskill into your GPS. The Birdsall House (the sister restaurant to NYC's beer-mad Blind Tiger Ale House) does killer charcuterie—often made with pigs fed on a diet of spent brewing grain—served alongside 20 taps of largely local craft beer. Down the road you'll find Peekskill Brewery, where former Ithaca Beer brewer Jeff O'Neil lets his creative impulses run wild, resulting in beers such as Zeitgeist Berliner Weisse and Shotgun Willie IPA, a tropical tribute to Nelson Sauvin hops. (He also uses a coolship to make wild ales.) Additonally, Birdsall's original chef, Matt Hutchins, has opened the Hop, his own chapel to beer and food a few towns up the Hudson River in Beacon.

6. **BRANCH OUT WITH BEER.** "Don't get stuck in a style. Branch out and try a wide amount of styles across the board," Dulye says. "Your favorite beer style may be limiting for a pairing. IPAs are great, but they do a pretty good job of covering your palate."

7. **HAVE A DRINK FIRST.** "If you're doing a pairing at home, you should really sample a beer first. Just because the bottle says IPA, it doesn't mean it's going to be the same IPA you had last week. Every beer is going to be different."

8. **BEER IS FOR DRINKING, NOT COOKING.** "I don't use much beer as an ingredient in cooking. It often gets lost in food," Dulye says. "For me, beer is more of a pairing tool. Craft beer is going to exciting places, and it's really no longer needed to be used as an ingredient. I like to take what brewers are doing with ingredients and match it to my food."

9. **IN LIGHTNESS, THEN DARKNESS.** "If you're doing multiple courses of pairings, start with lighter beers and then work your way to heavier, stronger beers," advises Dulye. Pouring a double IPA with an appetizer is an easy way to fatigue a palate.

10. **STRENGTH, MEET STRENGTH.** Robust flavors work well with robust beers, and lighter flavors work well with lighter beers. A salad and a barley wine will have a hard time finding common ground.

ADAM DULYE'S FIVE NO-FAIL PAIRINGS FOR FOOD AND BEER

1. ALTBIERS OR AMBER ALES WITH STEAK. "The smooth, caramel-driven beers go great with almost any kind of grilled steak and will get people on the road to beer pairing. Don't go with crazy steak rubs or sauces. Keep it simple with salt and pepper."

2. BELGIAN-STYLE WITBIERS WITH SHELLFISH. "This is always a crowd-pleaser. The delicate flavors of a crisp, elegant witbier like Allagash White are ideal for pairing with shellfish, especially any dish that includes citrus. Steaming mussels with witbier is also an excellent option."

3. PILSNERS WITH ROASTED ROOT VEGETABLES. "A classic pilsner's malt and characteristically spicy and clean Saaz hop go well with roasted vegetables, such as turnips. A pilsner is perfect for playing off root vegetables' caramelization."

4. DUBBELS WITH DUCK. "A dark, rich Belgian-style dubbel is ideal with a nicely caramelized duck breast. Depending on the dubbel, you can work in stone fruits such as apricots, peaches, cherries, or plums. That's a classic culinary tradition."

5. IPAS WITH CARROT CAKE. "This one is really fun. Look for a straightforward IPA, not one that's overly bitter or has more than 85 IBUs. The sweetness of the carrot pulls a little bit of sweetness out of the malt, and if you use cream cheese frosting, that will play off the hops as well. If the beer has citrus qualities, it will cleanse the palate at the end."

FOUR GREAT AMERICAN BEER CHEFS

SCHUYLER SCHULTZ

Building on his expertise as culinary director for San Diego's AleSmith Brewing Company, Schultz (right), an ingredient-driven cook and sommelier, has authored the terrific *Beer, Food, and Flavor: A Guide to Tasting, Pairing, and the Culture of Beer.* It's an invaluable resource that is informed by Schultz's extensive travel across Europe, Asia, Australia, and America.

SEAN Z. PAXTON

The "Homebrew Chef," as Sonoma, California's Paxton is known, is a giant in the world of beer cuisine—in stature, the size of his goatee, and his influential reach. Since the mid-1990s, he has orchestrated some high-wire multicourse dinners incorporating beer as an ingredient (short ribs braised in Trappistes Rochefort 10, Achilles Serafijn Grand Cru–cured pork belly), then paired with an additional brew. You can see what he's up to on his website, *homebrewchef.com.*

BRUCE PATON

Since 1995, San Francisco "Beer Chef" Paton has hosted the ongoing Dinner with the Brewmaster, which features a custom menu paired with beer from breweries such as Stone, Lagunitas, Moylan's, and Bear Republic.

TEDDY FOLKMAN

As culinary ambassador for Brewery Ommegang, Folkman crisscrosses the country, hosting beer dinners and singing the praises of brews and grub. He is also the chef at Dr. Granville Moore's in Washington, D.C., a beer-focused Belgian gastropub.

RESTAURANTS AND BEER

I dine at restaurants for several reasons (and yes, being hungry is one of them). First, there's convenience. Although cooking relaxes me, there are nights when tying on an apron and chopping vegetables seems as daunting as getting Democrats and Republicans to agree. I consider this dining out because I *need* to. Second, there's dining out because I *want* to. I patronize restaurants to eat food that I lack the skills or equipment to replicate. That's why I'll pay good money for pizza pulled from a wood-fired oven but blanch at buying a plate of pasta. I want an experience I can't have in my kitchen.

At restaurants that goes double for beer. Too often, an intriguing menu is coupled to boring bottles I can buy at my local beer shop. There are thousands of unique beers available across the country and around the world. Is it so tough to select a dozen interesting beers or to install a couple of taps dispensing local craft beers? If you do, I'll gladly open my wallet and make it worth your while.

At high-end restaurants, chefs classically have paired their fare with wine lists as thick as a phone book circa 1986. But that breed of white-tablecloth, hushed-conversation dining is an endangered species. Diners are embracing casual, quirky, rule-bending, and value-driven restaurants where the emphasis is on fun. It's an evolution of the culinary ecosystem for which craft beer is particularly well suited. Restaurants are finally embracing hops and stepping up their beer game, with many offering dozens of different beers by the bottle and plenty more on draft (as well as wine and barrel-aged cocktails, but that's for another book).

For example, Daniel Boulud's DBGB Kitchen & Bar in New York City offers up a bill of fare that includes burgers and homemade sausages as well as a beer list that takes up nearly eight packed pages on the drinks menu. Father's Office helped bring the gastropub concept (good beer, a bitchin' burger) to Los Angeles, and locally sourced meat, vegetables, and beer is an inalienable right at Portland, Oregon's Grain and Gristle—and just about anywhere in that town. The fun and funky pizzeria chains Mellow

Each year, the union of beer and food is celebrated at the Brewers Association's annual SAVOR: An American Craft Beer & Food Experience. The festival partners some of the States' best beers with custom-devised dishes. You'll come hungry—and leave tipsy and totally stuffed.

When traveling across the United States, the best tactic for finding top eats is to belly up to a bar and chat with fellow barflies. Beer lovers and culinary explorers are cut from the same cloth, and there is often overlap between the epicurean contingents. Hop tips while tippling have led me to Minneapolis's Tilia, where the crunchy fish taco torta is available alongside 21 mostly Midwestern drafts, as well as Longman & Eagle in Chicago, where whiskey, wild boar sloppy Joes, and craft beer are held in equal regard. A barstool suggestion led me to Philadelphia's Kraftwork Bar for a beer can–chicken sandwich, crispy pierogi, and my choice of two dozen craft beers, as well as Austin's Whip In. I filled myself with Indian eats, had several of the dozens of drafts available (including a few made at the in-house Namaste nanobrewery), and then bought bottles to take home. Random stranger at the bar, I can never thank you enough for your suggestions.

Mushroom and Flatbread Company put an equal premium on pies and craft beer. An even surer sign of the trend is that both Applebee's and T.G.I. Friday's are now offering draft craft beer at their outlets across the country.

Even more intriguing, restaurants are now enlisting breweries to make exclusive bespoke beers. This allows restaurants to partner their meals with specially formulated beers that are as singular as the cuisine they serve. The popular East Coast franchise Shake Shack has Brooklyn Brewery make its biscuity, burger-friendly ShackMeister amber ale. At the New Orleans restaurant Lüke, chef John Besh has Louisiana's Heiner Brau make its fruity, delicate Lüke Alt and crisp, light Lüke Fru kölsch, which is ideal with anything from the raw bar. Chicago's Goose Island regularly invites local chefs to collaborate on food-friendly curiosities such as Squid Ink, a black saison brewed with Giuseppe Tentori of GT Fish & Oyster, and Xocolatl, a barrel-aged chocolate barley wine brewed in collaboration with Rick Bayless.

I'll take that over a Corona any day.

SEVEN GREAT BEER-FOCUSED RESTAURANTS

AMERASIA (COVINGTON, KENTUCKY)

Most Chinese restaurants offer Tsingtao and stop there. Not so at unconventional AmerAsia, which combines mouth-on-fire Chinese fare with top-shelf craft beer. In a room decorated with graffiti-style murals and kung fu movie posters, master chef Rich Chu makes righteously spicy fare such as plump pork-and-ginger wontons anointed with incendiary red pepper sauce; cold beef salad marinated in sesame oil, smoky peppers, and ginger; and an incendiary General Tso's chicken that shames its gloppy namesake. What about the beer? There's great craft on draft and a constantly evolving list of 100-plus beers from the likes of Bell's, Three Floyds, Great Lakes, and Southern Tier. (In addition, Richmond, Virginia's Mekong mixes Vietnamese food with a mouthwatering beer list.)

EUCLID HALL BAR & KITCHEN (DENVER, COLORADO)

Stroll up the stairs of this historic brick building and you'll enter a realm dedicated to craft beer and the sort of deliciously unhinged food devised during an attack of the munchies. Start with Buffalo-style fried oysters and pad Thai–style pig ears before moving onto a hand-cut poutine topped with duck, a duck egg, and foie gras—duck, duck, goose. The hand-stuffed sausages are heavenly with a pint of a Colorado-made ale such as Odell IPA or Avery White Rascal. A deep bottle list that ranges across the nation and around the world allows you to sip a Berliner weisse followed by a Belgian IPA and a wild ale.

Whenever I visit Denver, I always make a pit stop to fuel up on the snappy homemade sausages (left) and pedigreed selection of Colorado craft beer at Euclid Hall (above). Fun fact: the building's previous tenant was Soapy Smith's Double Eagle Bar.

THE BREWER'S ART (BALTIMORE, MARYLAND)

Housed in a handsome old townhouse, The Brewer's Art is a masterpiece. The on-site brewery makes wonderful—and wonderfully inventive—beers such as the spicy Green Peppercorn Tripel, strong, Belgian-style Ozzy Ale, and Resurrection, a dubbel that tastes of caramel and brown sugar. Equally exemplary is the food, whether it's beer-braised lamb shoulder partnered with pumpernickel gnocchi, duck fat–poached monkfish or foie gras cured in a spiced winter ale. To finish the meal, look to the lengthy whiskey list or a chocolate torte made with a touch of beer.

THE MONK'S KETTLE AND THE ABBOT'S CELLAR (SAN FRANCISCO)

At his duo of Bay Area restaurants, Adam Dulye focuses on forward-thinking, beer-friendly American cuisine. The Monk's Kettle menu includes burgers made with chickpeas and spent brewing grain, three-day ale-marinated brick chicken, and fries showered with hop-infused salt, each offered with a beer suggestion to cut,

compare, or contrast against the dish (see "Know the Three C's" on page 273). Over at the Abbot's Cellar, Dulye devises rotating seasonal dishes matched to 20 draft beers and 100-plus bottles (many offered by the glass), including a number of vintage bottles pulled from the two-story cellar, served at the appropriate temperatures. The nightly three- and five-course prix fixe beer-pairing menus are your best bet.

BIRCH & BARLEY (WASHINGTON, D.C.)

One of this country's most formidable one-two punches of beer and food are Greg Engert and Kyle Bailey, respectively, the beer director and chef at Birch & Barley and its upstairs bar, Churchkey. Engert oversees a list of 500 bottles, 50 drafts, and 5 cask ales (upstairs and downstairs), which the staff will happily match to the nightly five-course dinner, which might include hand-cut tagliatelle

San Francisco's Adam Dulye (above left) is chef at both Monk's Kettle and the Abbot's Cellar (above right), two of the city's choicest spots for craft beer and food.

Behind the stove at Washington, D.C.'s Birch & Barley, chef Kyle Bailey (above left) turns out flawless, inventive fare such as seared striped bass with cucumber-mint purée and purple potatoes (left) and PB&J cheesecake with Concord grape sorbet and peanut powder (below left). His cooking is complemented by the beer selections of Greg Engert (above right), who oversees the upstairs ChurchKey bar. His suggestions and selections are always surprising and spot-on.

topped with baby squid or honey-glazed duck breast with brandied cherries. Also of note: the restaurant group runs Bluejacket Brewery, which specializes in exotic offbeat brews (such as a movie snack–themed beer flavored with dry-roasted peanuts, Florida sea salt, cacao nibs, and vanilla beans) and sour ales.

THE PUBLICK HOUSE AND MONK'S CELL (BROOKLINE, MASSACHUSETTS)

It's two bars in one at this Massachusetts jewel. While the Publick House caters to craft-beer fans, the Monk's Cell offers enough Belgian brews to transplant drinkers overseas. Add to this a menu featuring beer-infused foods—pork-beef-veal meatballs drowned in Duvel gravy, pulled pork painted with Dogfish Head Indian Brown BBQ sauce, Trappist meatloaf made with Orval and topped with Chimay cheese—and brew fans stay well sated long after the last call.

THE PUBLICAN (CHICAGO, ILLINOIS)

At the pork-heavy Publican, you'll find house-made charcuterie, split pig heads, duck heart and liver sandwiches, pairing dinners featuring breweries such as California's The Bruery and Michigan's Founders, and Berliner weisse mimosas for brunch. Every waiter and bartender is a certified beer server—helpful when navigating the list of 100-plus bottles, including a house-blended lambic.

One of the most seamless pairings of beer and food is Linden Street Brewery's Daily (B)red. The Oakland, California, brewery ferments the red lager with the sourdough starter from San Francisco's famed Tartine Bakery.

IN THE WASH

Washing, or brushing, cheeses with brine, wine, cider, or beer keeps them soft and moist. This encourages the growth of *Brevibacterium linens*, a bacteria that surface ripens the cheese, resulting in an orange-reddish rind, a stinky aroma, and a pungent flavor. Legendary breweries such as Belgium's Brasserie Dupont and Chimay have long washed homemade cheeses in their own beer.

THE BIG CHEESE

Wine and cheese have been presented as the ideal marriage, but a closer examination of that date-night coupling reveals a fatal flaw: cows do not eat grapes. The mammals devour grass. The base unit of beer is barley, a member of the grass family. Building on this natural affinity, dairies have begun incorporating craft brews into cheese production.

For dairies, one of the easiest methods of collaborating with a brewery is to use its beer to wash cheese. This does not mean that an IPA will impart biting citric bitterness or that an imperial stout will add tons of cocoa and coffee. Washing supplies accent notes of the selected beer's flavor profile that ideally will enhance the cheese. A great example of beer-washed cheese is found at Minnesota's blue-cheese specialist Caves of Faribault. It was once the site of Fleckenstein Brewery, which in the 1850s excavated a series of sandstone caves to age its beer. Although Prohibition felled the brewery, a series of cheesemakers have used its cool, arched caves—which are almost on the same latitude as the stinky-cheese Mecca of Roquefort, France—to age blue cheese.

Caves of Fairbault aligned with Minnesota brewery Summit to create the Blues & Brews, in which the dairy washes its cow's-milk St. Pete's Select blue cheese in Summit's seasonal beers. The Winter Blues is painted with

In one of America's more interesting examples of adaptive reuse, these former sandstone lagering caves were repurposed by Minnesota's Caves of Faribault to age its AmaBlu family of blue cheeses. Unfortunately, federal regulations prohibit tours of the caves.

nutty, caramel-nuanced Winter Ale, and the Summertime Blues is soaked in piney Horizon Red Ale; Oktoberfest Blau takes a bath in toffee-hinted Oktoberfest lager.

This technique also has been embraced in dairy-filled Wisconsin, where Sartori soaks a nutty cheese in New Glarus Brewing Co.'s fruity Raspberry Tart to make Raspberry BellaVitano. River Valley Ranch in Washington State bathes its raw-milk Naughty Nellie tomme in the same-named golden ale from Seattle's Pike Brewing. In Newburg, Pennsylvania, Keswick Creamery relies on the beers of fellow Pennsylvanians Tröegs Brewing. Historically, the Alpine-style washed-rind cheese known as tomme is bathed in brine. As a flavorful alternative, Tröegs supplied its trub, the layer of sediment and yeast that's removed after the initial fermentation. Trub is typically waste, but the yeast-rich by-product is exceptionally good at promoting rind growth. The trub from the Troegenator Double Bock helps create the malt-sweet, lightly hoppy Tommenator (which won gold at 2011's North American Jersey Cheese Awards), and the cherry and honey notes of Mad Elf Ale imbue Mad Tomme's rind.

USE YOUR INFUSION

Although washing cheese with beer only imparts subtle notes, infusing cheese with beer during the production process—and not just beer fondue or Kentucky's popular beer-cheese spread—provides fuller, more recognizable flavors of beer. This technique is popular in Ireland, where each bite of tangy Cahill's Irish Porter Cheese offers marbled swirls of dark beer, and a special version of Kerrygold's nutty-sweet Dubliner cheese is cut through with concentrated Irish stout. You'll also find this alliance in Oregon, where a brewery and a creamery are bonded by name.

Rogue Ales provides the unaffiliated Rogue Creamery with its Morimoto Soba Ale and Chocolate Stout, which are infused directly into cheddar cheese to create a line of same-named cheeses. Additionally, Rogue supplies the dairy with its homegrown Freedom hops, which are steeped in hot water, blended with curds, and pressed into Hopyard Cheddar.

Taking this coupling to the next level, Vermont's Cellars at Jasper Hill partners with its neighbor, Hill Farmstead Brewery, to make Winnimere. The base cheese is

BEER WITHOUT BORDERS

A central reason why ChurchKey and Birch & Barley, as well as excellent bars such as Pizzeria Paradiso and Meridian Pint, pour far-reaching beers that typically aren't distributed on the East Coast (Michigan's Short's Brewing Company, Oregon's Deschutes, Indiana's Upland) is that Washington, D.C., has one of the country's most permissive beer policies. Most states operate under a three-tier system that requires bars and beer stores to purchase their bottles, cans, and kegs from wholesalers, which receive beer directly from breweries or importers. In Washington, D.C., if wholesalers do not stock a sufficient amount of a brand, bars can import the beer by any means necessary, from road tripping to a distant brewery and loading up a rental truck to getting beer shipped directly to a bar.

Rogue Creamery's Hopyard Cheddar is infused with hops grown by Rogue Ales.

made during the winter, when the farm's Ayrshire heifers produce high-fat, protein-rich milk. The cheese then is washed with a special beer brewed by Hill Farmstead.

In the first several years of the project, freshly brewed buckets of wort were brought to Jasper Hill's cheese-ripening cellar, where the lurking microflora colonized the sugary broth, spontaneously fermenting the brew and producing a sour, lambic-like ale. The beer was blended with salt and then used to baste the raw-milk cheeses twice a week for 60 days. During that time, bacteria attracted by the moist surface and sugary beer settled into the rind, softening the cheese's interior. The finished fromage was a buttery, spoonable revelation: woodsy and smoky with robust notes of tropical fruit and an earthy aroma. The cheese was a delight. It was the beer that was the problem. Spontaneously fermented lambics can take years to develop fully. Currently, Jasper Hill is working with Hill Farmstead to find the perfect match.

The dairy's staff has developed special graphs to diagram flavor and is washing cheeses with a range of beers, exploring the specific impact of bitterness, booze, and residual sugar. The end goal is to create the perfect wash for a cheese that is also available to buy as a beer. It just might end up being the world's most harmonious beer and cheese pairing.

HAVE A COW

BARLEY WINES Sweetly potent barley wines have just the oomph to stand up to unapologetically pungent cheeses such as Gorgonzola, Limburger, or Stilton.

***BRETTANOMYCES*-INFECTED BEERS** The funky, earthy barnyard brews do divinely with washed-rind cheeses such as Taleggio, Livarot, and Jasper Hill Winnimere.

IPAS Generously bittered IPAs will get on like gangbusters with a sharp cheddar or a gym sock–stinky washed-rind cheese.

LAMBICS AND SOUR ALES To match the no-holds-barred acidity of these ales, go for a pungent and crumbly Gorgonzola or a tangy goat cheese such as Cypress Grove Chevre's Humboldt Fog. Alternately, sweet and fruity lambics are swell with a rich and creamy mascarpone.

PALE ALES As long as they do not veer too far into the bitterness zone, a pale ale is excellent with provolone as well as buttery cheeses such as Havarti and Muenster.

PILSNERS Brisk, herbal pilsners ably slice through a rich and creamy Brie or Camembert and will complement a mild cheddar.

STOUTS Dry Irish stouts are fine fits for an Irish cheese such as a nutty-sweet Dubliner, and imperial stouts have an affinity for aged Gouda, sharp cheddar, and Parmesan.

TRIPEL AND GOLDEN STRONG ALES Fruity, complex, spicy, and strapping, these Belgian beers are perfect puzzle matches for washed-rind cheeses (such as one from, fittingly, Chimay), Gorgonzola, and a decadent triple-crème such as L'Explorateur or Cowgirl Creamery's Mt. Tam (right).

WITBIERS AND HEFEWEIZENS The light, cloudy, and aromatic summertime refreshments do best with chèvre, feta cheese, or maybe an herb-freighted cheese spread. (Saisons are also excellent with fresh chèvre.)

BEER AND DESSERT

When it comes to dessert, I often serve beer as a sweet coda to the meal. A snifter full of rich, cocoa-flavored imperial stout can be just as rewarding as a slice of frosting-topped chocolate cake or, if you're feeling extra decadent, as half of a great one-two combo to sate your sweet tooth.

Still, a simple pairing is but the tip of beer's after-dinner potential. More and more, sweets specialists are using beer as a showpiece ingredient, incorporating it into candies, chocolates, and ice cream that for the most part you need not be 21 to purchase (see the box at the left).

One of the coolest (pun totally intended) dessert trends is beer partnered with ice cream or sorbet, creating a childhood indulgence with an adult edge. Every year, Sweet Action Ice Cream hosts the Denver Beer (Ice Cream) Fest, featuring unique mash-ups such as Maple Pale Ale, made with Odell Brewing's St. Lupulin Extra Pale Ale, and Double Chocolate Stout, infused with Fort Collins Brewery's Double Chocolate Stout. In Columbus, Ohio, Jeni's Splendid Ice Cream has created the tart, refreshing Cherry Lambic Sorbet, and Atlanta's Frozen Pints offers a line of craft beer–integrated desserts that include Honey IPA and Cinnamon Espresso Stout. You can try this at-home twist on the root beer float: pour your your favorite stout into a glass, then add a few scoops of vanilla or chocolate ice cream. (Adding the ice cream first will create a foamy disaster.)

CANDY IS DANDY

The cocoa-like characteristics of dark stouts and porters would seem like a natural fit for chocolate, but these Willy Wonkas are not taking the easy route. At Brooklyn's Nunu Chocolates, the shop pours craft beers on tap, which it turns into a "six-pack" of beer-infused chocolates. As expected, you'll find Southern Tier Choklat Imperial Stout and Two Brothers Red Eye Coffee Porter, but the rotating fillings also have included Bear Republic's

A handful of states forbid the underage sale of alcohol-laced confectionaries. They include Colorado, Florida, Hawaii, Kentucky, Louisiana, Maryland, Minnesota, Nebraska, New Hampshire, New Jersey, New York, Texas, and Washington.

Hop Rod Rye and the Ballast Point's Sculpin IPA. (Couple them with Nunu's spirit-infused chocolate for a neat twist on booze with a beer chaser.)

You'll also stumble upon beer chocolates at Montana's Sweet Palace, which makes Moose Truffles with Big Sky Brewing's Moose Drool Brown Ale, and Heavy Seas in Maryland has partnered with Parfections to create truffles filled with various stouts, porters, and barley wines. Chicago's Truffle Truffle uses Rogue Chocolate Stout in its Beer & Pretzel collection of marshmallows, brittle, caramels, and truffles.

That's not all. These days, if you name a dessert, someone's probably infusing it with beer. You'll find beer-infused cupcakes at San Diego's PubCakes, where every offering is blended with beers such as the Top Ten Cake made with Karl Strauss's Tower Ten IPA or the Beer for Breakfast containing AleSmith Wee Heavy, maple cream cheese frosting, and bacon. Moist chocolate Guinness cake is a Saint Patrick's Day standby (celeb chef Nigella Lawson even included a recipe in her cookbook *Feast*). Beer-infused milkshakes are so commonplace that I'd need another book to give every restaurant and bar credit.

When it comes to dessert, you can have your beer and eat it too.

AGING BEER

Let me be blunt: there is no need to age beer. Every bottle released by a brewery is fit for immediate consumption. Furthermore, most beers should be consumed lickety-split, before sunlight, heat, and Father Time's wrinkled hands work their ruinous magic.

Some beers, though, are stronger than others and embrace a ticking clock. As months slide away, these brews slowly begin to change. Flavors lessen. Flavors deepen. New flavors emerge. A beer will not undergo a wholesale transformation like mild-mannered Bruce Banner becoming the Incredible Hulk, but the changes will be perceptible. It's a beer you've always enjoyed, just different.

So set up the right environment, stock it with the right beer, wait a few years, and you'll be able to enjoy a brew that, like you, gets better with age.

The addition of Guinness makes the chocolate cupcake a rich, moist indulgence.

There's no need to build a separate cellar for your wine, which you can store alongside your beer. Optimally, red wine should be stored at 50 to 55 degrees, whereas white wine is best aged at 45 degrees.

When you sample a series of the same beer from different years, that's known as a vertical tasting. A horizontal tasting would be a sampling of like-minded styles of beer from the same year.

TIPS FOR CELLARING BEER

Aging beer is not as simple as shoving a bottle in the back of the fridge and forgetting about it. Here, with assistance from cellaring expert Bill Sysask, are tips to help your beer stand the test of time.

UNDERSTAND THE ENVIRONMENT

From cellars to closets, selecting your beer's new long-term home requires some careful planning.

1. **STABILITY IS YOUR FRIEND.** My wife does not like wild temperature fluctuations, preferring a constant, cool environment. Beer is much the same. The ideal environment is a cellar or a basement where the temperature remains low and steady. The sweet spot is 55°F with 5 degrees of wiggle room on either side. Just as crucial is a narrow range of temperature fluctuation, as swings of more than 20 degrees can devastate beer. Styrofoam works great as an extra layer of insulation, especially if you're using a closet. (Look for one away from windows, in the center of your house or apartment.)

2. **THINK LIKE A VAMPIRE.** Light is beer's mortal enemy, capable of transforming a lovely bitter beer into a skunky catastrophe. When you're searching for a place to store your beer, ask yourself this question: Is this where a vampire would happily nap?

3. **EVERYONE HATES HUMIDITY.** Warm, damp air makes most people cranky. Beer also hates humidity. It invites the development of mold, which can infiltrate a beer through a cork or an imperfectly sealed crown cap. If you live in a humid environment—heck, anywhere below the Mason-Dixon Line for nine months of the year—a dehumidifier is crucial. Alternatively, an arid climate will cause corks to dry out, so a humidifier might be a good investment as well. The ideal humidity range is somewhere between 50 and 70 percent.

MAKE THE RIGHT PICKS

Just like people, some beers do not want to grow old.

1. **IT'S A MATTER OF STRENGTH.** Lagers, pilsners, and other low- to moderate-strength beers should not marinate for years or even

months. These lower-potency beers are best fresh and will degrade as the days and months disappear.

2. **DON'T HOP TO IT.** I implore you, do not allow an IPA, imperial IPA, or hop-packed pale ale to gather dust. Hoppy beers are finest fresh, as the in-your-face aromatics diminish over time. I recommend that you follow the advice Vermont's The Alchemist inscribes on its 16-ounce cans of Heady Topper, one of the country's dankest, most craved double IPAs: DRINK THIS BEER IMMEDIATELY. WE ARE ALWAYS MAKING MORE.

3. **GIVE IN TO THE DARKNESS.** Look to dark, hearty, and malty beers, such as barley wines, imperial stouts, and Belgian strong ales, that have an ABV of at least 8 percent or more. Given time, the alcohol heat will diminish gradually, often creating a cashmere-smooth mouthfeel.

4. **THE CONDITION IT'S IN.** Bottle-conditioned beers that contain yeast are preferable to filtered beers. The fungi will help modify a beer's character.

5. **DOUBLE YOUR PLEASURE, DOUBLE YOUR FUN.** Aging beer is akin to a science experiment. You want to match a control group to a variable. I suggest aging at least two beers—more, if you can swing it. Taste the beer fresh, then at least six months down the line to gauge how it's evolving. If the beer's *really* good, you'll be glad you bought extra.

6. **UP WITH BEER.** Resist the urge to store beer on its side, a common practice with wine to keep the cork moist. Even if a beer comes corked and caged like Champagne, the bottle should be stored upright. This allows sediment and yeast to collect at the bottom and stay there when you open a bottle.

Michigan-based brewery photographer Michael Donk's cellar includes more than 300 bottles, including rarities from Three Floyds, 3 Fonteinen, De Struise, Kuhnhenn and countless more. (Find his pictures at brewbokeh.com.)

KNOW WHEN ENOUGH IS ENOUGH

When you are aging beer, the clock is both your best friend and a mortal enemy. Here are some tips on how to know how long is enough.

1. **WAIT—BUT NOT FOREVER.** Beer is not like dairy, its clock constantly counting down toward a machine-printed expiration date. Beer is fairly hearty, able to withstand the depredations of time better than most. But every beer has its limit. Most should be consumed within several years, though heartier barley wines and imperial stouts can be divine after 8 to 10 years. Still, five years is the point at which even strong beers dive off a flavor cliff.

2. **PAST THEIR PRIME.** Since they were in their early twenties, my parents collected wine, breaking out choice bottles for special dinners and the holidays. Opening one was a roll of the dice. Some had weathered the years wonderfully, and others were vinegar. Such are the hazards of aging. For every hit, there might be a miss. Dump it down the drain and carry on.

3. **CROWD-SOURCE WISDOM.** With beer, the Web offers a wealth of brewing knowledge and knowledgeable beer drinkers eager to impart their wisdom. If you're uncertain how long a beer should age, take to the lively aging forums on sites such as *Ratebeer.com* and *Beeradvocate.com*, where members are eager to add their two cents.

4. **IT'S ALWAYS TIME TO CELEBRATE.** Two or three times a year, when my beer closet bulges, I invite friends over, with a caveat: do not bring beer. Pull whatever you want from the closet and crack it open. The moral is: your stash is not a museum hidden behind DO NOT TOUCH signs. Every day is an excuse to celebrate, a reason to open a great beer and flood your evening with cheer.

TEN GREAT BEERS TO STASH

The nation's preeminent expert on aging beer is Southern California's "Dr." Bill Sysak, a certified cicerone (a sort of beer sommelier) and Craft Beer Ambassador for Stone Brewing World Bistro and Gardens. A walking encyclopedia of fermented knowledge, Sysak, who earned his nickname as a combat military medic, has spent the last 30-plus years crisscrossing the globe, visiting more than 1,000 breweries and amassing a collection of more than 2,000 bottles stored everywhere from a three-door cooler in the garage (the unplugged convenience-store artifact maintains temperatures between 62° and 65°F) to a cabinet beneath a bathroom sink—and beneath his home. Rare beers are popped during his extravagant private parties, but anyone is welcome to attend his Sour Fest and Oakquinox festivals (see page 222). Here, he imparts his wisdom on 10 beers to stock your cellar.

IMPERIAL STOUTS

"When I'm first starting to guide people, I tell them to look to beers that are 8 percent ABV or higher and are darker. They pick up fewer off flavors," Sysak says. "What's great about imperial stouts is that as they oxidize"—and all beers eventually oxidize—"they became vinous, or wine-like and get a little tart. But that adds a complexity that works well with the style."

1. **NORTH COAST BREWING COMPANY OLD RASPUTIN RUSSIAN IMPERIAL STOUT**: "This is a simple, relatively inexpensive beer," Sysak says. "I like to recommend to people that they, if possible, buy a case to drink one fresh, then monitor it on a three- to six-month schedule. There's nothing worse than waiting two to three years and saying, 'Oh, I have 23 beers that have gone bad.'"

2. **ALESMITH BREWING COMPANY SPEEDWAY STOUT**: "It's 12 percent ABV, which is perfect, and the coffee adds an extra nuance," Sysak says. "As the beer ages, the coffee and chocolate notes really blend together. In fact, all of the big AleSmith beers are great for aging."

3. **STONE BREWING CO. IMPERIAL RUSSIAN STOUT**: "Of all the Stone beers, the imperial stout is best for aging. It's 10.5 percent ABV, so it's in the sweet spot, and it's also fairly affordable."

BARLEY WINES

"I break barley wines into two major categories. West Coast barley wines are hoppier, with a lighter malt profile up front," Sysak says. "English-style barley wines start off sweeter, but as they age, more flavors come out. I believe that English barley wines have longer legs." Ample hops are never ideal for the long haul.

4. **ROGUE ALES XS OLD CRUSTACEAN**: "It's a legendary example of a West Coast barley wine," Sysak says. "When I used to do the Toronado Barleywine Festival [in San Francisco; see page 213], the 1994 Old Crustacean was the best of show year in, year out. I remember we tried Old Crustacean in 2001, and we said, 'Oh, the 1994 peaked.' A beer will not stay great forever."

5. **ANCHOR BREWING OLD FOGHORN BARLEYWINE STYLE ALE**: "It's just a classic English-style barley wine," Sysak says. "It's widely available and affordable as well."

In 2010, a Baltic Sea shipwreck that dated to the 1840s yielded a stock of still-drinkable Champagne and five bottles of beer that Finnish researchers hope to reverse-engineer and one day re-create.

"Don't be afraid to try aging any beer style," Sysak says. "I have saisons, tripels, and blonde ales in my cellar."

BARREL-AGED BEERS

"When you're cellaring nonsour, barrel-aged beer, brandy and bourbon barrels offer the best longevity, and bourbon is the most readily available," Sysak says. "They work perfectly for the imperial stouts and barley wines because they have complementary flavors of vanilla or toffee that, given time, create a really warming, enjoyable digestif."

6. **GOOSE ISLAND BOURBON COUNTY BRAND STOUT:** "In 1992, it was the first bourbon barrel–aged beer, and it has continually been a top performer for aging," Sysak says.

7. **THE LOST ABBEY THE ANGEL'S SHARE:** "Aged in bourbon or brandy barrels, this strong ale"—named after the spirits that evaporate from wood casks during aging—"is 12.5 percent ABV and has wonderful flavors of caramel, oak, and vanilla. It's a classic."

HIGHER-ALCOHOL AMERICAN WILD ALES AND SOURS

"Sour beers usually take years to make, and many bars want to carry them, so it can be tough to find readily available sours to buy," Sysak says. The silver lining is that higher-alcohol sour beers and wild ales inoculated with yeasts such as *Brettanomyces* can be cellared—with careful monitoring and sampling. *Brettanomyces* does not obey boundaries, and given too much time, it may turn a transcendent beer into an undrinkable drain pour. Beers soured with a blend of wild yeast and souring bacteria are a better bet, Sysak says.

8. **RUSSIAN RIVER BREWING COMPANY CONSECRATION, TEMPTATION, OR SUPPLICATION:** "One of the great things about these classic Russian River beers is that since they've been in the market so long, you can usually find them at the store," Sysak says. "They don't age into the 10- to 20-year range, but they do grow complex and amazing."

LAMBICS, FLEMISH REDS, AND OTHER LOWER-ALCOHOL SOURS

With aging, rules are meant to be broken. "Lambics are one of the few beers that don't need to be over 8 percent to age for 20 years," Sysak says. If you can find it, look for anything from Cantillon or perhaps New Belgium Brewing Company's celebrated annual sour ale La Folie.

BELGIAN BEERS

"Many Belgian beers work well for aging because of the yeast strains that the country's brewers use as well as the fact that most Belgian beers are bottle-conditioned," Sysak says. "Go to your local beer store, talk to your local beer seller, and find out which Belgian beers they have in stock that are 9, 10, 11, or 12 percent ABV. They lay down beautifully."

9. **TRAPPISTES ROCHEFORT 10:** "Strong Trappist beers like Rochefort 10 are great for aging and are also usually available," Sysak says, "but you can go for secular breweries," he adds, such as the Scaldis beers from Brasserie Dubuisson Frères and De Dolle Stille Nacht from Brouwerij De Dolle Brouwers.

SCOTCH ALES/WEE HEAVIES

"There are a lot of great Scotch ales that have the right ABV for aging," Sysak says of this nuanced, somewhat smoky style (see more on page 209). "If you find a nice Scotch ale, go ahead and age it. It's a darker beer with a malt complexity that's suited for aging."

10. **FOUNDERS BREWING COMPANY BACKWOODS BASTARD:** "It's more than 10 percent ABV, which makes it ideal for aging," Sysak says of the lightly peaty ale aged in bourbon barrels. "Seasonally, it's a great wintertime beer."

To celebrate Edward VIII's first year as the king of England, Britain's Greene King brewery brewed the strong celebratory Coronation Ale. Too bad Edward never made it to the one-year mark. He abdicated the throne after 325 days to marry the American Wallis Simpson—and Coronation Ale was never released. In 2012, brewery workers discovered a bricked-over cellar that contained about 2,000 bottles of royal ale.

EIGHT GREAT BARS AND RESTAURANTS WITH STELLAR CELLARS

ALTHOUGH VINTAGE WINE HAS LONG BEEN A STAPLE IN BARS, RESTAURANTS, AND COLLECTORS' HOME CELLARS, THE MOMENT FINALLY HAS ARRIVED FOR AGING BEER. FINE-DINING RESTAURANTS SUCH AS NEW YORK CITY'S GRAMERCY TAVERN AND ELEVEN MADISON PARK ARE SMARTENING UP AND SELLING VINTAGE BEER, AND BARS RANGING FROM LOS ANGELES'S BLUE PALMS BREWHOUSE TO LOUISVILLE, KENTUCKY'S SERGIO'S WORLD BEERS PAIR THEIR DRAFT PROGRAMS WITH A LENGTHY LIST OF AGED BEERS. I GUARANTEE YOU'LL HAVE A GRAND OLD TIME AT THESE RESTAURANTS AND BARS.

BLUE PALMS BREWHOUSE (LOS ANGELES, CALIFORNIA)

In the glittering heart of Hollywood, abutting the Walk of Fame, you'll find Blue Palms, a bar where the star is undeniably beer. The 24 taps pay lip service to Left Coast breweries such as Golden Road and AleSmith, as does the vintage-beer list, which features aged versions of great ales from Firestone Walker, Lost Abbey, Stone, and Port Brewing. To stave off the inevitable intoxication, try one of the exotic sausages (elk, pheasant, venison) and the decadent truffle burger cooked in duck fat.

EBENEZER'S PUB (LOVELL, MAINE)

Deep in rural Maine, down roads identified by numbers, not names, you'll find Chris and Jen Lively's pilgrimage-worthy Belgian-focused restaurant. Yeah, the 35 taps regularly count rare lambics from cult brewers Oude Beersel and Cantillon, but the real gems are found in the cellar, where Chris has amassed a "liquid Library of Congress" featuring 1,000 bottles, some stretching back a century. Ebenezer's sister pub, Lion's Pride in Brunswick, Maine, is equally top-notch.

DE KULMINATOR (ANTWERP, BELGIUM)

It doesn't look like much, a cluttered little pub decorated with plants, mugs, empty beer bottles, and a fine patina of dust. Don't be deceived. Since 1974, Dirk Van Dyck and his wife, Leen Boudewijn, have run one of the world's foremost repositories of vintage Belgian beers, with some dating to the early 1970s. Peruse the thick menu and be prepared to empty your bank account.

BRICK STORE PUB (DECATUR, GEORGIA)

After a revelatory trip to Belgium's De Kulminator, Dave Blanchard and the crew at the Atlanta-area nerve center of better beer decided to up their aging game, turning an adjoining underground bank vault into a cellar stocked with more than 750 rare, vintage beers. E-mail the bar ahead of time to prearrange a drool-worthy cellar tour.

Rare Belgian beers are the specialty at Maine's off-the-beaten-path Ebenezer's Pub (left). Brick Store Pub (above) is one of the choicest spots in the South to sample vintage beer.

THE BULL & BUSH PUB & BREWERY (DENVER, COLORADO)

On your next visit to the Mile High City, there's every reason to make the B&B a must-stop. The brewers make award-winning ales such as the citrus-smacked Man Beer and the fruity, toffee-nuanced Big Ben Brown Ale, which are complemented by owner Erik Peterson's stock of vintage beers, from a 1994 Samuel Adams Triple Bock to lambics and saisons from the turn of the millennium.

MONK'S CAFÉ (PHILADELPHIA, PENNSYLVANIA)

On the list of beer bars to visit before you kick the bucket, Tom Peters's long-running Belgian bar ranks high owing to his dedication to both beer cuisine (mussels steamed in Saison Dupont or a sour ale, stout-braised lamb) and enough vintage lambics and bottled Belgians to spin your head like a top. Of note: try the Monk's Café Flemish Sour Ale.

SERGIO'S WORLD BEERS (LOUISVILLE, KENTUCKY)

Brazil native and globetrotter Sergio Ribenboim has created, well, a world-class beer destination as unlikely as it is tough to find. Hidden beneath a sign reading FUSION RESTAURANT is a carbonated museum packed with coolers stocked with more than 1,400 beers culled from around the globe, plus 45 more rarities dispensed on draft.

THE HAPPY GNOME (SAINT PAUL, MINNESOTA)

The Twin Cities' beer scene has blown up thanks to bars and restaurants such as the Happy Gnome, which marries quirky American cuisine (tater tots with bacon ketchup, wild boar chops with fried corn pudding) with 76 craft drafts and a deep list of bottled and vintage beers. The Gnome also hosts the annual cask ale–focused Firkin Fest.

BEER WEEKS

Besides dumplings and a deep shoulder massage, there are few things I like better in life than a good beer festival. It's an educational buffet, offering up a variety of breweries and styles of beer that are doled out in two-ounce increments—drunkenness by the sip. But though these festivals are a fine meet-and-greet for craft beer, they're not a great introduction to your area beer scene. That's the role of beer weeks.

Across North America and, increasingly, the globe, beer-focused "weeks" (which sometimes stretch for 10 days or longer) have begun sprouting up, shining a spotlight on local beer culture. These collaborative, community-based celebrations bring together a city or region's bars, restaurants, breweries, and beer lovers, who curate craft beer–focused events such as pairing dinners (and breakfasts!), bike rides and runs to breweries, cask-ale festivals, and even burlesque shows and Skee-Ball tournaments.

Yes, craft-beer powerhouses such as San Diego, Philadelphia, and Portland, Oregon, have their festivities, but the concept also has taken root in lesser-known beer cities such as Nashville, Louisville, and Glasgow, Scotland. Pack your bags. These weeks are coming on strong.

CRAFT BEER WEEKS

The dates for the beer weeks may change. Contact organizers for current info.

AMERICAN CRAFT BEER WEEK, MAY

craftbeer.com

The Brewers Association's national craft beer week grew out of the longer-running craft-beer month.

ALABAMA

ALABAMA BEER WEEK, JUNE

alabamabeerweek.com

Launched in 2010, the statewide celebration is highlighted by the Magic City Brewfest, which is held at Birmingham's historic Sloss Furnaces.

ALASKA

AK BEER WEEK, JANUARY

akbeerweek.com

The festivities at this cure for cabin fever have included dinners paired with Alaskan Brewing Company's darkest beers, the Panty Peeler Strip Show (a risqué celebration of Midnight Sun's Panty Peeler Tripel), and, in Anchorage, the Great Alaska Beer & Barley Wine Festival.

ARIZONA

ARIZONA BEER WEEK, FEBRUARY

arizonabeerweek.com

The Grand Canyon State celebrates its week, which was founded in 2010, with events such as Phoenix's Strong Beer Festival, breweries turned into temporary art galleries, and beer-and-bacon dinners.

CALIFORNIA

L.A. BEER WEEK, SEPTEMBER

labeerweek.com

Given the exploding craft-beer scene in Los Angeles, it's understandable that the city's event stretches to 11 days. Highlights include the L.A. Beer Week Festival at the

CALIFORNIA (CONTINUED)

historic Union Station and Eagle Rock Brewing's annual collaboration beer, Unity.

SACRAMENTO CRAFT BEER WEEK, FEBRUARY/MARCH

sacramentobeerweek.com

Expect Skee-Ball tournaments, Rubicon Brewing's cask-focused Gravity Festival, and two big bashes: Sacramento Brewers Showcase and Capital Beerfest.

SAN DIEGO BEER WEEK, NOVEMBER

sdbw.org

The SoCal brewing powerhouse pulls out all the stops with more than 400 events, including a rare-beer breakfast, lunches with brewmasters, and a "beer garden" event partnering local breweries and chefs.

SF BEER WEEK, FEBRUARY

sfbeerweek.org

The Bay Area offers a sour festival at Berkeley's Jupiter and Triple Rock, group bike rides, and Sean Paxton's high-wire beer-pairing dinners, such as 2012's big top–themed Three Ring Circus. It was epic.

COLORADO

DENVER BEER FEST, OCTOBER

denver.org/denverbeerfest

Dovetailing with the Great American Beer Festival, the week's events include a beer-cocktail tour, the Colorado Beer Ice Cream Festival, and a bus tour of Oskar Blues' Hops & Heifers Farm.

DELAWARE

WILMINGTON BEER WEEK, JULY

wilmingtonbeerweek.com

The city's mayor leads a simulcast toast at all the beer-week venues, commencing eight days of citywide happy hours and prix-fixe menus paired with craft beer, including Delaware's Dogfish Head.

FLORIDA

JAX BEER WEEK, APRIL

beerweekjax.com

Founded in 2012, the Florida week's festivities have included beer-movie nights and the Grand Tasting party featuring local breweries such as Intuition Ale Works and Swamp Head.

GEORGIA

ATLANTA BEER WEEK, OCTOBER

atlantabeerweek.com

Consonant with the sprawling nature of Atlanta, this week (which began in 2010) focuses its festivities—offbeat beer-and-food pairings, tap takeovers, rare cask ales—on a different neighborhood each night.

ILLINOIS

CHICAGO CRAFT BEER WEEK, MAY

chibeerweek.com

The Windy City's winning roster of events typically includes the Faux BAB barrel aged–beer bash, Haymarket Pub & Brewery's Beerfly Alleyfight (a homebrewed beer is paired with food *and* a piece of art), and the Beer Under Glass festival at the leafy Garfield Park Conservatory.

INDIANA

INDIANA BEER WEEK, JULY

brewersofindianaguild.com/beerweek.html

The highlight of the week is Indianapolis's Indiana Microbrewers Festival, which features dozens of the state's—and nation's—best brewers, including the sublime sours of Bloomington's Upland Brewing.

KENTUCKY

LOUISVILLE CRAFT BEER WEEK, SEPTEMBER/OCTOBER

louisvillecraftbeerweek.com

Forget bourbon: this week, beer reigns supreme at events such as a "battle" of Indiana and Kentucky breweries, dog-friendly Yappy Hour at Apocalypse Brew Works, and the Feast of Fall Beers.

MAINE

MAINE BEER WEEK, NOVEMBER

mainebeerweek.com

The land of lobsters also loves its beers, as evidenced by the kickoff beer week in 2011. Events included a Maine-brewery tap takeover at Portland's Great Lost Bear (one of my favorite bars) and a nanobrewery dinner featuring beers from Rising Tide, Baxter, and Marshall Wharf.

MARYLAND

BALTIMORE BEER WEEK, OCTOBER

bbweek.com

The week features the Okto-BEAR-fest at the Maryland Zoo, crab-and-beer feasts, and Chesapeake Real Ale Festival.

MASSACHUSETTS

BOSTON BEER WEEK, MAY/JUNE

beeradvocate.com/bbw

Produced by the website Beer Advocate, the week is anchored by the East Coast's largest beer bash, the American Craft Beer Fest.

MICHIGAN

DETROIT BEER WEEK, OCTOBER

detbeerweek.com

Take a bike tour of the Motor City's historic and current breweries, go on a pub crawl, or hit the Detroit Fall Beer Festival.

GRAND RAPIDS BEER WEEK, FEBRUARY

facebook.com/grbeerweek

Local breweries such as Founders, Brewery Vivant, and the Hideout take the spotlight during festivities filled with beer dinners and rare brews tapped at bars, including the world-class Hopcat. Winter Beer Festival caps the week.

KALAMAZOO BEER WEEK, JANUARY

kalamazoobeerweek.com

Bell's fans, take note: the lauded Kalamazoo brewery hosts loads of events (smoked meat and aged beer pairings, tours, movie nights); elsewhere you'll find limited-edition tastings from Michigan breweries such as Right Brain, Arcadia, and New Holland.

MISSISSIPPI

MISSISSIPPI CRAFT BEER WEEK, JULY

raiseyourpints.com

The must-hit event is Jackson's Top of the Hops Beer Fest, featuring 150-plus beers and educational seminars.

MISSOURI

ST. LOUIS CRAFT BEER WEEK, APRIL/MAY

stlbeerweek.com

Attend symposiums on brewing, overdose on cask ales at the Firkin Fest, and sip some dubbels and tripels at Perennial Artisan Ales' Midwest Belgian Beer Festival.

MONTANA

MISSOULA CRAFT BEER WEEK, MAY

missoulabeerweek.com

This Montana city makes the most of its week with brewery bus tours, the annual Garden City BrewFest (arrive early!), and a fun run that starts and ends at a local brewery—there's a pint waiting for you at the finish line.

NEBRASKA

OMAHA BEER WEEK, FEBRUARY

omahabeerweek.com

Extremely vintage beer tastings (think the 1970s, 1980s, and 1990s), homebrew contests, and the Beertopia Extreme Beerfest have helped distinguish this Nebraska city's week of revelry.

NEVADA

NEVADA BEER WEEKS, MAY/JUNE

nevadabeerweeks.com

Reno, Las Vegas, and Henderson play host to events ranging from jazz brunches to beer dinners and a festival held at Barley's Casino & Brewing Company—escaping gambling is impossible in this state.

NEW HAMPSHIRE

PORTSMOUTH BEER WEEK, FEBRUARY/MARCH

portsmouthbeerweek.com

Although winter in this water-hugging town may be frigid, the Seacoast Winter Brew Fest, a rollicking pub crawl, IPA tap takeovers, and rare Smuttynose beers will warm you up this week.

NEW JERSEY

NEW JERSEY CRAFT BEER WEEK, MARCH/APRIL

newjerseycraftbeer.com

The lead-up events to the week-capping Atlantic City Beer and Music Festival typically include tons of tap takeovers and special beers from Jersey breweries such as Kane and Carton.

NEW MEXICO

ABQ BEER WEEK, MAY

abqbeerweek.com

Albuquerque's festivities include rare beer releases, a trolley-based brewery tour, and the Blues and Brews festival featuring local breweries such as Marble and Broken Bottle.

NEW YORK

BUFFALO BEER WEEK, OCTOBER/NOVEMBER

buffalobeerweek.com

Past events have included extreme-beer tastings, homemade sausage and craft-beer pairings, and a "beer geek" brunch.

LONG ISLAND CRAFT BEER WEEK, MAY

longislandcraftbeerweek.com

In 2011, Long Island launched its first beer week, an annual tradition featuring oyster fests, cask ale festivals, and special beers from the region's burgeoning breweries, such as Greenport Harbor and Port Jefferson.

NEW YORK CRAFT BEER WEEK, FEBRUARY/MARCH

nycbeerweek.com

The Big Apple goes all out with the Brewer's Choice beer-and-food festival, IPA tastings aboard yachts, and bashes inside four-star restaurants.

SARATOGA BEER WEEK, FEBRUARY

saratogabeerweek.com

The city of horse races and hot springs also has a big thing for beer. Expect the likes of seminars on hop growing and food pairings, plus an international brew festival.

SYRACUSE BEER WEEK, NOVEMBER

syracusebeerweek.com

The city features sampling sessions from upstate breweries such as Middle Ages and Empire, along with the Harvest Fest, which showcases New York wineries, food vendors, and plenty of breweries.

NORTH CAROLINA

ASHEVILLE BEER WEEK, MAY/JUNE

ashevillebeerweek.com

Asheville celebrates its brewing bounty (around a dozen breweries, with New Belgium and Sierra Nevada soon to open outposts) with the Just Brew It! Homebrew Festival and Beer City Fest.

CHARLOTTE CRAFT BEER WEEK, MARCH

charlottecraftbeerweek.org

The Best of the East vs. Best of the West beer tasting, the Common Market Freak Fest, and bars dedicating their taps to North Carolina's terrific beers help Charlotte shine.

RALEIGH BEER WEEK, AUGUST/ SEPTEMBER

raleighbeerweek.com

Launched in 2010, the week keeps getting better with beer cocktails, brewing panels at Busy Bee Cafe, and boatloads of exclusive beers from breweries such as Mother Earth.

OHIO

CINCINNATI BREW WEEK, FEBRUARY

cincinnatibeerweek.com

Launched in 2012, the Queen City's first week featured a collaboration barley wine, a state-to-state pub crawl that stretched across the Ohio River, and the Cincy Winter Beerfest.

CLEVELAND BEER WEEK, OCTOBER

clevelandbeerweek.org

Enjoy one-off collaborative brews, a nighttime bike ride ending at a brewery, a stout-beer brunch, and BREWzilla, a "monster of a beer tasting" featuring more than 80 breweries.

DAYTON BEER WEEK, OCTOBER

daytonbeerweek.com

When I grew up in Dayton, a good beer was hard to find. No longer. The city is awash in great brews, and during this week you'll sample them at AleFest Dayton and local bars such as South Park Tavern.

OHIO BREW WEEK, JULY

ohiobrewweek.com

The Athens-based week features the Brew-B-Q Sauce Competition, plenty of bands, and, oh yeah, lots of great Ohio breweries, including local all-star Jackie O's. P.S. I attended college at Ohio University.

OREGON

CENTRAL OREGON BEER WEEK, MAY

centraloregonbeerweek.com

To fete Bend's brewing bounty (Deschutes, Boneyard, GoodLife, 10 Barrel, etc.), this week was founded in 2012, featuring a half marathon, shuttles between breweries, and beer and BBQ at snow-capped Mount Bachelor.

OREGON (CONTINUED)
CORVALLIS BEER WEEK, SEPTEMBER
corvallisbeerweek.org

The week starts with a kickoff march, which leads into the barrel-matured beer "experience" and quirky events such as a paper-plate art contest powered by West Coast beers, bingo, and a disc-golf tournament.

EUGENE BEER WEEK, MAY
eugenebeerweek.org

During Eugene's week, you might learn how to build a kegerator, pucker up at a sour-beer festival, or pig out at a charcuterie pairing pitting beer versus wine.

OREGON CRAFT BEER MONTH, JULY
oregoncraftbeermonth.com

Launched as a week in 2005, the bash mushroomed into a monthlong celebration the ensuing year. Expect gobs of special beer releases, dinners, and fests, including Portland's legendary Oregon Brewers Festival.

PDX BEER WEEK, JUNE
pdxbeerweek.com

Portland celebrates its embarrassment of hoppy riches with the Fruit Beer Festival, Rye Beer Fest, and Olympics-inspired Brewers Summer Games, which includes a keg toss.

PENNSYLVANIA
PHILLY BEER WEEK, JULY
phillybeerweek.org

From pig roasts to beer-pairing seminars, festivals, and meet-the-brewer pub crawls, Philly offers it all. It's one of the East Coast's best beer cities.

PITTSBURGH CRAFT BEER WEEK, APRIL
pittsburghcraftbeerweek.com

Exclusive beers, meet-the-brewer events, and pairing dinners were the focus at the first PCBW in 2012, which highlighted smaller local brewers such as Church Brew Works, Penn Brewery, and East End Brewing.

RHODE ISLAND
PROVIDENCE CRAFT BEER WEEK, OCTOBER
facebook.com/providence.week

Beer dinners and brewer visits culminate in the enormous Beervana Fest, hosted at the historic Rhodes-on-the-Pawtuxet in nearby Cranston.

SOUTH CAROLINA
CHARLESTON CRAFT BEER WEEK, APRIL
charlestoncraftbeerweek.com

Come on down for the SweetWater Music Festival, rare-beer bar crawl, brew cruise, and kickball featuring brewery teams. Make sure you eat at Husk Restaurant.

TENNESSEE
NASHVILLE CRAFT BEER WEEK, MARCH
nashvillecraftbeerweek.com

With the Music City's beer scene on the upswing, this week launched in 2012 with the Homebrew Kickoff Extravaganza and East Nashville Beer Festival. You'll love the beers from Yazoo and Jackalope.

TEXAS

AUSTIN CRAFT BEER WEEK, OCTOBER

austinbeerweek.com

"No one leaves thirsty" is the motto at this Texas bash that has featured collaborative beers, unusual cask ales, the Beer Olympics, and special vertical tastings of Saint Arnold Brewing Company's Divine Reserve beers.

DALLAS BEER WEEK, NOVEMBER

dallasbeerweek.com

Tours of breweries such as Deep Ellum and Peticolas, tap takeovers, and band-fueled beer bashes are reason enough to make Dallas a destination.

HOUSTON BEER WEEK, NOVEMBER

houstonbeerweek.com

The Monsters of Beer charity festival, a brewing clinic with Mikkeller's Mikkel Borg Bjergsø, and bike-in movie nights have made past Houston beer weeks special.

SAN ANTONIO CRAFT BEER WEEK, MAY

sanantoniobeerweek.com

The city's beer week features pub crawls by foot and bus, a pro-am brewing competition (the winner gets entered into the Great American Beer Festival), and special nights at area breweries. The must-hit: Freetail Brewing Co.

VIRGINIA

RICHMOND BEER WEEK, NOVEMBER

richmondbeerweek.com

Beer-themed movie screenings, smoked-beer nights, and the Beer-istoric bus tour of Richmond have helped make the city's week a success since 2010.

WASHINGTON

SEATTLE BEER WEEK, FEBRUARY

seattlebeerweek.com

Past events have included the Tour de Pints bike ride, the Iron Brewer competition, and an IPA-fueled bull-riding night—mechanical, that is.

SNOHOMISH COUNTY BEER WEEK, AUGUST

snohomishcountybeerweek.com

Area breweries, including Diamond Knot, Scuttlebutt, Lazy Boy, and Big E, brew special beers for the week.

WASHINGTON, D.C.

D.C. BEER WEEK, AUGUST

dcbeerweek.net

Organized by chef Teddy Folkman and beer distributor Jeff Wells, this week's events have included a craft-beer cruise down the Potomac River and an oyster fest with Rogue Ales. ChurchKey bar is usually the epicenter.

WISCONSIN

MADISON CRAFT BEER WEEK, MAY

madbeerweek.com

Collaborative beers, craft beer–battered fish fries, a bike-based pub crawl (wear your helmet!), and a cask-ale festival have helped Madison's week stand apart.

MILWAUKEE BEER WEEK, APRIL

milwaukeebeerweek.com

The famous brewing city's events have included hard-to-find bourbon-barrel imperial stouts, a Firkin Friday cask-ale event around town, and a beer-sampling session at the Harley-Davidson Museum.

AUSTRALIA

MELBOURNE GOOD BEER WEEK, MAY

goodbeerweek.com

Founded in 2011, the Melbourne week has quickly proved to be one of the world's best. Must-hits include the Great Australasian Beer SpecTAPular, the region-specific Pint of Origin events, and the Kiwi Tap Invasion of New Zealand beers. Think of the frequent-flyer miles!

SYDNEY CRAFT BEER WEEK, OCTOBER

sydneycraftbeerweek.com

The celebration regularly counts tap takeovers, brewery tours, a cow-versus-bird beer dinner, and a trivia night called "Who Is the Ultimate Beer Wanker?"

CANADA

ONTARIO CRAFT BEER WEEK, JUNE

ontariocraftbrewers.com/craftbeerweek /index.php

Past highlights have included a "field to firkin" farm tour, a tasting event of Ontario's canned craft beer, and a battle of brewery bands.

TORONTO BEER WEEK, SEPTEMBER

torontobeerweek.com

Guided tours of Toronto's brewing history, a homebrewer competition, and multicourse beer-pairing dinners have made the city's week a hit since 2010.

VANCOUVER CRAFT BEER WEEK, MAY

vancouvercraftbeerweek.com

Head to Vancouver for events ranging from a multivenue beer-dinner "crawl" to a homebrew competition and the Hoppapalooza bitter-beer bash.

EUROPE

GLASGOW BEER WEEK, SEPTEMBER

glasgowbeerweek.com

Past events have included a homebrewing demonstration, a foraging expedition for edible plants to use in brewing a beer, and, not surprisingly given Scotland's spirits history, panels on the link between brewing and distilling.

NORWICH CITY OF ALE, MAY/JUNE

cityofale.org.uk

Real, or cask, ale is the star at this English 10-day celebration that has featured massive pub quizzes, political debates, and historical walks detailing the city's brewing heritage.

KULMBACHER BIERFEST/BEER WEEK, JULY/AUGUST

bierfest.de

More than 100,000 people flock to the German city's answer to Oktoberfest to enjoy parades, boatloads of beer, Bavarian folk music, and heaps of sausages.

SETTIMANA DELLA BIRRA ARTIGIANALE, MARCH

settimanadellabirra.it

Sorry, wine. This week, craft beer stars at bars, brewpubs, and restaurants across Italy. Expect brewery tours, pairing dinners, and guided tastings galore.

GLOSSARY

Abbey beer A Trappist-style ale made by a secular brewery. Also known as *bière d'abbaye*.

Adjuncts Fermentable substances that are substituted for the cereal grains (chiefly barley) that constitute beer. Adjuncts, such as rice and corn, are used for several reasons. First, they're cheaper than barley. Second, they can lighten a beer's body. That's why Coors Light is the color of watered-down urine. That said, *adjunct* may seem like an evil word, but deployed judiciously, adjuncts can create delicious beer.

Alcohol This mood-brightening by-product of fermentation is produced when yeasts devour sugars in the wort. Alcohol is measured in two categories: alcohol by volume (ABV) and alcohol by weight (ABW). In craft brewing, ABV is the standard measurement, but here's a quick tip on how to convert ABW to ABV: multiply by 1.25. Alcohol is about 80 percent the weight of water, making a 6 percent ABV beer about 4.8 percent ABW.

Ale One of two big families of beer, the other being lager. Like my great-aunt in Florida, ale yeasts favor warmer temperatures, hanging out at the top of a fermentation tank. An ale's flavors and aromas are typically a touch estery—that is, fruity—and thus ales can be sweeter and fuller-bodied than lagers. Ales encompass an enormous grab bag of styles, from stouts to IPAs to Belgian strong ales.

Alternating proprietorship An arrangement by which brewers and winemakers can make their preferred potions at wineries and breweries they don't own. It's a relationship favored by nomadic brewers such as Mikkeller or Evil Twin.

Aroma hops Hops that are used later in the boil for their bouquet, not their bitterness.

Astringent Refers to a drying, puckering taste. Can be a negative or a positive, depending on your taste buds.

Barley The predominant cereal grain used to make beer. After water, it's the biggest ingredient in brewing.

Barley wine A burly, warming, and often sweet beer that originated in Britain. American versions, especially those hailing from the West Coast, tend to be hoppier than their British counterparts. A variation on the style is the wheat wine, which, though similarly strong, tends to be smoother with less residual sweetness.

Barrel The standard term of measurement for brewing. A barrel equals 31 gallons. A half barrel, which is the standard keg you toted to parties in college, holds 15.5 gallons.

Beer engine A manually operated pump used to dispense cask ale.

Berliner weisse This ghostly pale, low-alcohol German wheat beer gets its sour, acidic tang from warm-fermenting yeasts and *Lactobacillus* bacteria. Drink it straight or add a shot of sweet syrup (*mit Schuss*) and slurp it through a straw.

Bière de Champagne A riotously effervescent beer that mimics Champagne's appearance, cork-and-cage packaging, and, typically, painstaking production technique. The style also is known as *bière brut*. I like to pop these bottles on New Year's Eve.

Bière de garde Translated as "beer for keeping," this strong, rustic farmhouse ale originated in northern France's Nord-Pas de Calais region. Traditionally, *bières de garde* were brewed in early spring and kept in chilly cellars for sipping during the warmer summer months.

Bitter A loose category of easy-drinking, moderately hopped British pale ales that are the standard-bearers in every pub. They climb the alcohol ladder from "ordinary" to "best" and "premium," which is also known as an "extra special bitter," or ESB.

Bittering hops Used early in the boil to add bitterness, not aroma.

Bock A strong German lager with a hearty malt character and dark hue. Look for a beer with a goat on the label. See *Eisbock*.

Boil This is the stage in beer making in which the wort is boiled to kill bacteria and yeast as well as to cause proteins to coagulate. Hops are added during this stage.

Bottle-conditioned Beer that's naturally carbonated by live yeast lurking inside the bottle.

Brewers Association Based in Boulder, Colorado, this trade organization is the country's preeminent craft-beer advocate. It curates Denver's annual Great American Beer Festival.

Brew kettle The vessel in which wort is boiled with hops.

California Common A rootin'-tootin', all-American lager fermented with a special lager yeast that functions better at toastier temperatures. The amber-hued brews are characterized by a bit of malt, fruit, and bitterness. The iconic example is Anchor Steam, which has copyrighted its moniker.

Cascadian dark ale The name that brewers in the Pacific Northwest want to confer on dark, hoppy ales. Myself, I prefer *black IPA*, and the Brewers Association recommends *American-style black ale*. Whatever floats your boat.

Cask A wooden, metal, or plastic vessel used to mature, ferment, or flavor beer.

Cask ale Also called *real ale*, cask ale is unfiltered, naturally carbonated beer that's best served at 55°F, which plays up its subtler flavors and aromas.

Cask-conditioned Beer that's fermented in a cask by a second dose of yeast.

Cicerone A beer sommelier who passes the Cicerone Certification Program.

Craft brewer A nebulous, controversial, confusing term that according to the Brewers Association describes a brewery that's small and independent and produces annually less than 6 million barrels of traditional beer. To me, craft brewers are any breweries that make flavorful, unique beer that you'll never see advertised during the Super Bowl. Since many microbreweries are no longer micro, *craft brewery* is the preferred descriptor.

Cream ale Don't have a cow: there's zero dairy in this indigenous American ale that, although it's fermented warm, is conditioned at lager temperatures.

Doppelbock A maltier, more potent bock. It's so rich, it's almost like drinking your dinner.

Dry hopping Hops that are added to beer that has finished fermenting or is conditioning. This step is what creates those intense, fragrant aromatic brews that make hops lovers swoon.

Dubbel This Trappist-style Belgian ale is a tour de force of rich malt and caramel flavors, with dark fruit and a whisper of bitterness to boot.

Dunkleweizen A dark wheat beer that, like a hefeweizen, boasts plenty of banana and clove notes.

Eisbock A strong, concentrated lager that's created by freezing a beer and removing water. Though eisbocks can verge on syrupy, they'll warm you like a wool coat.

America's killjoy government declares that the production process is a form of distillation, with the end product deemed hard liquor.

Extreme beers Extra flavor, extra alcohol, extra *everything*. These are beefy he-man beers that'll knock you for a loop. Extreme beers include double IPA, triple IPA, and Russian imperial stout—in fact, anything with the word *imperial* on it.

Fermentation The metabolic process during which yeasts devour the sugars in the wort like Pac-Man, creating alcohol and carbon dioxide.

Filtration The removal of all the floating proteins and yeasts, creating a clearer, more stable—and sometimes less flavorful—beer.

Firkin A wood, plastic, or, more commonly, metal keg that holds 10.8 gallons. You can also call it a cask.

Flanders This region of Belgium lends its name to several styles of beer: the dark, sour oud bruin and the similarly tart Flanders red, of which Rodenbach is a textbook example.

Fresh hop ale A delicate, ephemeral fall specialty that's made with just-harvested hops. It typically appears in September and October.

Gluten It's the protein present in many grains, including barley. Sufferers of celiac disease can't drink beers that contain gluten—sadly, most of 'em. See *Sorghum.*

Gose A specialty of Leipzig, Germany, this cloudy yellow wheat beer is dry and refreshing, with some coriander spicing and salt, which adds a sharp complexity. A dose of lactic acid or *Lactobacillus* bacteria gives gose a tart profile.

Great American Beer Festival Since 1982, this has been the Super Bowl of American brewing. Annually, nearly 600 brewers show up in hopes of garnering a bronze, silver, or gold medal in one of more than 80 categories. Winning could alter a brewery's fortunes forever. Attending the festival leaves you (well, me) drunk for days.

Grodziskie A rustic European beer made with 100 percent smoked wheat malt and hops aplenty. In Germany, the rustic ale is known as *grätzer*.

Gruit A medieval beer that was flavored with a mixture of herbs. Gruit predates the use of hops in brewing.

Gueuze This traditional Belgian beer is made by blending one-, two-, and three-year-old lambics, then letting the mixture age and continue fermenting in the bottle. The result is a dry, fruity elixir with a lip-scrunching sourness.

Hefeweizen A beer style from southern Germany made with 50 percent wheat or more. They're tangy, refreshing beers with notes of bananas and cloves thanks to the yeast strain. Some folks like to squeeze in lemons. As far as I'm concerned, it's as unnecessary as nipples on men. Bonus trivia: *hefe* means "with yeast."

Hopback A sealed, hops-stuffed vessel through which the wort circulates, snatching up heady aromas and flavors.

Hops The creeping bine (a bine climbs by wrapping its stem around a support, compared with a vine, which climbs with tendrils or suckers) *Humulus lupulus*, whose female flowers (called cones) flavor beers and provide bitterness. Each variety has its own unique flavor profile (see page 19). Hop resins possess two primary acids: alpha and beta. Beta acids contribute to a beer's bouquet. Alpha acids serve as a preservative and contribute bitterness when hops are added early in the boil, flavor later in the boil, and aroma in the last minutes of a boil. Oh, you might ask: Why do some hops smell like marijuana? The plants are related.

Imperial See *Extreme beers.*

India pale ale (IPA) A superbitter style of beer that has become craft brewing's missionary beer, converting drinkers around the globe. An imperial, double IPA, or triple IPA increases the hops and malt, creating a bitterer, boozier beer.

International bitterness unit (IBU) A scientific scale that measures bitterness in beer. A low IBU (Budweiser is around 11) means the beer isn't hoppy; when an IBU tops triple digits, you're in for a mouth-scrunching ride.

Kölsch This pale, elegant German ale receives its fruity, biscuity flavors from a warmer fermentation before it is lagered at cooler temperatures to smooth out the sweet malts.

Lager The second main style of beer. Like penguins, bottom-fermenting lager yeasts prefer cooler temperatures. They also take longer to ferment, hence the name; *lagern* means "to rest" in German. Lagers are typically crisp, delicate, and as refreshing as a dip in a lake in August.

Lambic Made with wheat, this traditional Belgian beer is spontaneously fermented with wild yeasts, resulting in a sour, tart, barnyard-leaning profile. Lambics can be broken down into three general classes: those made with fruit such as cherries (kriek), raspberries (framboise), or black currants (cassis); gueuze, which is a blend of young and old lambics; and faro, a lambic sweetened with candi sugar or brown sugar.

Macrobreweries MillerCoors, Anheuser-Busch InBev, and the other behemoths that rule global brewing with a watery fist. Contrary to common belief, macrobreweries do not make bad beer. Their brewing protocols are among the industry's most rigid. Rather, the problem is that they make lowest-common-denominator beer.

Maibock A lighter-hued, somewhat hoppier bock lager.

Malt To create malt, cereal grains are bathed in water. This jump-starts germination, allowing the grain to create the enzymes required to convert starches and proteins into fermentable sugars. The process is arrested when maltsters—the people who make malt—heat and dry the grain. Like coffee, grain can be roasted to create different flavors.

Märzen Since hot weather can muck up fermentation, this robust, full-bodied lager is brewed in early spring—*März* is the German word for "March"—then lagered into the fall, when it is traditionally served during Oktoberfest. Any beer sold as an Oktoberfest beer is a märzen.

Mash The initial step in brewing. Crushed grain is steeped in a big ol' pot of boiling water, transforming starches into sugars.

Mash tun The vessel in which brewers boil their mash.

Mouthfeel How the beer feels when you drink it—a combination of body, texture, carbonation, and flavor. Mouthfeel is as subjective as a Yelp review.

Nanobrewery A pint-size brewery that in my book brews on a three-barrel system or smaller. Care to convince me otherwise? I'm all ears: josh.bernstein@gmail.com.

Nitrogen tap A draft-beer system that sends nitrogen coursing through beers such as stouts, augmenting the creamy mouthfeel. The process is known as nitrogenation, which also can be applied to bottled beers such as Left Hand Milk Stout Nitro.

Noble hops European hop varieties that are aromatic and less bitter. That's not necessarily a negative. These hops, including Hallertauer, Tettnanger, Spalt, and Saaz, impart a spicy, herbal, zesty character. Commonly found in pilsners and European lagers.

Oxidation When beer is exposed to oxygen, it undergoes

a series of chemical reactions that create stale flavors sometimes described as "sherry" or "cardboard."

Pasteurization Murdering yeast through a serious application of heat. Unpasteurized beers retain their yeast, which means the beer will continue to evolve over time.

Pilsner In the 1840s, this beer style was born in the Czech Republic town of Plzen, aka Pilsen. The straw-gold brew is see-through and packs plenty of spicy floral notes and zingy bitterness—the trademark of the noble hops used to brew it.

Pitch Adding yeast to the cooled-down wort.

Porter This style originated in Britain as a strong, dark brew made from a blend of sour or stale mild and new ales. Though that style fell out of practice, porters still endure. They include the potent, dark-brown Baltic (originally shipped across the North Sea) and innovative American riffs that can incorporate smoked malts, vanilla, or a mountain of hops.

Priming Dosing a fermented beer with priming sugar after it has been bottled or kegged, spurring increased carbonation and flavor creation.

Quadrupel A decadent Trappist-style ale with an ABV residing in the double digits and decadent flavors of dark fruit. The Netherlands' Koningshoeven monastery created the first quadrupel in 1991 with its La Trappe Quadrupel. Also called *quad* or *Alt*.

Rauchbier This German beer is made with malts that have been smoked over a roaring beech wood fire, imbuing the malt with smokiness. (*Rauch* is German for "smoke.") It's a bit like drinking a liquefied ham or hunk of Texas BBQ.

Reinheitsgebot The German Purity Law dates back to 1516, when William IV, Duke of Bavaria, decreed that beer could be made only from hops, water, and grain; the law predated the discovery of yeast, which has since been added to the list. In 1993, the Reinheitsgebot was replaced by the *Vorläufiges Deutsches Biergesetz*, or Provisional German Beer Law, which lets brewers use yeast (how generous!), different grains, and, for top-fermenting beers, additional sugars.

Roggenbier Though closely related to hefeweizen (they use the same clove- and banana-like flavor-inducing yeast strain), roggenbier trades wheat for rye. (*Roggen* is German for "rye.") They're crisp and drying, with a bit of a spicy jolt.

Rye When used in brews, this grain can impart spiciness and a crisp character and help dry out a beer.

Saison Originally brewed to slake the summertime thirst of Belgian farmhands, earthy, spicy saisons inhabit a wide stylistic range. Some are fruity, and others are desert-dry, peppery, and aromatic. Also called a farmhouse ale.

Schwarzbier A dark, roasty lager that despite its dark tint remains megadrinkable.

Scotch ale A style of beer born in, you guessed it, Scotland. Expect flavors of caramel, toffee, and perhaps a teensy bit of smoke and a substantial ABV. Also known as *wee heavy*. The related Scottish ales are lighter and less sweet.

Session beer Beer low in alcohol, not in flavor. Best for sipping during a long-haul drinking session.

Skunked When UV light strikes beer, it causes isohumulones—chemicals released when hops are boiled—to break down, creating chemical compounds identical to those found in skunk spray. Never buy bottled beer that's been sunning in a store's window.

Sorghum An African grass with a high sugar content that, when turned into a syrup, is used to craft gluten-free beer. Sorghum is the salvation of beer-loving folks with celiac disease.

Sour beer See *Wild ale*.

Sparging Removing the grains from the mash, leaving behind hot, watery wort.

Spontaneous fermentation The technique of allowing wild, indigenous yeast to inoculate wort naturally. It's the signature process of brewing Belgian lambics. See *Wild ale*.

Steam beer See *California Common*.

Stout This dark ale originally was developed in Ireland and Britain and can be creamy, bitter, or coffee-like. Styles include the strong, full-bodied imperial; the sweet milk stout (made with lactose); the burly, roasty Russian imperial, which originally was brewed for that country's czars; the silky oatmeal stout; and the drinkable Irish dry stout, which includes Guinness.

Terroir The unique characteristics that soil, climate, and people give agricultural products. Though it once was a term reserved for wine and coffee, beer is making a grab for it.

Tripel This Trappist-style Belgian ale is a heavy hitter, often boasting a double-digit ABV. The pale golden ale boasts a creamy head, complex flavors of fruit and spice, and a sticky-sweet finish.

Wee heavy See *Scotch ale*.

Weizenbock A potent wheat beer. Dunkelweizen's big brother is often fruity, sometimes spicy, and always complex.

Wet-hopping Using fresh, sticky, undried hops. See *Fresh hop ale*.

Wild ale A catchall category of funky-tasting offbeat beers dosed with wild yeast such as *Brettanomyces* and perhaps a souring bacteria such as *Lactobacillus* or *Pediococcus* (see page 228).

Witbier An unfiltered Belgian wheat beer (also known as *bière blanche*) that's amply spiced with orange peel, coriander, and whatever herbs catch the brewer's fancy. They're crisp and lively and aces on an 80-degree afternoon. Drink it with a lemon slice if you must, but doing so is a little like coating filet mignon in ketchup.

Wort The hot soup that's extracted from the mash. It's an all-you-can-eat buffet for the yeasts that create beer.

Yeast The microscopic critters that craft your favorite beverage and make 5 p.m. the best hour of the day. Grains and hops notwithstanding, yeast drives about 90 percent of a beer's flavor profile. Each strain provides a different flavor profile, and breweries often develop their own idiosyncratic yeast strains.

INDEX

Note: Page numbers in *italics* indicate brews to try.

A

Abbaye d'Orval, 156, *163*
Abbey of Maria Toevlucht, 161
Abbey of New Clairvaux, 161
Abbey of Saint Sixtus of
    Westvleteren, 157, 159, *163*,
    164
Abita Brewing Company, *70*
ABQ Beer Week, 300
ABV (alcohol by volume), 25–27
ABW (alcohol by weight), 25
Acetaldehyde taste, 37
Acetic taste, 37
Achel Blonde 5°, *163*
Achel Bruin 5°, *163*
Acidity, 36
Adam, 67, 203, 205
Aecht Schlenkerla Rauchbier
    Märzen, *59*
Aftertaste, 37
Aging beer, 287–295. *See also*
    Barrel-aged beers
    about: overview of, 287
    aging time, 289–290
    bars/restaurants with best cellars,
        294–295
    brews to cellar, 290
    humidity and, 288
    light and, 288
    sampling, 288
    selecting beers for aging, 288–289
    stability and, 288
    storage environment, 288
    tips for, 288
Ahtanum hops, 19
AK Beer Week, 297
Alabama Beer Week, 297
Alaskan Brewing, 58, 80
The Alchemist, 16

Alcohol. *See also* ABV (alcohol by
    volume)
    carbonation and, 26
    low, 26
    measurement of, 25
    yeasts and, 26–27
AleSmith Brewing Company, 210,
    287, 291
Ale yeasts, 24
Allagash Brewing Company, *100*,
    166–168, 232
Allsopp's Arctic Ale, 112
Almond '22, 265
Altbiers, 81–83, 275
Alt-schwarzbier, 56
Aluminum cans, 29
Amarillo hops, 19, 103, *151*, 181, 204
Ambacht Ales, 268
Amber ale, 122–123
Amerasia (Covington, KY), 279
American Craft Beer Week, 297
American lagers. *See also* Lagers
    about, 70–74
    naming roots, 60
    revival, 73–75
    rice and, 72
    serving temperature, 31
American pale ales, 118–119
American pale wheat ale, 101–103
American porters, 178–179
American sour and wild ales,
    236–239
American stout, 192–193
American strong ale, 149
American-style barley wines,
    200–202
American wheat ales, 100–103
Anchorage Brewing Company, *237*
Anchor Brewing Company, 76, 77,
    119, 199, 201, 219, 291
Anchor Steam Beer, 77
Anderson Valley Brewing
    Company, 80, 218
Andygator, *70*

Ancient Ales, 187
Anheuser-Busch, 99
Apollo hops, 19
Appearance, in tasting, 34–35
Apricot Ale, *238*
Arizona Beer Week, 297
Aroma hops, 18
Aroma, in tasting, 35
Arrogant Bastard Ale, 149
Arthur, Tomme, 237–239
Artisan Ales, 207
Asheville Beer Week, 301
Astringent taste, 37
Atlanta Beer Week, 298
Atlantic Brewing Company, *257*
Attenuation, 25
Austin Craft Beer Week, 303
Aventinus, 93
Aventinus Weizen-Eisbock, *208*
Avery Brewing Co., *139*, 202, 237,
    256
Ayinger Bräu-Weisse, *88*
Ayinger Celebrator, *49*

B

Back in Black, *142*
Bailey, Kyle, 280, 281
Baird Beer, 268
Baird, Bryan, 267–268
Ballast Point Brewing, 69, 74, *132*,
    287
Baltic porters, 185–186
Baltika Brewers, *186*
Baltimore Beer Week, 299
Bananas and cloves taste, 39, 101
Barchet, Ron, 64–66
Barclay, Perkins & Co., 193
Bar Harbor Blueberry Ale, *257*
Barley. *See also* Hops
    about, 14
    malt classifications, 14–15
    roasted, 175
    unmalted, 15

*Barley Wine: History, Brewing
    Techniques, Recipes* (Allen and
    Cantwell), 199
Barley wine
    alcohol range, 27
    American-style, 200–202
    beginnings of, 198–199
    brews to taste, *200–201*
    cellaring, 291
    cheese pairings, 285
    English-style, 200
    festivals, 212–213
    maturity, 202
    serving temperature, 31
Barnyard aroma, 39
From the Barrel, 222
Barrel-aged beers
    about: overview of, 216
    barrel woods, 218–219
    beer festivals, 222
    bourbon barrels and, 217
    brews to taste, *220–221*
    cellaring, 292
    oud bruins, 235
Barrels, 30
Barrier Brewing, 268
Base malts, 14
Bass Brewers, *110*
Bass No. 1, 200
Bass Pale Ale, *110*
Bayerische Staatsbrauerei
    Weihenstephan, *92*
Bayou Teche Brewing, 56
Bear Republic Brewing Co., *148*,
    194, 286–287
Beatification, 232
Beer chefs, 276
Beer Judge Certification Program,
    142
Beer pairings
    about: overview of, 272
    Belgian ales, 274
    branching out, 274
    cheese, 285

PICTURE CREDITS

21st Amendment Brewery: 142 (right); 8 Wired Brewing Company: 261 (left); À l'abri de la Tempête: 246 (left); Abita Brewing Company: 70 (right); Alaskan Brewing Company: 58; Allagash Brewing Company: 100 (left), 166, 168, 232; Anchor Brewing/Dog and a Duck Marketing and Public Relations: 74-75, 76, 77 (right); Anchorage Brewing Company: 237 (right); Anderson Valley Brewing Company: 80 (right); Anheuser-Busch InBev; Deutschland/Spaten-Franziskaner-Bräu GmbH: 88 (right); Anne-Cathérine Dilewyns: 239; Aurora Productions, Inc./Great Alaska Beer & Barley Wine Festival: 212; Avery Brewing Company: 139 (left), 202; B.R. Rolya/Shelton Brothers: 249 (left); Baird Brewing Company: 268 (right); Baltika Breweries: 186 (left); Bass Brewers Limited: 110 (right),199; Bayerische Staatsbrauerei Weihenstephan: 92 (right); Bayou Teche Brewing: 56; Bear Republic Brewing Company: 148 (bottom left, top right), 149; Becca Dilley Photography: 122; Besh Restaurant Group: 278 (top); Bierbrouwerij De Koningshoeven/Artisanal Imports: 171 (right); BIERES DE CHIMAY S.A.: 156, 157 (top), 169 (right); Birra Del Borgo/Othmar Seehauser: 266; Blue Point Brewing Company: 54 (right); Bob Inman/Brauerei Schumacher: 83; Boulevard Brewing Company: 104-105; Brasserie Bourganel/Shelton Brothers: 249 (bottom right); Brasserie Cantillon Brouwerij/Shelton Brothers: 230 (right); Brasserie d'Achouffe: 151 (right); Brasserie d'Orval/Merchant du Vin: 157 (bottom), 158; Brasserie de Rochefort/Merchant du Vin: 171 (left); Brasserie De Saint-Sylvestre: 248 (left); Brasserie Dupont/Vanberg & DeWulf: 253 (left); Brasserie Duyck: 249 (top right); Brauerei Aying/Merchant du Vin: 49 (left), 88 (left); Brauerei Heller-Trum/B. United International, Inc.: 59 (left); Brauerei Hofstetten/ B. United International, Inc.: 208 (right); Brauerei Pinkus Mueller: 82 (right); Braustelle & Bierkompass.de/Freigeist Bierkultur: 81; Breckenridge Brewery: 48 (right); Brouwerij Huyghe: 117 (right); Brick Store Pub: 295; BridgePort Brewery: 138 (right), 140 (bottom); Brouwerij Bavik: 235 (right); Brouwerij Boon/Latis Imports: 231 (right); Brouwerij Bosteels: 250 (left); Brouwerij Corsendonk: 164 (right); Brouwerij De Dolle Brouwers: 191 (right); Brouwerij Duvel Moortgat: 117 (left); Brouwerij Liefmans: 235 (left); Brouwerij Lindemans/Merchant du Vin: 230 (left); Brouwerij Oud Beersel: 231 (left); Brouwerij Rodenbach/Latis Imports: 234 (right); Brouwerij Verhaeghe: 234 (left); Brouwerij Westmalle/Merchant du Vin: 164 (left) 165; Bryan N. Miller: 276; Budweiser Budvar: 60; Cambria Griffiths/Golden Road Brewing: 29 (top, bottom right); Cambridge Brewing Company: 129; Captain Lawrence Brewing Company: 115 (right); Cascade Brewing: 238 (left); Caves of Faribault: 282, 283; Central City Brewers and Distillers Ltd: 246 (right), 247 (bottom right); Charbay® Distillery & Winery: 219 (left);

Cigar City Brewing: 221; Cobra Beer Partnership Limited: 250 (right); Courtesy of Brooklyn Brewery: 52 (right), 131 (left); Cowgirl Creamery: 285 (bottom); Cypress Grove Chevre: 285 (logo, top); Dakota Fine: 281 (top two images) Dark Horse Brewing Company/Helix Creative Incorporated: 192 (right), 209 (right); Deschutes Brewery/Campbell Consulting: 125 (left), 144 (top), 145 (left), 179 (right), 195; DESTIHL® Restaurant & Brew Works: 238 (far left); Dogfish Head Craft Brewery: 143, 144 (bottom); Doug Nolan: 181; Drake's Brewing Company: 133; Duck-Rabbit Craft Brewery: 179 (left), 180; Einbecker Brauhaus/B. United International, Inc.: 48 (left); Elysian Brewing Company: 255, 256 (right); Euclid Hall Bar and Kitchen: 279, Ron Pollard (top), Marc Piscotty (bottom); Evan Semón/Euclid Hall Bar and Kitchen: 274; F.X. Matt Brewing Company/Saranac: 145 (right); FiftyFifty Brewing Company: 220 (middle); Firestone Walker Brewing Company: 120; Flying Dog Brewery: 150, 151 (left); Fort Collins Brewing: 59 (right); Fort George Brewery + Public House: 73 (right); Founders Brewing Company: 141 (right), 217, 293; French Broad Brewing Co.: 113 (right); Full Sail Brewing Company: 57 (right), 68; Fuller Smith & Turner; PLC/Paulaner HP USA: 111 (right),176 (right); G. Schneider & Sohn/ B. United International, Inc.: 208 (left); 97; Gasthaus & Gosebrauerei Beyerischer Bahnhof/B. United International; Goose Island Beer Company: 218, 219 (top), 79 (right); Great Divide Brewing Company: 125 (right), 194 (right); Great Lakes Brewing Company: 67 (left), 131 (right); Green Flash Brewing Company: 134, 135, 136, 137, 146 (right); Greene King PLC: 110 (left); Grupo Modelo S.A. de C.V.: 54 (left); Guinness Ltd: 183 (left); Hacker-Pschorr Bräu GmbH/Paulaner HP USA: 52 (left); 91 (left); Hair of the Dog Brewing Company: 204; Harpoon Brewery: 46 (right); Hill Farmstead Brewery/Bob M. Montgomery Images: 254 (top); Hofbrau Maibock ad design: Lori Yarnall. All other Hofbrau artwork is property of Hofbrau/Staatliches Hofbräuhaus: 70 (left); Hoppin' Frog Brewery: 141 (left); Hopworks Urban Brewery: 192 (left); International Trappist Association: 155; Ise Kadoya Brewery: 269 (top); J.W. Lees & Co./ B. United International, Inc.: 200 (left); James "Dr Fermento" Roberts: 213; Jeff Freeman Photography: 252; Jenene Chesbrough: 240; Jolly Pumpkin Artisan Ales/Irene Tomoko Sugiura/Northern United Brewing Company: 238 (right); Josh Shalek: 172 (HUB cap); Joshua M. Bernstein: 18 (top), 98, 167; Katherine Longly: 115 (left); Kiuchi Brewery: 100 (right); Kona Brewing Company: 184 (right); Köstritzer Schwarzbierbrauerei GmbH & Co.: 57 (left); Lagunitas Brewing Company: 61 (right); Lakefront Brewery, Inc.: 147 (top) Laurelwood Public House and Brewery: 138 (left); Left Hand Brewing Company: 188 (left); Lesley Louden/

Blameitonthefood.com: 294; Lew Bryson/The Session Beer Project: 26 (right); Lion Brewery Limited: 191 (left); Local Option: 236; Magic Rock Brewing Co. LTD: 259; Maine Beer Company: 119 (left); Meantime Brewing Company/Artisinal Imports: 130 (right), 176 (left); Michael Donk/BrewBokeh.com: 159, 227, 268 (bottom), 289; Midnight Sun Brewing Company: 146 (left); Mikkeller: 264 (left); Mondial de la Bière: 247, photo by CosmosImage; Mont des Cats: 160; Neighborhood Restaurant Group/Birch & Barley: 281 (bottom), middle image courtesy of Kyle Martell; New Belgium Brewing: 73 (left), 123 (left); New Holland Brewing Company: 206 (right); Ninkasi Brewing Company: 190 (right); Nørrebro Bryghus: 264 (right); North Coast Brewing Company/Colored Horse Studios: 194 (left); Odell Brewing Company: 101 (right), 140 (top), 220 (right); The Orkney Brewery/Sinclair Breweries Limited: 211 (right); Oskar Blues Brewery: 211 (left); Otter Creek Brewing: 82 (left); Oy Sinebrychoff Ab/B. United International, Inc.: 186 (right); Oyster House Brewing Company: 182; Paul Body/ Ballast Point Brewing Co.: 132 (right); Paulaner Brauarei/ Paulaner HP USA: 69 (right); Pelican Pub & Brewery/Kiwanda Hospitality Group: 80 (left); Pierre-Luc Gagnon: 245; Pilsner Urquell Brewery/RF|BINDER: 61 (left); Pretty Things Beer and Ale Project: 187; Privatbrauerei Gaffel Becker & Co./DIE KOELNER Public Relations: 79 (left); Private Weissbierbrauerei G. Schneider & Sohn GmbH/B. United International, Inc.: 92 (left); Professor Fritz Briem: 95 (right); Rachel Hirschey: 286; Radeberger Exportbierbrauerei/Baltz & Company, Inc.: 62, 63 (right); Redhook Brewing/LANE: 113 (left); Ridgeway Brewing/Shelton Brothers: 200 (right); Robert Gale, Beerlens.com: 203; Rogue Ales and Spirits: 17, 201 (right), 284; Russian River Brewing Company: 139 (right), 237 (left); Saint Somewhere Brewing Company: 253 (right); Samuel Adams/Devries Public Relations 49 (right); Samuel Smith/ Merchant du Vin: 130 (left), 189; Sara Lasha: 124; Savor Craft Beer Festival: Photo © 2012 Brewers Association: 277 (top); Savor Craft Beer Festival: Photo © 2012 Eddie Arrossi: 277 (bottom); Shipyard Brewing Company: 256 (left); Shmaltz Brewing Company/JP Cutler Media: 148 (left); Short's Brewing Company: 257; Sierra Nevada Brewing Co.: 119 (far right), 161, 201 (left); Ska Brewing Company: 186 (bottom left) Smuttynose Brewing Company: 206 (left); Spaten-Franziskaner-Bräu: 46 (left); Starr Hill Brewery, LLC: 183 (right); Steamworks Brewing Company: 77 (left); Stone Brewing Co./ StudioSchulz.com: 132 (left); Stoudt's Brewing Company: 69 (left); Stuart Mullenberg Photography: 205; Studio Dedée.be/Gueuzerie Tilquin S.A.: 230 (bottom left); StudioSchulz.com: 291; Surly Brewing Co.: 111 (left); SweetWater Brewing Company: 119 (right); The Bruery: 95 (left); The Caledonian Brewery Company Limited: 184 (left); The Kernel Brewery: 258; The Lost Abbey: 228, 292; The Monk's Kettle/Abbot's Cellar/Adam Dulye/ Jamie Law: 280; Three Floyds Brewing Company: 101 (left); Timothy Taylor & Co.; Limited/Ash Marketing: 109 (right); Traquair House/ Merchant du Vin: 210; Tröegs Brewery: 123 (right); Tucher Bräu GmbH/ Edelweiss Imports, Inc.: 91 (right); Two Brothers Brewing Company: 67 (right); Unibroue: 169 (right); Upland Brewing Company: 198; Vanberg & Dewulf: 233 (bottom right), 248 (right); Victory Brewing Company: 63 (left), 64, 65, 66; Wells & Young's Brewing Company Ltd: 188 (right);

White Labs, Inc.: 26, (left top and bottom); Widmer Brothers Brewing/ LANE: 102-103, 142 (left); Wolaver's Fine Organic Ales: 190 (left); Yazoo Brewing Company: 147 (bottom); Yeastie Boys: 261 (right); Yo-Ho Brewing Company: 269 (bottom).

Stock Images:
Viii: © Shutterstock/Valentyn Volkov; 15: © Benjamin Yu/Wortlock Brewery; 17: Shutterstock/Jita; 18: © iStockphoto.com/Dumitru Cristian; 28: © iStockphoto.com/Jiri Bursik; 29: © Shutterstock/ Ivancovlad; 30: bottles left to right: © Shutterstock/Tim UR, © Shutterstock/Nitr, © Shutterstock/Joao Seabra; 31: © Shutterstock/ jcjgphotography; 33: bottles © Shutterstock/TheVectorminator; 45: © Shutterstock/Pavel L Photo and Video; 47: © Shutterstock/PixDeluxe; 50: Christmas illustration © Shutterstock/Victorian Traditions; Oktoberfest horse carriage © Shutterstock/Kochneva Tetyana; 51: pretzel © Shutterstock/motorolka; Munich city center © Shutterstock/gary718; 53: © Shutterstock/gillmar; 55: © Shutterstock/Richard Lyons; 56: © Shutterstock/R. MACKAY PHOTOGRAPHY, LLC; 71: Library of Congress/Copyright by Leeland Art Studio, Pierre, S.D.; image of goat © Shutterstock/Dudarev Mikhail; 72: Library of Congress; 78: © Didi/ Alamy; 81: © Shutterstock/Christopher Meder; 87: © Shutterstock/ Bplanet; 89: © Shutterstock/cappi thompson; 90: © Shutterstock/ Rudchenko Liliia; 93: image of rye © Shutterstock/ Seregam, pretzels © Shutterstock/bogdan ionescu; 94: © Shutterstock/Sebastian Kaulitzki; 109: © Shutterstock/Stuart Monk; 114: © Shutterstock/ Antonio Abrignani; 116: Brewery Moortgat © Wikimedia/Dirk Van Esbroeck; 145: © Shutterstock/R. MACKAY PHOTOGRAPHY, LLC; 160: © Shutterstock/Antonio Abrignani; 163: © Shutterstock/ Antonio Abrignani; 174: © Shutterstock/Alexander Sayenko; 175: © Shutterstock/James Smart Photography; 177: © Shutterstock/Alexander Ishchenko, patent image via Google documents; 178: © Shutterstock/ Wollertz; 179: © Shutterstock/Madlen; 207: © Shutterstock/Nick Stubbs; 209: © Shutterstock/UnaPhoto; 211: © Shutterstock/Nicole Gordine; 223: © Shutterstock/tjwvandongen; 233: © Shutterstock/ Mik Lav; 251: cork image © Shutterstock/Sinisa Botas, confetti image © Shutterstock/Elena Itsenko; 254: © Shutterstock/Antonio Abrignani; 257: © Shutterstock/Hein Nouwens; 260: © Shutterstock/ ChameleonsEye; 261: © Shutterstock/Antonio Abrignani; 263: © Shutterstock/Andreas Gradin; 264: © Shutterstock/David Wilkins; 269: © Shutterstock/ Mila Petkova; 276: © Shutterstock/lynea; 278: © Shutterstock/Alexey U; 284: © Shutterstock/Morphart Creation; 287: © Shutterstock/Margoe Edwards; 296: © Shutterstock/Caroline Eibl

All other graphics and design elements sourced from Shutterstock.

BRAND

B

CASTELAIN

BLOND BIERE de GARD

CB
BEYOND THE BEST OF
DEUS
Brut des Flandres
Cuvée Prestige 2002
BIÈRE BIER BEER

SHORT'S BREW™

Handmade by people who care.™

ed & bottled by Short's Brewing Company

Rapids, MI

KEY

Beer brew

GOVERNMENT WARNING: (1) ACCORDING TO THE SURGEON GENERAL, WOMEN SHOULD NOT DRINK ALCOHOLIC BEVERAGES DURING PREGNANCY BECAUSE OF THE RISK OF BIRTH DEFECTS. (2) CONSUMPTION OF ALCOHOLIC BEVERAGES IMPAIRS YOUR ABILITY TO DRIVE A CAR OR OPERATE MACHINERY, AND MAY CAUSE HEALTH PROBLEMS.

伊

勢

ISE KADOYA BREW

750 ml / 1 pint 9.4 fl. oz.

Product of Belgium

ELYSIA

DARK O' THE

MOON

Pumpkin Stout

Vieille Provision
SAISON DUPONT
Belgian Farmhouse Ale   Bottle conditioned
tered   wed by Brasserie Dupont, Tourpes

B

Baird Beer